ANGEL ISLAND

ANGEL ISLAND

IMMIGRANT GATEWAY TO AMERICA

ERIKA LEE *&* JUDY YUNG

OXFORD

UNIVERSITY PRESS

2010

OXFORD
UNIVERSITY PRESS

Oxford University Press, Inc., publishes works that further
Oxford University's objective of excellence
in research, scholarship, and education.

Oxford   New York
Auckland   Cape Town   Dar es Salaam   Hong Kong   Karachi
Kuala Lumpur   Madrid   Melbourne   Mexico City   Nairobi
New Delhi   Shanghai   Taipei   Toronto

With offices in
Argentina   Austria   Brazil   Chile   Czech Republic   France   Greece
Guatemala   Hungary   Italy   Japan   Poland   Portugal   Singapore
South Korea   Switzerland   Thailand   Turkey   Ukraine   Vietnam

Copyright © 2010 by Erika Lee and Judy Yung

Published by Oxford University Press, Inc.
198 Madison Avenue, New York, New York 10016

www.oup.com

Oxford is a registered trademark of Oxford University Press.

Title page photo: Immigrants boarding the ferry
at Angel Island after passing inspection.
(Courtesy of California State Parks, 2010.)

Library of Congress Cataloging-in-Publication Data
Lee, Erika.
Angel Island: immigrant gateway to America / Erika Lee, Judy Yung.
p.   cm.
Includes bibliographical references and index.
ISBN 978-0-19-973408-5
1. Angel Island Immigration Station (Calif.)—History.
2. San Francisco Bay Area (Calif.)—Emigration and immigration.
I. Yung, Judy.   II. Title.
JV6926.A65L44 2010
304.8'7309041—dc22   2009054343

1 3 5 7 9 8 6 4 2

Printed in the United States of America
on acid-free paper

In memory of our great teachers Him Mark Lai, Ronald Takaki, and Jon Gjerde

For Mark, Benjamin, and Billy
—*E. L.*

For Eddie
—*J. Y.*

CONTENTS

Acknowledgments • ix
Preface • xv
A Note on Language and Terminology • xxi
Abbreviations • xxv

INTRODUCTION
1

CHAPTER ONE
GUARDING THE GOLDEN GATE
The Life and Business of the Immigration Station
29

CHAPTER TWO
"ONE HUNDRED KINDS OF OPPRESSIVE LAWS"
Chinese Immigrants in the Shadow of Exclusion
69

CHAPTER THREE
"AGONY, ANGUISH, AND ANXIETY"
Japanese Immigrants on Angel Island
111

CHAPTER FOUR
"OBSTACLES THIS WAY, BLOCKADES THAT WAY"
South Asian Immigrants, U.S. Exclusion, and the Gadar Movement
145

CHAPTER FIVE
"A PEOPLE WITHOUT A COUNTRY"
Korean Refugee Students and Picture Brides
177

CHAPTER SIX
IN SEARCH OF FREEDOM AND OPPORTUNITY
Russians and Jews in the Promised Land
211

CHAPTER SEVEN
EL NORTE
Mexican Immigrants on Angel Island
247

CHAPTER EIGHT
FROM "U.S. NATIONALS" TO "ALIENS"
Filipino Migration and Repatriation through Angel Island
273

CHAPTER NINE
SAVING ANGEL ISLAND
299

EPILOGUE
THE LEGACY OF ANGEL ISLAND
315

Appendix • 327
Notes • 333
Bibliography • 373
Index • 389

ACKNOWLEDGMENTS

IT HAS BEEN A PRIVILEGE to write this book and to work with so many people who care about preserving Angel Island's immigration history as much as we do. Documenting the histories of the major immigrant groups to pass through Angel Island has required extensive outreach into local communities as well as traditional archival research. This book could not have been completed without the generosity of many colleagues, research assistants, volunteers, librarians, archivists, families, and individuals who have shared their time, energy, knowledge, ideas, and stories with us.

The Angel Island Immigration Station Foundation staff and board have supported this project from the very beginning. Grant Din, Erika Gee, Daphne Kwok, Felicia Lowe, Julie Phuong, Katherine Toy, and Kathy Owyang Turner have been instrumental in assisting us with research, outreach, and marketing efforts. Executive Director Eddie Wong has been an especially supportive partner and advocate.

Our Scholars Advisory Board, including Robert Barde, Albert Camarillo, Catherine Ceniza Choy, Charles Egan, Steve Fujita, Jennifer Gee, Richard Kim, Bill Ong Hing, Maria Sakovich, and Jane Singh generously provided early counsel, research leads, and collegial support.

We received generous research funding from a number of institutions, including the Angel Island Immigration Station Foundation and Georges Van Den Abbeele, Office of the Dean, Division of Humanities, University of California, Santa Cruz. The Fesler-Lampert Professorship in the Public Humanities, a College of Liberal Arts Sabbatical Supplement, and an Arts

& Humanities Imagine Fund Award from the University of Minnesota also provided Erika Lee with much needed time and research support.

A team of committed research assistants in Minnesota and California tracked down photographs and documents, catalogued sources, and dug through archives with cheerful efficiency: Kelly Condit-Shrestha, Kimberly Foley, Marisa Louie, Ki Jung Nam, Kim Park Nelson, Maria Sakovich, Andy Urban, Jeannie Woo, and Elizabeth Zanoni.

In addition, we have been gratified to receive the research assistance of the following volunteers: Elizabeth and Joe Chan, Franklin Fung Chow, C. F. Kwok, Dana Lew, Jean Lew, Barbara Lutes, Alice Murata, Franklin Ng, Kio Tong-Ishikawa, Katherine Toy, and students in Carol McKibben's "Introduction to Public History" class at Stanford University, including Christine Cho, Victoria Gray, Laura Gutierrez, Ivan Jimenez, Jairo Marshall, and Sabine Moller. Many volunteers assisted us with the data entry of over 70,000 Angel Island case files, including: Leonard Chan, Lillian Chan, Angelina Chang, Craig Charnley, Helen Chin, Kenneth Chin, Melody Chin, Vincent Chin, Vana Curtis, Grant Din, Eddie Fung, Mary Geong, Lynette Choy Uyeda Gin, Yoshiko Ho, Jim Huen, John Jung, Elsie Lam, Denise Leo, Lillian Louie, Marisa Louie, Arlene Lum, Diana Lum, Matthew Lum, Rose Marr, Grace Toy, Pamela Wong, Jeannie Woo, Irene Yee, and Myrna Yee.

We were fortunate to have the following volunteers assist us with the difficult task of translating documents, articles, and poems from various Asian languages into English: John Akiyama, Christine Cho, Charles Egan, Marlon K. Hom, Jikyung Hwang, Yuko Konno, Jean Lew, Hyonggyu Rhew, Yoshiko Yokochi Samuel, and Brian Yang.

Many people also assisted us with research details and with locating families with Angel Island connections, including: Estrella Ravelo Alamar, Henry Hyungju Ahn, Jonathan Beecher, Nina Bogdan, Susan Briggs, Philip Choy, Dorothy Cordova, William Estrada, Hardeep Gosal, Jayasri Majumdar Hart, Yoshiko Ho, Harjit Gosal Khaira, Peter Klassen, Daphne Kwok, Casey Lee, Hyung W. Lee, Marie Matsumoto, Baylan Megino, Yuki Ooi, Amita Rodman, Vicki Ruiz, Grace Shimizu, Jane Singh, Harold and Sonia Sunoo, Kei Tanaka, Terri Torres, Michael Tripp, Katherine Toy, Richard Villegas, William Warrior, Gail Whang, William Wong, Ikumi Yamagisawa, Steve Yee, Connie Young Yu, Rev. Suk-Chong Yu, and Lydia Zaverukha.

The following people generously shared their Angel Island family histories with us: Estrella Ravelo Alamar, David and Kathy Ang, Jim Ariki, Rani Bagai, Liana Belloni, Elisa Brooks, Virginia Dilim, Ann Yuri Dion, Betty Kawamoto Dunn, Joyce Ellorin, Eliseo Felipe, Nick Friesen, Yaho Fujii, Jim Hullana, Mary Hyodo, Arliss Jann, Lourdes Kelly, Dick Jiro Kobashigawa, Don Lee, Michael Lopez, Donald Lyang, Sally Matsuishi, Mabel Meu, William Mock, Yoshio Murakawa, Janice Muto, Donald

Nakahata, Herbert Neufeld, Hiro Nishikawa, Ted Schulze, Nora Steiner, Tami Takahashi, Chie Yazuki Takeshita, Sheridan Tatsuno, William Warrior, Deak Wooten, Tomoyo Fujita Yamasaki, Yae Kami Yedlosky, Irene Yee, and Lily Zaima. Their time and cooperation have allowed us to tell a more complete and rich history of immigration through Angel Island.

Staff at numerous libraries and archives greatly assisted us in the research for this book: Asian American Studies Center, UC Los Angeles; Bancroft Library, UC Berkeley; California Department of Parks and Recreation Archives; California Historical Society; California History Room, California State Library; Center for Mennonite Brethren Studies, Fresno Pacific University; Center for Oral and Public History, California State University, Fullerton; East Asian Library, University of Southern California; East Asiatic Library, UC Berkeley; Ethnic Studies Library, UC Berkeley; Hoover Institution Archives, Stanford University; Immigration History Research Center, University of Minnesota; Japanese American Historical Society; Japanese American National Museum; National Archives, Washington, D.C.; National Archives, Pacific Regional Branch; Occidental College Library; Pacific School of Religion; Sacramento Public Library; San Francisco History Center, San Francisco Public Library; San Diego Historical Society; Society of California Pioneers; Special Collections and University Archives, California State University, Sacramento; Special Collections, UC Los Angeles; University of Notre Dame Press; and Visual Communications Photographic Archives. We are especially grateful to Bill Greene of the National Archives, Pacific Regional Branch, for pulling hundreds of records for us and answering our many queries; Tim Wilson and Christina Moretta of the San Francisco History Center at the San Francisco Public Library for helping us find and verify newspaper sources and photographs; Frank Gravier at McHenry Library, UC Santa Cruz, for sharing resourceful web sites with us; and Wil Jorae at the California Department of Parks and Recreation for providing us with many Angel Island photographs.

Numerous colleagues have generously provided time, research assistance, and support while we worked on this book. Maria Sakovich generously shared her research files on non-Asian immigrants at Angel Island. Kei Tanaka and Eiichiro Azuma sent us materials on Japanese picture brides. Charles Egan shared new poems and writings about Angel Island as he found them in various ethnic community newspapers. Robert Barde crunched data for us from his statistical analysis of passenger arrivals at San Francisco. Daniel Quan generously shared his archive of Angel Island photographs and documents. Marian Smith, Immigration and Customs Enforcement historian at the Department of Homeland Security, answered our many queries and provided us with immigration service data. Kelly Lytle Hernandez, Dawn Bohulano Mabalon, and Thomas Wolfe offered research suggestions and answered queries.

Eiichiro Azuma, Albert Camarillo, Gordon H. Chang, Catherine Ceniza Choy, Charles Egan, Steve Fujita, Jennifer Gee, Bill Ong Hing, Richard Kim, Kathy Lim Ko, Felicia Lowe, Ruthanne Lum McCunn, Mae Ngai, Gary Okihiro, Maria Sakovich, Jane Singh, Barbara Welke, Harold Sunoo, Rev. Suk-Chong Yu, members of the University of Minnesota Law School Faculty Work-in-Progress colloquium, and the anonymous readers for Oxford University Press and University of California Press offered helpful comments on parts of the manuscript.

Gail Dubrow offered early and good advice on writing public history. Elaine May and Mae Ngai read early proposals for this project. Todd Bontemps generously gave us sound legal advice. Vincent Chin compiled statistical data and scanned numerous documents and photographs for us. Mark Buccella painstakingly restored and enhanced old photographs and images for publication. Friends and colleagues at our respective universities listened to ideas, offered advice, and cheered on the project from beginning to end, including: Jigna Desai, Donna Gabaccia, Walt Jacobs, Josephine Lee, Rich Lee, Valerie Matsumoto, Elaine May, Ruthanne Lum McCunn, Kevin Murphy, Jean O'Brien, Peggy Pascoe, Georges Van Den Abbeele, and Barbara Welke.

Sandra Dijkstra has been an exceptional agent. Her enthusiasm for the project inspired us to think big. Along with Elise Capron, Elizabeth James, and others at the Dijkstra Literary Agency, she expertly introduced us to the world of trade publishing and cheerfully motivated us every step of the way.

We owe special thanks to several individuals at Oxford University Press whose staff has gone the extra mile in producing this book. Susan Ferber has been an extraordinary editor and advocate. She believed in our vision for this book from the very beginning and helped us turn it into a reality. Her editorial suggestions greatly improved the manuscript, and her support throughout the writing, production, and marketing stages has been invaluable. Publisher Niko Pfund's enthusiasm for the project launched us forward to publication. Copyeditor Patterson Lamb provided useful corrections. Keith Faivre guided us in the final production stages, and Christian Purdy developed a marketing and publicity campaign to reach a wide audience.

Our families' histories are tied to the Angel Island Immigration Station, and it is to them that we owe our deepest gratitude. Erika Lee thanks her parents and sisters for teaching her the importance of history and for their enduring support. Her mother, Fay Lee, deserves special thanks. Her weekly words of encouragement have meant more than words can say. Erika is especially grateful to Mark Buccella, Benjamin, and Billy who provide love and support everyday. As a former tour guide at the Angel Island Immigration Station, Mark was enthusiastic about this book from the very beginning. He gave advice, donated his time and design skills, read drafts, and took on even more parental duties to help Erika complete this project on time. His support has made this, and so many other things, possible. Ben and Billy Lee Buccella listened to many dinnertime discussions about Angel Island, offered encouragement, and were patient and understanding while their mom wrote upstairs in the attic office. They also happily accompanied her on research trips and to the Angel Island Immigration Station to visit the place where two of their great grandparents caught their first sight of America.

Judy Yung is grateful to her parents, Tom Yip Jing and Jew Law Ying, for making the journey to America, enduring confinement at Angel Island for the sake of their children, and nurturing her interest in Chinese American history. She thanks her five sisters for their unflagging support through many book projects leading to this one. And to Eddie Fung, she owes her deepest gratitude for being a supportive sounding board, diligent research assistant, generous benefactor, and devoted partner throughout.

Angel Island is dedicated to our families and to the memory of three important mentors, colleagues, and friends who were pioneers in the fields of Chinese American history, Ethnic Studies, and immigration history, respectively: Him Mark Lai, Ronald Takaki, and Jon Gjerde.

PREFACE

THE FIFTH DAUGHTER OF IMMIGRANT PARENTS FROM CHINA, I grew up in the 1950s knowing very little about my own family history, let alone the history of Chinese in America. Like everyone else in San Francisco's Chinatown, my family went by two different surnames. Among our relatives and friends, we were known as the Tom family, but at school and on our birth certificates, we were known as the Yung family. We always knew that if ever questioned by the *lo fan* (foreigners), we were not to reveal our real Chinese surname; otherwise, the family would be in big trouble. I never understood why until I found out about a place called Angel Island in 1975.

Word had been going around Chinatown that a park ranger named Alexander Weiss had seen Chinese poems carved into the walls of an old immigration building on Angel Island. That piqued my interest, and I set out with a few friends to see for myself. It was a beautiful day for a ferry ride across the bay to the island. The sun glistened on the deep blue waters as seagulls trailed behind us. Once the boat docked at Ayala Cove, we were greeted by a park ranger who took us on a steep climb up to the perimeter road that led around to the immigration station on the north side of the island. It was a one-mile walk and the panoramic view of the bay was breathtaking.

We finally arrived at the two-story wooden barracks that once served as a detention facility for Chinese immigrants. Some of the windows were boarded up, and the structure looked old and decrepit behind the barbed wire fence. We were told that the place had not been used since World War II, when it housed Japanese prisoners of war. The building smelled and the floor creaked as we entered. We were taken to the main dormitory where the poetry had been found. The room was empty except for the twenty-eight standing poles from which three tiers of beds had once hung. Sunlight streamed in through the dirty windows. The floor was covered with litter and the paint on the ceiling and walls was peeling. With the aid of a flashlight, we could make out the impressions of Chinese calligraphy on the walls. There were rows and rows of stately poems. I remember feeling as if I had walked back into the past. Touching the words covered by a thin layer of chipped paint, I could hear the voices of immigrants bemoaning their fate imprisoned on this lonely island. "Grief and bitterness entwined are heaven sent," wrote one poet. "Sadness kills the person in the wooden building," wrote another. I was moved to tears. And I wondered why I had never heard of this place before.

Later when I got home I asked my father, "Do you know of a place called Angel Island?" At first, he didn't want to talk about it. Then he finally said, "Yeah, that's where they kept us when we first arrived." I later learned that in order to circumvent the Chinese Exclusion Act, which barred all Chinese laborers from entering the United States, my father Tom Yip Jing came to this country in 1921 claiming to be Yung Hin Sen, the nineteen-year-old son of a Chinese merchant in Stockton, California. Detained on Angel Island for thirty-four days, he was grilled about his family background, details of the house and village he supposedly came from, and whatever he knew about his father's life in America. When the immigrant inspector found no discrepancies in his answers when compared to those of his father and brother, he was believed to be the son of Yung Dung and duly admitted into the country. Like my father, the overwhelming majority of Chinese immigrants who came during the exclusion period (1882–1943) were "paper sons" of merchants or U.S. citizens. They took this "crooked path" because that was the only way they could come. The price they paid was heavy. Many were forced to live a life of deceit and duplicity, under constant fear of detection and deportation, until the day they died. It was a well-kept secret, as was the harsh treatment accorded them at the immigration station. No wonder that they never wanted to tell their children about this damned place—Angel Island.

But I was determined to find out. For the next five years, I worked with historian Him Mark Lai and poet Genny Lim to collect and translate as many Angel Island poems as we could find and to conduct oral history interviews with former detainees and employees of the immigration station. Many of the poems on the walls had been partially obliterated by layers of paint and natural deterioration. We were fortunate to find two immigrants, Smiley Jann and Tet Yee, who had meticulously copied down close to 100 poems in their notebooks while detained on Angel

Island in the early 1930s. Convincing other people to talk about their experiences on Angel Island proved to be more difficult. We started with our own families and branched out to relatives of close friends in the Chinese American community. Only by promising anonymity were we allowed to record the interviews and publish their stories along with translations of 135 poems. The result of our labor was *Island: Poetry and History of Chinese Immigrants on Angel Island, 1910–1940*.

Island is a testament to the hardships, perseverance, and ultimate triumphs of Chinese immigrants on Angel Island. At the same time, it exposes a dark chapter in our country's immigration history and wipes clean the shame and humiliation that many paper sons like my father have kept locked within through the years. More important, *Island* calls on America to reckon with its past mistake of adopting and enforcing discriminatory immigration policies that belie its ideals of liberty and justice for all. The lessons of Angel Island are very present and real. As immigrants from around the world continue to come to the United States in search of freedom and opportunity, we must ensure that they be treated fairly and with dignity and respect. What happened to the Chinese on Angel Island was unconscionable and must never be repeated again.

Since the publication of *Island* in 1980, many historians, community activists, and preservationists have continued to research about Angel Island in an effort to document, preserve, and restore the immigration site and its history. The new research materials they have found, including photographs, wall inscriptions, personal stories and writings, and immigration records, have raised awareness of the great diversity of immigrants on Angel Island. Although the Chinese were the most numerous, we now know there were also immigrants and refugees from some eighty countries, including Japan, India, Korea, the Philippines, Russia, Spain, Mexico, Australia, and New Zealand. It is time for their stories to be told, compared, and interpreted within the larger context of U.S. immigration history. By expanding the Angel Island story to include a broad range of perspectives and experiences of gatekeepers and immigrants alike, Erika Lee and I have set out to write a comprehensive history of how Angel Island became the Pacific gateway to America, forever changing the lives of immigrants and of America itself.

Judy Yung

On June 3, 1918, my grandfather Lee Chi Yet boarded the *Korea Maru* steamship in Hong Kong and sailed for San Francisco. He traveled with a man named Yee Yook Haw, a Chinese merchant who claimed that my grandfather was his oldest son. In fact, my grandfather was a "paper son" and an orphan, who, after his parents' deaths, had survived as well as he could in his native village of Poon Leung Chun in the Sunning (Toisan) district near Canton, China. As an adult, he left his village to find work in Toisan City and got a job working for Yee Yook Haw. When his employer decided to go to San Francisco, he decided to go with him.

Because of the Chinese exclusion laws, the only way for my grandfather to enter the country was through deception. Upon arrival in San Francisco, Yee Yook Haw and my grandfather, who adopted the paper name of Yee Shew Ning, were taken with all other third-class passengers to the Angel Island Immigration Station. Yee Yook Haw answered the immigration officials' brief set of questions and showed them his visa from the American consulate in Hong Kong proving he was a reputable merchant. He was admitted into the country after six days of detention.

My grandfather was detained longer and subjected to a thorough medical examination and interrogation. He answered questions about his name, age, the Yee family, and the Yee family village. He had studied these details, including how many rows of houses there were in Lok Oh Lee village, the name of the nearest market, how often his "father" came to visit, the occupations and family makeup of various neighbors, and the size and location of the family's clock. My grandfather also had to pass a special medical examination to prove that his claimed age of seventeen years matched his physical description. The last hurdle was an eight-day hospital stay to treat hookworm, an excludable disease if left untreated. The day he was released from the hospital, my grandfather was officially admitted into the country.

I did not learn about my grandfather's journey to America while growing up in the suburbs east of San Francisco. Angel Island was just another landmark in the San Francisco Bay that my family passed on the Bay Bridge while driving into Chinatown for dim sum or to Little Italy for pasta. It was not until I was a college student learning about Asian American history for the first time that I thought to ask how my own family might be connected to laws like the Chinese Exclusion Act and to places like Angel Island. I interviewed my grandparents to find out. One grandmother refused to talk about it at all. The memories of those times were too painful for her to share. My grandfather who came through Angel Island described how he had left a life of nothing in China, dared to enter a country that did not want him, and pulled it off on the island. He was even able to change the family name back to Lee when he applied for naturalization in 1946.

The story of my grandparents—and those of countless other Asian Americans whose lives never made it into any American history textbook—inspired me to go to graduate school. Debates over immigration, border control, and undocumented immigration divided the country in the 1990s, and it seemed natural to start with researching Chinese immigration during the exclusion era. Specifically, I wanted to better understand what Angel Island said about America and its relationship to immigration and race. How did it compare to Ellis Island? And what was its legacy for modern immigration policy?

I tracked down clues in obscure government reports, and I found the private papers and correspondence of some of Angel Island's immigration officials. But the full history of Chinese immigration through Angel Island did not come alive to me until I visited the National Archives branch in San Bruno, California. There, staff archivist Neil Thomsen pointed me to nearly 70,000 recently declassified files on Chinese immigrants who entered the country through San Francisco and Angel Island.

When I found my grandparents' files, their faces peered out at me from old photographs I had never seen before. There was my grandfather's original 1918 application, with passport-sized photographs of himself and his paper father. He wore a traditional Chinese tunic, and his hair was combed back to reveal a self-assured young man. The next pages in the file revealed my grandfather's interrogation at the Angel Island Immigration Station, in which he fabricated a false identity, family, and life. And on the top of the file was my grandparents' wedding photograph. It was the only one that my grandparents had, but Angel Island officials had confiscated it during my grandmother's interview for admission in 1927. They scrawled her file number across a corner and slipped it back into the file jacket where it lay for over seventy years.

I spent the next several years researching and writing what would become my first book, *At America's Gates: Chinese Immigration during the Exclusion Era, 1882–1943*. I looked at over a thousand individual Chinese immigration files as well as hundreds of documents in the National Archives and other archives. Together, these records allowed me to piece together not only a social history of Chinese immigrants and Chinese Americans under the shadow of exclusion on Angel Island, but also a larger history of America's transformation into a "gatekeeping nation." But I knew that I was only scratching the surface. Time and again when I rifled through the dusty file boxes, I found not a Chinese immigrant's file, but that of another immigrant. Like Inder Singh, a Sikh laborer who applied for admission from the Philippines in 1913. Or Yoshi Nakayama, a Japanese "picture bride" coming to join her husband in 1911; Rafael Magno, a Filipino laborer reentering the United States in 1935; a twenty-seven-year-old Italian native named Dominco Rinaldo, who sailed north from a South American port in September 1914; and Esther Lopez, who gave birth to twins at the immigration station's hospital in 1913 before being sent back to Mexico. There were even a few scattered files of immigrants from Norway, Afghanistan, Persia, Nicaragua, Australia, French Indochina, and Tahiti. These were all people who had also passed through the Angel Island Immigration Station but whose histories were even less known than those of the Chinese immigrants who were there at the same time. I made copies of them and saved them in a file marked

"Angel Island—Other Immigrants," hoping that someday I would have the opportunity to revisit them.

When Judy Yung and I began talking about marking Angel Island's centennial, we knew it was time to share their stories and many others like them in a new comprehensive history of Angel Island's diverse immigrants. Their experiences have helped us see Angel Island in a new light.

But it is our hope that this book offers more than just a new set of stories about the immigration station and the people who came through it. We would like to illustrate how the Angel Island Immigration Station—now a National Historic Landmark—fundamentally changes our understandings of America and American immigration in the past and present. Angel Island is not just Chinese American history, or Asian American history, or California history, or immigration history. It is American history.

Erika Lee

A NOTE ON LANGUAGE AND TERMINOLOGY

WE USE THE TERMS *immigrant, migrant, migration, and immigration* broadly to describe the fluid movement of peoples across national borders for a variety of reasons. The term *immigrant* is a legal status that refers to an alien who comes for permanent settlement. We use *immigrant* and *immigration* to refer to foreigners coming to and residing in the United States, recognizing that these movements did not always result in permanent settlement. The terms *migrant* and *migration* reflect multiple types of movement, including temporary residence in a foreign country (students, travelers, temporary workers, for example), or circular, transnational migration across national borders or within an empire.

The U.S. government at times referred to temporary visitors, such as students, and ministers, or returning U.S. residents, and the spouses and children of U.S. citizens, as *nonimmigrant aliens,* or after 1924, *nonquota immigrants,* to indicate that their admission into the country was on a temporary basis and was not to count against their home country's annual quota set by the 1924 Immigration Act.[1] The U.S. government also classified persons traveling through the United States to a second country as *transients.*

Government records often refer to individuals through their legal status as *aliens,* persons who are not U.S. citizens; or *illegal aliens,* persons who are in the country in violation of immigration law. In recent years, the terms used to describe immigration have become highly politicized and are often manipulated to serve different purposes in the political debates over

U.S. immigration policy. There are derogatory and selective uses of the terms *illegal alien* and *illegal immigrant*, for example. While there are technically individuals from all over the world currently living and working in the United States without proper documentation, the "illegal" label mostly gets applied to persons from Mexico, Latin America, or to other immigrants of color. This selective usage helps further the racial dimensions of the contemporary debate over immigration. The terms *illegal immigration* and *illegal immigrant* are also problematic because they dehumanize individuals and ignore the large role that the U.S. government, U.S. immigration law, and U.S. businesses play in facilitating undocumented immigration. As in the past, immigration policies continue to favor some immigrants over others. Many working-class immigrants have very few opportunities to enter the country under current immigration law due to preference categories that privilege those with professional skills and because of visa backlogs for certain countries. At the same time, U.S. companies have hired and recruited workers regardless of immigration status, thereby encouraging and supporting undocumented immigration.

The term *undocumented immigrant* has been suggested as a more neutral description of immigrants who have entered without proper immigration documents or who do not have the federal documentation to show they are legally entitled to work, visit, or live in the United States. However, this term does not work for all immigrants across the time period that we cover in this book. The Chinese immigrants that we discuss, for example, were certainly "documented," in that they came with documents that allowed them legal entry and residence. In their case, the documents were often fraudulent, and their entry, though "documented," still circumvented the law. Given the imperfect choice of terms available to us, we try to be as specific, accurate, and neutral as possible in describing the type of entry immigrants have used in both the past and present while also representing our sources correctly. In the few instances that we do use the terms *illegal immigrants* or *illegal immigration*, we contextualize them within the patterns of discriminatory immigration laws that left few other migration options open to specific groups of immigrants. Our goal has been to stay true to history without condoning the use of inflammatory language.[2]

The category of the *U.S. national* is a result of American colonialism abroad following the Spanish-American War, during which the Philippines, Puerto Rico, and Guam became U.S. territories. The Philippines was annexed as American territory, but Filipinos were not made American citizens. American colonial policy created a new legal status of the "U.S. national," someone who owed allegiance to the United States, but who did not have the rights of a citizen. U.S. nationals could not vote or run for elected office. They did not have the rights of representation or trial by jury. But as American colonial subjects and "nationals," they were also not "aliens" and could thus enter the United States without an entry visa and were not subject to exclusion or deportation from the United States.[3]

We refer to newcomers arriving on Angel Island as *arrivals, immigrants* or *applicants*. We refer to the individuals who were detained at the immigration station as *detainees*. Although they were technically in the United States, detainees were not legally admitted into the country until their cases were finalized and an admission decision was given. They were subject to the rules and regulations set forth by the U.S. immigration service while in detention.

When individuals applied for admission into the United States, the government could *land* or *admit* them for legal residence permanently or temporarily, *debar, reject,* or *exclude* them from the country, or *admit on parole*, which meant allowing them into the country temporarily under bond and/or parole by a third party, usually a relative, acquaintance, or organization.

Deportation refers to the removal of aliens already in the United States. Immigration officials referred to deporting both foreigners residing in the United States and applicants for admission who had been denied entry. We use *deportation* to describe both the official action of barring applicants for admission and returning them to their port of embarkation *and* the removal or expulsion of immigrants already residing in the country.[4] Formal *deportation* differs from *repatriation*, which refers to the process of returning a person back to his or her place of origin or citizenship on a voluntary basis.

When we refer to groups in terms of their country or geographic region of origin, we use Chinese, Japanese, Korean, European, Asian, Mexican, and so on. We use Chinese American or Korean American to refer to all Chinese or Koreans in America.

We use the term *South Asia* in reference to the present-day countries of Bangladesh, Bhutan, India, Maldives, Nepal, Pakistan, and Sri Lanka. Prior to and during the immigration station's years of operation, the U.S. government categorized all persons from South Asia as "Indian," "East Indian," or "Hindoo." These terms are confusing and incorrect for this time period. Most immigrants from South Asia during the early twentieth century practiced the Sikh religion rather than Hinduism. The Indian subcontinent, under the colonial rule of Great Britain from 1612 to 1947, included all of the present-day countries of South Asia (not just India), and immigrants from all of these countries did come to the United States. The vast majority of migrants discussed in this book were from the Punjab region of the British Indian Empire, which in 1947 was split into East and West Punjab. East Punjab became part of India, while West Punjab became part of Pakistan. We thus use *South Asia* and *Indian subcontinent* to describe immigrants from this region, unless a more specific label, such as "Punjabi," was used in the original source. *India* and *Indian* are used in reference to nationalist activism related to that nation-state inside and outside the Indian subcontinent during this time period.[5]

Following standard practice, when using a person's Chinese or Korean name, we give the surname (family name) first, followed by the given name (usually two characters). For example, in the name Jung Look Moy, Jung is the surname and Look Moy, the given name. The appearance of *Shee* in a Chinese woman's name indicates that she is married. We use the Pinyin romanization system for Chinese proper nouns, except in cases where the names have been commonly spelled in a different romanization system.

We have chosen to protect the privacy and identity of certain Angel Island detainees by changing their names when their stories include sensitive information regarding immigration status and/or personal behavior. Even though the government sources that we use are part of the public record and are open to everyone, we understand that some Angel Island detainees and their descendants may not wish their real names used in these cases. Pseudonyms for these individuals appear in the text and are indicated as such in the endnotes.

Outdated and derogatory terms like "Oriental" or "Asiatic" often appear in this book as part of the historical record from which they were drawn and reflect the perspective of the times.

ABBREVIATIONS

AIISF	Angel Island Immigration Station Foundation
AIISHAC	Angel Island Immigration Station Historical Advisory Committee
AEL	Asiatic Exclusion League
BSI	Board of Special Inquiry
DAR	Daughters of the American Revolution
DHS	Department of Homeland Security
HIAS	Hebrew Immigrant Aid Society
ICE	Immigration and Customs Enforcement
INS	Immigration and Naturalization Service
IRCA	Immigration Reform and Control Act
IWW	Industrial Workers of the World
JAA	Japanese Association of America
KNA	Korean National Association
LPC	Likely to become a public charge
PMSS	Pacific Mail Steamship Company
SAT	Save America's Treasures
YMCA	Young Men's Christian Association
YWCA	Young Women's Christian Association

ANGEL ISLAND

INTRODUCTION

ON JANUARY 22, 1910, thirty-year-old Wong Chung Hong arrived in San Francisco on the steamship *China*. A Chinese merchant with partnerships in a general merchandise store and a dried fruit business in and around Canton, Wong hoped to expand his business in the United States. But first he had to pass the U.S. government's immigrant inspection. He was ordered off the *China* and onto a U.S. government ferry that took him to the brand-new immigration station on Angel Island. One of nineteen immigration stations operating around the United States in the early twentieth century, the Angel Island Immigration Station was the main Pacific gateway into and out of the country.[1]

Wong gave the uniformed immigrant inspectors his documents and answered their questions. He presented his "section-six" certificate signed by the Chinese viceroy and the American consul general in Canton that verified his status as a merchant exempt from the Chinese exclusion laws. The photograph that was attached showed Wong dressed in richly embroidered Chinese robes, a clear marker of his wealth and status. He told Inspector Lauritz Lorenzen that he was heading to Sang Wo & Co., a well-known Chinese grocery store in San Francisco's Chinatown and that he had $500 in U.S. currency with him. Wong's papers were all in order, and he made a good impression on U.S. immigration officials. Inspector Lorenzen noted that the applicant's appearance was "conclusively" not that of a laborer, a class that was excluded from the country, and Wong was admitted into the United States three days later. He would be the first

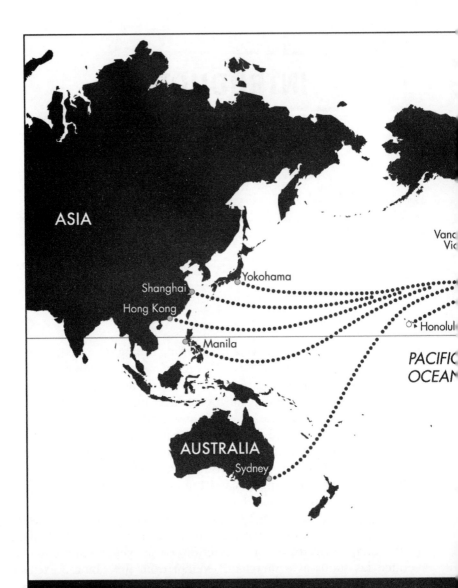

ASIA

Yokohama

Shanghai

Hong Kong

Manila

Vanc
Vic

Honolul

PACIFIC
OCEAN

AUSTRALIA

Sydney

ARRIVALS FROM

Afghanistan	Bulgaria	Denmark	French Indochin
Alaska	Burma	Dominican	Germany
Arabia	Canada	Republic	Ghana
Argentina	Cape Verde	Ecuador	Greece
Armenia	Chile	El Salvador	Grenada
Australia	China	Estonia	Guatemala
Austria	Colombia	Fiji	Hawaii
Belgium	Costa Rica	Finland	Honduras
Brazil	Czechoslovakia	France	Hungary

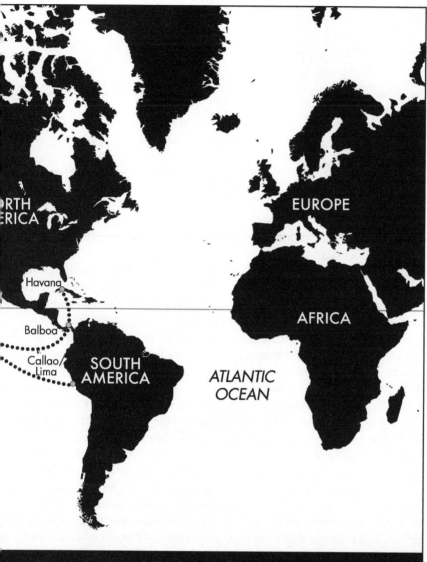

EUROPE

Havana

Balboa

AFRICA

Callao/
Lima

SOUTH
AMERICA

ATLANTIC
OCEAN

RTH
ERICA

UND THE WORLD

Luxembourg
Malaysia
Mauritius
Mexico
Netherlands
New Zealand
Nicaragua
Norway
Panama

Persia
Peru
Philippine Islands
Poland
Portugal
Puerto Rico
Romania
Russia
Samoa

Singapore
South Africa
Spain
Surinam
Sweden
Switzerland
Syria
Tahiti
Thailand

Turkey
United
   Kingdom
Venezuela
West Indies
Yugoslavia

Map of passenger ship routes to San Francisco. The Angel Island Immigration Station was a global crossroads for migrants from all over the world. (Courtesy of Daniel Quan.)

Photograph from Wong Chung Hong's "section six" certificate. (Scan by Vincent Chin. National Archives, Pacific Regional Branch.)

recorded person admitted into the country after being interviewed and detained on Angel Island.[2]

From 1910 to 1940, one million people were processed through the port of San Francisco on their way into or out of the country. These included over 341,000 aliens and returning residents and 209,000 U.S. citizens arriving in the United States. In addition, over 483,000 aliens and 183,000 U.S. citizens departed the country through San Francisco.[3] Deportees, repatriates, alien stowaways, deserting seamen, and migrants in transit also arrived at and departed from San Francisco during the same time period. About half a million people entered or departed the country through Angel Island. Some, like Wong, were admitted within a few days. Others, like Esther and Catarino Lopez and their three young children, were detained at the immigration station for months before being sent back home to Mexico.

The Lopez family arrived on Angel Island three years after Wong Chung Hong. Unlike Wong, they were working class, and immigration officials unanimously voted to exclude the entire family on the grounds that they were "likely to become public charges." Commissioner of Immigration Samuel Backus argued that the aliens did not look fit to support themselves and presented "a very poor appearance." Catarino was "thin, scrawny-looking and not at all rugged." Esther was in her last trimester of pregnancy and presumably unable to work due to her "delicate condition." The children also looked "illy nourished and poorly developed." The family's relatives in Sacramento organized a defense, but after a month, the exclusion order remained in place. While still on Angel Island, Esther gave birth to twins at the immigration station hospital. Methodist missionary Katharine Maurer, known as the "angel of Angel Island," bought clothes for the two children and some gowns for Esther. They were "not the plainest I could find, for I knew how she would appreciate a bit of ribbon and embroidery," Maurer reported. Esther was indeed appreciative. She caressed the garments and profusely thanked Maurer. Two months later, she and her family were deported back to Mexico.[4]

The same year that the Lopezes were deported from Angel Island, six Korean students from Shanghai arrived at the immigration station seeking refuge in America from persecution by the Japanese in their colonized homeland. They had two strikes against them. They did not have the required Japanese passport or identification verifying their status as students, and they were found to be afflicted with hookworm, an excludable medical condition. However, their arrival had been preceded by a letter from the American consul in Shanghai to the secretary of state in Washington, D.C., recommending that, given their family wealth and strong opposition to Japan, they be given special consideration. In addition, they had the support of the Korean National Association, which was willing to guarantee their stay in America. They were treated for hookworm and were admitted one month later.[5]

Soto Shee was not so fortunate, and she received no special consideration on the island. She arrived at the immigration station from Hong Kong in late July of 1924 with her seven-month-old son, Soon Din. While in detention, Soon Din died suddenly. His body was brought to San Francisco for burial while Soto remained detained at the station. Distraught, she asked to be released from the immigration station on bond to be with her husband. Her attorney, Joseph P. Fallon, described his client's "very nervous state of health." But immigration officials in Washington, D.C., denied the request, finding "no unusual hardship." Three weeks later, in the middle of the night, Soto hanged herself in the women's bathroom. She would have died had Matron Grace McKeener not found her unconscious and taken her to the hospital. As she lay in recovery, Soto's husband and attorney Fallon renewed their calls for her to be admitted into the United States. She was eventually allowed to leave the immigration station and enter the country temporarily on bond.[6]

Soto Shee would not have recognized Canadian Ivy Gidlow's description of the immigration station, as their experiences on the island were drastically different. Detained briefly on Angel Island five years after Soto Shee, Gidlow sent her sister a letter describing her clean, white room, the colorful people she encountered in the dining halls, and the comforts of the immigration station. She could take a hot bath whenever she pleased and she enjoyed the well-stocked library immensely. "I am almost content here," she wrote.[7]

How did Wong Chung Hong, Esther Lopez, the six Korean students, Soto Shee, and Ivy Gidlow all end up on Angel Island? And why were their experiences at the immigration station so different?

Angel Island: Immigrant Gateway to America explores the great diversity of immigrants who passed through America's Pacific gateway for the first time. Situated at the edge of the United States, the Angel Island Immigration Station was a place where global forces clashed with American national interests and identity. People from around the world were on the move as part of the era of global mass migration. Those seeking entry to the United States confronted U.S. immigration policies that treated immigrants differently based on their race, nationality, gender, and class as a way of identifying which ones were fit to enter the country and become Americans and which ones were not. These laws were just one part of a larger system of racial segregation and discrimination for immigrants and people of color in the United States during the twentieth century. The history of immigration on Angel Island illustrates the very real consequences that these policies had on immigrant lives and communities. But the significance of Angel Island's immigration history extends far beyond the island itself. The migration histories and experiences of the one million people who were processed through San Francisco and Angel Island reveals a world on the move and the making of America as both an inclusive nation of immigrants and an exclusive gatekeeping nation.

Immigration Policy and the Making of America

For much of its history, the United States had an open-door immigration policy. From the colonial era through the mid-nineteenth century, foreign immigration was encouraged to help settle newly colonized lands in an expanding America. Until the late nineteenth century, states still regulated foreign immigration into and out of their jurisdictions. The federal government began to keep track of immigrants in 1819 and passed its first federal law regulating immigration in 1875. From that point on, the United States' open door began to close, and Congress and the executive branch established executive authority over immigration as a sovereign right of the United States. Immigration policy became viewed as a tool to define just what it meant to be an "American." The first laws began to exclude certain groups from that definition by explicitly restricting immigrants based on their race, gender, and class. The 1875 Page Law forbade the entry of Chinese, Japanese, and other Asian laborers brought to the United States involuntarily and Asian women brought for the purpose of prostitution. The Chinese Exclusion Act followed in 1882. The 1875 and 1882 laws focused specifically on Chinese laborers and prostitutes, but they transformed modern American immigration policy and immigrant inspection and detention in general. They legalized the restriction, exclusion, and deportation of immigrants considered to be threats to the United States for the first time in the country's history. The Chinese Exclusion Act firmly established the need for federal immigrant inspection sites and inspection policies, as well as federal documentation such as passports and "green cards." It also firmly placed immigration regulation under the control of the government's immigration officials rather than the courts and designated penalties for unlawful or fraudulent entry. The Supreme Court upheld the constitutionality of these laws by arguing that the power to exclude and deport immigrants was an "inherent and inalienable right of every sovereign and independent nation" and was "essential to its safety, its independence, and its welfare."[8]

With these laws, the United States began to close its doors to a wide range of people. Beginning in 1882, a general immigration law barred criminals, prostitutes, paupers, lunatics, idiots, and those likely to become public charges (LPC) from entering the United States. The Alien Contract Labor Law was passed in 1885. In 1891, Congress further forbade the entry of polygamists and aliens convicted of a crime involving "moral turpitude" and gave the federal government unprecedented power to decide immigration matters. In 1903, another immigration law excluded anarchists, and four years later, Congress barred all women coming to the United States for "immoral purposes." A diplomatic accord, known as the "Gentlemen's Agreement" between the United States and Japan, also effectively ended the immigration of Japanese and Korean laborers after 1907.[9]

By the early twentieth century, Americans largely supported the call to "close the gates" to immigration in general. The Immigration Act of 1917 reflected growing anti-immigrant sentiment across the country and enacted a wide range of new provisions, including a literacy test for all adult immigrants and restrictions on suspected radicals. In response to anti-Asian sentiment, the act also denied entry to aliens living within a newly conceived geographical area called the "Asiatic Barred Zone." All immigrants from India, Burma, Siam, the Malay States, Arabia, Afghanistan, part of Russia, and most of the Polynesian Islands were thereafter excluded.[10]

During and after World War I, new passport controls were instituted by the U.S. government. As the campaign to restrict immigration intensified in the 1920s, new laws also followed. The Quota Act of 1921 placed numerical limitations on immigration for the first time and set temporary quotas for each immigrant group based on national origins. Three years later, the 1924 Immigration Act reduced the total number of admissions even more and revised the quota formula. Both laws were designed to limit arrivals from Southern and Eastern Europe and favor immigrants from Northern and Western Europe. No restrictions were placed on immigration from the Western Hemisphere, but the 1924 act closed the door on any further Asian immigration by denying admission to all aliens who were "ineligible to citizenship," a legal classification that applied only to Asians. The act also required visas to enter the country and shifted the burden of immigrant inspection to overseas personnel at American embassies. The Border Patrol was established in 1925 to increase surveillance and immigrant inspection along the U.S.-Mexico and U.S.-Canadian borders. In 1929, immigration into the United States was limited to 150,000 individuals a year based on an even more restrictive national origins quota system that continued to favor immigration from Northern and Western Europe. This system would remain in place until 1965.[11]

The economic depression of the 1930s sharply curtailed immigration into the United States. At the same time, there was an increase in arrests and deportations of immigrants already in the country, particularly Filipinos and Mexicans. An estimated one million Mexicans, including American-born children, were returned to Mexico during the decade. The 1934 Tydings-McDuffie Act subjected the immigration of Filipinos to the quota system, and the 1935 Repatriation Act enabled the voluntary repatriation of Filipinos to the Philippines.[12]

As the United States continued to close its door to an ever-widening group of immigrants, regulation of immigration on Angel Island became a complex, multifaceted process. Like Ellis Island, the Angel Island Immigration Station was one of the country's main ports of entry for immigrants in the early twentieth century. But while Angel Island was popularly called the "Ellis Island of the West," it was very different from its counterpart in New York. Mainly a processing center for European immigrants, Ellis Island enforced American immigration laws that restricted, but did not exclude, European immigrants. In fact, one of the goals of Ellis Island was to begin the process of turning European immigrants into naturalized Americans. Angel Island, on the other hand, was the main port of entry for Asian immigrants and was characterized by American immigration policies that excluded Asians and barred them from becoming naturalized citizens. Most European immigrants processed through Ellis Island spent only a few hours or at most a few days there, while the processing time for Asian, especially Chinese, immigrants on Angel Island was measured in days and weeks.[13]

Although the Angel Island Immigration Station was designed to address San Francisco's unique status as the primary entryway for Chinese coming to the United States, an increasingly diverse group of immigrants from Europe, Asia, and Latin America arrived at the station over the years. Between 1915 and 1920, non-Asians represented approximately one-third of the immigrants applying for admission at the port of San Francisco. After 1924, non-Asians represented about 15 percent of all arrivals.[14] Russians and Mexicans came to America seeking refuge from the revolutionary violence and disorder ravaging their homelands; Japanese "picture brides" and Chinese "paper sons" crossed the Pacific to join their families; Sikh and Filipino laborers sought work in the fields of California's Central Valley; and Korean, Russian, and Jewish refugees hoped to find freedom from religious and political persecution.[15] Some crossed the Pacific Ocean directly from their homelands. Chinese from the Pearl River Delta could easily board a trans-Pacific steamship in Hong Kong that would take them to family and relatives in *Gam Saan*, or Gold Mountain, the name that Chinese used for

California. Others took more circuitous routes to San Francisco and traveled great distances by land and sea before arriving in the United States. South Asians came through the Golden Gate after working in Manila, Hong Kong, or Tokyo. Filipinos ended their contracts on Hawaiian plantations and then came to San Francisco to try their luck on the mainland. Russian refugees crossed Siberia and Manchuria before boarding ships in Yokohama and Kobe bound for the United States. Spanish laborers arrived in the city after working in Panama, Mexico, Cuba, Guatemala, and Hawaii. Salvadorans traveled through Guatemala and Mexico to board steamships in Mazatlan bound for *el norte*.[16]

The Angel Island Immigration Station also played a key role in removing and deporting immigrants already in the United States on charges of prostitution, LPC, criminal offenses, and radical politics. The deportation hearings for Harry Bridges, the Australian-born labor leader accused of being a communist, took place at the Angel Island Immigration Station in 1939 and lasted over nine weeks before the judge ruled that he was not a member of the Communist Party. Many Filipinos were also detained and deported from Angel Island during the repatriation campaigns of the 1930s. Although this history is not as fully documented as the immigration station's role in processing new arrivals, this work was an essential part of United States immigration policy. Angel Island was both an entry point for immigrants seeking better lives in America and a last stop on a forced journey out of the country.[17]

Angel Island: Immigrant Gateway to America is the first full history of the Angel Island Immigration Station and the diverse immigrants who passed through its doors on their way into and out of the United States. It connects Angel Island to global histories of migration, war, colonialism, and revolution, as well as to American histories of race, ethnic, class, and gender relations. As America's Pacific gateway, it tells a different story from that of Ellis Island, one that fundamentally changes the way we think about immigration in the past and in the present.

Building the "Finest Immigrant Station in the World"

The largest island in the San Francisco Bay, Angel Island has a long and varied history. According to archaeological evidence and artifacts, the Hookooeko tribe of the Coast Miwok American Indians lived on the island for at least 1,000 years and used it as a temporary hunting and fishing camp. In 1775, a Spanish expedition led by Juan Manuel de Ayala anchored on the island and named it *Isla de Los Angeles*, Angel Island. Thereafter, Spanish, French, Russian, and British explorers, sealers, whalers, and navy crews often used it as a base for their operations or a place to obtain fuel and fresh water after making the difficult passage through the Golden Gate. The European presence was disastrous for the Miwok. Contagious diseases brought by the new European settlers greatly reduced the small number of natives on the island.[18]

Under the ownership of the Mexican government after 1821, Angel Island was home to a large cattle ranch. After the U.S.-Mexican war, the United States gained control of the island, and in 1850, the federal government designated Angel Island a military base. The Camp Reynolds army post was established there in 1863 during the Civil War, and in 1900, all of the army facilities on the island were renamed Fort McDowell. Until 1946, Angel Island served as an overseas assignment and discharge depot for troops bound to and from Hawaii and the Philippines. A quarantine station operated at Ayala Cove on the island from 1891 to 1946. Over 700 German enemy aliens were housed at the immigration station for a brief period during World War I, and federal prisoners and prisoners of war were also detained there in subsequent years.[19]

Although the immigration station on Angel Island did not open until 1910, its history dates back to 1882 when the federal government established new immigrant inspection procedures under the Chinese Exclusion Act. The law declared that passengers would not be allowed to land in the United States until they had been inspected and approved for admission by a "Chinese inspector." The problem was that the act did not indicate where any detainees would be housed if their inspections took longer than one day.

Immigration officials and steamship companies bringing Asian passengers to the United States were forced to piece together a makeshift detention system. In August 1882 when the *City of Sydney* steamship arrived in San Francisco with the first Chinese passengers after the Exclusion Act went into effect, sixteen Chinese crewmen needed to be detained while immigrant inspectors studied their papers and their claims for admission into the country. But there was nowhere to house them. They were transferred to another ship docked nearby in the San Francisco Bay. Other steamship companies followed suit and transferred Chinese passengers from ship to ship until the final decisions in their cases were made. The San Francisco county jail, located on Broadway near Dupont Street, was also used as a detention facility for those who could not post bond or who had been ordered deported. Young women traveling alone were often sent to one of the mission homes in San Francisco, such as the Chinese Presbyterian Mission Home, established to "rescue" and convert Chinese prostitutes. But steamship detention continued to be the main system of detention for almost twenty years, and immigration officials complained of the "large floating Chinese alien population in the Bay."[20]

In 1898, the Pacific Mail Steamship Company (PMSS), one of the main transporters of goods and people across the Pacific Ocean, converted some of its general offices on Pier 40 into a detention facility, and Chinese detainees were moved there. The "detention shed," as it came to be known, was a two-story wooden building, measuring only 100 feet by 50 feet. Although it had been built to house 200 inmates, at times it held more than twice that many. Men were held on the ground floor, women on the second. Additional bunks were added, but they were placed in the aisles, which only exacerbated the chronic overcrowding in the shed.[21]

Located at the end of the wharf, where city sewage odors were "most offensive," the shed was extremely unsanitary. Ventilation was poor, and the inmates often fell sick. A few even died. One immigrant inspector declared the place a "veritable fire trap," while another referred to the detention shed as having "inhuman" conditions. Immigrants themselves referred to it generally as the *muk uk*, "wooden barracks," but more commonly as the "iron cage" and "Chinese jail." Wong Ngum Yin, a Chinese immigrant detained in the shed, charged that the American "barbarians" had "neither mercy or compassion and are like the lions and the tigers. Our countrymen hate them." The *Chinese World*, a Chinese-language newspaper in San Francisco, reported that one detainee committed suicide inside the detention shed "due to unbearable misery." In 1902, Chinese frustration with the conditions at the shed neared riot proportions. Several immigrants, in transit from Latin America back to China, had been detained for over seven months. Loy Yuen Wing spoke for the group in a mass meeting and threatened to "tear the shed apart" unless they were immediately returned to China on the very next boat. Other Chinese grew so frustrated that they risked their lives to escape. Between September and November of 1908 alone, thirty-two Chinese succeeded in escaping from the shed.[22] In 1902, Commissioner-General of Immigration Frank Sargent admitted that the detention quarters were so "disgraceful—cramped in dimensions, lacking in every facility for cleanliness and decency that it is necessary to insist upon an immediate remodeling thereof." San Francisco, being the "principal port for Japanese and Chinese aliens" into the country, needed better facilities, he reported. These protests did result in some slight improvements to the detention shed in 1903, but it remained in use until 1909.[23]

The numerous complaints about the conditions at the detention shed helped sway government officials in Washington, D.C., to find a better solution. In 1904, Congress appropriated $250,000 to construct an immigration facility in San Francisco. With the successful operation on Ellis Island in mind, lawmakers suggested that San Francisco build a similar immigration station on an isolated island. Angel Island was seen as a logical choice.[24] In 1905, the Department of Commerce and Labor requested twenty acres of land on the north side of the island from the War Department to establish the immigration facility. Chinese community leaders protested against the location, arguing that it would be difficult for witnesses to travel so far from the mainland. However, federal officials were eager for the station to be completed. As San Francisco Commissioner of Immigration Hart Hyatt North explained, the new station would provide immigration officials with larger offices and Chinese immigrants with better detention quarters. Most important, the island location would also be the most effective means of keeping a watchful eye over the newly arriving Chinese. They would be separated from friends and family who might try to coach them on how to pass the interrogations, something that was common to the "wily Chinee," North said. With the island reachable only by a forty-five-minute ferry ride from the mainland, Chinese detainees would also be segregated from the rest of the nation, thereby protecting Americans from any contagious diseases or danger represented by their threatening presence. Plus, the island was escape proof. Angel Island, North explained, was "ideal," for "it is impossible for anyone to escape by swimming to the mainland."[25]

Architect Walter J. Matthews from Oakland, California, was hired to design the new immigration station. He hoped to build a station similar to the one on Ellis Island and drew up plans for the facility after a visit to New York. Matthews was particularly drawn to the "cottage system" and campus setting on Ellis Island, where buildings were devoted to specific functions, such as administration, medical services, and detention, and were grouped together. Work began in 1907, and by 1908, construction of the major buildings had been completed. But problems during the final construction phase led to numerous delays. A 1909 government inspection found that the facility suffered from a long list of deficiencies, including shoddy construction, a lack of fire protection, and a limited water supply.

U. S. IMMIGRATION STATION, ANGEL ISLAND, CALIFORNIA

Sketch of the Angel Island Immigration Station by architect Walter J. Matthews, c. 1907. (Courtesy of the California History Room, California State Library, Sacramento, California.)

Architect Matthews was abruptly let go in July 1909, and the future of the station was placed in doubt. However, immigrant detention at the PMSS shed could not continue either. The conditions were deplorable, and the escape of thirty-one Chinese aliens in 1909 provided further evidence that better, more secure facilities were needed. California politicians petitioned President William Howard Taft on his visit to San Francisco in October of 1909. The president expressed support for the "immediate opening" of the immigration station on Angel Island, and soon thereafter, the station was being prepared for its opening day.[26]

Local newspapers gushed about the future immigration station. The *San Francisco Chronicle* predicted that it would be the "finest Immigrant Station in the World." "Newcomers from foreign shores will probably think they have struck paradise when they emerge from steerage quarters of an ocean liner and land at the summer resort which the Immigration Bureau has provided for them," it claimed. Other descriptions of the immigration station in the local press described how "San Francisco's New Ellis Island" would be "one of the finest and best equipped immigrant stations in the country." Its European quarters would have "excellent accommodations" and "most of the conveniences of a first-class hotel." The design of the "Oriental quarters" assured "the perfect scheme of sanitation," and the hospital would be as well equipped as "the most modern hospitals in the world."[27]

In reality, with only a few months left before the station was to open, the immigration station was far from complete. Roads, employee housing, paths, sidewalks, retaining walls, gutters, and fences all needed to be built. Telephone service, lighting, and sewers needed to be installed. Blankets, furniture, and kitchen equipment needed to be purchased. Ferry service to and from the mainland needed to be established,

San Francisco Commissioner of Immigration Hart Hyatt North (right) in the administration building of the Angel Island Immigration Station, c. 1910. (Courtesy of the Bancroft Library, University of California, Berkeley.)

and both immigrant detainees and immigration personnel and records needed to be transferred to the new immigration station.[28]

All of these daunting responsibilities fell to San Francisco Commissioner of Immigration Hart Hyatt North. A native Californian, former lawyer, and Republican California state representative from Alameda County, North had served as commissioner since 1898. A graduate of the University of California, Berkeley, he considered himself an expert on Asian immigration matters and was an early supporter of building the immigration station on the island.[29] But in the frenzied weeks and months leading up to the station's opening day, North faced constant obstacles. As he wrote to the commissioner-general of immigration:

No one who has not been here since October…can have any conception of the difficulties under which I have struggled in carrying out the regular work, and in equipping and occupying this station.

The responsibility of the work we have been doing since October has been so great that I have never been able to get rid of my work even on leaving the office and going home; in fact the responsibility has stayed with me day and night, so much so that I have been suffering for some months with insomnia, an absolutely new physical disorder to me, and the cause of which I can only attribute to an overstrained nervous condition…

I had to overcome the silent but nevertheless forceful opposition of a large number of the employees of this Service, who either because of disinclination to cross the bay twice a day, or for worse motives, preferred to stay in San Francisco. I have had to overcome the persistent and steady opposition of the Chinese people and their representatives who would not hesitate to do anything in the world to prevent the occupancy of the station, as the same meant a proper enforcement of the Chinese exclusion law…

In addition to all this mechanical equipment and reorganization of the Service, I have managed to carry on all the regular immigration and Chinese business with scarcely any delay notwithstanding the fact that immigration during the winter and spring months up to the 1st of May, was unprecedented for those periods of the year.[30]

When opening day for the immigration station on Angel Island came on January 21, 1910, North was exhausted. He conceded to his superiors in Washington, D.C., that the station was too small and inadequate to the task at hand, and that renovations and enlargements were needed immediately. The Chinese community, he also observed, were "still holding meetings of protest and so forth." He suspected that Chinese shipping agents and others had endeavored to "rush in all the Chinese possible

The administration building was the focal point of the entire immigration station. Situated at the end of the dock and wharf, its formal architecture, terrace, and landscaping reflected the power of the Bureau of Immigration and the U.S. government. It had three separate sets of stairs leading to a covered, colonnaded porch. New arrivals would enter through the center, or main doors into the main examination room, where they would wait to be processed. The left entrance led to the dining rooms, detention quarters, inspectors' rooms, and the stenographers' pool. Interrogations most likely took place in this space. The right entrance led to the commissioner's office. (Courtesy of the California State Parks, 2010.)

before we got to the station." The large numbers of Chinese arrivals during Chinese New Year was unprecedented, and he surmised that they wanted to avoid the new station and its tougher procedures at all costs. North read the sentiments of the Chinese community correctly. The *Chinese World* marked the opening of the Angel Island Immigration Station with a special editorial on the treatment of Chinese immigrants under the exclusion laws. At the Pacific Mail Steamship Company detention shed, the editors noted that the "mistreatment of us Chinese confined there was worse than for jailed prisoners." The barren offshore island immigration station, they predicted, would be no better.[31]

Immigration officials began working at the new immigration station on January 21, 1910. The next day, 101 Chinese detainees and "one lone and gloomy Hindu" were brought from the PMSS detention shed to the detention barracks on the island. Over 400 new passengers, mostly Chinese, were also transferred from the *China* and the *Manchuria* steamships without incident. By February 3, North reported that there were 566 aliens in detention and that he was expecting between 600 and 700 more the next day. The vast majority was Chinese, but there were also 150 South Asians, twenty-five Japanese, and a "scattering" of other nationalities. The Angel Island Immigration Station was officially open for business.[32]

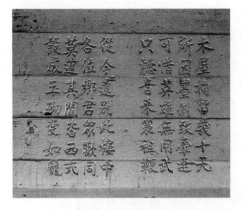

The walls literally talk at the Angel Island Immigration Station. Hundreds of poems and inscriptions can be found carved or written into the walls of the detention barracks. This Chinese poem (see translation below) was carved by an anonymous poet into the walls of a lavatory room on the first floor of the detention barracks. (Photograph by Mak Takahashi. Courtesy of Philip Choy.)

New Histories from America's Pacific Gateway

Until recently, the literature on Angel Island has centered almost exclusively on the Chinese immigrant experience. This has made sense in many ways. As the main port of entry for Chinese immigrants applying for admission into the United States, the Angel Island Immigration Station was largely built to fulfill the country's need to enforce the Chinese exclusion laws. It was designed with exclusion, not admission, in mind, and on the island, Chinese were singled out for long detentions and intense interrogations to prove their legal right to enter the country. For them, Angel Island was a symbol of exclusion, or a "half-open door at best." The poems written and carved into the station's walls by angry, frustrated, and homesick immigrants are especially powerful reminders of the costs and hardships of immigration under such a discriminatory regime. Their discovery by California State Park Ranger Alexander Weiss in 1970 inspired community efforts to preserve the immigration station and its history and to designate it a National Historic Landmark. The poems are also evidence of immigrant resistance and perseverance, and it is this immigrant spirit that draws hundreds of thousands of visitors to the island every year.[33]

Detained in this wooden house for several tens of days,
It is all because of the Mexican exclusion law which implicates me.
It's a pity heroes have no way of exercising their prowess.
I can only await the word so that I can snap Zu's whip.

From now on, I am departing far from this building.
All of my fellow villagers are rejoicing with me.
Don't say that everything within is Western styled.
Even if it is built of jade, it has turned into a cage.[34]

As important as the Chinese immigrant experience on Angel Island is, there are many more immigrant stories that need to be recovered and preserved. The Angel Island Immigration Station was a global crossroads, and it played a central role in the overall development of U.S. immigration and refugee policy in the twentieth century. People from all over the world passed through its doors, but we have known almost nothing about them or their experiences. *Angel Island* examines the great diversity of immigrants who passed through America's Pacific gateway and asks: Who were the immigrants of Angel Island? Where did they come from and why? What were their experiences at America's Pacific gateway and why were they so different from each other? What does Angel Island tell us about America and its conflicted relationship with immigration?

A few tantalizing clues came to our attention early in the process of writing this book. The faces looking up from photographs in the California State Park archives include Japanese women in kimonos, Russian refugees, Sikh farmers, and a mother and son from Turkey. Japanese poems written by labor organizer Karl Yoneda while he was detained on the island in 1927 describe the "different sounds of voices from the next room; Chinese, Russian, Mexican, Greek, and Italian." Coverage of leading Indian nationalist Har Dayal and his deportation hearing on Angel Island in 1914 landed on the front page of San Francisco newspapers. An article in the *Russkii Golos* newspaper describes a group of Russian students who wrote poems and gave theatrical performances during their months-long detention on Angel Island. In his autobiography, Chicano historian Ernesto Galarza recalls his visit to the island and the "gringo" immigration officials that denied entry to his Mexican relatives in the 1910s. Recent feasibility studies conducted by the Angel Island Immigration Station Foundation have revealed a treasure trove of over 187 Chinese poems, 33 graphic images, and 156 inscriptions in Japanese, Korean, Russian, Punjabi, Spanish, Italian, German, and English.

But before we could start exploring this great diversity of immigrant passages, we needed to find out how many immigrants were detained at the Angel Island Immigration Station and their ethnic backgrounds. One major challenge is that the 1940 fire that destroyed the administration building also destroyed most of the immigration station's administrative records. After hundreds of hours digging through Immigration and Naturalization Service (INS) reports, ship passenger lists, Board of Special Inquiry (BSI) registers, and immigration case files at the National Archives, we could only say with certainty that over one million people passed through the port of San Francisco between 1910 and 1940: 550,469 people arrived and 665,430 departed (see Appendix, Table 1). We could not determine exactly how many of the arrivals had to go to Angel Island for immigrant inspection. We estimate 300,000 based

ANGEL ISLAND LEAGUE OF NATIONS.

No. 2, is an African; No. 3, Japanese, (too bad he is almost hidden); No. 4, German; Nos. 7 and 8, two Russian stowaways; No. 9, Mohammedans; No. 11, Argentinean. The others are Samoans and South Sea Islanders, who were taken from an Alaskan ship and sent back to their native isles.

The detainees on Angel Island made up their own "league of nations." (Scan by Vincent Chin. *Woman's Home Missions*, October 28, 1920.)

Turkish mother and son, c. 1910. (Courtesy of the California State Parks, 2010.)

An African woman and two children standing on the rooftop of the administration building, c. 1916. (Courtesy of the California State Parks, 2010.)

Japanese women on the rooftop of the administration building, c. 1915. (Courtesy of the California State Parks, 2010.)

Two immigrant children, a Chinese toddler and a Canadian boy named Earl, on the rooftop of the administration building, c. 1915. (Courtesy of the California State Parks, 2010.)

Immigrant women detainees posing outdoors in the recreation yard behind the detention barracks, c. 1930. (Courtesy of the California State Parks, 2010.)

Group of five Sikh immigrants, c. 1916. (Courtesy of the California State Parks, 2010.)

on Robert Barde's study that 70 percent of alien arrivals (and some U.S. citizens) were detained at Angel Island. Of the 300,000 detainees, we estimate that there were 100,000 Chinese, 85,000 Japanese, 8,000 South Asians, 8,000 Russians and Jews, 1,000 Koreans, 1,000 Filipinos, and 400 Mexicans based on immigration statistics for the entire United States, the BSI registers, and the immigration case files at the National Archives. Even the latter two sources are incomplete. With the exception of the Chinese, most immigrants were not interviewed by the BSI or were interviewed only briefly, and through the years, many immigration files have been lost, destroyed, or consolidated into other types of INS files. Thanks to the help of many volunteers who laboriously went through all the Angel Island case files at the National Archives, we now know that detainees were born in and came from eighty different countries in the world (see Appendix, Table 2).[35]

This book focuses on the experiences of Chinese, Japanese, Korean, South Asian, Russian, Mexican, and Filipino immigrants on Angel Island. They were the largest immigrant groups to come through the immigration station, and their experiences highlight particularly important chapters in Angel Island and American immigration history. We drew upon fifty previously conducted oral history interviews and interviewed forty more people who either entered the country through Angel Island or had family members who did so. They have generously shared their time, family histories, documents, and photographs with us. These oral histories, along with the autobiographies and other writings by immigrants, visitors, and immigration officials, have helped us to better understand the impact of immigration policies on immigrants and immigrant communities. Government documents, including the central files of the INS in Washington, D.C., and the immigration arrival case files for San Francisco and Angel Island in San Bruno, CA, shed light on why and how policies were made and implemented at both national and regional levels. Archival collections housing the papers and records of immigration officials, social workers, and organizations allowed us to examine the life and business of the Angel Island Immigration Station from a variety of perspectives.

At the center of this book are the stories of immigrants themselves and the ways in which immigration laws were translated into real decisions and actions on Angel Island. We have dug through thousands of immigration documents for those who applied for admission or readmission into the country through Angel Island. Many of these immigrants would be admitted; some would be turned back or detained for months to await decisions on their legal appeals; still others would later be arrested and deported. Together, their stories offer a more complete and complicated history of immigration on Angel Island than we have ever known.

Debates over American race and class relations and the proper roles for women and men were played out every day in the decisions made on Angel Island. Immigration laws and their proper enforcement had great significance for the nation. Many Americans believed that only the right kinds of immigrants could help America maintain its greatness and become a world power. Admitting the wrong kind would lead to racial, economic, cultural, and moral decline and the ruin of the country. Thus, new arrivals were sifted according to how well they fit the nation's definitions of who could and should be an American. Angel Island's immigration history is ultimately about the ongoing struggle to define what it means to be an American and the nation's complicated relationship with immigration.

For immigrants themselves, the immigration experience transcended Angel Island. The policies enforced there categorized some immigrants as "aliens ineligible to citizenship," while others were automatically set on the path toward naturalization. These legal classifications came with tangible rights such as the ability to vote or own or lease property. They also helped define a national American identity that included some while excluding others.

Angel Island's history complicates our understandings of America as a celebratory "nation of immigrants." It forces us to ask these essential and timely questions: Is the United States a "nation of immigrants" that welcomes newcomers and helps them to achieve their dreams? Or is it a "gate-keeping nation" that builds fences and detention centers to keep out certain groups of immigrants who are perceived as undesirable and dangerous aliens?

Angel Island shows how the United States has simultaneously welcomed and restricted immigrants. Certainly, Angel Island did become the gateway into America for thousands of immigrants who went on to strive for the opportunity, freedom, and fortune that the American Dream represented—if not for themselves, then for their children and grandchildren. Koreans, Russians, and Mexicans all found refuge from political persecution and revolutionary chaos in their homelands. Chinese, Japanese, Koreans, South Asians, and Filipinos found work as farm laborers, and some eventually owned their own farms or businesses. For them, Angel Island was a stepping-stone to better lives in America, and their journey was made easier by the social workers, immigrant aid societies, and religious organizations that assisted them on and off the island. These Angel Island immigrants went on to help build this nation of immigrants.

However, as the recent debates over immigration vividly illustrate, the United States has not always been at ease with the number of newcomers—especially non-European—coming to and staying in the United States.

From the colonial era to the present, Americans have debated whether immigration is beneficial or detrimental to the country. And more often than not, they have supported the passage of restrictive and exclusionary immigration laws and border control measures. As an immigrant detention facility, the Angel Island Immigration Station turned away countless newcomers and processed the deportation of thousands of U.S. residents in the country without proper documentation. Chinese "paper sons," Sikh laborers, Mexican families, and women suspected of prostitution were denied entry, sometimes after harrowing interrogations and long detentions. Indian nationalists, Filipino repatriates, and others were hounded by immigration authorities and either denied entry or arrested and deported from the country. The "gatekeeping" functions of the immigration station reflected the U.S. government's efforts to manage an unsurpassed wave of migration from around the world. Angel Island thus directly helped to maintain two Americas: one that allowed immigrants to make better lives for themselves and become Americans, and another that treated immigrants as unwanted foreigners who were to be denied entry and removed.

The fact that immigration policy could both welcome and exclude immigrants led to fascinating contradictions at the immigration station. Chinese laborers were excluded, but Chinese merchants were not. Commissioner of Immigration Hart Hyatt North wrote about the "wily Chinee" but earned the nickname of "Sahib North" when he refused to exclude South Asians without cause. Immigrant Inspector Frank Ainsworth led the charge to exclude as many unassimilable "Hindus" as possible but came to the defense of Korean refugee students. Australians and New Zealanders were able to bypass the quota laws, but Assyrian and Russian refugees could not. Meanwhile, America's involvement in World War I and President Woodrow Wilson's public statement advocating relief for Europe's refugees translated into differential treatment of refugees at Angel Island. Russian and Jewish refugees received special consideration for their status fleeing persecution, while Korean and Mexican refugees did not. Women of all backgrounds faced aggressive interrogations that focused on their sexual histories, while men did not. And even though they immigrated to the United States during a period of intense anti-Japanese sentiment, the Japanese had the lowest rejection rates among all the immigrant groups (see Appendix, Table 3).

These two contradictory sides of American immigration history are rarely told together. Indeed, for many Americans, the celebratory story of the twelve million immigrants, most of them European, coming through Ellis Island resonates with Emma Lazarus's famous couplet, "Give me your tired, your poor,/Your huddled masses yearning to breathe free," and has come to represent America's immigration history in its entirety. Ellis Island has become synonymous not only with America's immigrant heritage but also with its national identity in general. But in its celebration of how European immigrants were welcomed into and remade America, the popular Ellis Island mythology eclipses more complicated histories, like those from Angel Island.[36]

The Angel Island Immigration Station was not the "Ellis Island of the West," and *Angel Island: Immigrant Gateway to America* tells this different immigration history. It is the story of both America's welcome to immigrants *and* its history of immigration restriction. It pointedly examines the contradictions inherent in America's celebratory mythos of immigration and the reality that immigration policies reinforced race, class, and gender hierarchies in the country. It is a rich, and sometimes, tragic history that helps to explain the full complexity of both American immigration and America itself.[37]

In comparing the varied experiences of detainees on Angel Island, we can clearly see that applicants for admission shared some similar experiences. Immigrants wanted to enter the United States. Immigration officials were charged with protecting the nation from undesirable and dangerous aliens. How both sides interpreted the intent and application of immigration laws often resulted in conflict. Lawyers, family members, employers, social workers, and government officials in Washington, D.C., sometimes became involved, extending the conflict far beyond the island.

Despite these similarities, immigration regulation on Angel Island was also extremely complex. International relations, histories of colonialism, and U.S. immigration policies that treated individuals differently according to their race, class, gender, and nationality all influenced how different immigrant groups came to Angel Island and how they fared once there. Chinese immigrants were judged solely through the terms of the Chinese exclusion laws. Japanese, Koreans, and South Asians eventually became excluded by race-based laws, but they were also subjected to class-based and general immigration laws. For Russian and Jewish refugees, class, nationality, and political convictions, but not race, were the criteria for exclusion. Immigrants with wealth, education, and powerful friends from all backgrounds almost always faced less scrutiny than their fellow countrymen and entered the country after only minimal inspections. Women were judged by their morality, their role in the family, and their race. Women traveling alone or who had checkered sexual pasts encountered more difficulties than others traveling with their husbands and who were deemed to be "respectable." For all immigrants, race, class, and gender-based laws worked together to either open the gate to America or keep it closed.[38]

Immigrants actively challenged their treatment on Angel Island and their exclusion from the country, but the ways that they did so also varied. Some, like the Chinese, Koreans, and Russians, were able to marshal strong ethnic organizations to come to their defense. Chinese were the most active litigants and routinely hired the best lawyers to represent their cases to the U.S. government. Jewish refugees relied upon a highly organized network of religious and ethnic organizations to come to their defense. Others like the Japanese depended on their home governments as a counterweight to American discrimination. Many, such as the Mexicans, Chinese, and Filipinos, called on family, friends, neighbors, and employers to verify their claims for admission. Others, like South Asians, had fewer ethnic organizations and an unresponsive, or even hostile, home government that facilitated their exclusion from the United States.

The differences between immigrant groups, their migration histories, and the immigration policies used to regulate their admission or exclusion from the country played out on every level. They influenced which groups were more likely to be detained and how closely they were scrutinized by immigration officials. They determined how much was budgeted for their meals, the type of food offered, and where they would sleep. Men and women were treated differently, as were people of different classes, but race was the most important factor shaping different immigration laws and immigrant experiences on the island. A strict policy of racial segregation separated Asians from non-Asians, and a difference in detention rates reflected immigration policies that privileged whites over Asians.

The half a million immigrants who were processed through the Angel Island Immigration Station is substantially fewer than the twelve million who were processed on Ellis Island. But with its diversity of immigrants, Angel Island—perhaps more than any other site—allows us to best understand how U.S. immigration policies and their hierarchical treatment of immigrants played out in daily practices at the nation's borders.

This book is organized to highlight new histories from Angel Island. The history of the immigration station provides the organizational spine of the book, beginning with the building of the immigration station and ending with its rebirth and restoration as a National Historic Landmark. The chapters on specific immigrant groups are the centerpiece of the book. They illustrate the diverse migration histories and experiences on Angel Island that, together, revise both our understandings of immigration through Angel Island and American immigration history in general.

Chapter One focuses on the life and business of the immigration station and the ways in which U.S. immigration policies were applied to an increasingly diverse population of immigrants. While there were some common procedures that all arrivals at the immigration station followed, Angel Island's immigration history is best characterized by the diversity of immigrant experiences. Immigrants' class status, gender, nationality, and especially race, determined who was more likely to be detained at the station and for how long, as well as who would be admitted and who would be excluded.

While the first chapter focuses on comparison, the next chapters separately examine specific immigrant groups in order to capture their full, diverse, and complex histories of migration to America and their unique experiences on Angel Island.

The majority of Chinese who immigrated to the United States during the so-called exclusion era from 1882–1943 came through San Francisco, and they were the largest immigrant group to pass through the Angel Island Immigration Station. Chapter Two explores the experiences of the approximately 100,000 Chinese detainees on Angel Island and the wide range of legal, political, and migration strategies they used to immigrate during this restrictive era.

Chapter Three tells the stories of the second largest group at Angel Island, the 85,000 Japanese who immigrated as picture brides or as the children of Japanese residents. Under the protection of a strong home government, their stay on the island was much shorter than that of the Chinese and their exclusion rate was the lowest of all the immigrant groups. Still, many Japanese detainees remember Angel Island as a prison and a place of anguish and anxiety.

Approximately 8,000 South Asians entered the United States through Angel Island. Many came just as the Angel Island Immigration Station opened its doors, and their arrival created a controversy that put the new station and its officers to the test. Chapter Four explores how South Asian immigrants, immigration officials, and anti-Asian activists clashed over the meaning and enforcement of U.S. immigration policy. South Asians faced discrimination and anti-immigrant sentiment on and off the island and chafed at the inability of their homeland to protect them. As a result, many became involved in the Gadar (Rebellion) movement to fight against inequality in the United States and British imperialism on the Indian subcontinent.

Only 1,000 Koreans—mainly refugee students and picture brides fleeing Japanese colonial rule in their homeland—applied for admission into the United States through Angel Island. Chapter Five traces the immigration process for these "people without a country" as they came face to face with gatekeepers at the Angel Island Immigration Station, and with the support of the Korean National Association, found a way to circumvent the Asian exclusion laws and enter the country.

Economic conditions, ethnic and religious persecution, and the Bolshevik Revolution drove three million Russians and Jews to leave their homes for the United States in the late nineteenth and early twentieth centuries. Most went west and entered through Ellis Island, but approximately 8,000 people chose to escape via the vast territory of Siberia, cross the Amur River into Manchuria, board a ship in Japan, and enter the United States through Angel Island. Chapter Six follows their arduous journey east to America and their experiences as (white) European refugees at the immigration station.

From 1900 to 1930, one and a half million Mexicans migrated north to the United States. While the vast majority chose to migrate by rail across the U.S.-Mexico border, a small number of Mexicans came via the sea and Angel Island. Many were refugees fleeing the political chaos and violence gripping their homeland during the Mexican Revolution. Chapter Seven explores these migrants' journeys *el norte*, their encounters with immigration officials on Angel Island, and the ways in which Mexican immigration became increasingly viewed as the latest "immigration problem" in the early twentieth century.

As colonial "U.S. Nationals," Filipinos were generally admitted into the country after a primary inspection on board the steamship and bypassed the interrogations, examinations, and detentions that other immigrants faced on Angel Island. After 1934, when the Philippines received nominal independence from the United States, however, Filipinos' immigration status changed. Chapter Eight focuses on how Filipinos' changing legal status from "U.S. nationals" to "aliens" brought them to Angel Island and influenced their experiences there.

The immigration station closed after a fire in 1940, and the remaining buildings fell into disrepair for many years. Chapter Nine examines how, beginning in the 1970s, two separate groups of community activists and descendants of Angel Island detainees struggled to recover Angel Island's immigration history, preserve and restore the immigration station site, and lobby for its recognition as a National Historic Landmark.

One hundred years after it first opened its doors, the Angel Island Immigration Station remains critically important, both as a historic site and as a way to understand our contemporary society and culture. Debates over immigration continue to divide us in the twenty-first century, and immigrant detention is the fastest growing form of incarceration in the United States. The epilogue discusses the continuing significance of Angel Island and the ways in which its history resonates with current debates over immigration, national security, and the future of America. While some experts claim that we have opened a new chapter in American immigration history, we see echoes of Angel Island's past.

View of the Angel Island Immigration Station administration building and detention barracks. (Courtesy of California State Parks, 2010.)

CHAPTER ONE

GUARDING THE GOLDEN GATE

THE LIFE AND BUSINESS OF THE IMMIGRATION STATION

ON JUNE 1, 1916, the Reverend Hugh Linton and his wife Lillian arrived in San Francisco from Australia. Their steamship, the *Tenyo Maru*, docked in the late afternoon. The Lintons and all other second- and third-class passengers were taken by ferry to the immigration station on Angel Island. Because business on the island had closed for the day, there were no immigrant inspectors to clear the Lintons for landing. Following standard policy that required men and women, including married couples, to be detained separately, the minister and his wife were taken to different detention quarters and were told to wait until morning when their immigration documents could be inspected. The couple was incensed over what Mr. Linton referred to as "outrageous red tape." They also chafed at their treatment at the station. "The authorities refused to permit any conversation between us," the minister explained. "When my wife attempted to speak to me through the iron grating that separated us she was rudely restrained by officials." But most upsetting to the Lintons was how they were forced to go to the immigration station along with "Chinese, Japanese, and Hindoos." Many of them, Reverend Linton explained with disgust, "showed traces of having infectious diseases." The conditions at the station were also deplorable. The beds in the European detainee quarters were "filthy," and the food was "nauseating," he charged. The Lintons were inspected the next morning and then released. "They simply asked us our names and then permitted us to leave," the minister explained. Nonetheless, the couple believed that their treatment at the immigration station was unjust, and the Reverend Linton took his complaints to the San Francisco media. "The United States immigration law treats a man as if he were a criminal, imprisons him for a length of time to suit the fancy of the authorities, and herds him with the lowest type of Oriental races," he angrily told the *San Francisco Chronicle*.[1]

Arriving in San Francisco on the same ship as the Lintons was Jung Look Moy, a Chinese merchant's wife and her three children: seventeen-year-old son Louie Kuhn, thirteen-year-old daughter Louie Ah Len, and four-year-old son Louie Kan Foo. They had sailed on the *Tenyo Maru* from Hong Kong to join their husband and father, Louie Gar Fun, who ran a lodging house and mercantile store in Boise, Idaho. Unlike the Lintons, who were detained for just one night and were asked just a few simple questions, Jung Look Moy and her family had a very different experience on Angel Island. Because they were Chinese, their applications to enter the country fell under the purview of the Chinese exclusion laws, and they could only be admitted under very specific circumstances. Louie Gar Fun had to first verify his status as a Chinese merchant, a class of immigrants who were exempt from the exclusion laws and who could sponsor their wives and children into the country. Then Jung Look Moy and Louie Gar Fun had to convince immigration officials that they were legally husband and wife. Last, the couple had to provide evidence that the three children were indeed their own. The immigration investigation involved five interrogations of Jung Look Moy that lasted almost three months during the summer of 1916. In total, immigrant inspectors asked her 255 questions about her husband, his occupation, his previous marriage, their children, their home in China, and the layout of their village. Some of the questions involved intricate details and directions: "What kind of floor did your husband's house have in the home village?" "How far is your village from See Gow railway station?" "Is the old Ying village near the See Gow Market or farther away as compared with your village?"

Louie Gar Fun was also brought before immigrant inspectors on Angel Island and in Boise over the same three-month period and was asked 298 questions in five separate interrogations. Officials asked him about his business and residency in Boise, his previous entries into the United States, his marriages, the death of his first wife, and many other details about his family and native village. They examined the children carefully to see if they could detect any physical resemblance between parents and children. They conducted several other interviews with witnesses for the family in Boise, Hong Kong, and China.

In turn, Jung Look Moy and Louie Gar Fun provided copious amounts of documentation to verify their claims of admission. They gave the immigration service notarized affidavits from white acquaintances in Idaho, including one from the chief of police in Boise and another from the U.S. commissioner for the district of Idaho. They also hired the prominent immigration law firm of Stidger and Stidger to represent them. After enduring months of interrogation and detention, the family was admitted into the country on parole and left the immigration station on August 10, 1916, almost three months after they had arrived with the Lintons in San Francisco. The three children were permanently admitted into the country a few weeks later, but it took more than an additional year for the government to do the same for Jung Look Moy. Until that time, immigrant inspectors conducted a series of visits to the Louie family residence in Boise to observe whether or not they acted and lived together as a family.[2]

How could the Angel Island experiences of Jung Look Moy and her children be so different from those of their shipmates, the Lintons? For Jung and other Chinese immigrants, the long detentions and rigorous examinations at the immigration station were routine consequences of the discriminatory Chinese exclusion laws and the ways in which the government enforced them. In contrast, the Lintons faced no legal restrictions to their entry, for in 1916, there were only limited barriers on immigration from Australia or Europe. Their brief interrogation and overnight stay in the European detainee quarters did not compare to Jung Look Moy's more arduous detention experience. Nevertheless, Reverend Linton was incensed to have been taken to Angel Island at all. Expecting the privilege of unrestricted immigration granted to Australians and other whites, he was outraged to be treated like a nonwhite, like "the lowest type of Oriental."[3]

In the course of the daily life and business of the immigration station, immigrants as different as the Lintons and Jung Look Moy could disembark from the same steamship and end up on Angel Island together. Once there, however, their experiences could be radically different. The immigration station acted as a hub where these different immigrants and immigration laws met and sometimes clashed. Immigration officials screened thousands of new arrivals. They admitted those they deemed fit to enter the country and integrate into American society and excluded and deported others whom they judged to be undesirable and dangerous to the United States. Comparing the varied experiences of detainees on Angel Island illustrates some of the common inspection, examination, and detention procedures that immigration officials followed for all new arrivals. However, just as U.S. immigration policies treated individuals differently, immigration regulation on Angel Island also varied—sometimes dramatically—across groups.

Primary Inspections

After seventeen days of traveling north on a slow boat from Salina Cruz, Mexico, Jean and Bertha Gontard finally caught sight of the golden yellow coast of California. Soon the *San Jose* passed through the Golden Gate

Primary inspection on board a ship in San Francisco, n.d. (National Archives, Washington, D.C.)

to land in the foggy harbor of San Francisco. The date was October 3, 1914, and the French couple were tourists on their first visit to the United States. As Jean Gontard recounted, there had been very few passengers on the steamship:

> In first class were several fat businessmen from Central America, haughty, unapproachable, as it pleased them. However, a Mexican doctor was more sociable and deigned often to come have a chat with me. Run out by the revolution, he abandoned his vast properties, coffee and sugar cane plantations in the State of Tabasco, and was taking his whole family to San Francisco: his wife and four senoritas with dark eyes and clear complexions whom I met sometimes on deck.
>
> My companions in second class: two Chilean students going to study engineering at Stanford University; some Chinese, so comical in their way of murdering Spanish; some Hindus [more likely Sikhs], ceaselessly in prayer when they are not cooking some unknown dish in their little, strangely shaped pots; Mexicans hoping to find work in California.... Certain of these Mexicans brought with them women and infants, not to speak of their parrots, to have with them in their exile among the detested gringos something to remind them of the lost homeland.[4]

After the ship docked, the Gontards noticed that the first-class passengers were given a cursory medical exam and allowed to land while they, along with the other second-class passengers, were loaded onto a "foul" ferry boat to be taken to Angel Island for inspection.

What Gontard had just witnessed was known as the "primary inspection," the government's first step in processing new arrivals in San Francisco. Whenever a new ship docked at Meiggs' Wharf, a cutter with immigrant inspectors, clerks and interpreters, doctors and nurses met the ship's officers on the steamships and were given the ship's passenger list. The immigration and medical officers attached to the U.S. Bureau of Immigration and the U.S. Public Health Service examined passengers to determine whether they needed additional inspections on the island. Sick passengers were automatically sent to the immigration station hospital.[5]

Arriving aliens were generally asked the same identifying questions that were on the ship's manifest—name, age, marital status, and occupation. But nationality, race, and immigrant and economic status all played a part in determining whether further medical and immigration inspections took place on board the ship or at the immigration station. For certain classes of arrivals, the immigration service aimed "to conduct a rapid examination between quarantine and the wharf so that as many as possible get off there," explained Acting Commissioner of Immigration Luther Steward in 1911. Thus, first-class cabin passengers, who were mostly white, wealthy U.S. citizens, or European visitors, received preferential treatment and were given a visual medical inspection in the privacy of their rooms. Foreign officials and some elite European travelers and returning Asian residents of the United States traveling in second class might also be examined on the boat. Public health officers believed that these upper-class passengers were less susceptible to disease because they could afford better sanitary conditions and nourishment. They were thus spared the invasive and humiliating physical examinations as well as the exhaustive immigration inspections on the island to which most second- and all third-class and steerage passengers were subjected. Any individual whose eligibility to enter the country was in doubt was also ordered to the station for further investigation.[6]

The Gontards were traveling with Mexican, Sikh, and Chinese passengers in second class, and after a few hours in port, they were rerouted to

The *Angel Island* ferry brought new arrivals and employees to and from the station. It made four round-trips across the San Francisco Bay every day. (National Archives, Washington, D.C.)

the immigration station on the *Angel Island* ferry, which traveled between Angel Island and San Francisco.[7] Although Gontard did not make note of it, the U.S. government instituted a strict policy of racial segregation on the ferryboats and at the immigration station that would have separated the Gontards from their fellow Asian passengers. Similar to the Jim Crow laws that mandated de jure segregation in all public facilities in the American South, Angel Island's racial segregation policy was an attempt to create spatial distance between the races. It also tried to protect non-Asians from Asians and the contagious diseases that they allegedly spread. Separate entrances and spaces ensured that whites and Asians would have minimal contact. Superior detention quarters and dining facilities for whites also reflected the favoritism in U.S. immigration policies.

Accordingly, the *Angel Island* had separate cabins for all classes of passengers. Asians were directed to the main deck, while Europeans like the Gontards used the upper deck. When the ferry docked at Angel Island, arrivals deposited their bags in the baggage shed at the end of the wharf and then walked to the administration building, a two-story wood-framed structure that contained inspection, examination, dining, detention, and administrative areas. The main examination room, where passenger documents were examined and where the intake process began, dominated the ground floor of the building. There were four separate waiting areas, each designated for a different class or group of individuals. Asians congregated in the largest room which was filled with rows of wooden benches. Men and women were separated as well, including husbands and wives. They were not allowed to see or communicate with each other again until they were admitted into the country or deported. Children under the age of twelve stayed with their mothers, while boys over twelve were detained in the male section.[8]

The main examination room inside the administration building contained different waiting areas for different races. The largest was reserved for Asian immigrants. (National Archives, Washington, D.C.)

Any arriving passenger who appeared ill was sent directly to the doctor's office located behind the main examination room. They then proceeded to the hospital for further treatment. Other applicants for admission were ushered up a half flight of stairs to the registry division room, which was partitioned into four large, caged areas with benches lining the two long sides and a processing desk. These areas were also segregated by race. Individuals who needed to be detained on the island were taken here to receive identification numbers and barracks assignments. Subjected to such procedures, new arrivals' first impression of America was not one of welcome. Mrs. Woo, a Chinese detainee who was twenty-three when she arrived on Angel Island in 1940, recalled that Angel Island officials "locked us up like criminals in compartments like the cages at the zoo."[9]

"Here Come the Doctors"

The next morning after breakfast, Jean Gontard and a group of new arrivals were shepherded to the two-story hospital located on the hillside northeast of the administration building for the medical examination, which he described in great detail:

> Here come the doctors in white shirts, followed by a bevy of nurses. The nurses presented to each one of us a numbered wash-basin.... And each one waits with his wash-basin in his hands. One of the doctors, by voice and gesture, attempts to make clear what is being asked of us.... And, squatting down behind the protective barrier of the beds, the astonished patients do their business, for the most part with great effort to produce something on the immaculate bottom of the wash basin. It would have been better to prepare us in advance so as not to catch us unawares, don't you think!
>
> The nurses, very serious, are there distributing to the most unfortunate some purgative salts. "You aren't doing anything? Ah, that's bad, very bad! You won't be allowed to leave here without having done something! Take another purgative, it is necessary, it is necessary, that's the law! You won't be going anywhere until you produce something, no matter how little!"
>
> Impassive, without even turning the head, the gentle nurses carried the basins at arms' length to the laboratory of the doctor whom I had noticed downstairs, in the midst of microscopes and tests, absorbed in his devilish duty.[10]

Indeed, medical officers on Angel Island were kept very busy, and the high number of patients and examinations sometimes stretched the hospital facility beyond its capacity. In 1910, they examined more than 11,000 immigrants. In 1920, 25,000 people were given medical examinations.[11]

The imposing hospital building sat on a hill connected to the administration building by a curved path. In the distance to the right are employee houses. (Courtesy of California State Parks, 2010.)

By the time the Angel Island Immigration Station opened its doors in 1910, a number of "contagious and loathsome diseases," as well as other mental and physical conditions, had already been established as legal causes for exclusion. Immigrants could be excluded for having trachoma, tuberculosis, syphilis, gonorrhea, and leprosy. Those found to be "insane" or "idiots" were also excludable. Aliens who were afflicted with a condition that would affect their ability to earn a living, such as heart disease, hernia, pregnancy, "poor physique," "nervous affections," senility, and more, could also be excluded. The medical screenings for these conditions and diseases were designed to protect Americans from disease and to ensure that only the fittest and most able-bodied immigrants were allowed into the country.[12]

The hospital contained patients' wards, a surgery facility, a mortuary, administrative offices, and communal spaces, including a kitchen, large dining room, small private dining room, and limited sleeping quarters for employees. A "disinfector room" was also located on the first floor, where passenger belongings were fumigated.[13] The hospital reinforced the racial and ethnic segregation policy at the immigration station. It had separate entrances for whites and Asians and separate stairs to keep the different races apart once they were inside the building. On the second floor, separate patient wards for European men, European women, Japanese and Chinese women, Japanese men, and Chinese men were all spaced far apart. The Chinese and Japanese men's wards were located at the south end of the building, while the European men's and women's wards were located in the north. The joint Japanese and Chinese women's ward was located in the middle of the building. Several small rooms, including dressing rooms, bathrooms, nurses' rooms, the doctor's office, the operating room, and the stairwells separated each patient ward from the next.

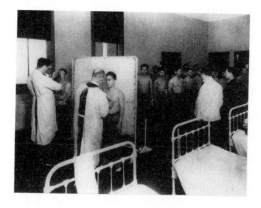

Public Health Service examination, c. 1923. Public health officials generally inspected the men's teeth, ears, and nose and conducted a stethoscope examination of the chest. They then took the individuals behind a hospital ward screen, where each man was stripped naked in order to reveal any abnormalities. Officers did not ask women to disrobe unless they detected specific signs of disease. The clothes that arrivals had worn on their journeys were sent to be disinfected. (National Archives, Washington, D.C.)

Officials explained that the original intent in the design of the hospital was to provide "practically...two distinct buildings" for Asians and whites.[14]

Public health officers first conducted a line inspection to detect the presence of excludable diseases and medical defects. Eyes were particularly scrutinized for ailments such as trachoma, which might impair the sight and lead to an inability to support oneself. Medical screenings could also involve a physical examination of the naked body to search for abnormalities or symptoms. Finally, the public health officers examined blood and waste products to detect traces of parasitic diseases that were classified as dangerously contagious. In 1910, uncinariasis (hookworm) and filiariasis (threadworm) were categorized as excludable diseases, and in 1917, clonorchiasis (liver fluke) was added to the list. The hospital on Angel Island had a state-of-the-art bacteriological laboratory, and bacterial examinations of blood and feces samples from applicants became a vital technique in the health screenings of Asian immigrants. During certain years, all second- and third-class passengers, including non-Asians, were brought to the immigration station and also required to take the stool examination.[15]

While Jean Gontard described his ordeal with a sense of detached and amused resignation, other hospital patients had very different reactions. Gontard's own wife was forced to stay at the station an extra weekend after he had been released. She cried so much during that time that "she was nearly unrecognizable" when her husband came to pick her up. She also recalled with horror how a Spanish woman had been detained at the station for six months and subjected "to all sorts of tests and experiments."[16]

Still others resented the medical officers who treated them as if they were already diseased, and they questioned the officers' own sanitary habits. Anna Dill, an arrival from Russia in 1936, recoiled as the doctor tried to examine the inside of her eyelid after examining her toes (and those of the others in the line before her). According to her daughter, she "slapped his hands...and she said in Russian, 'don't you touch me after you have touched dirty feet.'"[17]

Lack of proper sanitary procedures was just one problem at the hospital. Although the facility had been designed to foster healthful conditions and to enhance patient recuperation, it suffered from a lack of hot water, proper toilet facilities, overcrowding, unsanitary walls and floors, and poor ventilation. Only eleven months after the immigration station had opened, Assistant Surgeon M. W. Glover of the Public Health and Marine Hospital Service complained that "in no way does the hospital meet the requirements for this Station. At best it is and always will remain a makeshift." Some immigration officials conceded that the conditions of the station, while admittedly poor, were good enough for Asian immigrants. In 1915, Special Immigrant Inspector A. Warner Parker offered his opinion that the hospital was "fairly well adapted to the *present* needs of the Station," a reference to the "Oriental" nature of the detainees. Should European immigration increase, Parker suggested, segregated (and better) facilities would be necessary for these individuals.[18]

Unsanitary conditions had at least one fatal consequence in the winter of 1914, when three patients were infected with spinal meningitis after being transferred into a ward that had not been properly disinfected. The outbreak had begun with the arrival of Honda Suichi, a returning Japanese resident of San Francisco. After being diagnosed with the fatal disease, he had been transferred to an isolation hospital in San Francisco and subsequently died. Angel Island hospital officials reported that Suichi's ward had been disinfected after his departure, but apparently not thoroughly enough. Shortly after Suichi's death, John A. Stevens, classified as "African (West Indies)," and two "Spaniards," Jose Guiterrez and Miguel Gonzalez, arrived from Colon, Panama, on the *City of Sydney*. Placed in Suichi's old hospital ward for treatment of hookworm, they soon contracted spinal meningitis. Stevens died less than two weeks after first arriving in San Francisco.[19]

The immigration station's attention to the unique medical and other challenges that Asian immigrants allegedly posed set the San Francisco facility apart from other immigration stations. Both public opinion and medical theory assumed that Asians were more susceptible to dangerous diseases and therefore posed a greater health risk to the public. Samuel W. Backus, commissioner of immigration on Angel Island, explained that the immigration station had been planned with special regard for the "great hordes coming from Asia." The *San Francisco Chronicle* similarly observed that the station was designed to combat the "consistent menace from Oriental plagues and diseases." While most European immigrants on Ellis Island were only subjected to cursory "line inspections," consisting of "six-second physicals," Asian immigrants on Angel Island were subjected to more intensive and invasive examinations. Chinese men and women were especially scrutinized, both to detect disease and to confirm claims of age when requested by the Board of Special Inquiry.[20]

Because of poor sanitation in rural parts of Asia, the exclusions based on parasitic diseases primarily affected Asians. Public Health Service officers specifically targeted South Asians and Chinese passengers for mandatory bacteriological exams after Dr. M. W. Glover found hookworm ova in over 70 percent of South Asian patients in 1910. Later, Japanese "picture brides" were also required to submit to the examinations. Because scientists believed that "Orientals" carried more serious and harmful strains of diseases that would cause damage to white Americans, Asian immigrants had higher rates of medical exclusion than their European counterparts. Statistics from the Public Health Service, for example, indicate that while European immigrants were generally more vulnerable to acute trachoma infections than other groups, Asians and Middle Eastern immigrants were more commonly diagnosed with them and denied entry.[21]

Asian immigrants, especially the Chinese, reacted strongly to what they believed were invasive and unfair medical procedures and bacteriological tests. Mr. Lee, a detainee in 1930, expressed the sentiment of many Chinese immigrants: "When we first came, we went to the hospital building for the physical examination. The doctor told us to take off everything. Really though, it was humiliating. The Chinese never expose themselves like that. They checked you and checked you. We never got used to that kind of thing—and in front of whites." Community protests did result in some changes to medical policies. The U.S. government eventually reclassified some parasitic diseases, such as hookworm and liver fluke, and lifted the penalty of exclusion for anyone with these diseases.[22]

The "Keepers of the Gate"

A large number of individuals were required to keep the station functioning, immigrants processed, buildings and grounds maintained, and detainees fed and cared for. The Angel Island Immigration Station employed immigrant inspectors, stenographers, guards, clerks, deckhands, transportation employees, engineers, telephone operators, plumbers, carpenters, laundrymen, and cooks. There were also unarmed guards who watched the station at night and during the day assisted in handling aliens at the examinations, monitored Chinese crews on vessels, and searched arriving ships for stowaways. The number of employees grew as the work of the immigration station increased in volume and complexity. Six months before the immigration service moved from San Francisco to the island, the total number of employees was around thirty. By 1920, the Angel Island Immigration Station had 137 employees. After immigration restrictions were put into place during the 1920s and the global economic depression of the 1930s decreased migration worldwide, the number of immigration station employees decreased. In 1934, there were 104.[23]

Some Angel Island Immigration Station employees and their families lived on the island year-round. This cottage was assigned to Albert Thau, the immigration station's electrician, and his family. (Courtesy of California State Parks, 2010.)

Most Angel Island employees commuted daily from the mainland, but some lived on the island in employee cottages provided by the government. These residents included staff that maintained and operated the immigration station facilities on a daily basis, such as the station engineers, gardener, electrician, and others. Chinese cooks and hospital workers also lived on site in the cottages. Originally, there were three employee cottages built behind the powerhouse. By 1920, nine additional cottages and a two-story horse stable had been added. The cottages were located close together, but employees often enlarged their backyards to plant vegetable gardens and to dry clothes. There were at least four families living at the immigration station in the 1920s. The Mooneys and Perrys were the families of the station's engineers, Hugh Mooney and Alonzo Perry. The Thaus were the children of the station's electrician, Albert Thau. The Garcias were the children of the station's laundryman, Philip Garcia, Sr.[24]

Immigrant detainees came into contact with those employees most involved in the bureaucratic work of processing their applications—immigrant inspectors, clerks, and interpreters. They were the most numerous at the immigration station, and their work was the most difficult, as they were called upon to interpret and enforce a wide range of complex immigration laws and policies. Viewing themselves as the "keepers" or "guardians" of the Western gate into the United States, these employees of the U.S. Bureau of Immigration and later, the Immigration and Naturalization Service, took their responsibilities seriously.[25] Immigration officials enforced not only federal immigration laws regulating the admission and exclusion of aliens applying for entry but also participated in the arrest and deportation of aliens in the country without proper documentation. Some cases were clear-cut. Others required additional paperwork, documentation, cross-examination of witnesses and applicants, even extensive man hunts. Attorneys, courts, and community organizations were sometimes involved. Overwork and low morale were not uncommon among the staff.

Immigrant Inspector John Sawyer (with clipboard), another immigrant inspector, and an interpreter question Chinese aboard an arriving ship in Portland, ca. 1904–10. (Courtesy of the Bancroft Library, University of California, Berkeley.)

By 1910, the Bureau of Immigration was a powerful, centralized agency of career civil servants. Unlike earlier immigrant inspectors whose appointments were often politically motivated, the employees in the new bureau were selected by merit and promoted for upholding standards of expertise and efficiency. Appointments to the immigration service were based on results of civil service examinations that tested mental ability and knowledge of immigration laws and rules. Angel Island's first commissioner of immigration, Hart Hyatt North, boasted that "the personnel of our force is better than almost ever before; most of the dead timber has been eradicated and we have additional new men who bid fair to be first rate."[26]

North might have been thinking of Immigrant Inspector John Birge Sawyer, who first entered the Chinese Bureau in Portland in 1902. Sawyer was a graduate of the University of California at Berkeley and had passed the civil service examination easily. He reflected a new breed of career government bureaucrats who viewed their work not as a stepping-stone to an elected political office but as a career. Upon his appointment to the bureau, Sawyer recorded in his diary that he had "high hopes of the opportunity in government work."[27] Unlike many of his predecessors who had been active in the anti-Chinese movement, Sawyer expressed an earnest desire to perform his duties in an efficient and just manner.

The immigration station on Angel Island would challenge and disillusion Sawyer. He served as an inspector of the Chinese division of the immigration service on Angel Island from January 1916 to June 1918, a time of immense corruption within the service. His diaries record his misgivings about the overwhelming caseload that awaited officers at the immigration station, the inefficient system of Chinese exclusion enforcement, and the culture of suspicion that permeated the station:

November 6, 1916: Two days ago, I was in a veritable panic at the prospect of going to work in the San Francisco office. I have been struggling with a voluminous record in a tangled Chinese case from San Francisco and as I worked I could think of nothing but the horror of being kept at that one thing month and month and perhaps year after year.

February 8, 1917: After 2 weeks of work at A.I. what has impressed me most is the remarkable system that has been developed to protect the gov't against its own officials. 1) No inspector can know in advance of a hearing what case he will have for investigation.... 2) Interpreters are changed with each witness.... No interpreter acts for more than one witness in any case and each interpreter can have no knowledge of the testimony given by a previous witness. Th[ese] method[s] seem most admirable protection against crookedness but also most obstructive to the efforts of conscientious officers. It causes interruptions, delay and confusion and centers the attention of the officers on forms instead of on vital work. Work is paralyzed while the shift [in interpreters] is made and inspectors adjust to conflicts. I feel that the government's inspectors should be trusted or fired. They should have the right to set their own cases and take any necessary time for preparation in advance of the calling of witnesses....

I am having plenty of experience with the wastefulness of methods at Angel Island. Here an inspector may have completed his investigation and digested his evidence and be on the point of setting down a report when he will be handed another case for investigation which he must take up at once. Perhaps this will happen twice before he finds leisure time to return to the original case. By that time, he has forgotten his impression of the witnesses in the first case. I sincerely believe that I could do 50% more work or do my work 50% better if I could be allowed to...stick to a case until finished.[28]

John Birge Sawyer's commitment to enforce the laws fairly was not shared by all. Despite claims of reform and the end of racism in the immigration service, many officials dealing with Asian immigration matters still held prejudices that affected their handling of Asian cases. Commissioner of Immigration Backus publicly admitted at an immigration conference in 1915 that he was opposed to "Oriental immigration" from "all its standpoints." Unrestricted Asiatic immigration was a clear threat, he continued, and "God help our beloved country if it could not be stopped in some measure."[29]

Yet, there were also inspectors like Emery Sims. He believed in carrying out the law, but he also wanted to give every immigrant "a square deal." Sims found his job interesting and rewarding. Originally from North Dakota, he came to San Francisco at the beginning of the Great Depression in search of work. He started out as a clerk assigned to the records vault and was promoted to immigrant inspector after he passed the civil service examination. He had not intended to stay long with the immigration service, but the salary was good and he enjoyed matching wits with the applicants. Sims remained on Angel Island until he retired in 1957. Edwar Lee, who served as an interpreter on Angel Island for thirteen years, observed that some inspectors on Angel Island were known to do whatever they could "to trip you up and deny you admission." But "by and large," he added, "I think that many of the inspectors were quite fair. For instance, [Inspector] George Washington Kenney used to say, 'I don't care how false they are. If they can pass my examination, they are eligible to land.'"[30]

Along with the immigrant inspectors, the many interpreters on Angel Island were indispensable members of the immigration service. Few inspectors were fluent in any language other than English, and both officials and applicants relied upon the accurate translation of questions and answers during any interaction with each other, especially in the official hearing that determined the applicant's case for admission into the country. Considering that there could be as many as thirty nationalities speaking different languages on Angel Island at one time meant that there was always a shortage of interpreters to handle the diverse population of applicants. At times, crewmen, fellow passengers, witnesses, and other staff were called upon to help out. For example, Watchman H. Mayerson and Deaconess Katharine Maurer sometimes helped the inspectors interpret in Russian and German. Interpreters were also expected to translate incoming mail and newspaper articles, serve as court interpreters, and assist in investigations on the mainland.[31]

Immigrant Inspector and Interpreter John Endicott Gardner. (Courtesy of Susan S. Briggs.)

During the beginning of the Chinese exclusion era, the hiring of Chinese employees was expressly prohibited. Government officials believed that they could not be trusted in immigration work and would translate incorrectly or be susceptible to bribes to help as many fellow Chinese as possible. Similar policies applied toward Japanese immigrants as well. Someone like B. C. Haworth, a white missionary who had spent nineteen years in Japan and who was fluent in the Japanese language, was perfect for the job. Haworth was hired by the immigration service in 1907 and served on Angel Island from 1910 to 1914. By the time the Angel Island Immigration Sation had opened, government policies had changed to allow for the hiring of Asian employees, partly because it was nearly impossible to find enough qualified whites to fill the positions.[32]

John Endicott Gardner was one Angel Island interpreter who was hired under the whites-only policy in 1896 and stayed until 1915. Son of a white American father and biracial (Chinese/white) mother from Macao, Gardner was born in Canton, China, and in 1882 moved to San Francisco, where he taught Chinese language classes and worked occasionally as a court interpreter. He applied for a position in the immigration service at a time when the government was in dire need of interpreters who were fluent in Chinese. Gardner came highly recommended by some of San Francisco's most prominent clergymen and politicians. He was widely considered the "best Chinese interpreter and translator on the Pacific Coast and one of the best in the country." In 1896, however, the official policy prohibiting Chinese employees was still in place. A government investigation solved this problem by pronouncing that Gardner was an American citizen through his father and that his integrity and credentials were beyond dispute. He became an instrumental force in enforcing the Chinese exclusion laws and calling the government's attention to Chinese strategies to enter the country under fraudulent pretenses.

However, Gardner's part-Chinese heritage hindered him in his initial years in the service. His superiors conceded that Gardner's intelligence and his knowledge of the Chinese language were invaluable to the service, but because he was part Chinese, he was not fully trusted by all staff. In later years, Gardner was accused of extorting bribes from immigrants and their attorneys. Facing a transfer order to New Jersey in 1915, Gardner retired from the service, but he remained the subject of official government scrutiny. In 1917, federal agents raided his Berkeley home and reportedly found "several hundred pounds" of immigration files belonging to the Angel Island Immigration Station.[33]

Most of the Chinese interpreters who were hired to work at Angel Island had been recommended by white American social workers or missionaries. Many, like Edwar Lee, were college graduates, devout Christians, and fluent in English and several Chinese dialects. At a time when even highly educated American-born Chinese faced intense discrimination in the job market, working for the immigration service was considered a plum job. Entry-level interpreters earned a monthly salary of $130 compared to the paltry sum of $30 that Chinatown grocery clerks were making. This is how Edwar Lee remembers being hired:

I had just graduated from U.C. Berkeley with a Master's degree in political economics and was looking for a job. I tried several commercial firms without success. My friend, Deaconess Katharine Maurer, asked me if I would like to work as an interpreter on Angel Island since I couldn't find any other work, and I said yes, I'll give it a try. So she made an appointment for me to see the head inspector, R. B. Jones. He interviewed me and immediately hired me. That was in 1927 and that was how I landed the job, not knowing that I would stay there for the next twelve years.[34]

According to Lee, the interpreter post had its advantages and disadvantages. Most days were spent in the interrogation rooms. "We are supposedly impartial," he explained. "We just interpret what the man says, or the question that is asked. We have no decision-making power, but we do render an opinion as to that person's dialect." The job could be quite tedious, especially when some of the inspectors were "long-winded, drawn out, and overly detailed." Moreover, the interpreters were always under suspicion. They were not trusted to be alone with the immigrants for a long period of time, and they were regularly shifted around during interrogations for fear of collusion between them and the applicants. "So in order to play it safe," Lee recalled, "one case may have two to three interpreters. You hear a portion of the testimony, say from the father...and when it comes to the applicant, they ask for a change in the interpreter."[35] Another problem for the interpreters was racial discrimination in the immigration service. Many were more qualified than the inspectors they served under. But, as Lee remarked, "There's not a ghost of a chance of a Chinese being an inspector." He added, "I realized that one could render a service in spite of the fact that there are many handicaps. There's a service I could provide not only for the government, but for the immigrants and others."[36]

Notably, immigrant inspectors and interpreters on Angel Island continued to be predominantly male. Women were regularly employed as stenographers, clerks, and matrons, and a few were hired on as interpreters—Emily

Angel Island Immigration Station employees in front of the administration building, 1930s. Emily Austin is second from the left in the second row; Mable Lee is fourth from the right in the second row; Emery Sims and Edwar Lee are third and fourth from the right in the fourth row. (Courtesy of California State Parks, 2010.)

Austin (French and Japanese), Fuku Terasawa (Japanese), Tye Leung (Chinese), Mary Chang (Chinese), and Mabel Lee (Chinese)—but none was ever appointed immigrant inspector. Female interpreters were often asked to help the matrons supervise and assist women detainees.[37]

Enforcing the Law

The main responsibility of Angel Island staff like John Birge Sawyer, John Endicott Gardner, and Edwar Lee was to enforce the nation's immigration laws. The interrogation of immigrants was a central component of this work. In these hearings immigration documents were examined and questions were asked and answered. Applicants tried to make the strongest case for admission. Immigration officials sought to detect fraud.

In the early years of the immigration station's operation, enforcement of the Chinese exclusion laws was the primary business of Angel Island officials. Not only were Chinese applicants the most numerous, but their cases and the complexity of the laws made them labor-intensive. A huge paper trail consisting of identification documents, interrogations, photographs, legal records, and official correspondence was created and maintained for every Chinese applicant. In 1911, Commissioner of Immigration Samuel Backus explained that "the proper disposition of one Chinese case may require stenographic work equal to that required in the handling of several hundred aliens of other races." The large fireproof vault that was kept at the center of the inspectors' wing of the administration building held close to three-quarters of a million Chinese records in 1914, and Commissioner Backus boasted that because San Francisco was the main port of entry for Chinese coming to the United States, "any question regarding the status of a Chinese any place in the United States is likely to trace back to this room."[38]

Over the years, the number of applicants from other Asian countries and from around the world increased. World War I in particular brought an increasing number of immigrants and refugees from Russia, Mexico, Australia, New Zealand, and Central and South America. These new arrivals and the passage of additional immigration laws increased the workload and the complexity of immigration work on the island.

Newcomers applying for admission were subjected to a number of routine procedures: medical and immigrant inspections; waiting periods while their cases were being decided; and appeals, if necessary. Any question about an applicant's eligibility to enter the country resulted in a hearing before the Board of Special Inquiry. The boards consisted of three inspectors, one of whom acted as chair, an interpreter (if necessary), and a stenographer. Immigrant inspector Emory Sims recalled how the process worked:

The interrogation rooms were bright, airy rooms. There would be the stenographer's desk and another desk or two. When the applicant was brought in, he would be given a seat where he could be at ease and talk as he wished and where the interpreter would communicate with him. The testimony was taken directly on the typewriter.

After the board heard the testimony, they would be pretty much in accord as to what was right and what was not. If two voted to land him and one voted to deny him, the dissenting member could appeal the case. But if he didn't wish to appeal, the person was landed. If the testimony were in accord, the file would be sent to the detention quarters and the person ordered to land. If denied, the person was not notified until the testimony was all summarized, but he would be given that notice eventually. If the applicant wished to appeal, the copy of the testimony would be sent to the central office in Washington, and the attorney handling the case would be given a copy from which he made his appeal. Washington would probably make its decision based on the transcript alone.

More than 75 percent passed the interrogation at Angel Island. There could have been indications of fraud in some of them, but nothing that would stand up in court to debar them. Of those that were denied here, there was always an appeal to Washington and probably only 5 percent of those denied were ever really deported. Some who were deported came back and tried again, and made it.[40]

Applicants themselves experienced the interrogation quite differently. Whereas immigrant inspectors recounted the work of the boards as routine and even mundane, French tourist Jean Gontard's recollections emphasized the imbalance of power between inspectors and applicants and the invasive, aggressive questioning that characterized the hearings:

> After having followed the endless corridors, our group now came before the door of the inspector's office. Two solemn fellows were enthroned there and as in the confessional, each of us awaited his turn. When mine came, I entered. They had me sit down and the most solemn of the two bureaucrats proceeded to interrogate me....
>
> Where do you come from? What are you going to do here? Do you have any money? About how much? How long did you stay in Mexico and what did you do there? Do you have any relatives in the United States? Lacking relatives, do you have any friends or acquaintances? And so forth for half an hour, while the other man wrote down all my answers in his papers.[41]

The boards asked additional questions and heard testimony from witnesses. They then decided to admit, exclude, or admit with conditions or bonds. All decisions, except for some medical conditions, such as tuberculosis, could be appealed to the San Francisco commissioner of immigration or to the commissioner-general of immigration in Washington, D.C.

Lee Puey You was detained on Angel Island for twenty months in 1939 while her attorney appealed and took the case all the way to the U.S. Supreme Court. She recalled feeling scared and nervous during the interrogation. "Many of the questions pertained to my family background—who my grandparents and parents were. But they also asked me questions that I could not answer, like how many feet was our house [in the village] from the house next door. I couldn't say exactly." This went on for three days. "Sometimes the interpreters were cranky," she said. "When I said I wasn't sure or I didn't know, they would tell me to say yes or no. They just treated us like criminals."[42]

While immigration officials primarily used the Chinese exclusion laws to regulate Chinese immigration into the country, they used the general immigration laws to screen non-Chinese applicants. The literacy clause of the 1917 Immigration Act, for example, required that immigrants aged sixteen and older be able to read in their own language. The law's intent was to help reduce the numbers of immigrants from Southern and Eastern Europe, but almost all aliens were tested. The U.S. government tested applicants' literacy with test cards printed in several different languages. In 1917, there were thirty-six different language test cards. In 1927, there were forty, including Hebrew, Armenian, Dutch, Finnish, Romanian, Lithuanian, Armeno-Turkish, Chinese, and Japanese. The routine inspection of new arrivals became more complicated after Congress established a passport/visa system in 1918 that required entering aliens to carry passports and to "make a written declaration before [an] American consul."[43]

Immigrant processing changed once more with America's entry into World War I and the renewed xenophobia that increased during the 1920s. New arrivals were more heavily scrutinized, and increased concern about espionage and sabotage brought the Bureau of Immigration in close cooperation with the Departments of State, Treasury, Justice, War, and Navy, as well as local police departments to monitor, arrest, and deport alien radicals and anarchists. Russian immigrants arriving in San Francisco after the Russian Revolution and Germans arriving during World War I especially found themselves under increased scrutiny.[44]

The passage of new laws, such as the 1921 Quota Act and the 1924 Immigration Act, required still more procedures on Angel Island and increased the already heavy staff workload. The quota law allowed 20 percent of the year's allotment for each country to be used each month. But immigrants did not know in advance whether they would arrive before a quota was filled. With the arrival of each ship, the commissioner of immigration in San Francisco had to communicate with his superiors in Washington, D.C., to determine what was left in that month's allotment for each country. On several occasions, Assyrians, Australians, New Zealanders, and Russians arrived on Angel Island after their countries' quotas had been filled. They were detained until they could be admitted under the following month's quotas. Those who arrived after the annual quota for their particular country had already been met were faced with longer detentions, or worse, had to turn back. The law, one social worker reported, caused "untold misery and hardship among the immigrants.... We were told last year that those who desired to come, sold their homes and all their household effects, expecting to establish new homes permanently in this land of promise. To be denied admission and to be deported or kept in detention for months, was like a death-blow to hope and caused them to cry out in despair, 'we have nothing to go back to—nothing, nothing.'"[45]

The new immigration policies and the complexities associated with their enforcement initiated a reorganization of the immigration service on Angel Island. In 1921, there were six divisions: law (two inspectors); files, records, accounts, and statistics (one inspector); Chinese immigration (eighteen employees); non-Chinese immigration (five inspectors); boarding and primary inspection (three inspectors); deportation and detention (one inspector). There were also seven inspectors who were stationed in the city office in San Francisco. Sixteen years later, the "Oriental Division" had replaced the Chinese division and had a staff of fourteen immigrant inspectors, eight clerks, seven Chinese interpreters, and two Japanese interpreters. Reflecting the new focus on repatriation and deportation that was a focus of immigration policy in the 1930s, there was also a "Detention and Deportation Division," which had one clerk, one telephone operator, twenty-four guards, and four matrons.[46]

Comparing Immigrant Experiences on Angel Island

While the procedures of immigrant inspection and detention were generally the same, there were stark differences in the level of scrutiny immigrant inspectors paid to specific groups. Immigration files reveal that European applicants, such as Germans, Greeks, Spanish, Italian, and British, were briefly interrogated about their financial situations, occupational backgrounds, and contacts in America and were then generally admitted within a day or two. The same was true of Japanese and Korean picture brides and returning residents who had the proper documentation. Chinese applicants, however, were subjected to exhaustive interrogations. The detailed questions designed to confirm relationships and immigrant status could last up to three or four days and total forty or fifty pages of typed testimony.

Race continued to be a determining factor in how immigrants were treated differently from each other on Angel Island. One stark example of racial bias in the interrogation process occurred in 1910, when

Commissioner-General of Immigration Daniel Keefe considered whether South Asian and Russian laborers were excludable under the "likely to become a public charge" (LPC) clause of the immigration laws. At the time, South Asians were the targets of a well-organized and passionate exclusion campaign led by the Asiatic Exclusion League. Feeling the pressure from exclusionists to bar South Asians by any means possible, Keefe ordered Angel Island inspectors to exclude them as a whole on the basis that American prejudice would make it difficult for them to secure work and cause them to become public charges. In contrast, when considering the cases of Russian laborers seeking entry into the mainland from Hawaii that same year, Keefe personally interviewed each of the applicants. While he concluded that they were indeed at risk of becoming destitute should they be landed in San Francisco, he nevertheless ordered their admission. As Maria Sakovich aptly concluded in her study of non-Asian immigration on Angel Island, "penniless Russians at this time was acceptable; penniless Asian Indians were not."[47]

The same can be said about the racial bias of immigration officers toward African applicants, few as they were. Twenty-two-year-old George Griffith, born in Dutch Guiana and of the "African race," arrived as a stowaway on a steamship from the Panama Canal Zone. He told the Board of Special Inquiry investigating his case that he had only $2 on his person and that he hoped to find work in the United States or on an American ship as a sailor. He was deemed LPC and ordered deported. Although he was physically fit for work, the board concluded that "it is believed on account of his race, that it might be difficult for him to immediately secure employment." Two years earlier, nineteen-year-old Paul Kofend had also been caught as a stowaway. According to his case file, he said he was a Danish sailor and did not have a single cent on him. But the board, believing that he would reship as soon as he was landed, admitted Kofend the next day.[48]

Other accounts indicate that Australians and New Zealanders might have received preferential treatment and were not always subject to the restrictions of the quota laws. In July 1921, orders were passed down to San Francisco from Washington, D.C. that all aliens from Australia and New Zealand should be landed expeditiously, "regardless of quota." San Francisco Commissioner of Immigration Edward White was ordered to act first and "report facts later." At least twenty-seven Australians were landed on personal bonds of $500. In contrast, twenty-five Assyrian refugees were detained on Angel Island for over a year pending a decision on their appeal because their country's quota had been used up.[49]

Racial bias can be found even among the immigration lawyers who represented clients on Angel Island. Some wrote publicly of their great belief in the American tradition of immigration and took on clients from around the world. Others expressed their distinct preference for European immigration. Joseph P. Fallon, a prominent attorney who represented a great number of Chinese immigrants, openly communicated this opinion to immigration officials. In 1914, he passionately argued that European immigrants like his Spanish client Juan Rechy Gonzales helped to make the great country of the United States and that they should continue to be admitted. "The American people are great because they are sprung from all the peoples of Europe," Fallon declared. "It is the purpose of the American people to increase the efficiency of the race by encouraging, stimulating and increasing European immigration to our shores...the Finn, the Bohemian, the Italian, the Greek, the Spaniard, the Russian, the Pole, the Israelite, the Magyar, we need them all."[50] Fallon was a committed attorney to both his European and Asian clients, but by tracing America's greatness to European immigration alone, he lent his support to U.S. immigration policies that privileged European immigrants as future U.S. citizens, rather than the many Asian immigrants he represented in his practice.

Immigration laws also favored those of higher economic standing, and accordingly, inspection processes on Angel Island gave preferential treatment to those traveling in first-class cabins. The official records provide ample evidence that immigration officials looked favorably upon immigrants of all racial backgrounds who demonstrated "refinement," wealth, and status. Mexican applicants who showed bank statements or property deeds, for example, could convince immigration officials that they were members of the middle, rather than laboring, class. Many immigrants arriving from Guatemala through Angel Island in the early twentieth century were wealthy, well-connected people who were coming for vacation, education, or permanent residence. With supporting letters from the Guatemalan consul general and ample funds in their bank accounts, they were readily admitted.[51]

Temporary visitors denied admission for minor infractions under the immigration laws could also be admitted on bond if they had sufficient funds. It was not an uncommon practice to take out a bond with a surety company and pledge to return to one's home country after the time allotted for their visit had expired, but these bonds were expensive and thus available only to those with ample resources. Erbon Delventhal, who collected the bond money for a surety company in the 1930s, collected $1,000 bonds from hundreds of visitors who passed through the immigration station. As he recalled years later:

> One at a time the immigrants would come in. I would write the bond for them and hand the bond to the government man and they'd give me the thousand dollars in cash. God knows, where they got the money. It was a stack of bills—a thousand dollars in fives and tens, a big stack of money. I'd give them official receipts and I told them, "Don't lose this, it's worth a thousand dollars to you when you get back home."[52]

In contrast, working-class immigrants were often excluded from the country because immigration officials considered them "likely to become a public charge." The vague definition of the LPC category made it an effective tool with which to exclude a broad range of people. An LPC decision not only implied that applicants were currently unable to support themselves but also that they would not be able to support themselves in the future. Thus, immigrant inspectors routinely measured an immigrant's appearance, skill set, and work history against the current labor market, racial attitudes, and more. Appearance was used as evidence of poverty in the present and in the future.[53]

Immigration officials also treated female arrivals differently from males. Immigration policies like the Chinese exclusion laws and the Gentlemen's Agreement explicitly allowed only Chinese and Japanese women to enter the country as dependents to a husband or father. But all female applicants were also subjected to gender-based policies that favored the admission of valuable laborers (mostly men) and "respectable" women who were wives and mothers, that is, women who were dependent upon husbands and who conformed to middle-class standards of domesticity. It was rare for women to be admitted independently, and most of these cases involved women visiting the country temporarily as students or travelers. Working-class women were at a clear disadvantage under these terms, and the LPC clause was disproportionately applied to women who were seen as both moral and economic risks. Those traveling alone or who had suspicious moral pasts were routinely excluded as LPC. Those traveling with husbands who were suspected of not being able to support their families were also excluded regardless of their own abilities to support themselves and their families.

Take, for example, the case of Rose Louis, a white Englishwoman married to Emile Louis, a black ship's steward from the island of Mauritius off the southeastern coast of Africa. The couple arrived in the United States with their seven-week-old son Alfred in February of 1918. As subjects of Great Britain, the couple had been living and working in Hong Kong as

Rose and Emile Louis and their infant son were detained on Angel Island for six months in 1918. (Scan by Vincent Chin. National Archives, Pacific Regional Branch.)

a ship steward and stewardess and sought entry into the United States in order to enter Canada to find steady employment. Even though the Louises clearly stated that they had no desire to remain in the United States and that they had arrangements for an agent to meet them in Vancouver, Angel Island immigration officials applied U.S. immigration policies to their case and excluded Emile as an illiterate. Despite the fact that Rose could also continue to work for wages to support the family, she was deemed to be "entirely dependent" upon her husband for support, and all family members were excluded as "persons likely to become public charges." Emile and Rose appealed the decision. Both immigration officials on Angel Island and in Washington, D.C., supported the appeal as long as the U.S. government could receive assurances that Canada would admit the family. For unknown reasons, the Canadian government refused. The Louis family remained stuck in detention on Angel Island for six months. The fact that Emile was black did not come up in the official record as being a cause for exclusion, but other cases indicate that black immigrants did not fare as well as their white counterparts. The U.S. government proceeded with plans to deport the family back to Hong Kong. Rose pleaded with immigration officials to find a different solution "for the sake of my baby." In April, she wrote to the commissioner of immigration that "to be deported to Hong Kong would mean starvation as it is all Chinese labour in that Port." The next month she wrote again asking officials to at least allow her husband to leave the station and find work as a steward alone on "any vessel in this port" heading to foreign lands. The family hoped "to obtain a Little Money to Maintain Self and Children," including a four-year-old son in England to whom she had not been able to send any money in several months. There is no record that immigration officials replied to Rose Louis, and in July 1918, the family was deported to Hong Kong.[54]

Women from all countries also encountered a gendered immigration inspection process, whereby immigration officials held them to higher moral standards than their male counterparts. Female applicants were subjected to interrogations that included personal, invasive questioning about their moral behavior and sexual activities. In contrast, the same type of questioning or level of invasiveness was rarely applied to male applicants.[55] Immigrant women were especially vulnerable to exclusions based on crimes of moral turpitude, which had been defined by a federal district court in 1913 as an "act of baseness, vileness, or depravity." The Bureau of Immigration included a wide range of behaviors as immoral, including perjury, indictment for murder, and conviction of criminal libel. But the realm of immigrants' private sexuality came under the most scrutiny. Fornication, premarital sex, adultery, and homosexuality were all listed as cause for exclusion. On Angel Island, enforcing the nation's immigration laws meant upholding middle-class ideals of female respectability that did not include sexual relations outside the bounds of marriage. Women suspected of having "immoral relations with men prior to…arrival in the United States" were commonly excluded as committing crimes of moral turpitude.[56]

When Swedish vaudeville artist Maria Holmgren was interrogated in 1914, for example, immigration officials aggressively pursued questions meant to uncover immoral behavior. Holmgren, a former resident of San Francisco, arrived on Angel Island on the last day of December in 1914 from Australia. During the voyage, she traveled with her swimming partner Steven Herron, who claimed to be her husband. The ship's manifest recorded the two as sharing a stateroom during the trans-Pacific voyage. But when Holmgren was questioned by the Board of Special Inquiry, she claimed no relation or cohabitation. The board proceeded with a highly personal, aggressive line of questioning:

Q. Have you ever been engaged to be married to anybody? A. No.

Q. Have you ever lived with any man? A. No.

Q. Remember you are under oath now; we want a truthful statement; have you ever lived with any man as his wife? No answer.

Q. Answer the question, please? A. Yes.

Q. Why did you not marry him? A. We did not have money.

Q. Now let us get down to it. As a matter of fact on the voyage over you cohabited as man and wife did you not? A. What do you mean by cohabited?

Q. Were you in bed together? A. No.

Q. You are positive of that? A. I could swear to that; I can take my oath; we never slept together, we were in the same room but we never slept together.

Q. Did you have sexual intercourse? A. No.

Q. Did you have sexual intercourse at all with Mr. Herron? A. No, never in Australasia and never here.

Q. Were you a virtuous woman when you first arrived in the United States from Sweden? A. No.

Q. Who was the cause of your losing your virtue in Sweden? A. A young man.

The board continued to question Holmgren and called upon Steven Herron and a former neighbor from San Francisco. The officers ordered Holmgren to be excluded as a "person admitting a misdemeanor involving moral turpitude…having had immoral relations with men prior to [her] arrival in the United States." Holmgren was detained on the island for three and a half months while she appealed the decision. Finally, upon the recommendation of Mrs. Barfield, a special agent assigned to investigate the case, and Kate Barrett, president of the National Council of Women, she was paroled to the Florence Crittenton Home, a mission home for women and children, and was later landed without bond.[57] By judging Holmgren against middle-class norms of sexual behavior, immigration officials tried to enforce certain standards of morality at the nation's borders. In other cases, immigration laws were used to reinforce the belief that women's primary roles in the nation were those of wife and mother. Women of color, disadvantaged by both their gender and their race, faced additional hurdles. By regulating why and how immigrant women could enter the country, immigration laws sought to mold both the American family and the American nation.[58]

Life in Detention

Imprisoned in the wooden building day after day,
My freedom withheld; how can I bear to talk about it?
I look to see who is happy but they only sit quietly.
I am anxious and depressed and cannot fall asleep.
The days are long, and the bottle constantly empty; my sad mood,
   even so, is not dispelled.
Nights are long and the pillow cold; who can pity my loneliness?
After experiencing such loneliness and sorrow,
Why not just return home and learn to plow the fields?[59]

Such sentiments carved into the barrack walls by an anonymous Chinese immigrant were shared by many other detainees who found themselves imprisoned on Angel Island and anxiously waiting decisions on their applications for admission into the country. Yet like other areas of the immigration station, the detention facilities and the experiences of immigrant

A view of the detention barracks in 1928. The covered stairway connected the barracks to the administration building. (San Francisco History Center, San Francisco Public Library.)

detainees differed. The two separate buildings in which immigrants were detained were explicitly designed to maintain the segregation of different classes, races, and genders of detainees. "Occidentals" were generally housed in the administration building on the second floor, where there were detention quarters for around 100 male and female European detainees. A separate "European" recreation yard was attached. There was general agreement that the detention quarters for white and European immigrants were more comfortable than those for Asians. Assistant Surgeon M. W. Glover of the Public Health and Marine Hospital Service observed in 1910 that the quarters for European immigrant men were "in better condition than any other." There was a modest visiting room where detainees could visit with relatives, friends, and attorneys. When the number of white immigrant detainees increased as a result of the 1921 and 1924 immigration laws, local newspapers called for improved conditions on Angel Island. "The immigration station was designed to receive Orientals," an article in the *San Francisco Chronicle* explained in 1922. Citing a number of complaints from Australian detainees who found the food and quarters on the island to be intolerable, the paper suggested that immigration officials offer "better accommodations" for white immigrants.[60]

"Orientals" were housed in the detention barracks, a two-story building set on the hillside above the administration building, that could house 300 to 400 males and 100 females at one time. During busy times, it often held even more detainees. The initial plan was to separate Chinese, Japanese, men, and women into four different living areas. Japanese were to reside on the first floor, men in the east wing and women in the west. Chinese were to be placed on the second floor, with men in the east wing and women in the west. Mary Bamford, a missionary visitor to the station in 1917, described South Asians as having their own room. In practice, the building was almost always an all-male detention facility, separated by nationality. Japanese, South Asian, and Korean men were detained on the second floor of the barracks. When the station was crowded, Russian men were also housed there. Chinese men were housed on both floors in separate dormitories from non-Chinese. By 1911, Chinese and Japanese women and young children were moved to newly remodeled quarters in the administration building so they could be supervised by a live-in matron. Maintaining racial segregation was a consistent goal over the years. In 1938, journalist Nellie Margaret Scanlan observed that Chinese women and children were kept in one room while Russians occupied the next dormitory. The British and other nationalities had separate dormitories. Only the children crossed the segregated spaces. Crowds of Chinese children often raced "up and down the corridor," she noted.[61]

The first and second floors of the detention barracks held sitting rooms, storage closets, washrooms, and lavatories. A fence enclosed the barracks and a recreation yard. A guard tower was added in the 1930s, probably to provide better security for the federal prisoners who were housed at the station during this time. A covered stairway, similar to one built on Ellis Island, connected the building to the administration building. While the covered passageway in New York was primarily used to protect people from inclement weather, the passageway on Angel Island was used to provide security and to prevent detainees from escaping. Security measures took precedence over safety. There were no fire escapes, and all windows were grated and locked.[62]

Each dormitory housed large numbers of metal bunks. Four rows of bunks, two wide, were stacked in tiers of two or three and took up almost the entire dormitory space. Each bunk came with a mattress, pillow, and blanket. Sitting rooms and lavatories were adjacent to the dormitories. Soon after the station opened, the sitting rooms were renovated into five rooms and an office for guards to use in the barracks. In 1912, a new toilet wing was added to improve sanitary conditions and to turn the old lavatories into new dormitory space.[63]

An estimated 70 percent of all passengers arriving in San Francisco were brought to Angel Island; the remaining passengers, including returning residents and citizens, were landed directly from the steamships. Of those detained on Angel Island, nearly 60 percent were confined for up to three days. This rate of detention contrasts dramatically with Ellis Island, where only 10 percent of all arrivals were detained for legal reasons and another 10 percent were detained for medical treatment. Eighty percent of applicants passed the Ellis Island immigrant inspection and medical examination and were released to the ground floor of the administration building to wait for ferries to transport them to Manhattan or to the Jersey City railway terminal. Most of those detained stayed only one night, awaiting money or relatives to pick them up. Others stayed a few days or weeks, including those who needed medical treatment.[64]

Rates and length of immigrant detention on Angel Island were also determined in large part by race, nationality, legal status, and class. Most non-Asians (Hispanics, Russians, Germans, and English) avoided Angel Island altogether or had a very short stay there. Seventy-six percent of all Chinese applicants were ferried over to the island, compared to only 38 percent of non-Asians. Chinese also had the highest and longest rates of detention. Quok Shee, who was detained on Angel Island from September 1916 to August 1918, holds the record for the longest known detention at the immigration station. She claimed to be the wife of a Chinese merchant, but immigration officials suspected that she was being brought in for "immoral reasons" and debarred her. After her attorney filed three appeals on her behalf, she was finally admitted into the country.[65]

Regardless of their racial and ethnic backgrounds, all immigrants resented being confined like criminals behind barbed wire fences, locked doors, and wire netted windows. "I had never seen such a prison-like place as Angel Island," recalled Kamechiyo Takahashi, a young Japanese bride in 1917. Many questioned as she did, "Why I had to be kept in a prison?" As Katharine Maurer observed in 1921, a French woman reacted even more strongly to her surroundings: "Oh, they put me in pree-zohn," she shrieked, "give me a rope, I will kheel myself!"[66] The loudest protest came from the Chinese, who were detained on the island the longest. Many of the poems they left behind on the barrack walls referred to the immigration station as a prison.

Families also resented being separated while in detention, including during meal times. The Isaak family, Mennonites who had fled Russia to escape political and religious persecution in 1929, found the segregated living and eating arrangements disconcerting. "What is wrong in this honorable America, that they separate families as soon as they entered the country?" H. P. Isaak wrote in his memoirs years later. Although the family was detained on the island only for a weekend to prove paternity through a blood test, family members were overwhelmed with grief and anxiety the whole time.[67]

There was limited privacy in any part of the immigration station, and despite the government's intent to keep the different groups separated, the close quarters and forced confinement meant that Chinese, New Zealanders, Italians, and others often bumped up against each other. In 1915, Michi Kawai, general secretary of the YWCA of Japan, observed during her visit to Angel Island that the Chinese, Japanese, Hispanic, and European women all ate together in one dining room. The carefully laid-out plans of racial segregation were also tested during World War I, when an increased number of immigrants came to Angel Island. In August 1917, Commissioner Edward White warned the commissioner-general of immigration in Washington that they had "no room at all. The Russians were doubled up in bunks normally reserved for the Japanese, and more passengers were expected to be arriving in mere days."[68]

Some cases of intermingling led to conflict. In 1917, Acting Commissioner of Immigration M. Boyce explained to his superiors in Washington, D.C., that it was necessary to place an overflow of Japanese women in the same detention room as Chinese women. This situation turned out to be "most objectionable to both classes, and is the cause of many complaints, protests, etc." When German crew members from German merchant vessels were housed in the detention barracks that same month, they demanded separate facilities. "Some relief must be given us that we do not have to live in the company of Chinamen, with whom we are obliged to take even our meals in the same room. This destroys our appetite, which is not improved by the monotonous fare," they told immigration officials. Both Asian and European women of "respectable character" also chafed when forced into close contact with prostitutes and other women of suspicious morals, and the immigration service tried to separate the two classes of women from each other. For others, mixing with detainees of other races and nationalities proved to be a colorful and exotic experience. In 1929, Ivy Gidlow wrote her sister about her experience eating with "two Japanese women who look like China dolls" while the Chinese women ate "chow-chow" with chopsticks at the other table in the dining hall.[69]

Life in detention tended to follow a mundane routine of endless waiting that was occasionally interrupted by periods of anxiety, even terror. But again, detainees' experiences on Angel Island differed. Non-Asian detainees described the conditions at the station as tolerable when the barracks were not crowded. Russian students who were stuck on Angel Island in 1923 because of the quota laws wrote about their great pleasure in receiving visitors from 11:00 A.M. to 2:00 P.M. on certain days. Smaller rooms for "special cases" and first-class female passengers were also available at least for some years. Canadian Ivy Gidlow described a room that she shared with an Italian roommate as being "large, white, bare-looking... [with] four white beds in a row." She wrote her sister about the comforts of her detention at the station and the pleasant times she experienced there. The *San Francisco Chronicle* reported that a French Canadian family even looked upon their four-month detention in 1930 as a welcome respite from the harsh Canadian winter and the usual toil of work. David and Maria Trudeau and their five children reportedly left the station in March "with thanks for the workless winter they had spent in California."[70]

In contrast, Chinese detainees, who faced both higher rates of detention and longer detention periods than other groups, chafed at the injustices they experienced. In interviews conducted decades after their detention on Angel Island, detainees recalled, often emotionally and angrily, the feelings of frustration and hopelessness that characterized their time on the island. They were confined to the barracks except for meals and two exercise periods daily. Only the women could go for walks under guard. In addition to the discomfort of detention, the dormitories themselves were extremely crowded. Rows of rods supported three metal bunks and lined the rooms. When fully occupied, there was hardly any room to move. "It was like being in prison," said Mock Ging Sing. "Everyone suffered great pain and mental anguish, worrying about whether or not we will be allowed to enter the U.S. The living space was so small and confining, it just made us feel more depressed." He added, "Of course we were mad but what can we do?"[71]

Some non-Asian detainees echoed the Chinese protests of inhumane treatment, overcrowdedness, and unsanitary conditions. A British Army officer and two Dutch businessmen reported to the local press in 1917 that due to overcrowded conditions in the European men's detention quarters, they were "herded like cattle" into a locked hospital room with German prisoners for one night. Wladimir Pruszyaski, a Polish stowaway who was detained for seven weeks in 1919, described his "indefinite confinement" as "worse than the life in prison." In August 1922, half a dozen immigrants from Australia were detained at the immigration station because that country's quota for the previous month had already been exhausted. They aired their disgust over the bare sleeping quarters, inedible food, strict regulations, and lack of freedom to the San Francisco newspapers. Likening his stay at the immigration station to the California state prison at San Quentin, detainee W. B. Parker claimed that "convicted criminals in San Quentin get better fare." Alexandra Dill also complained about being herded like a guarded "flock of sheep" when she and her mother were detained at the station in the 1930s. Even officials at the immigration station warned that the detention barracks were "unfit for habitation by reason of vermin and stench." Assistant Surgeon M. W. Glover offered pointed criticism of the building in 1910: "We bring aliens to this Immigration Station and confine them here against their will. While perfectly within our rights to do so, we are also under obligation to give them the best that modern methods will permit."[72]

One of the detainees' biggest sources of complaint concerned the poor quality and lack of variety of food served in the dining facilities. Meals took place in the immigration station's dining rooms located in the administration building and connected to the detention barracks by a covered stairway. Like other aspects of the immigration station, food service was also strictly regulated by racial segregation. Four dining rooms occupied the entire south wing of the administration building's second floor. One public dining room, one officers' dining room, a European dining room, and the Chinese and Japanese dining room separated detainees from immigration officials and visitors and also segregated the detainees

This rare photograph shows the interior of the mess hall at mealtime. Waiters served the food in the dining rooms, which contained long wooden tables and backless benches. The tables in the Asian dining room, shown here, were set with large earthenware serving dishes, crackers, chopsticks, and rice bowls. (California Historical Society, FN-23697.)

by race. Conditions also differed. The European dining room had table-cloths; the Asian dining room did not.

The logistics of feeding three different meals per day to hundreds of detainees and employees in different shifts was immense. Meals were served at regular times. Records from 1917 indicate that these were at 7:15 A.M., 1:00 P.M., and 4:15 P.M. Between 600 and 700 people were fed at one time.[73] The kitchen staff accomplished this feat by careful orchestration. As Mr. Low, a kitchen helper on the island in the 1920s, described:

> There were 33 tables in all, which seated six or eight people apiece. When I was there, there were over 700 Chinese inmates, so they had to eat in shifts. Each meal took half-an-hour. It went very fast. We would place the food on the table before they came. Then voom, they ate and left. Everyone ate at the same place each time. Two guards accompanied the group to the dining room. They would count heads on arrival and before departure.[74]

Both immigrants and immigration officials agreed that the quality of the food offered to the detainees was generally poor all around. European detainees complained that their food was served cold and had no variety. Seventeen Russian Jews refused to eat the non-kosher food during Passover week. In 1915, Japanese women detainees cried when they told a visiting social worker about the food served to them on the island. Chinese detainees flatly called the food inedible, and two food riots erupted over food in 1919 and 1925. Even Commissioner of Immigration Backus admitted that the Chinese criticism was "manifestly well grounded." Moreover, the dining rooms were often unsanitary. The tables, chairs, and dishes were dirty, often with caked-on food from many previous meals.[75]

The poor food quality, especially for Asian detainees, was a result of inequality at the immigration station. The government required that the private firms hired to prepare all meals for the immigration station staff and detainees spend less on meals for Asian detainees than for Europeans or staff members. In 1909, concessionaires were allotted 14 cents per meal for Asian detainees, 15 cents per meal for European detainees, and 25 cents for employee meals.[76] There was also a vast difference in the variety of food offered to detainees. This was partly to accommodate different palates and diet preferences, but the specific menus and cost requirements set by the government also point to a disparity in quality and variety of food. A 1909 restaurant contract form illustrates how the system worked:

> The following meals shall be furnished to detained passengers other than Asiatics as and when directed by the Commissioner of Immigration, port of San Francisco, and shall be supplied in such quantities as said passengers may individually desire:

Breakfast: (a) Boiled rice, oatmeal, farina, cracked wheat, or corn-meal mush, served with the necessary milk and sugar or sirup [*sic*]; (b) Meat hash or baked pork and beans (fried fish in lieu of meat hash or baked pork and beans on such days as may from time to time be officially designated); (c) Fresh bread, spread with wholesome butter; and (d) A bowl of tea or coffee (the individual alien's preference being consulted), with milk and sugar, served separately.

Dinner or Midday Meal: (a) Vegetable, pea, bean, lentil, tomato, ox-tail, or macaroni soup; (b) Fresh bread, spread with wholesome butter; (c) Roast or fried beef, pork or mutton, or corned beef, served with mashed potatoes, peeled baked potatoes, or peeled boiled potatoes and one other vegetable—lima beans, mashed turnips, carrots, peas, corn, or succotash; and (d) A bowl of tea or coffee (the individual aliens' preference being consulted), with milk and sugar, served separately. For those who prefer: Kosher meat or fish, with potatoes and one other vegetable as above; and fresh fish, baked or boiled, in lieu of roast or fried meat, on such days as may from time to time be officially designated.

The food to be supplied to Asiatic passengers shall consist of the following:

Breakfast: Bean soup, boiled rice, relishes, bread and tea; and in cases where Chinese are among the detained, boiled beef, pork or fish to be supplied upon request.

Midday Meal: Boiled rice, cooked vegetables, with fish or meat, or salt salmon, pickles, bread, tea.

Evening Meal: Boiled rice, cooked vegetables with fish or meat, or salt salmon, pickles, bread, tea.[77]

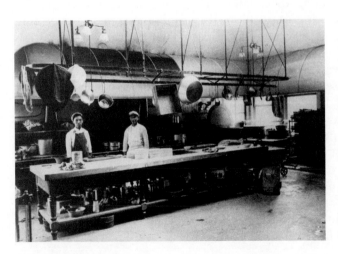

The cooks at the immigration station were often Chinese, though a few white cooks were employed during the station's operation as well. The kitchen was outfitted with refrigerators, an oven, and a large cooking range. (National Archives, Washington, DC.)

With such poor quality meals and little distractions, many detainees languished inside their dormitories. Chinese detainees were not allowed visitors until their cases were settled, but other detainees were allowed to see friends and attorneys on Saturdays and relatives on Sundays. Visitors were carefully monitored and were required to follow specific guidelines. A 1923 notice given to all visitors instructed them not to "give anything or to receive anything from an inmate." Any money, letters, or other items were to be handed to the captain of the guard, presumably so that they could be searched. All conversations were monitored by a government officer.[78]

The monotonous routine and the endless waiting took its toll, especially on the Chinese, who had the longest detentions. Many Chinese male detainees found ways to occupy their time gambling, reading newspapers, and listening to phonograph records. Some expressed their frustrations through poetry written or carved into the barracks walls. Recreation time in the small, fenced, outdoor yards allowed them to enjoy some sunlight and fresh air. Once a week, detainees were escorted down to the storehouse on the dock to retrieve personal items from their luggage. In contrast, women and European detainees were permitted to go for walks

Like all other aspects of life at the immigration station, recreation was segregated. European immigrant detainees used the so-called European recreation yard (top photo), while Chinese detainees used a separate facility (bottom photo). (Photograph of the European recreation yard, National Archives, Washington, DC. Photograph of the Chinese recreation yard, courtesy of California State Parks, 2010.)

outside the detention center, use the library, attend English classes, and visit with family on weekends. A group of Russian students wrote about going on walks twice a week, playing chess, singing, and organizing concerts for the administrators and "all white" detainees.[79]

Lending Comfort and Assistance

Besides relatives, friends, and attorneys, other visitors to Angel Island included missionaries and representatives of immigrant and social service organizations who provided religious services, occasional cultural programs, English classes, and comfort and assistance to distressed immigrants. Missionaries from the mainland began to visit the station soon after it opened. The most influential missionary at the immigration station was Katharine Maurer.

Born the youngest of nine children in Ontario, Canada, Katharine Maurer was raised as a devout Christian by a father who was a Bible teacher and a mother who had a Huguenot and Quaker background. In 1912, after completing two years of the deaconess program at the San Francisco National Training School, Maurer accepted the post of deaconess at the Angel Island Immigration Station, a position that combined faith-based ministry with social justice advocacy. For the next twenty-eight years, she took the ferry every day from San Francisco to the immigration station to distribute religious teachings, hold English classes, and visit both men and women in the barracks and in the hos-

Katharine Maurer with Chinese woman and children on rooftop of the administration building, 1929. (Courtesy of California State Parks, 2010.)

pital. In addition, she served as interpreter for German speakers during the interrogations and as witness in the weddings required of picture brides until 1917.

Dressed in the traditional deaconess garb of black dress and bonnet, Katharine Maurer devoted herself to the welfare of all immigrants regardless of race or creed. In her reports to the Woman's Home Missionary Society, Maurer described holiday parties that brought immigrants from diverse backgrounds together in a multipurpose area in the administration building. At an Easter service in 1916, "Chinese lined up on the right; Japanese on the left, while Europeans stood about in various groups" on the recreation grounds. The annual Christmas parties followed a similar pattern. During some years, both Chinese and Japanese attended the same celebration. Other years, the celebrations were very diverse, with "about fifteen nationalities" represented in 1921.[80]

Maurer did not have an official position in the immigration service, but she worked closely with immigration officials. By 1929, the immigration service had given her two rooms on the second floor of the administration building for use as a library and office. Because of her long-standing commitment to the immigrants on Angel Island, she became known as the "Angel of Angel Island." Maurer's 1937 report to the Woman's Home Missionary Society described not only the multiracial character of detainees at the immigration station but also her progressive belief in breaking down racial, national, and political barriers through her work:

Angel Island: "Keeper of the Western Gate"
Every day at Angel Island brings us into contact with folk who reflect the traditions of other lands: Chinese, Japanese, Filipino, East Indian, British, European, Hebrew, Mexican, and Latin-American. Upwards of one hundred people are in detention always—applicants for admission, passengers in transit, those awaiting deportation and repatriates—representing an average of twelve nationalities, inward and outward bound.
[In discussing the many requests for her help from detainees, Maurer described receiving notes and letters on her desk.] A little crumpled note, painstakingly written in lead pencil, lay on the desk of the deaconess...requests for handwork, needed clothing, for interviews to discuss personal problems—"would Miss Maurer give them a little time?" A Japanese gentleman wrote: "The sweater has done already. It is very long to pass these days. Please call me any time and kindly favor to give me some wool again." From a Korean family: "Kim's trunk with all his wearings is at the Island. Please look it up and express it to us." An Australian wrote: "I wish to thank you for your kindness in bringing Tommy down to the boat to see me." "I have gotten my bearings here at Angel Island during these weeks of waiting," wrote an Englishman. "May you be spared to carry on your great work for years to come and

know that wherever we are, a prayer will go to Miss Maurer." Welfare work at an Immigration Station is one of personal service in all its ramifications, not only national, but international in scope. One works closely with the Government officials who recognize the work and cooperate fully.

In these daily activities we find that whatever the native tongue may be, barriers seem to crumble in a friendly and understanding atmosphere. Here we have a testing ground for the theory that the similar desires and characteristics of men are stronger than national, racial, or political differences.

During the twenty-five years of my continuous service at Angel Island, a procession of folk has come and gone through this Immigration Station. True, you cannot educate a procession, but a procession can be guided. Often in an interview there is little one can do except listen, without trying to comfort, without trying to give anything, just helping to bring that release which comes from sharing troubles, and sometimes in the telling one finds the solution.[81]

Other organizations, such as the Daughters of the American Revolution (DAR), the Young Men's Christian Association (YMCA), and the Young Women's Christian Association (YWCA), assisted Katharine Maurer in her work at the station. The DAR established an emergency fund and contributed boxes of clothing, books, toys, wool and knitting needles, fabric to make clothes, and a radio. The YMCA and YWCA sent staff and volunteers out to the station to teach detainees about American customs; provide reading materials, movies, games, and recreational equipment; and perform small services for the detainees. Ethnic organizations and religious institutions such as the Chinese Six Companies, Japanese Association of America, Korean National Association, Hebrew Immigrant Aid Society, Mennonite Church, and Sikh Temple were all instrumental in advocating for improved conditions on the island and providing material and legal assistance to shorten the detainees' stay on Angel Island. The combined efforts of these social service organizations, missionaries, and immigrant aid societies helped to alleviate the monotony of detention, provided an important connection to life off the island, and for those who were eventually admitted into the country, helped immigrants make the transition to America.

It could take several hours or several months for the U.S. government to make a final decision about whether to admit or exclude an applicant for admission. For those who were admitted, Angel Island became the gate that opened up to new lives in America. For those who were excluded, the island represented an impenetrable wall barring them from families, work, and the promise of riches or freedom on the other side. Whether admitted or deported, the time on Angel Island was memorable for many. Over the years, detainees, social workers, immigration officials, and visitors recorded their recollections in interviews, personal collections, autobiographies, and official documentation. Some detainees expressed themselves by writing or carving their names, dates of their detention, or other thoughts and feelings onto the walls of the immigration station itself. Carved into the barracks walls of the detention building is one poem written by a Chinese detainee on the eve of his deportation back to China. He expressed his hopes that fellow detainees from his native village would remember their time together. But the poem also stands as a testament to how close the author came to a new life in the United States.

> For half a year on Island, we experienced both the bitter and the sweet
> We only part now as I am being deported
> I leave words to my fellow villagers that when they land,
> I expect them to always remember the time they spent here.[82]

Just as the outcomes of cases differed for people passing through Angel Island, so too did their experiences of being examined, inspected, and detained. While some reacted with bemused resignation at the phalanx of bureaucratic regulations and procedures, others were terrified and humiliated. Their reactions were formed in large part by the different treatment that various groups received on the island. U.S. immigration policies that privileged men over women, whites over Asians, and elites over workers manifested themselves in the daily practices of the work at the Angel Island Immigration Station.

Chinese immigrants arriving in San Francisco, n.d. (National Archives, Washington, DC.)

CHAPTER TWO

"ONE HUNDRED KINDS OF OPPRESSIVE LAWS"

CHINESE IMMIGRANTS IN THE SHADOW OF EXCLUSION

CARVED DEEP into one of the walls of the men's detention barracks of the Angel Island Immigration Station is a Chinese poem written by an anonymous detainee on the island.

> I clasped my hands in parting with my brothers and classmates.
> Because of the mouth,[1] I hastened to cross the American ocean.
> How was I to know that the western barbarians had lost their hearts
>   and reason?
> With a hundred kinds of oppressive laws, they mistreat us Chinese.[2]

We do not know when this poet might have carved it, how long he was at the immigration station, or whether he was admitted into the United States or sent back to China. What we do know is that his poem echoed many of the feelings of frustration, anger, and despair that other Chinese detainees on Angel Island experienced. Although Chinese immigration to the United States had been almost totally prohibited by the Chinese Exclusion Act, it did not end altogether. From 1910 to 1940, over 178,000 Chinese men and women were admitted into the country as new immigrants, returning residents, and U.S. citizens. The majority came through San Francisco and Angel Island, and approximately 100,000 Chinese were detained there. The immigration station was inextricably tied to the "hundred kinds of oppressive laws" that discriminated against Chinese immigrants. Thus, from the time that immigration officials boarded an arriving steamship to the time when an immigrant or returning resident was finally "landed," or officially admitted into the country, Chinese were subjected to longer examinations, interrogations, and detentions than other immigrants. Seventy-six percent of all Chinese applicants were ferried over to the island, compared to only 38 percent of non-Asians. Chinese also had the highest rates of detention compared to other groups. They made up 70 percent of the entire detainee population at the immigration station, and their average stay was for two to three weeks, the longest of all the immigrant groups coming through Angel Island.[3]

Oppressive as the Chinese exclusion laws were, Chinese immigrants, returning residents, and Chinese American citizens employed a wide range of legal, political, and immigration strategies to enter and return to the United States during this restrictive era. Immigration officials on Angel Island responded with stricter enforcement measures that expanded the scope of exclusion and revealed any false claims to admission. They asked more questions, called more witnesses, and required more evidence in Chinese cases than any others on Angel Island. As a result, interrogations became extensive, exhaustive ordeals, and Chinese faced long detentions at the immigration station. The angry, homesick poems carved into the walls of the immigration station's barracks are just one symbol of the hardships Chinese endured on the island.

In Search of Gold Mountain

Chinese immigration to the United States began during the California Gold Rush in the mid-nineteenth century and continued long after the rush ended. Those who arrived during the late nineteenth and early twentieth centuries came almost exclusively from the Pearl River Delta in Guangdong Province. The region had been drastically altered by both European and American imperialism and internal domestic crises. Unequal treaties and economic relationships between China and Western imperial powers resulted in higher taxes on local peasants. Western imperialism also brought traders, missionaries, and regular trans-Pacific steamship routes. A dynamic market economy sprang up around Canton, a busy metropolitan city and international trade center. A population explosion, natural disasters, and rebellions and wars like the brutal Taiping Rebellion (1850–64) and the Opium Wars (1839–42) wreaked havoc on local populations. As Chinese became displaced from their farms, they migrated to the cities where they came into contact with American merchants, missionaries, and labor recruiters, and were introduced to the idea of America. Just a short distance away in Hong Kong, trans-Pacific steamships waited to take them even further to San Francisco, Seattle, Vancouver, and other ports along the West Coast of the United States.

By the early twentieth century, China experienced further economic, political, and social instability as attempts to restore order under the Qing dynasty faltered and Japan defeated China in the Sino-Japanese War (1894–95). European imperialist powers tightened their grip on China's economy by forcibly occupying more territory and port cities. The 1911 Chinese Revolution led by Sun Yat-sen failed to bring stability. Powerful warlords emerged as the dominant power brokers in many parts of the country, and foreign imperialism continued to hinder China's economic development. Internal rivalry between the Guomindang (Nationalist Party) and the Communists beginning in the late 1920s and a full-scale war with Japan in the 1930s continued to foster economic, social, and political insecurity and provided additional incentives for Chinese to seek work and permanent resettlement abroad.

At the same time, industrialization and the expansion of American capitalism drove an incessant need for workers in the United States. A massive labor force was particularly needed in the developing western states to build a transportation infrastructure and to exploit natural resources. Chinese immigrant laborers quickly became "indispensable" as miners and as railroad and farm laborers. They were hired again and again for jobs that were believed to be too dirty, dangerous, or degrading for white men and were paid on a separate and lower wage scale than whites. By the end of the nineteenth century, Chinese immigrants had constructed an intricate irrigation system and turned marshland in California's Central Valley into some of the most productive and fertile farmland in the country. By the early twentieth century, the Chinese had been pushed out or had left agriculture and manufacturing and increasingly entered domestic service or started small businesses such as laundries, restaurants, and stores. The wages earned in these occupations continued to be enough for even a low-paid laundry worker to support his family in China. With these odds, Chinese immigrants kept on finding ways to immigrate to the United States.[4]

The Chinese who left the Pearl River Delta were not the poorest members of society. Rather, they had some limited capital and viewed immigration as a way to accumulate additional wealth and to maintain their family's prosperity and status in China for future generations. Eighty to ninety percent of Chinese immigrants in the late nineteenth and early twentieth centuries were young, able-bodied men who could work and send money home. Mr. Wong, who came through Angel Island in 1933, was one of them. "They told me that anyone who comes to *Gam Saan* will make money fast and go home a rich man," he explained. "Anyone who comes to America is well respected in China. My family pushed me to come. They wanted me to make a better living."[5] Jann Mon Fong, another Angel Island detainee, echoed these sentiments in an essay he wrote home in 1935:

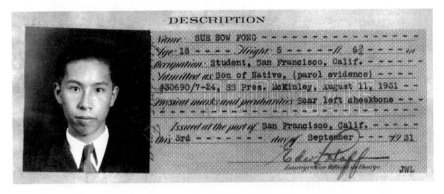

Jann Mon Fong's certificate of identity, 1931. All Chinese residents in the United States were required to possess "certificates of identity" that served as proof of their legal entry and lawful right to remain in the country. (Scan by Vincent Chin. National Archives, Pacific Regional Branch.)

> Every time a big steamer tooted into the harbor, carrying back fellow villagers with their loaded suitcases, we couldn't help but watch with envy the wealth they brought back, the power that could be wielded with money, and the dreams that were realized with it. I, for one, was impressed by their stories of life in the Gold Mountain, which kindled in me the desire to go overseas at a young age. As the worldwide depression in those days set in and we all felt the pressure for money, I decided it was time to go abroad to seek my fortune.[6]

Those who came in the late 1930s had another reason to leave China. "The Japanese took Canton and the country went to pieces," related Mr. Dea, who was detained on Angel Island in 1939. "We did not want our communication lines abroad cut, which would have meant no more remittances from my father in America; we would have starved to death. So I wrote Father to make arrangements for me to come to America."[7]

Chinese women immigrated to the United States, but in much smaller numbers. Patriarchal cultural values, traditional patterns of male sojourning, and anti-Chinese legislation in the United States all discouraged Chinese women from immigrating to America. As a result, transnational split-household arrangements became a common way of life for many Chinese families, separating husbands and wives and fathers and children for decades. Over time, however, the easing of cultural restrictions on Chinese female emigration and the desire for the economic security that some *gam saan haak* (Gold Mountain men) could offer prompted women to immigrate as the wives of Chinese merchants and U.S. citizens.[8] Among them was Law Shee Low. As she explained,

Before the bandits came, living conditions were not that bad. We had a bit of money because my grandfather owned land. Then when I was twelve years old, the bandits came and took everything. They destroyed our farmland and property and we became so poor that we had no food to go with rice, not even soy sauce or black bean paste. Some of our neighbors even had to go begging or sell their daughters, times were so bad. That was when my parents decided to marry me off to a *gam saan haak* from the next village. They thought I would have a better future in Gold Mountain. My husband was thirty-four years old to my eighteen years. We had an American minister perform the ceremony. Nine months after we were married, we left for America in 1922.[9]

The majority of Chinese immigrants traveled to the United States in the steerage class of trans-Pacific liners sailing from Hong Kong to San Francisco and other West Coast ports. A first-class steamship ticket cost $350–$400 and a second-class ticket was about $250. Traveling in steerage cost $85. Steerage accommodations were crowded, noisy, and dirty. "We stayed in one big room that had beds stacked three high," recalled Mr. Wong, who came in 1933. "In those days they treated us Chinese like cattle."[10] The voyage itself took three weeks and was often uncomfortable. Mr. Low remembered that his journey on the steamship *Siberia* was rocky and that access to fresh water was limited. "I was not used to the wind and waves and was seasick in bed the entire voyage. I stayed in the steerage and slept on a canvas cot. We had to use sea water to wash ourselves."[11] Soto Shee, who arrived on Angel Island in 1924, was in her first trimester of pregnancy during the voyage from Hong Kong to San Francisco. She later told her eldest daughter that during the sea voyage, she was seasick the whole time, and she believed that it was a miracle that she did not suffer a miscarriage.[12] Still, most believed that the difficult, long, and expensive journey was worth the chance for a new

Wedding portrait of Law Shee Low and husband Low Gun taken in Shekki, Zhongshan District, 1921. (Courtesy of Victor Low.)

beginning in America. They dreamed of riches that would allow them to settle in the United States or return to China wealthy and successful. Instead, they found discriminatory immigration laws that kept the door to their new lives only half-open.

The Chinese Exclusion Laws

Chinese immigrants were initially welcomed in the United States as valuable laborers and investors in the expanding American economy during the Gold Rush. But when the economy faltered and the gold ran out, Chinese men and women became targets of racist stereotyping, discriminatory laws, and racial violence. Chinese immigrants were seen as foreigners who could never assimilate into American life and who would always pose a moral and racial threat to the United States. At a California Senate

This cartoon published in *The Wasp* in 1881 captured white Californians' fears of Chinese immigration and invoked a comparison between San Francisco and New York. While New York welcomed European immigrants to America's shores, San Francisco feared the disastrous effects of Chinese immigration. As a result, a statue of a Chinese male coolie in San Francisco Bay mocks New York's Statue of Liberty, then under construction. His ragged robes, rat tail-like queue, stereotypical facial features, and opium pipe symbolize the inassimilability and immorality of the Chinese. The message that Chinese immigration would bring destruction to California and the entire nation is made clear with the skull upon which the statue rests his foot, the rats scurrying around the pedestal, the capsized ships and crumbling statue foundations, the slant-eyed moon, and the rays of light emanating from the coolie's head informing readers that Chinese brought "filth," "immorality," "diseases," and "ruin to white labor." (By George Frederick Keller, *The Wasp*, November 11, 1881. San Francisco History Center, San Francisco Public Library.)

committee hearing on Chinese immigration in 1876, Chinese immigration was described as an evil, "unarmed invasion" that endangered both the state of California and the United States as a whole.[13]

Beginning in the 1850s, discriminatory taxes targeted Chinese miners, laundrymen, prostitutes, and fishermen. California state laws denied Chinese basic civil rights, such as the right to immigrate, give testimony in court, be employed in public works, intermarry with whites, and own land. Discrimination against the Chinese escalated during the 1870s when California and other Western states fell into a deep economic recession. Chinese laborers were blamed for taking jobs away from white workers and for working for cheaper wages. An organized anti-Chinese movement began in earnest under the leadership of Irish immigrant Denis Kearney and the Workingmen's Party of California. Founded in 1877, the party's rallying cry was "The Chinese Must Go!"[14]

The small numbers of Chinese women in the United States during the late nineteenth century were also singled out for scrutiny and discriminatory treatment. Chinese prostitution was a lucrative and successful business that catered to both a Chinese and non-Chinese clientele in San Francisco. In 1870, 71 percent of Chinese women in the city were listed as prostitutes in the U.S. census. As social reformers railed against the practice of Chinese prostitution and the "moral and racial pollution" that it caused, the anti-Chinese movement used it as a justification for Chinese exclusion. During the 1870s, Chinese settlements were attacked by bloodthirsty mobs that looted, lynched, burned, and murdered Chinese residents—men and women—in an effort to drive them out of the American West.[15]

In 1875, the anti-Chinese movement gained momentum at the national level when Congress passed a law excluding Asian contract labor and prostitutes. The resulting Page Law represented the country's first—albeit limited—regulation of immigration on the federal level, and served as an important step toward general Chinese exclusion. In 1882, Congress passed the Chinese Exclusion Act, which barred all Chinese laborers from entering the country for ten years and prohibited Chinese immigrants from becoming naturalized citizens. It expressly allowed only Chinese students, teachers, diplomats, merchants, and travelers to continue to immigrate to the United States. In other words, Chinese could come to visit and conduct business, but they were not welcome to stay and settle in the United States. Court cases later initiated by the Chinese in America allowed families of merchants and native-born citizens of the United States to apply for admission (or readmission) into the country, but the general restrictions on Chinese laborers, and by implication their wives and children, remained in place and grew even more restrictive. The act was renewed in 1892 and 1902, extended to the U.S. territories of Hawaii and the Philippines, and made permanent in 1904.

Chinese immigration, particularly of women, was also affected by the 1924 Immigration Act. Aimed at stopping Japanese and all other "aliens ineligible to citizenship," it effectively barred foreign-born Chinese wives of U.S. citizens and merchants. As a result of lobbying efforts by Chinese organizations in America, the U.S. Supreme Court ruled to allow Chinese merchant wives to enter beginning in 1925. It was not until 1930 that the policy was reversed for wives of U.S. citizens, but only for those who were married prior to May 6, 1924. The Chinese exclusion laws were not repealed until 1943.[16]

Under the Shadow of Exclusion

The Chinese in America consistently challenged the constitutionality of the exclusion laws and protested the ways in which they were enforced. They also found ways to circumvent the laws and bring family and relatives to the United States as members of the exempt classes. From 1882 to 1943, an estimated 303,000 Chinese successfully gained admission into the United States, a figure that is greater than the 258,000 Chinese who were admitted during the pre-exclusion era from 1849 to 1882.[17] Chinese men most often applied for admission as returning laborers, merchants, U.S. citizens, or the sons of merchants and U.S. citizens. Chinese women applied as either the wives or daughters of Chinese merchants or U.S. citizens.[18]

The Chinese experience on Angel Island became a contest of wills and wits that began as soon as a ship carrying Chinese passengers arrived in San Francisco. Like other immigrants arriving in San Francisco, Chinese were first subjected to a primary inspection on board the steamship. Returning residents and those traveling in first or second class might be landed from the ship. All others were taken by ferry to Angel Island to have their baggage searched, receive their identification numbers, and await medical examinations and interrogations. Jann Mon Fong described his arrival in San Francisco on the *President McKinley* in 1931:

> Braving the winds and waves for twenty days, the ship finally entered the harbor. Old timers were allowed to land after the immigration inspection. We newcomers had to board another small boat that took us to the detention barracks on Angel Island. We were totally deprived of freedom as soon as we boarded the boat. Indeed, those blue-eyed Yankees treated us like pigs and goats!
>
> My cloth sack on my back and suitcase in my hand, I entered the detention barracks with tears soaking my eyes and cheeks. Resistance? It would not work. First, this was their land, and secondly, I couldn't even speak their language. Immediately, they locked us up in a small room barricaded with barbed wire. I was then made painfully aware of

Chinese immigrants walking toward the administration building, 1910. (National Archives, Washington, D.C.)

the weakness of our Motherland, the helplessness of myself, and the changes in circumstance, all of which had transformed us from a herd of cattle into hapless birds confined in a cage, waiting to be slaughtered.[19]

After receiving identification numbers, the new arrivals were sent to the hospital for the medical examination. The medical staff examined Chinese applicants for physical defects and even measured body parts to determine age. They looked for evidence of the so-called parasitic "Oriental diseases," which were grounds for exclusion if untreated. Chinese detainees found the entire medical examination process to be extremely humiliating. The examinations were conducted in a strict military style by uniformed white public health inspectors who called out orders in English. The procedures were hardly ever explained and the requirements to strip down naked and provide stool samples were especially embarrassing for the women. As Lee Puey You explained, "When the doctor came, I had to take off all my clothes. It was so embarrassing and shameful. I didn't really want to let him examine me, but I had no choice." Jann Mon Fong also objected strongly to the medical exam. "The physicians had us stripped to the skin and exposed to the chilly sea breeze for several hours before he routinely tapped our chest and spine and ordered us to jump up and down like monkeys. Was it really a physical exam or was it designed to insult our entire race?"[20]

Many felt that medical exclusion based on common parasitic diseases in Asia was an "arbitrary barrier" established to exclude Asian immigrants. Wong Shee, the widow of an American-born citizen who was returning from China with her six children, was barred from landing because she was afflicted with liver fluke. Immigration officials also ruled that the death of her American-born husband meant that she had no status entitling her to enter the country. Her children were all admitted, but Wong Shee was stuck on Angel Island for sixteen months until her lawyers convinced the U.S. Circuit Court that she had all the proper documents for reentry and that liver fluke was not a dangerous disease. Wong Shee was allowed treatment at the hospital on Angel Island at her own expense. Once cured, she was released and put on probation for two years. Her case later helped Dr. Frederick Lam of Hawaii persuade public health officials in Washington, D.C., that liver fluke, along with hookworm, was not a contagious disease and that patients should be allowed to stay in the United States for medical treatment.[21]

Asian patients, their advocates, and some journalists complained of the "humiliating or mutilating practices" associated with these examinations. But public health officers insisted that they were necessary to identify "infected," and therefore, undesirable and excludable immigrants. By 1913 and 1916, 57 and 69 percent of all immigrant exclusions nationwide were medically based.[22] But in addition to the routine medical exam given to all new arrivals, Chinese immigrants and returning residents who applied for admission or readmission had to contend with the exclusion laws themselves and how they were enforced on the island.

Since the primary intent of the Chinese exclusion laws was to bar Chinese laborers, class status was a major lens through which immigration

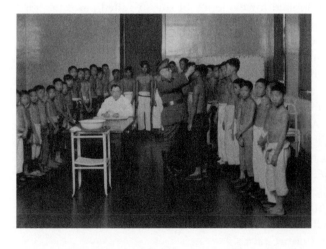

Medical examination at the Angel Island Immigration Station hospital. (National Archives, Washington, D.C.)

officials viewed Chinese arrivals. Although Chinese merchants, students, officials, and tourists were all exempt from the exclusion laws, they were never automatically admitted or given special treatment. Chinese merchants, by far the largest group of Chinese professionals who applied for admission, were required to provide detailed documentation of their business activities, the volume of merchandise, and lists of all partners. Returning merchants also had to have "two credible witnesses, other than Chinese" to testify on behalf of the applicant's status and state of business. The regulations did not specify that these witnesses were to be white, but, in practice, only white witnesses were used. The government's rationale was that white, but not Chinese, witnesses were considered trustworthy. Despite the fact that the majority of Chinese businesses catered mostly to the Chinese community, immigration officials also believed that only reputable businesses would have regular contacts with white customers, suppliers, and fellow businessmen.

Immigrant inspectors also relied upon their own ideas about class status to determine who was a merchant and who was not. They first expected Chinese merchants to look and act like members of the middle or upper classes. What this actually entailed, of course, was extremely subjective, but it is clear that officials believed that bona fide merchants were elites whose wealth would be apparent in their dress and appearance. Immigration officials were inclined to admit returning merchant Lee Kan, for example, because he had "the appearance of an exempt." In contrast, one Chinese immigrant applying as a merchant in 1912 was denied entry in part because officials judged his appearance to be "exceedingly poor." His handwriting, also "particularly poor," only confirmed immigrant inspectors' suspicions, and when the applicant's trunk was searched for additional evidence to be used in the case, his "poor quality" clothes were used as the final evidence to deny him entry. The hands of Chinese merchants were also often examined to detect any calluses caused by manual labor, which they believed was evidence that the applicant was a laborer in disguise.[23]

The experiences of Chinese women were sharply different from those of their male counterparts on Angel Island. Due to the limited educational and professional opportunities available to Chinese women in the early twentieth century, most could not apply for admission as one of the professional classes of students, teachers, merchants, or diplomats that were exempt from the exclusion laws. Instead, they primarily entered the country as the dependent wives or daughters of a Chinese merchant or U.S. citizen already in the United States. In other words, Chinese women derived their right to enter and remain in the country from their relationships to men.

Wives and children of merchants and citizens first had to prove to immigration officials that their husband or father still qualified as a person

Katharine Maurer with Chinese women in the administration building. (California Historical Society, FN-18240/ CHS2009.09I.tif.)

exempt from the exclusion laws. They also had to prove that their relationship was real. Since the Chinese government, unlike that of Japan, did not provide official records confirming applicants' identities, relationships, and eligibility for entry, U.S. immigration officials tried to verify Chinese identities through intensive and excruciatingly detailed interrogations and paper trails.

Both Chinese men and women were subjected to these rigorous procedures, but women were placed at a comparative disadvantage due to the gender bias embedded in the questioning. Chinese men were asked about their own families and villages in order to corroborate their identities. Chinese women, on the other hand, were interrogated about their husbands' villages and families instead of their own. Intimate knowledge about their husband's neighbors, the location of the village school, the well, or the furniture within their in-laws' house were considered proof that the marital relationship existed. Many women did not readily remember such details. Following Chinese custom, wives moved to their husband's villages only after marriage, and some stayed there for only a short time before arriving on Angel Island. Jee Shee, a newly married woman applying as a merchant's wife in 1911, for example, had lived in her husband's village for less than two months. Yet she was expected to know minute details about the place.[24]

Given the moral temper of the times and the efforts of social reformers to eradicate prostitution, Chinese women, like other immigrant women applying for admission into the country, were also scrutinized for any evidence of immoral behavior. They were judged according to how well they conformed to middle-class standards of respectability. Although Chinese prostitution had declined considerably by the beginning of the twentieth century, newspapers still called attention to cases of Chinese "slave girls" being smuggled into the country, arrested for practicing prostitution, or rescued by Protestant missionary women. The

assumption that Chinese women were still coming as indentured prostitutes continued to influence how Chinese wives and daughters were
treated on Angel Island. Women's appearance, age, clothing, demeanor,
and sexual history were all used as evidence of respectability or immorality. Interrogations were used to uncover any past or future immoral
behavior. Women who were suspected of being prostitutes were subjected to long interviews to determine whether the marital relationship
existed or whether they were being brought into the country for prostitution.[25]

Quock Shee, an applicant for admission in September 1916 as the wife
of merchant Chew Hoy Quong, was repeatedly interrogated at the immigration station, because immigration officials suspected that she was part
of a "concerted move to import Chinese prostitutes" into the United States.
She was denied entry into the country a few weeks after she had arrived
on the island. Quock and her husband hired attorneys Alfred Worley and
George McGowan to represent them. The attorneys sent an appeal to the
secretary of labor in Washington, D.C., and then took the case to the federal district court after the appeal was denied. The court upheld the government's position, and the lawyers turned to the Circuit Court of Appeals
in San Francisco. This court reversed the decision and allowed Quok Shee
to enter the country, but the entire process of denials and appeals took
almost two years. Quock Shee was detained at the immigration station for
nearly 600 nights while waiting for a decision on her case, making hers the
longest known detention at the Angel Island Immigration Station.[26]

Commissioner of Immigration Hart Hyatt North was so concerned
about stopping Chinese prostitution that as early as 1910 he sought to
hire "a person of their own sex and race" to look after the women and
assist the immigration service in this effort. Tye Leung, an interpreter and
assistant in the rescue work of the Presbyterian Mission Home in San
Francisco, came highly recommended by Donaldina Cameron, superintendent of the Mission Home.

Born in San Francisco's Chinatown in 1887, Tye Leung escaped an
arranged marriage at the age of twelve by seeking refuge at the Presbyterian Mission Home. She stayed on to help rescue and interpret for Chinese
prostitutes. In 1910, she became the first Chinese woman employed by
the U.S. government. Personally recommended for her reliability and
good character by Commissioner North, Leung was hired as an interpreter and assistant matron for Chinese women detainees. She was also
specifically instructed to stay on the alert for Chinese prostitutes attempting to enter the country. One of her specific duties was to gather "definite
evidence of the intentions" of the women arriving in San Francisco and
to give "unwilling slave[s]" an opportunity to alert immigration officers of
their predicaments. North noted that Leung had already "rendered great
service" to the immigration service in matters of these kind, and because

Tye Leung worked as an interpreter and assistant matron at the Angel Island Immigration Station from 1910 to 1913. She is pictured here with Deaconess Carrie Pierson in 1911. (Courtesy of Chris K. D. Huie.)

of her "intelligent and fearless" character, he was optimistic of her contributions to the government's efforts.[27]

While at Angel Island, Tye Leung met and fell in love with immigrant inspector Charles Frederick Schulze, who was of German and Scottish descent. Because interracial marriage was prohibited in California, they were married in the state of Washington. Both were forced to leave their civil service jobs at Angel Island "because of the racial prejudice," Leung later explained. Schulze had difficulty finding work, but he was finally hired by Southern Pacific Company as a mechanic. Tye Leung went on to work as a telephone operator at the Chinatown Telephone Exchange and spent many years providing interpreting and social services to the Chinese community in San Francisco.[28]

Despite their legal right to reenter the country, returning Chinese American citizens also faced intense government scrutiny at Angel Island. After the exclusion laws were first passed—based in large part on the argument that Chinese, as a race, were inassimilable—government officials questioned whether native-born Chinese should really be considered U.S. citizens in the first place. After many Chinese immigrants began to issue false claims of citizenship in order to enter the country, Chinese American citizens faced great scrutiny and found that their citizenship status offered only limited protection from the exclusion laws. One person who learned this firsthand was Wong Kim Ark.

On October 14, 1913, Wong Kim Ark, a forty-three-year-old Chinese American citizen, was interviewed by immigration officials on Angel Island

Wong Kim Ark's certificate of identity, 1914. (Scan by Vincent Chin. National Archives, Pacific Regional Branch.)

prior to a trip to China to visit his wife and three sons. He told Inspector Willard Becktell and Interpreter Chin Jack that he had been born in San Francisco on July 7, 1873, was the father to three sons, worked as a cook, and had traveled back and forth to China four times. The purpose of this official interrogation was to facilitate Wong's readmission into the United States. He dutifully filled out all of the necessary paperwork and attached his photograph to the U.S. government's form no. 430, "Application of Alleged American-born Chinese for Preinvestigation of Status." If Wong's application for preinvestigation was approved, he was to be permitted to reenter the United States without delay.

Although he was a U.S. citizen by birth and had the legal right to reenter the United States, Wong was extremely conscientious in making sure all of his paperwork was in order. The preinvestigation application, interview, and government approval were all that were formally required of Chinese American citizens traveling in and out of the country. But Wong was anxious. He hired the law firm of Stidger and Kennah to add to his application the court documents that confirmed his status as a "native" citizen. He wanted to ensure that there would be no problems when he returned to the United States.

Wong Kim Ark knew from experience that U.S. citizenship did not always guarantee an easy readmission into the United States if you were Chinese American. In 1895, he had been denied reentry into the United States by immigration officials in San Francisco after returning from a trip to China. Immigration officials rested their decision on the claim that Wong—though born in the United States—was not a U.S. citizen because his parents were Chinese persons ineligible for citizenship under the country's naturalization laws. Wong challenged his exclusion from the United States by hiring prominent San Francisco attorney Thomas Riordan to represent him. Riordan argued that Wong was entitled to readmission to the United States because of his status as a U.S. citizen under the Fourteenth Amendment, which declared that all persons born in the United States were citizens thereof. The U.S. District Court for the Northern District of California ruled in Wong's favor, but U.S. District Attorney Henry S. Foote appealed the decision and the case was argued before the United States Supreme Court. The high court confirmed that Wong Kim Ark was indeed a U.S. citizen under the Fourteenth Amendment and could not be excluded from the country, a ruling that firmly secured the constitutional status of birthright citizenship for all persons born in the United States.

Despite his clear victory, the legal ruling did not offer Wong Kong Ark total protection from government scrutiny or second-class treatment under the Chinese exclusion laws. Wong's immigration records reveal that he made three additional trips to China after his Supreme Court victory: once in 1905, again in 1913 through Angel Island, and a last trip in 1931. He was not placed in detention on Angel Island when he returned in 1913, but for each return trip, he laboriously filled out the routine paperwork, had his attorneys check it, and submitted himself to the same interrogations by Angel Island immigration officials who questioned his right to return to the land of his birth. In what must have felt like an enormous insult, Wong still had to fill out the government's form 430, "Application of *Alleged* American Citizen of the Chinese Race for Preinvestigation of Status," even though his status as a citizen had been affirmed by the highest court in the land. There is no mention of his Supreme Court case in any of the records.[29]

"The Crooked Path": Paper Sons and False Identities

The exclusion laws and the government's strict enforcement practices led many Chinese immigrants to adopt migration strategies that allowed them to continue immigrating during this restrictive period. As Mr. Chan, a former detainee on Angel Island explained, "We didn't want to come in illegally, but we were forced to because of the immigration laws. They particularly picked on the Chinese. If we told the truth, it didn't work. So we had to take the crooked path."[30] For many Chinese, taking "the crooked path" offered the only means of entering the United States while the Chinese exclusion laws were in effect. Both former detainees and immigration officials estimated that 90 percent of all Chinese had false papers.[31]

The most common strategy that immigrants used was to falsely claim membership in one of the classes that were exempt from the exclusion laws, such as Chinese merchants or native-born citizens of the United States. A lucrative business in false papers sprang up on both sides of the Pacific Ocean. Chinese companies, for example, regularly sold multiple partnerships (and the merchant status that accompanied such partnerships) to prospective immigrants. The exempt status of Chinese American citizens was another loophole in the laws that was relatively easy to exploit, because the 1906 San Francisco earthquake and fire had destroyed all of the city's birth records. By the 1920s and 1930s, more Chinese entered as U.S. citizens than as members of any other class, a fact most likely explained by false claims to U.S. citizenship.[32]

Identification papers for children, known as "paper sons," of exempt-class Chinese were useful, because the immigration service often lacked reliable documentary evidence verifying births and marriages occurring either in the United States or in China. A Chinese immigrant entering the country for the first time could easily claim more children than he actually had and then sell those "slots" to prospective migrants. Papers usually cost $100 per year of age of the applicant. "The trick is this," explained Mr. Yuen, a former detainee on Angel Island and a paper son, "You tell the immigration officer, 'I have been in China three years, I have three sons, these are their birthdays, the names and so forth.' Few years later, if you do have your own [sons,] then you bring them over here, if not, then you could sell these papers, you know. There's always a lot of buyers ready to buy. You try to sell to your own village, or a similar last name."[33]

Although false papers allowed Chinese to apply for admission into the United States, the mere possession of these papers did not guarantee the actual right to land. Chinese applying for admission still had to convince immigration officials that they were indeed the same individuals that their papers claimed them to be. By the time that the Angel Island Immigration Station opened in 1910, immigration officials were well aware of Chinese attempts to evade the exclusion laws. The immigration service viewed the skewed sex ratio of Chinese children and the preponderance of sons rather than daughters applying for admission as evidence of fraudulent entry. Published government guidelines instructed immigration officials to judge Chinese applicants "excludable until they could be proven otherwise," and officials readily admitted that they were "on guard from the time the Chinese arrives at the station until he is either admitted or deported."[34]

As immigration officials attempted to distinguish false claims for admission from real ones, long and detailed interrogations became commonplace. Because of the popular use of the paper son system, Angel Island officials particularly scrutinized cases involving families. As a routine part of the interrogations, family members were questioned about a wealth of minute details concerning their family history, relationships, and everyday life in the home village—what immigration officials believed should be "common knowledge" to all parties. Typical questions asked of the applicant were: What are the marriage and birth dates of your family members? Where are your paternal grandparents buried? How many steps lead up to your house? How many rows of houses in your village? Who lives in the third row? Of what material is

A Chinese applicant being interrogated at Angel Island, 1923. Interrogations could last from a few hours to several days. Rigid enforcement of the exclusion laws by the U.S. government and the proliferation of false documents used by Chinese immigrants turned interrogations into a battle of wits. In one extreme case, an applicant was asked almost 900 questions. (National Archives, Washington, D.C.)

the ancestral hall built? Is the name of the hall over the door carved or painted? The same questions were asked of his or her relatives. If any discrepancies were discovered in the testimonies, immigration inspectors concluded that the claimed relationship did not in fact exist, and the entire case was discredited.

Some inspectors used intimidation and even threats to test applicants. An immigrant inspector on Angel Island bluntly admitted to visitors in 1911 that many of the questions in the interrogations were "not material to the point at issue" but were necessary "to draw [the Chinese] out." The intention was to intimidate applicants and "to make them aware that we have some indirect means of finding out [the truth.]" In 1927, San Francisco Commissioner of Immigration John D. Nagle further conceded that his officers were "reluctant to accept defeat" and would reexamine applicants and witnesses on "every conceivable point" until they had found a discrepancy.[35] As the following excerpt illustrates, officials were especially hard on Fong Hoy Kun, who applied for admission as a son of a U.S. citizen in 1918:

Q: Which direction does the front of your house face?
A: Face west.
Q: Your alleged father has indicated that his house in How Chong Village faces east. How do you explain that?

A: I know the sun rises in the front of our house and sets in the back of our house. My mother told me that our house and also the How Chong Village faces west.

Q: Cannot you figure this matter out for yourself?

A: I really don't know directions...

Q: How many rooms in all are there on the ground floor of your house?

A: Three; (changes) I mean there is a parlor, two bedrooms and a kitchen. There are five rooms in all downstairs. The two bedrooms are together, side by side, and are between the parlor and kitchen.

Q: Do you wish us to understand you would forget how many bedrooms are in a house where you claim to have lived seventeen years?

A: Yes, I forgot about it.

Q: Did you visit the Sar Kai Market with your father when he was last in China?

A: No.

Q: Why not, if you really are his son?[36]

From the perspective of immigration officials, such actions were necessary to ferret out discrepancies. Chinese, however, viewed these questions as unreasonable and unnecessarily harsh, especially because they applied only to Chinese applicants. In many cases, the questions asked by immigrant inspectors were too challenging for even close blood-related relatives. Mr. Leung, who came to join his father in 1936, failed to answer correctly during his interrogation about his family and their house in China.

When it was my turn to be interrogated, they first made me wait in a small room. After awhile, they called me in and started asking me this and that, this and that, until I had a headache. After three or four hours of this, they confined me to a downstairs room where I stayed overnight. The next day, they questioned me again. They very seldom question you one day only and allow you to return upstairs. One strange question they asked me was: 'What is your living room floor made of?' I replied, 'Brick.' They said, 'Okay. What is the floor under your bed made of?' So I thought if the living room floor was brick, then the bedroom must also be brick. So I said, 'Brick!' They typed the answer down and didn't say anything. The next day, they asked the same question and I replied, 'Brick' again. They said my father had said it was dirt. What happened was that the floor was dirt at first, but later, after my father left for America, I changed the floor myself to brick. Where I really went wrong was in answering the question about who gave me the passage money. My father had written that he would send the money home to my mother to give me so that's what I said. But what happened was my father didn't really have the money and another relative loaned the money to my mother. So although I was a real son, I failed the interrogation. My deepest impression of Angel Island now was the rudeness of the white interrogators. They kept saying, 'Come on, answer, answer.' They kept rushing me to answer until I couldn't remember the answers anymore. And it wasn't just the whites. The Chinese interpreters did too.[37]

Chinese wives and husbands were interrogated separately, sometimes for hours. Immigration officials expected the answers to match in order to prove that the relationship existed. The level of scrutiny and detail in these interrogations intimidated many Chinese women at the immigration station. Law Shee Low recalled the anxiety and despair in the Chinese women's detention quarters. "One woman who was in her fifties was questioned all day and then later deported, which scared all of us. She told us they asked her about life in China: the chickens and the neighbors, and the direction the house faced. How would I know all that? I was scared." Ten days after arriving at the immigration station, Law was brought to the administration building for her interrogation. She answered the first questions about her marriage date, surname, and age easily. Then the interrogation became more difficult:

When the interpreter asked me whether I had visited my husband's ancestral home during the wedding I said no because I was afraid he was going to ask me which direction the house faced like the woman told me and I wouldn't know. Evidently, my husband had said yes. So when they asked me again (this time in the presence of my husband) and I said no again, my husband said, "*Choi* [For fortune's sake]! You went; why don't you say so?" The immigration officer hit the table with his hand [in objection] and scared me to death. So I quickly said, "Oh, I forgot. I did pass by in the wedding sedan chair, but I didn't go in."

Law Shee Low was certain that her mistake would prevent her from entering the country, but immigration officials ruled in her favor, and she was allowed to join her husband in San Francisco.[38]

The efforts by the immigration service to stem fraudulent entries certainly impacted Chinese immigration, but not in the ways officials had planned. Instead of putting an end to the paper son practice, the tougher inspection procedures merely motivated Chinese to take greater risks and invest more money and time to circumvent the exclusion laws. A new arm of the paper son business sprang up in the form of coaching book production and distribution. As Mr. Dea, who was detained on Angel Island in 1939, explained, Chinese came to rely on these books that contained answers to questions that would likely come up in the interrogations:

Before a son or daughter comes, the father must prepare coaching information to send them, which includes the family tree, descriptions of the village and living quarters, etc. But it can be very tricky, especially when they don't ask the essentials, but instead ask questions such as: Is there a clock? Who is in the family photos? So if they want to trip you, they can.

There were coaching specialists in San Francisco who pointed out the important questions and details. Sample standard questions were for sale. When you received the coaching information, you calculated how long it would take to memorize it and worked your departure date around that. Many took the papers on board the ship, but as soon as they approached Hawaii, it was torn to pieces and thrown overboard or flushed.[39]

Sometimes, immigration officials asked questions that were not covered by the coaching book. Other times, immigrants forgot important details in their fictitious identities and lives. "Who counts the number of steps in front of their house?" asked Mr. Tom, who was detained on Angel Island in 1921. "And even if you counted them, who knows whether your father will give the same answer? I could say forty and my father could say thirty. They interrogated my brother and my father—that's three people who have to agree. Even real sons could fail."[40]

To address these problems, Chinese found ways to acquire the right information by relying on outsiders to send notes to detainees. Government officials confiscated a handful of U.S. quarters and nickels with Chinese characters carefully written on one side of the coins. When read together, the characters translated into the answers to an immigration interrogation: "When Immigration officials ask you if your maternal grandmother is living, be sure that you say that she has been dead for more than ten years." Several peanuts, whose shells had been carefully pried apart and glued back together again, contained tiny scraps of paper with dates and names written on them.[41]

Coaching notes were either passed to immigrants in food packages sent by relatives or by the Chinese kitchen staff. According to Mr. Low, who worked in the kitchen in the 1920s, "Every week we each had one day off. We would drop by a certain store in San Francisco and ask if there was any coaching information to take back to the island. Each time we did this, we were given five dollars. We never got caught."[42] Upon return, the kitchen staff would hide the coaching note in the special dishes that they served to the officers of the Angel Island Liberty Association, a mutual aid organization formed by Chinese male detainees. Everyone was instructed to help destroy the evidence should anyone be caught passing a note. On two occasions, riots broke out in the dining hall when a mess hall attendant and chief matron tried to confiscate the coaching material. Corrupt

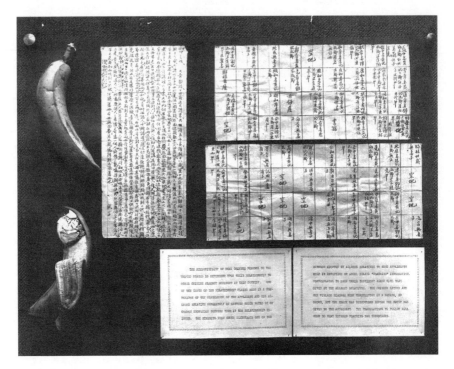

Coaching note inside a banana with detailed village map, n.d. (National Archives, Washington, D.C.)

immigration guards were also known to help smuggle in notes during meal times or in packages, all for a fee.[43] Coaching notes were an essential strategy to circumvent exclusion, but they also revealed just how dependent Chinese immigration had become on lies, false documents, and corruption.

Challenging Exclusion

The enforcement of the Chinese exclusion laws on Angel Island were so harsh that Chinese spokespersons regularly complained that the immigration service regarded "every Chinese applicant...as a cheat, a liar, a rogue and a criminal." Ng Poon Chew, editor of the Chinese daily newspaper *Chung Sai Yat Po*, charged immigration officials with examining Chinese "with the aim in mind of seeing how [they] may be excluded, rather than of finding out whether [they are] legally entitled to land." The high standards of proof in admission cases and the ways in which applicant and witness testimonies were read against each other turned the exclusion law into "an extermination law," Ng claimed. Charles Jung, who worked as an interpreter at Angel Island from 1926 to 1930 and as an immigration attorney for thirty-three years, remarked, "The only place in the United States where a man is guilty until he is proven innocent is at the immigration station."[44]

The Chinese on Angel Island responded with a variety of strategies. They researched the laws and the requirements for admission. They made sure that their paperwork was in order, and they hired lawyers to facilitate their entry or reentry into the country. More than any other immigrant group, Chinese went to great expense and trouble to exhaust the legal system in appealing exclusion decisions. Indeed, Chinese immigrants' most valuable resource during the exclusion era was an organized network of immigration lawyers who kept track of the necessary paperwork, lobbied on behalf of clients, and facilitated entry and reentry. By the 1930s, almost all cases of Chinese aliens applying for admission for the first time involved lawyers, and even returning Chinese residents secured the services of an attorney as a safeguard. Commissioner of Immigration John D. Nagle commented in 1927 that attorneys remained "indispensable" allies to the Chinese.[45]

Several lawyers and law firms represented Chinese clients on Angel Island. Some of the most active were Joseph P. Fallon, George A. McGowan, Alfred L. Worley, and Oliver P. Stidger III. With son Jason and former immigrant inspector Henry C. Kennah, Stidger built a formidable Chinese immigration practice, which reportedly handled 85 percent of the Chinese immigration business on Angel Island. Stidger spent his career defending Chinese immigrants and counseling the Chinese consulate and a variety of Chinese organizations, including the Chinese Six Companies and the Chinese Chamber of Commerce in San Francisco. He famously defended Chinese revolutionary leader Sun Yat-sen from the U.S. government's attempts to deport him, and as a legal advisor to the leader, he helped to draft the Republic of China's declaration of independence. He was a passionate and vocal critic of discrimination in immigration law, especially when it came to Chinese and other Asian immigrants.[46]

An attorney to hundreds of individual Chinese immigrants and a legal advisor to Chinese organizations in San Francisco, Oliver P. Stidger III impacted many Chinese immigrants and helped defend the rights of the Chinese in America during his fifty-year career. (O.P. Stidger, n.d. Copyprint. The Society of California Pioneers.)

Stidger's reputation was tarnished in 1916 when government investigators charged him and other immigration lawyers, Angel Island

Immigration Station employees, and Chinese immigration brokers with operating an international smuggling ring that netted hundreds of thousands of dollars each year. When the investigation concluded in 1917, thirty people were indicted by a federal grand jury, including Stidger and his partner Henry Kennah. Both were disbarred from practicing on Angel Island or at any other immigration station by the secretary of labor. Stidger vehemently denied any wrongdoing. In 1921, when a new commissioner of immigration was assigned to San Francisco, Stidger was allowed to represent immigrants and practice immigration law again. He continued to be a defender of Chinese immigration, and after the United States passed the 1924 Immigration Act, the Chinese Chamber of Commerce hired him to analyze how the law would affect Chinese Americans. Stidger issued a stinging indictment against the U.S. government and its persistent discrimination against the Chinese. "Will it only stop when every person of Chinese descent residing in the United States has been driven from its borders?" Stidger angrily asked. He advocated forceful action by the Chinese in America "in the name of justice" to ameliorate some of the harshest provisions of the law. Stidger remained an active advocate for the Chinese community until his death in 1959.[47]

Lawyers like Stidger were instrumental in helping Chinese immigrants exercise their legal rights on Angel Island. If an applicant was denied entry by a Board of Special Inquiry, they were given ten days to hire a lawyer and appeal the decision. If the board upheld its initial exclusion decision, the applicant had five days to appeal to the secretary of commerce and labor. Immigration lawyers were crucial during the entire appeal process. They helped to gather additional evidence, including witnesses who could travel to the immigration station to testify on behalf of their client. They also examined the immigration records, studied the government's case against their client, and prepared the formal appeal before the Department of Commerce and Labor. If the department upheld the exclusion decision, immigrants could appeal to the federal court.[48]

Chin Sing, a U.S. citizen returning to the United States in 1911 after a two-year absence, relied upon his attorneys George McGowan and Alfred Worley to appeal the immigration service's decision to deny him reentry into the United States. Despite the fact that Chin could speak English and demonstrated a "good knowledge" of his hometown of Dutch Flat, California, he had neither the necessary certificate of identity that proved his status as a returning native (it had been burned in a fire) nor any witnesses (preferably white) who could identify him and confirm his birth in the United States. Immigrant inspectors thought him an imposter. McGowan launched a search in Dutch Flat for any old acquaintances who could come and testify on his behalf. After a two-month search, the lawyers located two witnesses and brought them to Angel Island, where they and Chin immediately recognized each other. The additional testimony was added to Chin's record and appeal to the Department of Commerce and Labor, and he was finally landed in July 1911, five months after his return to the United States.[49]

Chinese immigrants' persistent legal challenges paid off. From 1910 to 1924, over 76 percent of Chinese rejected by immigrant inspectors on Angel Island hired attorneys and appealed to the Department of Commerce and Labor and federal courts. Immigration attorney Charles Jung explained that Chinese immigrants fought these legal battles because "nobody wanted to give up...they would exhaust all legal rights" even if it meant more money and detention time on Angel Island. Thirty-nine percent of those appeals were successful. In many cases, the department or court found that the interrogation process employed at the Angel Island Immigration Station was unfair. Jung recalled, "I had a case where the kid was twelve years old and the hearings took eighty-seven pages of testimony, and the kid was denied entry. The decision of the federal court was that *anyone* could make a mistake in eighty-seven pages of testimony and admitted the boy." In the end, only 7 percent of all Chinese applicants at the Angel Island Immigration Station ended up being excluded. Legal representation in cases involving women might also explain why only one Chinese woman was excluded for prostitution from 1910 to 1930 in spite of the government's scrutiny of Chinese women's sexuality and morality.[50]

Nevertheless, the appeal process came at great emotional and financial cost and explains why the Chinese had the longest detentions on Angel Island. Appeals could take three months. If the case was denied, the applicant could appeal to the federal district court, which usually took another five to six months, and beyond that, the appeals court. Exhausting all legal rights of appeal could take eighteen months or longer. Lee Puey You, an applicant for admission in 1939, for example, was detained at the immigration station for twenty months due to the lengthy appeals process that went through three different courts, including the U.S. Supreme Court.[51]

Lee Puey You was twenty-three years old when she arrived at Angel Island on April 13, 1939, claiming to be Ngim Ah Oy, the daughter of a U.S. citizen. "I didn't want to come to America but I was forced by circumstances to come," she said. "After my father died and left us nothing, my mother arranged a marriage

Lee Puey You in 1939. (National Archives, Pacific Regional Branch.)

for me to a Chinese immigrant in America. She wanted me to come so that I could bring the family over later. Because of that, I was afraid to oppose the arranged marriage. I had to be a filial daughter." The plan was for her to immigrate as the daughter of Ngim Lin, a son of a native. Then once admitted into the country, she was to marry Woo Tong, a man who was thirty years her senior.[52]

Two weeks after her arrival, Lee Puey You was called for the interrogation. "It took all of three days," she recalled. "They asked me about my grandparents, which direction the house faced, which house I lived in, how far from one place to another. It took a long time because they had to interrogate my father, my uncle, and two other witnesses." According to her immigration file, Lee Puey You and her alleged father were each interrogated for two days and asked 170 questions, the two witnesses for one day, and her uncle for another day. A week later, the father and uncle were called in for further questioning regarding Ngim Lin's claim to U.S. citizenship. The immigration officials found numerous discrepancies between Ngim Lin's prior and present testimonies as well as between him, Lee Puey You, and the other witnesses, leading them to conclude that the father's claims of American citizenship and paternity were based upon fraud. Lee Puey You was denied admission according to the Chinese exclusion laws.[53]

As she recalled thirty-five years later, "My relatives told me that they would appeal my case to the higher authorities in Washington, D.C. They told me to be patient. My appeal failed the first time and then a second time. They were hoping that when the war finally hit the United States, I would be released. But instead, I was stuck on Angel Island for twenty months. Most people stayed three weeks or so. Those on appeal left after a few months. But my case was more crooked because my paper father had reported twins and it wasn't true. So I wasn't landed."

Woo Tung wasted no time and spared no expense to get his bride into the country. He hired attorney Walter Lynch to immediately appeal the case to the INS Office in Washington, D.C. Two months later, INS dismissed the appeal. Although they conceded Ngim Lin's citizenship, they did not believe Lee Puey You was his real daughter. Three days later, Lynch filed a petition for a writ of habeas corpus in the U.S. District Court, arguing that Lee Puey You had not been given a full, fair, and impartial hearing by the Board of Special Inquiry. After studying the case quite closely, the District Court found serious discrepancies in the alleged father's testimony and denied the petition. Lynch then took the appeal to the Circuit Court of Appeals. Six months later, the Circuit Court rendered its decision to affirm the District Court's decision. Most immigrants would have stopped there, but not Woo Tung. He had Lynch file a writ of certiorari in the U.S. Supreme Court to review the lower court's decision. It took the Supreme Court two months to deny the petition. Having exhausted all legal channels, Lynch wrote District Director Edward Haff to request a stay of deportation under bond because of the "grave danger" that his client would face if she were returned to war-torn China. Quite coldly, Haff replied that it was impracticable for the government to receive inadmissible aliens into the country just because there was a war in progress. Lee Puey You was deported back to China on November 8, 1940.

In Detention

All Chinese immigrants applying for admission invariably spent some time in detention, waiting to be called for the interrogation or for decisions on their cases. Also detained were returning residents with questionable documents, transients on their way to neighboring countries, and immigrants who had been arrested and awaited deportation. At any one time, between 200 and 300 men were kept in the two-story detention barracks while thirty to fifty women and children under the age of twelve were housed on the second floor of the administration building. The quarters were crowded, noisy, unsanitary, and sparsely furnished with rows of double- or triple-deck steel bunks. Privacy was minimal. Their daily routine was marked by "wake-up" calls in the morning, three meals a day in the dining hall downstairs, and "lights out" in the evening.

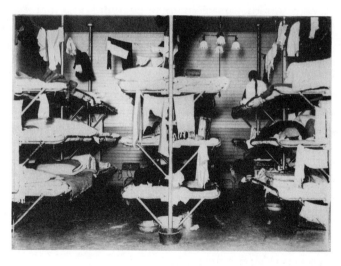

This image appears to be the only existing illustration of an occupied dormitory at the immigration station. It is not clear whether this image is of the dormitory in the detention barracks or in the administration building, but it does illustrate how crowded the detention facilities were and gives us a glimpse of everyday life in the barracks. Detainees had to wash their own clothes in the bathroom sinks. They were required to supply their own soap. They dried their clothes by draping them over the radiators or on ropes hung between the bunks. In the early years, detainees reportedly hung their laundry from the new chandeliers in the detention quarters. (Courtesy of California State Parks, 2010.)

Detainees were kept under lock and key and behind barbed wire fences except during meal times when they were escorted by guards to the dining hall. "After we ate," said Lee Puey You, "they took us back and locked the doors. Just like in jail. Followed us out and followed us back, then locked the doors. They treated us like criminals."[54]

Almost everyone complained about the Chinese food served at the immigration station, which was filling but not very tasty. According to Mrs. Jew, a merchant's wife who was detained on Angel Island for two weeks in 1922:

> At the sound of the bell, we all went down together, about twenty of us in a group escorted by two guards. The melon was chopped in pieces thrown together like pig slop. The pork was in big, big chunks. Everything was thrown into a big bowl that resembled a washtub and left there for you to eat or not as you wished. They just steamed the food till it was like a soupy stew. There was cabbage, stewed vegetables, pork, bits of stewed meat of low quality, that kind of thing. After looking at it, you'd lose your appetite![55]

Although the detainees blamed the cooks, the problem actually lay with the steamship companies (and U.S. government) that wanted to pay as little as possible to the contractors to feed the detainees, explained Ira Lee, one of the Chinese interpreters. There was only so much the cooks could do with the cheap grades of rice, meat, and vegetables that they were given to work with. Another problem, he pointed out, was that the kitchen was equipped with steamers to cook American food, but no woks to cook Chinese food properly.[56] Fifty years later, Mr. Low, one of the kitchen helpers, still remembers the food riot that broke out in 1925:

> Everyone started throwing dishes around the dining hall. The immigration people called the Chinese Consul General, who sent a representative down to explain that the food was set by an agreement with the government. The cooks could not change the menu. But they still thought it was our fault and wanted to beat us up. The white boss then pointed a gun at them and said, whoever comes in first, gets it first. No one dared. Soldiers were called over from Fort McDowell and everyone was forced back upstairs. Did you know they refused to come down to the dining hall to eat for the next three days? We cooked as usual, but they refused to eat. So the boss closed the food concession that sold sandwiches and crackers to punish them.[57]

Those who had money could buy food items from the store at the back of the dining room—canned fish, fermented bean cakes, fresh fruit, ice cream, and peanuts, or pay the cooks to make extra dishes for them. "We

Dining hall and concession in the administration building, where the Chinese had their three meals a day, 1929. (Courtesy of California State Parks, 2010.)

would put a little money in a napkin on the table and the cook would give us the best they had," recalled Gerald Won, who was eleven years old at the time. "One time it was spare ribs—wow!"[58] Many relied on relatives to send them food packages of roast duck, chicken, or sausage to supplement their meager diets. They would heat it up over the radiators or ask the kitchen staff to warm up the food during mealtime.

The poor quality food at the immigration station and crowded living conditions made long detentions difficult. A ban on visitors only increased the sense of isolation and anxiety felt by detainees. To prevent collusion and the smuggling of coaching information to detainees before the hearing, no visitors were allowed for Chinese detainees until after a judgment had been rendered. "Sometimes the only time you could have visitors is when you are about to be deported," said Charles Jung, interpreter and attorney. "And the father and son would cry like anything." Even when visits were allowed, they were not leisurely affairs. During the sixteen months that her mother Wong Shee was detained on Angel Island, Mary Lee Young was allowed to see her three times a week. She recalled waiting for hours until an interpreter could be found to sit in on the visit. "Visits had to be short—fifteen or twenty minutes," Young said. "Sometimes we wrote notes down so we would say what was the most important." Always on these visits, she would bring some tasty dish like homemade soup, rice and salted duck eggs, to cheer her mother up. But a pallor of uncertainty and anguish over the outcome of her mother's case made the visit a sad ordeal.[59]

Both the long detentions and the harsh treatment by immigration officials took their toll on Chinese detainees. Mrs. Jew observed that many Japanese arrived and left on the launch within twenty-four hours. "But us, we were confined inside so long. I kept thinking in my heart, what a worthless trip coming here, confined all the time! It's just like being in jail! I kept thinking, had I known it was like this, I never would have wanted to come!"[60] Mr. Ma also remembered a general air of animosity while incarcerated. "The guards at the wooden building disliked the new Chinese arrivals intensely. Night rules were strict: lights were shut off at 9 P.M., noise was not allowed. The tight security exceeded those for a prisoner and talking about it now, I cannot help but sigh deeply."[61] Even children who enjoyed playing and eating the whole time they were detained on Angel Island were aware of the injustices. According to Mr. Wong, who was twelve years old at the time, "It was a beautiful island with beautiful scenery. Most of us kids had a good time and were not a bit scared. Even the food tasted good to me because I had never tasted such things before. It was just the way they confined you, like in a prison, that made us feel degraded."[62]

Life in detention for the Chinese differed for men and women. Men had access to an exercise yard during the daytime where they could play ball or just breathe in the fresh air and enjoy the ocean view. There were also numerous indoor diversions and activities to keep them busy: Chinese gramophone records, musical instruments, singing, a small library of books and four Chinese daily newspapers, chess, and gambling. One detainee even set up a barbershop in the barracks and returned to China a rich man without ever setting foot on the U.S. mainland. Although Douglas Wong resented being "locked up like in jail" while he waited to be called for his hearing in 1939, he said that the time passed rather quickly for him because he had brought a suitcase full of books to read—translations of Shakespeare, *Treasure Island*, and other literary classics. He recalled that every Monday after breakfast, the men were allowed to go down to the storehouse by the pier to retrieve items from their luggage. "That was what saved me during those thirty-one days of confinement."[63] Then there were the periodic visits from the Chinese YMCA and Chinatown churches that helped to relieve the tedium of detainment. Staff and church members brought movies to show, reading material, toys for the children, and recreational equipment. "We talked to them about what they should expect when they landed in Chinatown and referred them to churches that had English schools," said Henry Tom, YMCA director in 1939. Usually a minister came along to preach to the inmates. "When we finished speaking, they asked us to come back again," recalled Tom. "Kind of boring over at the island, you know."[64]

The Chinese men were better organized than the women. In 1922, they formed the Zizhihui (self-governing organization) or Angel Island Liberty Association, which sought to provide mutual aid and maintain order in the barracks. The association welcomed new arrivals and oriented them to life and the rules in the dormitory and on the island. Funds collected from membership dues were used to buy books, school

A Chinese minister from the Chinese Baptist church in San Francisco talking to detainees in the recreation yard, c. 1910s. (Courtesy of Chris K. D. Huie.)

supplies, phonorecords, and recreational equipment. The group also scheduled musical concerts and entertainment. The association's elected officers, usually longtime detainees, acted as liaisons between the government officials and the inmates, relaying any complaints or requests they had. They also helped arbitrate any fights or arguments that broke out in the barracks. During his two terms of office as chairman of the Zizhihui in 1932, Tet Yee successfully negotiated with the immigration officials to provide the Chinese detainees with toilet paper and soap as they did for other immigrant groups. He also put a stop to gambling in the barracks. "No *fan tan* or *pai gow*, but *mah jongg* was alright within certain limits," he ruled. Yee also started a Chinese school for the children in an adjacent room to the men's barracks. "There were many Chinese children around the ages of eight and nine," he recalled. "Those of us with some education took turns teaching them reading, writing, and math." As an officer, Yee was also responsible for receiving coaching notes from the kitchen staff during mealtimes. "The officers got to sit at the front table and were served special dishes. If the waiter came by and said, 'the chicken is especially good today,' most likely there would be a note wrapped in wax paper and taped to the bottom of the dish." In these ways, the Angel Island Liberty Association reflected the united and collective spirit of the male detainees and helped to make life on the island more bearable.[65]

But day in and day out, the men mostly waited to be called for their interrogations, worried about whether they would be allowed to enter the country, and suffered the indignities of incarceration. As Mr. Lowe, a detainee in 1939, explained:

I had nothing to do there. During the day, we stared at the scenery beyond the barbed wires—the sea and the sky and clouds that were separated from us. Besides listening to the birds outside the fence, we could listen to records and talk to old-timers in the barracks. Some, due to faulty responses during the interrogation and lengthy appeal procedures, had been there for years. They poured out their sorrow unceasingly. Their greatest misery stemmed from the fact that most of them had had to borrow money for their trips to America. Some mortgaged their houses; some sold their land; some had to borrow at such high interest rates that their family had to sacrifice. A few committed suicide in the detention barracks. The worst part was the toilet. It was a ditch congested with filth. It stank up the whole barracks. We slept on three tiers of canvas bunks. The blankets were so coarse that it might have been woven of wolf's hair. It was indeed a most humiliating imprisonment.[66]

Chinese women marked the time in detention in different ways from their male counterparts. Many lacked formal education and were unable to read Chinese newspapers or books sent over from San Francisco or left behind by others. Some knitted or did needlework. Others attended the English and Americanization classes offered to them by social service workers, such as Katharine Maurer. Women and children were allowed to walk the grounds in a supervised group, a privilege denied the men. But mostly, they waited. This is how Lee Puey You described life in the women's barracks:

Chinese women were allowed to take walks around the island. Here, three women stop to pose before the hospital building. (Courtesy of California State Parks, 2010.)

There was nowhere to go. Just a little hallway that was fenced in for us to sun, exercise, or play ball. There was a long table put there for us to use for writing or sewing. From the windows we could see the boats arrive daily at about 9:30 or 10:00 in the morning. At the end of the day we would watch the inspectors and newly released immigrants leave the island on the same boat. Once a week they allowed us to walk out to the storage shed where our luggage was kept. We were allowed to walk around a bit and breathe in some fresh air before returning. There was no mah jongg, no recreational activities for the women. Sometimes I read or knitted, made some clothes, or slept. When you got up, it was time to eat again. Day in and day out, eat and sleep. Many people cried. I must have cried a bowlful of tears at Angel Island. It was so pitiful!

Although the women did not have a comparable organization like the Angel Island Liberty Association to unite them, they found other ways to bond in an effort to cope with the harsh conditions. "Sometimes people didn't get along," said Lee Puey You, "but because we were in the same fix, we became good friends." They chatted with one another, shared whatever food they had, dressed one another's hair, wrote letters for those who were illiterate, consoled those who failed the interrogation, and accompanied one another to the bathroom after hearing stories of women who had committed suicide there.[67]

Most of the detainees on Angel Island tried to swallow their disappointment and simply awaited their fate. A few were so full of despair and frustration that they tried to take their own lives. In October 1919, Fong Fook, a thirty-two-year-old immigrant en route from China to Mexicali, Mexico, hanged himself with a towel tied to a gas fixture after just a few days in detention.[68] Both Lester Tom Lee and Gerald Won said they witnessed a suicide in the men's barracks in 1931 and 1936, respectively. "The guy who hung himself knew that he was going to be deported after questioning and if he had gone back to China he would have been seen as a failure," explained Lee. "He was about forty. I can still remember his face. His tongue was sticking out and his eyes were open."[69] Won recalled that this older man who had married a young woman had so much trouble with the interrogation that he committed suicide. "He was so depressed he used a necktie and hung himself."[70] Interpreter Edwar Lee told the story of a Chinese woman who was so distraught about being deported back to China that "she sharpened a chopstick and stuck it in her brain through the ear and died."[71]

We have the most detailed information about the suicide attempt of Soto Shee, who arrived at the immigration station with her husband Lim Lee, a son of a U.S. citizen, and their seven-month-old son, Soon Din, in July 1924. The voyage from Hong Kong to San Francisco had been difficult,

Soto Shee and her infant son Soon Din. (Courtesy of David Ang.)

and Soto Shee was in her first trimester of pregnancy. The family had left Hong Kong prior to the passage of the 1924 immigration act, which placed new bans on Chinese wives of U.S. citizens, but landed in San Francisco after it was put into effect.[72] At her Board of Special Inquiry hearing in August, Soto Shee was ordered excluded as an alien ineligible to citizenship. Five days later, her son, Soon Din, died at the immigration station. His immigration file lists the cause of death as gastroenteritis. His body was brought to San Francisco for burial while Soto Shee remained at the station. She was two months pregnant and was distraught over the loss of her child. After immigration officials in San Francisco and Washington, D.C., denied her request to be released on bond to be with her husband, Soto Shee hanged herself in the women's lavatory. Matron Grace Mc Keener found her and cut her down. Soto Shee was semiconscious and was taken to the hospital. Once she recovered, she was eventually admitted into the country temporarily on bond. The family struggled financially and continued the legal battle to remain in the country. When she did give birth to her second child, she and her husband decided to name their daughter May Ho (May as in *mei gwok*, America; *ho* as in good). As May Ho (Mabel) recounted, "They reasoned that now they were starting anew in America—everything will be very good for them now." Soto Shee remained close to the other wives who came to America with her on the same ship. She eventually raised ten children and lived to be ninety-six years old.[73]

Cries of Complaints and Sadness

Other detainees vented their anger and frustrations by writing or carving poems into the barrack walls. Their feelings of hope and despair, self-pity and resentment, homesickness and loneliness filled the walls of the detention building. Some poems dwelled on wives and family left behind and debts incurred in making the voyage. Others decried the exclusionary laws and bemoaned a weak motherland incapable of protecting them from the injustices at Angel Island. There were also angry poems that spoke of revenge as well as farewell messages that offered advice and encouragement to fellow travelers.

Many of the poems were written in black ink with calligraphy brushes. Within a few months of the immigration station's opening, Commissioner North ordered the walls repainted to cover up what he considered graffiti. Undeterred, the poets began carving around the outlines of the Chinese characters and hollowing out the centers to create an impression of each word. The maintenance crew, ordered to cover the writing, filled in the words with putty before applying a new coat of paint. Although the putty and paint succeeded in obliterating many of the carved poems, they also served as sealers that helped to preserve the wood from further deterioration. Through the years, the putty shrank and the paint cracked to reveal the carved poems on the wall. Remarkably, over 200 poems are still visible today, having survived several layers of paint, natural deterioration, overwriting, and alterations in the building.[74]

Fortunately, two detainees recognized the importance of the poems and recorded as many as they could into notebooks. When Jann Mon Fong arrived in 1931 and Tet Yee in 1932, they both noticed right away that the walls were covered with poems, "wherever the hand could reach, even in the toilets and out on the porch where the wood was softer."[75] Jann remembered feeling "overwhelmed with grief and bitterness" as he copied down ninety-nine poems into his notebook during the two months that he was on Angel Island. Tet Yee, who was detained for six months with little else to do, copied down ninety-six poems. "The people who wrote the poems did not know what would become of them on Angel Island or if they would ever get off the island and make it to San Francisco," he explained. "The poems were their only means of expressing their inner feelings. Many of the poems were full of sorrow, resentment, and even bitterness. I felt very sad for them."[76]

All of the poems were written in the classical style of Chinese poetry, the traditional medium of self-expression and protest used by scholars in China for centuries. Most of the poems adhered to the strict form of regulated verse and were written with four or eight lines per poem and five or seven characters per line. The Chinese character at the end of every even-numbered line had to rhyme. The poets borrowed liberally from one another, using the same literary phrases and allusions to heroic figures in Chinese history. In his exhaustive study of the Angel Island poems, Charles Egan envisioned the writers as forming a Chinese "poetry society" that continued over time. "Early poets set the tone and themes, and later poets added responses in the same vein, and thereby joined the group," he explained. Although the Angel Island poets were not scholars in the traditional sense, the fine calligraphy, the poetic form, and the content of the inscriptions indicate that they had at least received a solid education.[77]

The majority of the poems were undated and unsigned, probably for fear of retribution from the authorities. More than likely, those who were detained on Angel Island for a long time or those awaiting deportation wrote the poems. Judging from the few that were dated and signed, as well as the fact that 80 percent of the poems in the Jann and Yee collections were found on the barrack walls by a team of scholars in 2003, a great number of the poems were probably written before the 1930s by Cantonese immigrants from the Pearl River Delta. Because the Chinese women were kept in the administration building that was destroyed in the 1940 fire, there are no records of poems written by women. For a long time, it was assumed that they probably did not write poetry on their barrack walls; however, Mrs. Loo, who was detained on Angel Island in 1924, remembered seeing "lots of women there and plenty of poems on the wall." She added, "Some of the women were really educated."[78] Lee Puey You recalled seeing the bathroom filled with sad and bitter poems. She wrote the following poem in response:

> Crossing the faraway ocean to arrive in America,
> Leaving behind my hometown, family and friends—
> Who would have expected to be stranded in a wooden building,
> Not knowing when I can hold my head up with pride?[79]

Often haunting and poignant in their directness and simplicity of language, the Angel Island poems express an indomitable spirit never before associated with the stereotypic image of a docile race. As the earliest literary expressions of Chinese immigrants in America, they not only bear witness to the indignities that these people suffered in coming to Gold Mountain but also serve as a reminder of the futility and folly of the exclusion laws themselves.[80]

> There are tens of thousands of poems composed on these walls.
> They are all cries of complaint and sadness.
> The day I am rid of this prison and attain success,
> I must remember that this chapter once existed.
> In my daily needs, I must be frugal.

Aside from poems, Chinese immigrants also carved drawings of ships, birds, horses, fish, flags, and altars on the barrack walls to express their longings to escape confinement. (Courtesy of the Architectural Resources Group.)

Needless extravagance leads youth to ruin.
All my compatriots should please be mindful.
Once you have some small gains, return home early.
By One from Xiangshan[81]

Beyond Angel Island

While detained in the barracks of the Angel Island Immigration Station, Chinese immigrants dreamt of the day when they might finally be admitted into the United States. Passing through America's gates, however, did not mean freedom from the exclusion laws. For many, the shadow of exclusion haunted them for years. Widespread "paper son" immigration and enduring anti-Chinese sentiment motivated U.S. government officials to increase their efforts to track, arrest, and deport Chinese immigrants who had entered or remained in the country in violation of the law. Immigration raids in Chinese American communities took place in neighborhoods, in places of business, and in schools and churches. No site was beyond the government's reach. After the Immigration Act of 1924 explicitly required all Chinese merchants, travelers, and students to maintain the exempt status under which they were admitted, government investigations of Chinese immigrants increased. Recognized as the country's first "illegal immigration" problem, Chinese immigrants were more vulnerable to deportation than other immigrant groups. During the 1920s, the San Francisco Chinese community complained of a "veritable Reign of Terror" against them. Chinese immigrants and Chinese American citizens lived their lives in the shadows, anxious about their immigration status, harassment by immigration officials, and personal safety.[82]

Although the Chinese exclusion laws were repealed in 1943, the Chinese in America continued to feel the impact of exclusion for many years thereafter. Those who came in under fraudulent identities were forced to live out lives of deceit and duplicity under constant fear of detection by immigration authorities. After China became a communist country in 1949, American anti-communism, combined with concern over fraudulent entries, led the federal government to conduct large-scale investigations in Chinese communities across the country. In an effort to prevent the mass prosecution and deportation of Chinese immigrants, the Chinese Six Companies opened negotiations with the immigration service. The result was the "Confession Program," a legalization program established in 1956 to allow Chinese who had entered the country by fraudulent means to make voluntary confessions of their status. Upon doing so, they could be made eligible for an adjustment in their status at the discretion of the Immigration and Naturalization Service (INS). Aliens who had served in the U.S. Armed Forces for at least ninety days could also become naturalized citizens once they confessed.[83]

While the program ostensibly offered some protections to those who confessed, each individual who entered the program did so at great risk and expense. By confessing to entering with fraudulent documents, Chinese automatically became aliens once again, dependent on the immigration service to allow them to become legal residents. Additionally, because confessors were required to implicate all of their family members, the confessions wreaked havoc in the Chinese American community. Immigrants who were in a position to legalize their status could negatively affect their paper relatives or even real relatives who were reluctant to confess or who were in the process of sponsoring family to come on the basis of their fraudulent admission. Moreover, the Federal Bureau of Investigation and the INS took this opportunity to hunt down and deport "pro Communists" in the Chinese community. Although 30,530 Chinese ultimately gave confessions to the government, many Chinese described the Confession Program as a "no win situation."[84]

Lee Puey You, who was deported in 1939, returned to the United States to marry the same man, Woo Tong, in 1947; this time she posed as the war bride of his friend Sai Chan. She was immediately admitted. Eight years later, she got caught in the INS dragnet and was arrested on the grounds that her immigration visa had been procured by fraud. Encouraged by her attorney Jackie W. Sing to confess, she told Officer Engelskirchen at her hearing her sad story—how she had been raped by Sai Chan upon their "paper marriage" in Hong Kong, how she became the concubine and slave to Woo Tong's family after she learned he was already married, and finally, how she divorced Sai Chan and married Fred Gin in 1953. In conclusion, she said:

I just wish to say that you give me a chance so that I can remain in the United States to be with my family. I found happiness after I married Fred Gin. Prior to that time the wrongdoing was not due to my fault. I was just obeying my mother, which she make all the arrangements with Woo Tong that I apply for a marriage certificate as the wife of Sai Chan to come to the United States.[85]

Officer Engelskirchen was evidently not moved by her confession and ordered her deported on the additional charge that she had committed a moral crime by living in an adulterous relationship with Woo Tong while still married to Sai Chan. Lee Puey You did not give up. She hired another attorney, Lambert O'Donnell, to appeal her case, and he was able to persuade the Board of Immigration Appeals to terminate the deportation proceedings. Lee Puey You became a naturalized citizen in 1959, which paved the way for her to send for her family from China. "It cost me thousands of dollars, but my mother's hopes have finally been fulfilled!" she said. "Everyone is happy and my responsibility to them is finally over." For many years, Lee Puey You operated a grocery store with her husband in San Francisco. She invested wisely in real estate, raised four children, and lived to be eighty years old.[86]

Jann Mon Fong (Smiley Jann), who had written to his classmates in China about his hardships at Angel Island, chose to put the bitter experience behind him and forge ahead with his life in America. He started out in Santa Barbara, California, where he worked in his paper father's dry goods store and then as a houseboy for a wealthy white family while he attended school. Jann eventually returned to San Francisco, where he got married, started a family, and ran a grocery store in the Western Addition neighborhood for thirty years. He broke the racial barrier when he became the first Chinese member of the San Francisco Wholesale Grocers Association. Jann took pride in seeing all four of his children graduate from college and become successful professionals. He never once mentioned Angel Island to them, not even after he voluntarily participated in the Confession Program and cleared his name. According to his son Arliss Jann, "We did not even know that he had gone through the Confession Program until he said we are changing our last names from Sue to Jann." Nothing more was said, but his children did notice that following this event, their father was able to return to China periodically for visits. Jann passed away in 1997, never having shared his immigration story with his children. But he did leave behind his notebook of Angel Island poems, which he titled, "A Collection of Autumn Grass: Voices from the Hearts of the Weak."[87]

Tet Yee, who was admitted as a merchant's son after a six-month delay on Angel Island, did not have to hide behind a paper name like many others. "My papers were all real," he said in an interview fifty years later.

Private Tet M. Yee at the time of his honorable discharge from the U.S. Army in December 1944. (Courtesy of Irene Yee.)

"I never had to lie." But he was forever changed by the many injustices he witnessed while on Angel Island. Putting aside his original plans to go to school and find a good-paying job, Yee became a political activist and labor organizer. As an officer of the Chinese Workers Mutual Aid Association in San Francisco, he spent many years fighting discrimination against the Chinese in the Confession Program, in the union hiring halls and workplace, and even in the U.S. Army after he enlisted during World War II. The exclusion laws had kept him separated from his wife and daughter in China for fourteen long years. Only after repeal and his honorable discharge from military service was Yee finally able to become a U.S. citizen and sponsor them to come under the War Brides Act of 1945. He worked as a butcher and grocer in Oakland, California, while raising a family of four children. Tet Yee died in 1996 at the age of eighty-five, but his parting words in the form of a Chinese poem live on in Felicia Lowe's film, *Carved in Silence*:

On Re-visiting Angel Island

I cannot forget my imprisonment in the wooden building.
The writing on the wall terrifies me.
Returning here after forty-four years,
I seek out poems now incomplete.
But still I remember the memories of sadness, anger, and frustration,
Memories we have kept from our children.
The memories are etched in my bones and in my heart.
Today we can stand proud as Chinese Americans,
But I will never forget what happened here on Angel Island,
Where our pain was carved in silence.[88]

For Chinese Americans like Tet Yee, detention on Angel Island symbolized the broader discrimination that they faced on and off the island. The "one hundred kinds of oppressive laws" created memories of "sadness, anger, and frustration" that lasted for decades. But Chinese immigrants were not the only detainees at the Angel Island Immigration Station. Many Japanese immigrants arrived in the United States on the same steamships that brought Chinese across the Pacific and into the Golden Gate. Yet their experiences on Angel Island were quite different. Although there was a similar ban on Japanese laborers entering the United States, there were no other restrictions on Japanese immigration until 1924. Like Chinese immigrants, Japanese also chafed at being detained at the immigration station, but they were often released after a few days, while Chinese detainees continued to wait out the weeks and months until their fate was known. If Angel Island represented America's "half-open" door for Chinese immigrants, it was a much larger entryway for the Japanese.

Newly arrived picture brides in the registry room at Angel Island, 1916. Kichiko Okada (third from the right) recalled putting on her silk kimono "to look her best" for her husband Jiro Okada just before the ship landed in San Francisco. (Courtesy of California State Parks, 2010.)

CHAPTER THREE

"AGONY, ANGUISH, AND ANXIETY"

JAPANESE IMMIGRANTS ON ANGEL ISLAND

ON A WINTRY DAY IN NOVEMBER OF 1926, a young Japanese man named Goso Yoneda boarded the *Shinyo Maru* in Yokohama and began his journey back to America. He was a *kibei* (born in the U.S. but educated in Japan) and was leaving his family and sweetheart in Japan to avoid conscription into the Imperial Army. After sixteen days crammed in steerage quarters filled with foul sweaty air and the smell of pickled radish, he finally arrived in San Francisco, only to find that his cousin in Los Angeles was too busy with spring planting to come testify on his behalf. Although a U.S. citizen with a birth certificate to prove it, Goso would spend the next two months locked up on Angel Island with other detainees waiting to be landed or deported. As he wrote years later in his autobiography, *Ganbatte: Sixty-Year Struggle of a Kibei Worker*:

> Inspecting my surroundings, I found that the two-story detention house was on a knoll overlooking the bay lined with trees and flowers. The house was divided into six sections. The three cells on the second floor were for men and assigned on an ethnic basis—one for Chinese, one for Japanese, and one for non-Orientals. I found nine Japanese men already confined in the cell reserved for us. The downstairs quarters consisted of a cell for Oriental women, another for non-Oriental women, and a huge dining room in which men and women were fed separately. There was a small commissary in one corner where if one had money, one could purchase candy, tobacco, and toilet items.[1]

Goso found life in the detention barracks "very monotonous and lonely except on Christmas and New Year's, when special lunches with all kinds of trimmings were served on both holidays, and Europeans awaiting deportation entertained us."[2] To pass the time, he read the *Nichibei* (Japanese American news) and his own copy of Rousseau's *Confessions*. He also wrote *waka* (thirty-one-syllable Japanese poems) in his diary. Some of his poems, including the ones below, were later published in the *Nichibei* under the pseudonym, Kiyohi Hama.

Angel Island Detention Station

Angel Island—what a beautiful name
I would play with her until I die
But there are no angels on this island.

Angel Island—what a sweet name
But there are no angels here
Only nameless immigrant prisoners.

Today is gone, but
Agony, anguish, and anxiety stay with me
Through the dark night until dawn.

Tears in my eyes have dried up
After several days of incarceration
No more tears of sadness, no more tears of anguish.

[I] watch through the wired window toward evening
See the sky light up with the splendor
Of the setting sun as if the world explodes.

America is my country
So my birth certificate says
But America doesn't want me here.

[I] hear sounds of different voices from the next cells
Chinese, Russian, Mexican, Greek, and Italian
Voices of sorrow, nostalgia, rage, and passion.

On one of the sad days
I [felt the] closeness of my village sweetheart
Through a newspaper from Japan.

New Year's Day on Angel Island
Is silent like a graveyard and nine Japanese deportees
Sitting together wrapped in blankets while I write poetry.

New Year's Day came quietly and left silently
I will soon be age twenty-one
No one can stop the sun.

Gazing at the picture of Daisuke Namba[3]
In the Japanese paper on the wall
They do not utter a single word.

Suddenly a thought flashed through my mind
Would she be at the Yokohama dock
If I were to be sent back to Japan?

Pain and ache have disappeared in this detention room
After writing several poems
For the first time in a month.

Since detention here, [I have forgotten] the villagers
Who hated and some who loved me
Freedom is the only thought in my mind.[4]

Finally, his cousin Saiji Okumura showed up in January to testify, but the Board of Special Inquiry (BSI) was not satisfied with his statements. Further investigation involving Yoneda's sister Emi in Los Angeles was conducted before Goso was finally released from the island.[5]

Goso Yoneda was but one of 85,000 Japanese to arrive in San Francisco between 1910 and 1940, making them the second largest group after the Chinese to be processed through Angel Island. Most Japanese had an easier time than Chinese arrivals in terms of the interrogation process and length of stay at Angel Island. That was because Japan, by defeating a European power in the Russo-Japanese War of 1905, had earned the diplomatic respect of the United States and was thus able to better protect the interests of its citizens abroad. Whereas China had failed to stop Congress from passing the Chinese Exclusion Act in 1882, Japan was able to negotiate a Gentlemen's Agreement with the U.S. in 1907–08, whereby it agreed to stop issuing passports to laborers. Immigrants coming to the United States with Japanese passports in hand were generally admitted within a day or two. Less than 1 percent were excluded or deported.[6] Nevertheless, for those who had to stay

Goso "Karl" Yoneda carrying *Memoirs of a Revolutionary* under his arm in Hiroshima, 1923. (Photo by Peter Kropotokin. Scan by Vincent Chin from *Ganbatte: Sixty-Year Struggle of a Kibei Worker*. Courtesy of Asian American Studies Center, UCLA.)

on Angel Island for weeks and sometimes even months to undergo medical treatment or appeal decisions to exclude them, their days were full of "agony, anguish, and anxiety," as expressed in Yoneda's poems.

Before Angel Island

For over two centuries, the Japanese people had been forbidden by law from emigrating. But after Commodore Matthew Perry forced Japan open to trade in 1854, the Japanese government had difficulty enforcing the law. In 1884, they gave in to the pressures of Hawaiian planters to recruit contract laborers, and large-scale Japanese immigration to America began. By the time the Angel Island Immigration Station officially opened in 1910, the Japanese population in the United States had grown from 148 in 1880 to 72,157.[7] Some of the early immigrants were students, merchants, political exiles, and women lured into prostitution, but most were farmers and laborers from the southwestern prefectures of Japan hit hard by the economic policies of the Meiji Restoration intent on rapid modernization. They had left their homeland to escape depressed conditions caused by increased taxes, land forfeitures, and unemployment, in addition to droughts, floods, and famines in the region.[8] Some had also left, as Goso Yoneda did, to avoid the three years of military service required of men over eighteen. Almost everyone had the same dream—to make it rich in America. Thousands had been drawn to the sugar plantations of Hawaii first, and later to the U.S. mainland, by labor contractors, emigration companies, and Japanese imperialists who advocated emigration as a way to expand the Japanese empire. "First sons, stay in Japan and be men of Japan," they had been taught in school. "Following sons, go abroad with great ambition as men of the world."[9]

Because the Chinese Exclusion Act had effectively stopped the flow of Chinese immigrants to the United States, there was a growing need for cheap labor to replace them in the railroads, mines, lumber mills, fish canneries, farms and orchards, and domestic service. According to one advertisement in the *Hawaii-Japan Chronicle* on March 22, 1905, "Employment offered in picking strawberries and tomatoes, planting beets, mining, and domestic service. Now is the time to go! Wages $1.50 a day."[10] Considering that a carpenter in Japan was making only 65 sen (30 cents) a day and that an American dollar was worth twice as much as a Japanese yen, it is no wonder that prospective immigrants thought that money grew on trees in America.[11] Between 1901 and 1907, 42,000 Japanese immigrated directly to the United States, while another 38,000 Japanese, attracted by the higher wages and better job opportunities on the mainland, remigrated from Hawaii.[12]

Before long, their increased numbers and presence in the American West became a thorn in the side of white workers, small farmers, and anti-Asian exclusionists. Highly organized as a workforce and particularly successful at farming, the Japanese were accused of displacing white workers, depressing wages and working conditions, and creating unfair competition to white farmers and small businesses. Because the Japanese did not want to be characterized as inassimilable like the Chinese, they worked hard to learn English, become Christians, adopt American customs, and resist gambling and prostitution. But they were still regarded as racially inferior and unfit to become Americans. In fact, their efforts at Americanization often backfired. The first attempt to exclude Japanese immigration occurred in 1900, when the Chinese Exclusion Act was up for renewal. At a mass rally in San Francisco organized by the American Federation of Labor and led by then mayor James D. Phelan, a resolution was passed urging Congress to stop all classes of Japanese other than diplomats from immigrating. According to the resolution, "Such a law has become a necessity not only on the grounds set forth in the policy of Chinese exclusion but because . . . the assumed virtue of the Japanese—i.e., their partial adoption of American customs—makes them the more dangerous as competitors."[13] The following year, California governor Henry Gage, arguing that cheap Japanese labor was as much a menace to American labor as Chinese labor, convinced the state legislature to send Congress a memorial to restrict Japanese immigration. Moreover, all three political parties in the 1900 election—Republican, Democratic, and Populist—ran on exclusion planks against admitting any more Asian laborers into this country.

Seeing the handwriting on the wall, the Japanese government attempted to curb the emigration of "low class" laborers in an effort to avoid the humiliation of a Japanese exclusion law.[14] But Congress was slow to respond. As Japanese immigration continued unabated, the *San Francisco Chronicle* began a series of articles attacking Japanese immigration in 1905. One front page story, "JAPANESE INVASION, THE PROBLEM OF THE HOUR," warned of an impending "brown stream of Japanese immigration" once the Russo-Japanese War was over. The newspaper claimed that at least 100,000 Japanese were already here undercutting white labor, and that they were "no more assimilable than the Chinese."[15] That same year, organized labor formed the Asiatic Exclusion League (AEL) for the sole purpose of stopping Asian immigration on both racial and economic grounds. According to the preamble to its constitution: "The preservation of the Caucasian race upon American soil, and particularly upon the west shore thereof, necessitates the adoption of all possible measures to prevent or minimize the immigration of Asiatics to America."[16] Boasting of 100,000 members in California alone and of branches in Washington, Oregon, Idaho, Colorado, and Nebraska, AEL organized boycotts of Japanese businesses and supported efforts to drive Japanese laborers out of the lumber industries and coal mines.

In 1906, the anti-Japanese campaign came to a head after the San Francisco school board, under pressure from AEL, ordered all Japanese and Korean pupils to be transferred to the segregated Oriental Public School that had been established for the Chinese. Considering this an affront to its national honor, Japan immediately launched a protest. President Theodore Roosevelt, fearful of offending Japan, a growing military power, personally interceded. To appease the exclusionists, he issued Executive Order 589 on March 14, 1907, to stop the entry of Japanese laborers from Hawaii, Mexico, and Canada to the continental United States. Then he negotiated the Gentlemen's Agreement with the Japanese government. In exchange for revoking the school segregation order, Japan agreed to stop issuing passports to laborers. As with the Chinese Exclusion Act, merchants, diplomats, students, visitors, and returning U.S. residents would be exempted, but the Gentlemen's Agreement differed in one important respect: Japanese immigrants already in the United States would be allowed to summon family members, whereas Chinese immigrants needed to be of the exempted classes such as merchants to bring their families to America.[17] The Japanese government, wary of the growing anti-Japanese movement and wanting to maintain good relations with the United States, took it a step further. They initially did not allow laborers in the United States to summon wives. Then, after 1915, only laborers who had $800 in savings were eligible to do so.

The impact of the Gentlemen's Agreement was felt immediately— Japanese immigration dropped from 9,544 in 1908 to 2,432 in 1909. But far from any semblance of exclusion, the terms of the Gentlemen's Agreement actually allowed another 120,000 Japanese into the country before the Immigration Act of 1924 effectively stopped Japanese immigration in its tracks.[18] The Japanese came to call this period of immigration *yobiyose-jidai*, "the period of summoning families."[19]

The largest group to be summoned were "picture brides," young women in Japan who had been married to Japanese immigrants in America through the custom of arranged marriage. The established custom was an expedient and legal way for Japanese immigrants to get married and establish families in America without the trouble and expense of making a trip home to look for a bride. There was also the threat of conscription looming over the men. If a Japanese man under thirty-five returned to Japan and stayed for more than thirty days, he would lose his deferment from serving in the Japanese Army. So when it was time, parents in Japan would secure a go-between or relative to find a suitable bride for their son in America. There would be a thorough investigation of the character, family background, health, and education of the prospective bride and groom, followed by an exchange of photos and a wedding ceremony. Once the bride's name was entered into the groom's family register, the marriage was considered legal and valid as far as Japan was concerned. The husband in America had only to pay a certification fee to the Japanese consulate and his bride's passage to America.

As early as 1905, Christian organizations and immigration officials had been opposed to U.S. recognition of these "proxy" marriages, arguing that it would result in an influx of Japanese prostitutes and laborers disguised as picture brides.[20] In response to these fears and criticisms, the Japanese government instituted a rule that all new brides had to live with their in-laws for at least six months prior to applying for a passport. The U.S. secretary of labor also directed all immigration stations to be on the lookout for Japanese prostitutes and anyone "likely to become a public charge." In addition, all picture brides had to be remarried according to U.S. laws before they could be admitted. This practice continued until 1917, when Japan finally convinced the United States to recognize picture brides as legal wives so that they would be exempted from the literacy test required by the Immigration Act of 1917. All throughout this period, the Japanese government encouraged the emigration of women, cultural assimilation, and permanent settlement in America as a way to counter anti-Japanese sentiment and to influence American public opinion about the superiority of Japanese immigrants in comparison to the despised Chinese.[21] The Gentlemen's Agreement and U.S. recognition of picture brides as legitimate immigrants paved the way for this to happen.

The Voyage

In March of 1919, Shizu Hayakawa left her home in Fukuoka and traveled alone to the United States to live with a man she had never met. "Everyone told me I was brave!" she said, although inside, "I was very much afraid." Coming from a poor family that ran a dairy, she was married to her step-mother's younger brother, Shunkei Hayakawa, who was a window washer in America. "My husband was sixteen years older than I," she said. "I did not think about whether he would be a suitable husband or not. In Japan it was the custom for parents to arrange marriages. This being so, there was no alternative." After stopping in Yokohama long enough to clear the physical examination for hookworm and trachoma and to obtain her passport from the Japanese Foreign Ministry, she boarded the *Korea Maru* for the month-long journey to San Francisco. There were many other young brides on this ship and Shizu took solace in talking to them about their future husbands and life in America. Almost all had agreed to the arranged marriage out of filial duty or economic necessity. When the ship stopped overnight in Hawaii, they were allowed to go ashore. "We all dressed in Japanese kimonos and went *shan shan* [walking with pride] to a restaurant where we ate delicious *sukiyaki*," she happily recalled. Then upon arrival in San Francisco, Shizu was taken to the Angel Island Immigration Station for processing. "It was somewhat frightening," she said. "We all had to go into the clinic for a physical examination. Well, the immigration authorities were on a holiday. What with one thing and another, it took a whole week before I was cleared."[22]

Iyo Tsutsui, who was detained at Angel Island for two weeks in 1915, agreed to an arranged marriage to Taro Tsutsui, a farmer in Stockton, California, because it was the only way she could get to America. "When I was fifteen, I had already made up my mind to come to America, even before my parents made their decision." As a student she had been inspired by a geography teacher to go abroad. He had told them, "If Japan does not change its course, she will not develop. Look at England. It is a small country, but it has many colonies and it is an industrialized nation. That's why England is said to be the most powerful country in the world. Young people must go abroad and develop themselves." Iyo found the opportunity to do so when a go-between and Taro's mother came to her house to propose a match. "They had brought his picture and everyone agreed with me that he looked like a man of steady and earnest character," she recalled. "It was at that time that I decided to become his bride, and sent him my picture." After the wedding, Iyo lived and farmed with her in-laws for over a year before leaving for America with a shipload of picture brides. "As soon as we landed," she said, "we were taken to the immigration office on Angel Island, where we were examined for hookworm." There, her deception earlier in Yokohama, when she had borrowed a stool sample from another woman, would come back to haunt her. Found with hookworm, a contagious disease that denied her entry, Iyo had to stay at Angel Island for two weeks to undergo medical treatment.[23]

Shizu Hayakawa and Iyo Tsutsui were but two young brides among the estimated 10,000 who were summoned by their husbands to America between 1908 and 1920, when the so-called Ladies Agreement between Japan and the United States put a stop to the immigration of picture brides.

Most of them were daughters of farmers, between the ages of eighteen and twenty-three, with seven to eight years of schooling, and married to Japanese immigrants ten to fifteen years their senior. Those lucky enough to marry wealthy husbands were able to travel comfortably in first class, and upon arrival, be inspected aboard the ship rather than at the Angel Island Immigration Station. However, the majority, including Shizu and Iyo, came in second-cabin or third-class steerage. The former meant sharing a cabin with a few passengers. The latter—the cheapest of all—meant sleeping below deck on double-tiered bunk beds "arranged like shelves in a silk-worm nursery," breathing stagnant air, served a poor diet of dried fish with rice, plagued by lice and seasickness, and without privacy or bathing facilities.[24] Although men and women were kept in separate quarters, cabin boys were known to prey on innocent women, molesting or seducing them. As Shizu observed, "They would say to the girls, 'Why don't you come with us rather than marry a man who is fifteen or sixteen years older than you?' That created all kinds of problems on the ship."[25] The *Shin Sekai* (New world) newspaper reported in 1916 that "there are quite a few immigrating Japanese women who behave shamefully in public on the steamship and are even unfaithful to their husbands during the trip."[26] In support of Japan's effort to project a positive image to the West, guidebooks were published by the YWCA and Japanese Association of America (JAA), which was founded in 1900 to help the Japanese government regulate Japanese immigration. The guidebooks, which were distributed at ports of departure, instructed young women going abroad for the first time to dress and behave properly and to resist temptations that might compromise their good reputation, or worse, disgrace their country. "It is extremely important for you to act as a refined, virtuous woman and do nothing to invite the scorn of foreigners."[27] In 1916, Japanese community leaders even convinced the Toyo steamship company to place a "ship matron" aboard their ships to chaperone the women.

Upon arrival, the ship would be greeted at the San Francisco dock by anxious husbands with photos of their brides in their hands. Equally anxious would be the young brides on board the ship searching for the matches to the photos they were holding. Some men were known to have sent younger or touched-up photographs of themselves or to have lied about their economic status, leading to disappointments and difficult, if not failed, marriages. A few disillusioned brides even asked to return to Japan on the next ship. Fortunately for Shizu and Iyo, they were not disappointed. Shizu was pleased that her husband had thought to bring her some delicious sushi when he came to meet her at the dock. Likewise, Iyo was touched by her husband's offer to help carry her luggage when they finally met on Angel Island. "I thought, 'Oh, he is very kind! If this is my real husband, everything will be fine.'"[28] However, before the women could be released to their husbands, they had to go to the Angel Island

Japanese women wearing both traditional and modern dress walking toward the administration building, c. 1910. (Courtesy of California State Parks, 2010.)

Immigration Station for the physical examination and interrogation. The process usually took a day or two, and very few of the picture brides were ever excluded or deported.[29] At most, they might be found with hookworm and have to stay at the Angel Island hospital for a week or two to undergo medical treatment at their husband's expense.

Life on Angel Island

Although their stay at Angel Island was short compared to that of Chinese immigrants, it was still a frightening experience for these young women coming from a different cultural and sheltered environment. At first sight, they may have all thought the immigration station, surrounded by California poppies and azaleas, was "a peaceful paradise quite becoming of the name Angel Island."[30] But once inside, they would feel otherwise. "I had never seen such a prison-like place as Angel Island," said Kamechiyo Takahashi, who had been summoned by her husband in 1917. Taking note of the barbed wire fence that surrounded the barracks on the outside and the grated windows and locked doors on the inside, many wondered as Kamechiyo did, "why I had to be kept in a prison."[31] Teiko Tomita, who was on Angel Island in 1921, remembered a lot of crying. "We didn't understand the language, and though they gave us three meals a day, their food did not agree with us. We all cried and cried because we didn't know when we'd be free and because we couldn't understand anything they said to us."[32] Shizu Hayakawa recalled how she got into trouble for bathing one day. "We bathed as we did in Japan. We washed ourselves outside the tub and then soaked. We got into trouble because there was water all over the place!" The water even leaked through the floorboards into the administration offices below. "Fortunately for the women," Shizu added, "Rev. Terasawa's wife was working at the immigration office on Angel Island, and she looked after us."[33]

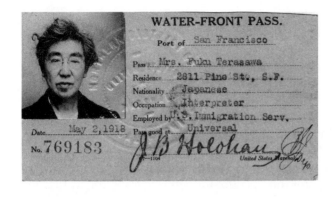

WATER-FRONT PASS.

Port of ... San Francisco

Pass... Mrs. Fuku Terasawa

Residence ... 2811 Pine St., S.F.

Nationality ... Japanese

Occupation ... Interpreter

Employed by U.S. Immigration Serv.

Date ... May 2, 1918 Pass good at ... Universal

No. 769183 J B Holohan United States Marshal

Fuku Terasawa was employed as a Japanese interpreter and matron at the Angel Island Immigration Station from 1912 to 1925. (Courtesy of Donald Nakahata.)

Fuku Terasawa worked as a matron and interpreter at Angel Island from 1912 to 1925, and many of the Japanese women who were detained there remembered her kind assistance. Born in 1863 and educated in an Episcopal mission school in Japan, she was married to the Reverend Barnabas Hisayoshi Terasawa, an Anglican priest. He immigrated to California in 1902 and she and their nine children followed in 1908. During the years that picture brides were required to be remarried according to U.S. laws, Fuku served as a witness in many of the weddings performed by her husband.[34] In 1926, she was interviewed by Clara Cahill Park, the wife of sociologist Robert E. Park, as part of the Survey of Race Relations project. Asked about her role as matron and interpreter at the immigration station, Fuku had this to say about picture brides and race relations:

People have a great many wrong ideas about Japanese picture brides and Japanese women coming to America. I know that Japanese do not send women to America to be prostitutes. They are married and usually they are happy. Sometimes when the age is very different they are not so happy, but with us Japanese love comes after marriage. Just a little while ago I had a crate of grapes sent me from some one whose name I did not remember, but a letter came with it, so: "I was a bride and came to this country years ago. You were very good to me, and I wanted you to know that I was happy and prosperous." I hear many stories like that.

I think people say a great many things about the Japanese when they don't know anything about them. For instance, they say the Japanese have taken all the best land in the Imperial Valley. But when they went in there, all the land was worthless. After they had made the land fit for cultivation and were raising crops then the white people began coming in and they said, "Look here, the Japanese are taking all the best land." Some white man who are friends of the Japanese said, "Why not come down to Texas. In our state of Texas we need the Japanese." So one family that I know sold everything and moved the whole family down to Texas, where they had been invited to come. But before they could even unpack their goods the American Legion called on them and said, "We will give you so many hours to get out of town."[35]

Methodist Deaconess Katharine Maurer, whom the Japanese women called "A.B.C. Mama" because she taught them English, was also available to help them. It was because of the "pitiful sight of forlorn picture brides waiting in a bare room for their picture husbands to claim them" that the Women's Home Missionary Society had asked the immigration service for permission to place a deaconess there in 1911.[36] Maurer provided the women with clothing, sewing material, sundries, holiday celebrations, and Japanese reading material donated by newspapers and bookstores in San Francisco.

In addition, YWCA staff was on hand to help the women at the docks and at the Angel Island Immigration Station. Sarah Ellis, secretary of the Japanese YWCA in San Francisco, made regular visits to Angel Island to comfort the new arrivals, prepare them for American life, and arrange for temporary landings under YWCA guardianship.[37] In 1915 Michi Kawai, general secretary of the YWCA in Japan, made three visits to Angel Island to investigate conditions there and to offer her assistance. A graduate of Bryn Mawr College and founder of Keisen Jogakuen (Girls School) in Tokyo, Kawai was a strong advocate of women's education and moral reform. It was largely through her efforts that the YWCA became directly involved in transforming "ignorant country girls" into refined women so that they would be worthy representatives of a civilized East Asian nation abroad. To this end, the YWCA in Yokohama and Tokyo helped emigrant women find suitable lodgings in the port cities, taught them conversational English, Western customs, cooking, sewing, and hygiene, and advised women on how to conduct themselves aboard ship and upon landing. A report by Kawai offers us a rare glimpse of what life was like for Japanese women on Angel Island. At the same time, her criticisms of the picture brides' shabby appearance and conduct reveal the class bias and condescending attitude of some Christian women toward the women they were trying to help.[38]

On the second floor [of the administration building] are one hundred or so [Japanese] women gathered in one room. Bunks in tiers of three occupy the greater part of the room. Some of the women are lying down, others are changing their clothes, and still others are sitting on a bench as if waiting for someone to come. All of them are anxiously awaiting the physical examination for trachoma and hookworm as they

Michi Kawai, YWCA Grand Secretary in Japan, visited the Angel Island Immigration Station three times in 1915. (Scan by Vincent Chin. Courtesy of Keisen Jogakuen.)

carefully guard their passports done up in *furoshiki* wrapping-cloths. It is no wonder that they are nervous. I hear that even those who passed the same exams three times in Japan have been stopped by the Immigration Service, because they did not take care of their health while on board the ship.

In general, the women represent a cross-section of lower-middle class Japanese—a hair-dresser, a middle-aged geisha and a dancing mistress, all with Japanese coiffure and clothes; a group of dancing girls going to the Exposition; several older country women; a refined looking mother with two children; wives who have been sent for by their husbands; some who are returning from visits in Japan; and a few "picture brides." The brides are mostly from rural communities and appear shamelessly in public with uncombed hair, no stockings, and with grubby and smelly clothes. Their efforts to beautify themselves with an excessive use of powder results only in giving an impression of uncleanness.

When the lunch bell rings, they go downstairs to the dining room along with the Chinese, Spanish, and European women—all housed in separate quarters. The room is bare, save for eight rows of long tables and benches. On each table is a large pan filled with slices of bread, some small bowls of jam and white sugar, and cups for tea. The Europeans have meat, beans, and even better silverware. Only a few of the Japanese women are served one or two extra dishes, which they had ordered and purchased beforehand. Within five minutes, they finish eating and head back upstairs. Some stop along the way at the small food stand to purchase pickled vegetables and other snacks. At four o'clock

Three women
dressed in kimonos
enjoy the scenery
from afar, c. 1910.
(Courtesy of
California State
Parks, 2010.)

for their supper they have steamed Chinese rice and greens cooked with scraps of pork in a salty broth. Some of the Japanese women tell me with tears that the food is awful.[39]

As Kawai concluded in her report, after dinner the women were allowed out to view the ocean scenery and get some exercise. They returned by 7 o'clock, took a bath, and prepared for bed. The next morning, Kawai comforted the women who were nervously waiting for the results of their physical exams. She talked to them about American customs, the likes and dislikes of the American people, and of the Japanese people's responsibility to the land they had come to live in—basically the same advice that was given by the YWCA to women before they left Japan and after they arrived in America. The emphasis was always on how to become disciplined homemakers and adapt to the American way of life in order to earn the respect of white Americans and prevent the same antagonisms visited on Chinese immigrants. At stake was the reputation of Japanese womanhood and that of Japan as a rising world power.

The Interview and Appeal Process

Once the women passed the physical examination, they were interviewed by a Board of Special Inquiry with the assistance of a Japanese interpreter.[40] According to Iyo Tsutsui's recollections, "I met Mr. Tsutsui for the first time—well, in the very beginning they called my husband's name and made him sit down in the waiting room. Then the immigration officers came to get me and questioned me. They also asked if I had *mise gane* [show money]. Then they called my husband and asked him questions. They had to make sure that he was the right man."[41]

A young couple appearing before the Board of Special Inquiry, 1916. Until 1917, a civil wedding was required of Japanese picture brides and grooms. (Courtesy of California State Parks, 2010.)

Although she did not mention it, Iyo probably had to show the inspector her passport and a certified copy of her husband's family registry. Her husband, in turn, had to produce a letter from the Japanese consulate attesting to his good character and ability to support a wife. And before being released, they would have to agree to be remarried in an American wedding ceremony to be certified by the Japanese Association of America.

Yoshi Nakayama. (National Archives, Pacific Regional Branch.)

Sakaki Nakayama. (National Archives, Pacific Regional Branch.)

Unlike the interrogations of the Chinese, in which they were asked hundreds of detailed questions about their family background as well as about their sponsors in America, the BSI interviews of picture brides and their husbands were relatively simple and brief—usually no more than twenty questions. The line of questioning was intended to ensure that the applicant was not "likely to become a public charge," as indicated by the initials "L.P.C." at the beginning of the transcript.

Immigration Service

In re Yoshi Nakayama, ex S.S.	:	Angel Island, Cal.
Mongolia, Dec. 31, 1910	:	Jan. 3, 1911
L.P.C.	:	

Board of special inquiry appointed by Act. Commissioner to consider this case. Present: H. Kennah, Chairman; Insprs. J. A. Robinson and C. Schulze. Intpr. J. L. Gardiner. Stenog. E. A. Carroll.

By Chairman: Sworn.
Q. What is your name and age? A. Yoshi Nakayama, age 20.
Presents passport No. 8454, issued for U.S., Dec. 7, 1910.
Q. Did you arrive at this port on S.S. Mongolia, Jan. 31, 1910? A. Yes, from Nagasaki; I have never been in U.S. before; I am now going to my husband, Sakaki Nakayama, at Guadalupe, Cal, to whom I have been married by photograph since Sept. 1910; he is a farmer, but I never saw him. Produces photo of husband.
Q. Were you ever married before? A. No.
Q. Was your husband ever married before, to your knowledge? A. No.
Q. What were you doing in Japan? A. I was a farm laborer, living with my parents at home. If admitted here I will assist my husband and do household duties, and will marry according to the laws of U.S.
Q. How much money have you? A. $50 (Showing).
Alleged husband called. Sworn.
Q. What is your name and age? A. Sakaki Nakayama, age 30; I am a farmer at Guadalupe, Cal., and have been in U.S. 9 years, and spent 4 years in Hawaii.
Q. For what purpose do you appear here? A. For my wife Yoshi (producing her photograph), whom I married by photograph in August, 1910.
Q. How much money have you? (Produces $180 and states he has $700 in bank, but did not bring his bank book with him.)
Q. Do you own or lease a farm? A. I work a farm by contract. (Presents a labor agreement dated Dec. 6, 1909 with the Routzahn Seed Co. of Arroyo Grande, Cal., showing agreement between said company, the witness and other Japanese, to perform labor on 350 acres of land.)
Q. Have you ever been married before? A. No.

Q. Has your wife ever been married before, to your knowledge? A. No.

Q. Are you willing to marry according to the laws of U.S. if your wife is admitted? A. Yes. I have never seen my wife, but if she is admitted we will marry according to the laws of U.S., and she will do only household duties. I have one room prepared for her.

To witness: Q. Is this the woman you intend to marry? A. Yes.

To applicant: Q. Is this the man you intend to marry? A. Yes.

Inspr. Schulze: I move that the applicant be admitted conditional upon her marriage to the witness in accordance with the laws of U.S., and the receipt of satisfactory proof of the marriage by the office.

Inspr. Robinson: I second the motion.

Inspr. Kennah: I concur; applicant is admitted under the conditions specified.[42]

In accordance to the conditions of the Gentlemen's Agreement, the wife's passport and family registry was considered adequate proof of her identity and marriage, while the certificate signed by the Japanese consul was sufficient to satisfy the requirements of U.S. residency and economic status of the husband. To be sure, the men were well aware of the class biases of the Gentlemen's Agreement and often produced bank account books, employment letters, and land titles or leases as further evidence of their financial standing. When asked what the wife would be doing in America, both knew to answer, "Housework," thus confirming she was not going to be a laborer but a proper middle-class housewife. This practiced response reflected intersecting requirements of gender and class respectability in order to make the entry of a despised group acceptable to immigration officials.[43] Unless there were problems with the husband's proof of prior lawful entry into the United States or suspicions of immoral behavior on the part of either spouse, the wife was released to her husband at the conclusion of the interview. But if the bride were a minor, she would most likely be released to the Ellen Stark Ford House for Japanese and Korean Women and Children in San Francisco. Established in 1904 by the Methodist Episcopal Home Missionary Society, the home assumed the responsibility of investigating the groom's background, serving as a witness to the marriage, and keeping in touch with the woman until she became of age. Until 1917, photos of the couple were kept on file at Angel Island for possible use in future investigations of immigration or prostitution cases.[44]

Not everyone had it so easy. A review of over 200 case files of Japanese who were detained on Angel Island for more than a week show that immigration inspectors were closely following Commissioner-General of Immigration Anthony Caminetti's directive: "Because of the racial antipathy and the non-assimilative character and prolific tendencies of this class [resident Japanese], their increasing number on the Pacific coast is a menace to the peace and prosperity of our citizens, and it is felt that a strict adherence to the spirit of the so-called 'gentlemen's agreement' should be required."[45] Not only were immigration inspectors diligent about enforcing the Asian exclusion laws, but they also sought ways to reject the Japanese on moral, medical, or economic grounds according to the general immigration laws.[46]

Returning U.S. residents as well as wives and children of Japanese aliens in America were generally subjected to longer interviews and detention time than picture brides, especially when they had to appeal adverse decisions. Upon his return from Japan in 1915, Shichitaro Ikeda was excluded and ordered deported for a past "crime involving moral turpitude." He had admitted to living in "concubinage" with a white woman in the past and to having three children by her. His wife Sumiyo Ikeda, in turn, was excluded on LPC charges because of her perceived dependent status. The underlying assumption was that the wives were wholly dependent on their husbands for financial support. The Ikedas were detained on Angel Island for thirty-eight days pending the results of their appeal. They were finally admitted on a legal technicality—a prior crime of moral turpitude can not be used to exclude a returning alien.[47]

Compared to the Chinese, there were few cases of Japanese women who were suspected or accused of being prostitutes, most likely because Japanese prostitution, thanks to the efforts of the Japanese government and community organizations, never became as rampant as Chinese prostitution. One of the last Japanese brothels in Fresno, California, was closed down in 1914 after immigration officers raided the place and arrested twenty-three Japanese women and eight white women on prostitution charges. Two years later, an investigation by Commissioner Edward White at the request of matrons of the Women's Home of the Episcopal Church, showed that all of the eighty picture brides who had already been admitted into the United States were leading respectable lives.[48]

Those found with illnesses that prevented them from making a living, such as tuberculosis or a heart condition, were almost always deported. In a borderline case, the applicant could be given temporary landing after s/he posted a bond. Wasaku Honji, an alien resident returning to the United States after an absence of nine years, was not given this opportunity. In 1913, he was excluded under the LPC clause because he had arteriosclerosis and limited resources. JAA tried to appeal on his behalf, arguing that the same illness had not stopped others from earning a living and that Honji had invested $500 in his son's farm in Mountain View, California, to which he was heading for work. But the appeal failed and Honji was deported after a month's delay at Angel Island.[49]

Whereas applications for medical treatment of hookworm were usually granted, the same was not always true of trachoma, which took longer to cure. When Sadaye Hisakuni and Masaya Onisuke, both married to Japanese alien residents, arrived at the immigration station two months apart in the summer of 1915, they were diagnosed with trachoma that was curable within sixty days. Both were excluded and denied hospital treatment. Both chose to appeal, retaining the same attorney to represent them—Frank Ainsworth, who had left the immigration service to work for JAA. Even though Commissioner of Immigration Samuel Backus recommended granting Hisakuni hospital treatment "as in similar cases in the past," the Immigration Bureau in Washington, D.C., instructed him to deny her treatment. She was subsequently deported after being detained on Angel Island for forty days. Learning from this experience, Ainsworth adopted a different strategy in the appeal of Onisuke's exclusion, arguing first, that her parents were deceased and she had no home to return to; and second, that she was not a picture bride but had married and lived with her husband for six months before coming to the United States. During the time it took Ainsworth to file an appeal to the secretary of labor and a writ of habeas corpus to the U.S. Circuit Court of Appeals, Onisuke was given medical treatment for "humanitarian reasons" at the Angel Island hospital and cured. She was landed after being detained at the immigration station for over two months.[50]

The case of Yoshitsugu Fujita, a fifteen-year-old son of a laundryman in Alameda, California, illustrates the extent to which the immigration service would go to exclude a Japanese immigrant they suspected of being brought into the country to work. When Fugita's father was asked what he planned to do with his son, he made the mistake of answering, "have him work in my laundry." He later changed his answer to, "I expect him to go to school in the day time, and work after school hours. He is only a child and can not do much in the laundry anyway." Inspector Edsell did not believe him and recommended that the boy be excluded, not for being a laborer but for having hookworm. The father's request for hospital treatment for his son was denied by Commissioner Backus, who wrote: "The application for admission was an attempt on the part of the Japanese father to take his fifteen-year old son, fresh from the influences of his mother and home surroundings in Japan and place him at laboring pursuits in the United States." JAA stepped in and appealed to the secretary of labor, arguing that the father really did not need the son to work and that hookworm was usually considered a treatable disease. Failing that, attorney Frank Guerena filed a writ of habeas corpus, requesting that the boy be released on the basis that Commissioner Backus's treatment of his case had been "wholly unjust and inequitable." Judge Maurice T. Dooling of the U.S. District Court refused to intercede, stating that granting hospital treatment was at the discretion of the immigration service. Yoshitsugu was deported on July 11, 1914, after being detained for six weeks on Angel Island. Unlike other cases of sons, even adopted sons, who were initially excluded but allowed to post bond and be released so that they would not be separated from their families, Yoshitsugu was not given this option supposedly because he had family in Japan.[51]

When denied entry, a Japanese immigrant's first line of defense was often the Japanese Association of America. All immigrant men were required to register with their local JAA branch in California, Nevada, Utah, or Colorado and pay an annual fee of $2. When it was time for them to make a trip to Japan or summon family members to America, they applied for the necessary paperwork at the local JAA. Two secretaries, one white American and one Japanese American, were employed by JAA to meet new arrivals at the port of San Francisco and help them get landed. This could involve giving legal advice, writing letters of character reference, certifying marriages of picture brides, posting bonds, and filing legal appeals. An important part of their immigration work was to advocate better treatment, food, and sanitary conditions at the Angel Island Immigration Station. Because of their efforts, a Japanese matron was hired to attend to the needs of the women, the dining hall began serving Japanese food in 1919, and a significant number of Japanese immigrants who were initially excluded successfully appealed the decision and were admitted to the country.[52]

Closing the Gate

The continued increase in the Japanese population in America, combined with the success of Japanese in agriculture, rekindled the fires of Japanese exclusion after World War I. The Gentlemen's Agreement had failed to curb Japanese immigration, and the Alien Land Law, passed by the California legislature in 1913 to prohibit Asian immigrants, from owning or leasing land, had been successfully evaded by the *issei*. They did so by purchasing land in their *nisei* (American-born) children's names or through corporations consisting of white American friends. California State Senator James D. Phelan, who made Japanese exclusion central to his reelection campaign, led the charge against picture brides as the crux of the problem. "These women are not only wives but laborers; they go to work with the children strapped upon their backs and accomplish the dual purpose of defeating the [immigration] law by getting in actual laborers and of defeating the land law by getting [through] the birth route persons eligible to hold land," he was quoted as saying in the local newspapers. Phelan raised the alarm that California was rapidly becoming a Japanese colony and he vowed to change the laws and "exterminate this menace as a matter of self-defense."[53]

Major newspapers on the West Coast like the *Sacramento Bee, San Francisco Examiner, Los Angeles Examiner*, and *Seattle Star* added fuel to the fires by publishing articles criticizing picture marriages as a barbaric practice

HOME MAKERS OR LAND GRABBERS?

Original caption from the *San Francisco Examiner*, March 9, 1919: "Here are a number of "picture brides" from the land of cherry blossoms, photographed on the deck of a ship just pulling into the San Francisco harbor. They are destined to be the wives of Japanese residents of California. The system has been attacked by Senator Phelan as an organized plot to gain possession of valuable State land and crowd out the whites. The Japanese vigorously deny this." (Scan by Vincent Chin. Courtesy of the Bancroft Library, University of California, Berkeley.)

in which women were coerced into marriage without regard to love or morality. Front-page headlines, such as "JAPANESE PICTURE BRIDES ARE SWARMING HERE," called attention to the boatloads of "strange-looking" and "simple-minded" women landing on the Pacific shores while the story lines exaggerated their fertility rates: "It is these brides who rear five children to every babe born to American parents."[54] V. S. McClatchy, owner of the *Sacramento Bee*, was as fervent as Phelan in advocating Japanese exclusion. In a series of newspaper articles, he accused the Japanese of "peaceful penetration," or using picture brides to facilitate a Japanese takeover of California. "The 'picture bride' plan [has] increased most rapidly and effectively the number of loyal and faithful sons and daughters of Nippon in this country with the added advantage of American citizenship, thus insuring the permanent establishment on American soil of the great Yamato race."[55]

Try as they did, the Japanese consulate and JAA could not counter the negative publicity nor stop the mounting anti-Japanese campaign. In the fall of 1919, a new group called the Oriental Exclusion League formed with the express purpose of excluding picture brides and all Japanese immigration, and forever banning Asians from acquiring U.S. citizenship. After the Exclusion League announced its plan to make a negative film about picture brides and Senator Phelan moved to convene a special session of the California Legislature to deal with the Japanese problem, Japanese Consul General Ohta Tamakichi decided it was time to act. He first wired the Japanese Foreign Ministry and pleaded with them to terminate the emigration of picture brides. "Such a measure," he argued, "would take away the most effective source of agitation from the exclusionists."[56] He next persuaded the JAA executive board to take a public stand against the picture-bride practice. Without consulting its local branches and to the utter dismay of its membership, the central board issued a press release declaring that the practice "should be abolished because it is not only in contravention of the accepted American conception of marriage, but is also out of harmony with the growing ideals of the Japanese themselves."[57]

Although the Japanese government and JAA had always defended the practice of picture brides in the past, they were now willing to abandon the cause and sacrifice the welfare of Japanese immigrants out of diplomatic necessity. Local members felt betrayed and protested loudly, but to no avail. On December 13, 1919, the Japanese Foreign Ministry, after receiving assurances from the Department of State that the United States would do what it could to prevent the enactment of any anti-Japanese measures, issued what became known as the "Ladies Agreement." Japan would cease issuing passports to picture brides effective March 1, 1920. But because the passports were good for six months, a few hundred more Japanese women were able to immigrate before the picture bride system came to an official end on September 1, 1920. Even so, there were still 24,000 unmarried *issei* men in America. They would now have to make trips to Japan, if they could afford it, to get married and return with their wives. To make things easier for them, the Japanese government extended their visits home from thirty days to three months before they would risk conscription into the Japanese Army.[58]

Japan's hope that the Ladies Agreement would placate anti-Japanese exclusionists proved wrong. Phelan and McClatchy, with the support of nativist organizations, labor unions, and farmers, were able to get voters in California to approve the Alien Land Law of 1920, which effectively stopped *issei* farmers from acquiring land through their *nisei* children. Worse yet, in the heat of nativism, scientific racism, and antiradicalism after World War I, Congress passed the Immigration Act of 1924 to reduce the flow of immigrants from Southern and Eastern Europe. A delegation of California politicians, led by Phelan and McClatchy, was able to persuade Congress to add an exclusion clause that would prohibit the admission of any "alien ineligible to citizenship." The 1924 act thus succeeded in abrogating the Gentlemen's Agreement and ending Japanese immigration once and for all.

Post-1924 Immigration

When word got out that the act had been signed into law on May 26 but that it would not take effect until July 1, there was a mad dash of Japanese bachelors for Japan to get married and bring their brides to America while the Gentlemen's Agreement was still in effect. Japanese immigrants who had postponed summoning family members from Japan, and others who had returned to Japan for a visit all rushed to book passage. To accommodate this rush, the Foreign Ministry waived its six-month waiting period required of new brides applying for passports and got Japanese shipping lines to put additional ships in service during the month of June. As a result, at least 5,000 passengers embarking from Kobe and Yokohama made it to the United States before the deadline. Among them were 442 brides who entered the country through Angel Island during the months of May and June.[59]

Once the 1924 Act went into effect, aside from those claiming U.S. citizenship, only returning residents and temporary visitors—such as ministers, students, government officials, merchants, and tourists—were admitted into the United States. As "aliens ineligible to citizenship," all other Japanese were excluded. Moreover, as with the Chinese Exclusion Act, the definition of temporary visitors reflected the U.S. preference for the elite and nonlaboring classes. Even so, another 20,000 Japanese qualified under these terms and arrived at the port of San Francisco between 1924 and 1940. Under the new law, applicants seeking admission into the United States were examined at the port of departure instead of the port of entry. For the Japanese, this meant applying for their visas at the American consulate instead of the Japanese Foreign Ministry. Then upon their arrival in the United States, all that the immigrant inspectors had to do was to make sure their documents were in order. Returning residents were required to show proof of prior lawful admission to the United States, and students had to provide a valid visa, letter of admission to an approved school, proof of financial support, and a healthy medical record. Other temporary visitors, in addition to their visas, needed to show evidence of their financial resources and letters of reference. As a result, there were fewer delays and most applicants were either admitted right off the ship or within a day or two from Angel Island.

Those excluded for medical or economic reasons could post bond—as much as $1,000—to guarantee their departures from the United States by a specific date. As it turned out, the Japanese had the highest rate of bond forfeitures among all nationalities at Angel Island. In 1929–30, they posted 197 out of a total of 268 bonds for that fiscal year and forfeited 84 out of 90 bonds. They just simply disappeared and never returned to Japan to claim the bond money.[60] As far as the immigration service was concerned, this made perfect sense. According to the San

Francisco Commissioner's Annual Report in 1931, "Where aliens come from countries where their economic power is consistently less than it is here, $500 or even $1,000 is not sufficient to affect the financial advantage arising out of increased earning power which the Japanese non-immigrant alien acquires after coming to this country,—in other words, he would rather lose the bond money than give up employment in the United States."[61]

One of the largest groups of Japanese to sail for America in the post-1924 period were *nisei* and *kibei* like Goso Yoneda, because as American-born citizens they were entitled to return at any time. Many had been taken to Japan as children for education. Others had chosen to go to Japan as adults for higher education or professional jobs denied them in the United States because of racial discrimination. In 1935, when it became apparent that immigration exclusion was depleting the Japanese workforce, thereby threatening the continued success of Japanese agriculture in the American West, JAA launched a "Back-to-America" campaign, sending envoys to Japan to encourage an estimated 40,000 to 60,000 *nisei* and *kibei* there to return and work the fields. In one pamphlet titled *Kibei no shiori* (Guide to returning to America), *issei* leaders compared the "perilous state" of Japanese agriculture to that of the Chinese after the Chinese Exclusion Act of 1882 was passed: "With the shortage of Nisei successors, our agriculture has already lost the labor market to Filipinos and Mexicans because older Japanese laborers cannot compete.... Our farms, which we, the pioneers of this new land, established in the last four decades, despite anti-Japanese exclusion, are panting under the shortage of racial successors; now we face the same fate our Chinese counterparts succumbed to forty years ago." Although it is difficult to gauge the effectiveness of the campaign, 850 *nisei* and *kibei* did return to the United States during the first nine months of 1936, as compared to the yearly average of 500 in previous years. Then as war broke out in China, many more returned to escape conscription into the Japanese Army and wartime conditions in Japan.[62]

As long as the *nisei* and *kibei* had documentation and a guardian or credible witness who could verify their identities, they were usually examined on board the ship and immediately landed. Otherwise, they were taken to Angel Island for further investigation or to await an adult relative to claim them. As unaccompanied minors, Jiro Kobashigawa, age sixteen, and Masayuki Ariki, age fourteen, were both detained on Angel Island when their relatives did not show up at the San Francisco docks. Seventy years later, both still remembered the feelings of anguish and anxiety at being locked up on Angel Island, not knowing when relatives would come to testify on their behalf.

Born in Phoenix, Arizona, Jiro was taken by his parents to Okinawa when he was six years old. There, he was given a good education. But in

1931, during his second year of high school, his family ran into financial problems and decided to take him out of school and send him back to Phoenix to work on his brother's farm. He was sad about leaving school but happy about returning to America. "All of my classmates were jealous of me," he said, "because at that time only certain people could come to America." Dressed in his cotton middle school uniform, Jiro boarded the *Tatsuta Maru* in Yokohama "with Mt. Fuji behind and a full playing band." His father, wanting to save money, had bought him a third-class ticket to San Francisco instead of Los Angeles. "Because of my father's mistake, I landed at San Francisco and was kept for three weeks at Angel Island." His brother had lost the farm in the Depression and did not have enough money to make the trip to San Francisco. By then there were fewer Japanese detainees on Angel Island, and Jiro was placed in the men's barracks with the Chinese and South Asians. All that he remembered was "chow time," when everyone would dash into the dining room to eat. "It was Chinese food and it was terrible," he said. "The soup, made with old meat, smelled and the rice was hard like day-old steamed rice, very hard to swallow." He did not encounter another Japanese until he went out to the exercise yard and met a group of Japanese men who were waiting to be deported. Feeling sorry for Jiro, they petitioned the immigration authorities, explaining that he was a U.S. citizen. As a result, Jiro was called for an interview and then moved to a private room in the administration building, where he got to eat better food with the employees. A week later, the Japanese Salvation Army, at the request of Japanese interpreter Emily Austin, came to get him released. They not only gave him a nice dinner at their San Francisco offices, but also put him on a train to Arizona the next day.[63]

Masayuki Ariki was not so lucky. Born in Fresno, California, he was taken to Japan by his parents when he was three years old. But because he was "nothing but trouble," always getting into fights and disobeying his parents, they decided to take him out of high school and send him to live with his sister and brother-in-law in San Francisco. Masayuki was not so happy about returning to America. "My parents never said why, but I knew they just wanted to get rid of me. That's what they use to do in Japan with someone who won't fit into their way of life." When he arrived in San Francisco in 1937, no one

Passport photo of Masayuki "Jim" Ariki, 1937. (Courtesy of National Archives, Pacific Regional Branch.)

was there to pick him up. Masayuki found out later that his brother-in-law knew about his troublesome background and intentionally snubbed him. He would spend the next twelve days locked up in the men's barracks, the sole Japanese among forty to fifty Chinese and Filipino men. "I couldn't talk to anybody and I was just worried the whole time—what the hell am I going to do?" he recalled. "But at the same time I was always hungry, so when meal time came, I sat down with the others and ate what they ate." Masayuki passed the rest of the time out in the exercise yard, napping on his bunk, and worrying about when his family would come to get him released. He wrote one letter to his parents from Angel Island. "I told them I got here in October and nobody came for me, so now I'm here on a small island." He did not even know the name of the island. A Filipino inmate helped him address the envelope to his parents in Hiroshima, the same Filipino who had taught him how to use the flush toilets. Finally, Masayuki's sister, Shizuye Yokoji, came to Angel Island, and he was called for the interview. "I noticed right away that they were very cordial to me," he recalled, "not harsh like my mother." After showing the *hakujin* (white) inspector his birth certificate and family registry and answering a few questions about his family background, he was released from the island that same day. The first thing he remembered saying to his sister was,

This family portrait of the Shiibashi family, taken in 1910 before they departed for Japan, was not sufficient evidence to prove that Kaoru Shiibashi (the baby in the picture) was born in Hawaii and entitled to reenter the country. (Courtesy of National Archives, Pacific Regional Branch.)

"That's not the kind of place you want to go and stay, especially when I can't even speak their language."[64]

Applying the tactics they had developed in dealing with Chinese applicants, the immigration service went to great trouble to catch Japanese fraudulent entries. They utlilized an international system of investigation. Like the Chinese, most Japanese had the financial resources to defend their immigrant rights through the appeal process, and they usually won. Japanese *kibei* who were suspected of making false claims to U.S. citizenship could be kept on Angel Island for months while the American consulate cross-examined their families in Japan. Such a case involved twenty-three-year-old Kaoru Shiibashi. When he arrived in the United States in April of 1931, he had a birth certificate showing that he was born in Hawaii and thus a U.S. citizen. He also had a photograph taken of him as a baby with his parents and older sister in Hawaii before the entire family left for Japan in 1910. His uncle came to testify on his behalf, but because he had never seen Kaoru before, immigration officials did not deem him a credible witness and asked the immigration office in Honolulu to investigate Kaoru's family background and birth. They found three witnesses in Hawaii who knew his parents, but no one who could identify Kaoru as the baby in the photo. There were further delays while the American consulate in Nagasaki interrogated Kaoru's father twice. Because of discrepancies in the answers of the father and son about Kaoru's age, his wages as a factory worker in Japan, and the scars on his body, the Board of Special Inquiry denied him admission, stating that "the evidence submitted does not satisfactorily establish that he is a citizen of the U.S." The Shiibashis did not give up. They hired attorney M. E. Mitchell to appeal the decision, and the secretary of labor ruled in their favor. Kaoru Shiibashi was finally landed after being detained on Angel Island for almost five months.[65]

The case of Miyono Nojima, who was detained on Angel Island for six months, demonstrates the great lengths that some Japanese immigrants, like their Chinese predecessors, took to circumvent the exclusion laws and gain entry into the United States. It also shows how alert and adept immigration inspectors had become at detecting fraudulent entries among the Japanese. On July 4, 1931, Miyono Nojima returned to America with her two daughters to join her husband, Fukujiro Nojima, who operated a laundry in Elko, Nevada. She had first immigrated as a picture bride in 1912 and given birth to two girls in Baker, Oregon, before the family left for Japan in 1915. Her husband returned to America alone the next year, leaving Miyono to take care of his ailing mother in Japan. He made two more visits to Japan, and the couple bore another daughter and a son. Because Miyono became sick with pleurisy and their son was hospitalized for a bone disease, Fukujiro did not make arrangements for his wife's return until 1930.

Passport photo of Miyono Nojima, 1931. (National Archives, Pacific Regional Branch.)

Upon landing in San Francisco, the two American-born daughters were admitted immediately, but Miyono was sent to Angel Island for further questioning. Something was wrong with her immigration visa. Under intense pressure to tell the truth, she finally admitted that she was first unable to obtain a visa from the American consulate in Kobe because she had been away from America too long for her absence to be considered temporary. It was out of desperation that she had listened to a clerk at the Iwakuniya Hotel in Kobe and paid 400 yen to secure the visa. Following his instructions, Miyono was to insist that she had departed from Seattle for Japan on October 29, 1930, and was now returning to the United States less than a year later. According to a memo in her case file, when told that the immigration office in San Francisco could easily contact the Seattle office to verify her departure date, she "reached a point bordering on hysteria, and she tearfully explained that her husband had nothing to do with her false claims and that she, herself, was entirely to blame." Two weeks later, her husband sent a telegram to Inspector August Kuckein on Angel Island, which read, "Please protect her for she may commit suicide."[66]

The board finally reached a decision on October 20, 1931, to deny Miyono Nojima admission on the grounds that she could not be considered a returning resident or nonquota immigrant under the Immigration Act of 1924; and that she had committed a crime involving moral turpitude by using an immigration visa procured by false claims and by making false statements under oath. Her attorney, Mark Coleman of the prestigious law firm, Thomas, Beedy, Presley and Paramore, was unsuccessful in securing probation for her from the District Court of Northern California and in appealing the exclusion decision to the secretary of labor. Miyono was deported on January 7, 1932, after being detained on Angel Island for six months. The scam by which Miyono had obtained a visa evidently involved hundreds of Japanese immigrants coming from Kobe with visas as returning residents obtained fraudulently from a well-organized ring that was under investigation by the Bureau of Immigration. Miyono Nojima was among seventeen applicants who admitted to falsifying their departure date from the United States to circumvent the Immigration Act of 1924. All were prosecuted and denied entry for obtaining visas by fraud and for committing perjury.[67]

Fukujiro Nojima did not give up easily. Soon after Miyono was deported, he retained the same law firm to find a way to bring her back. Although distraught by what had happened to her on Angel Island, Miyono was willing to try again. It is unclear from her case file what special arrangements were made, but this time, someone from the American consulate came to her home to advise her on how to secure a new visa and bring her two other children, sixteen-year-old Hideko and twelve-year-old Tetsuo, to America. On November 15, 1932, Miyono arrived in San Francisco with the two children, and they were all immediately sent to Angel Island. This time she appeared more confident and straightforward when interrogated by the BSI. She was excluded on the same grounds—her stay in Japan from 1915 to 1930 did not constitute a temporary visit abroad as contemplated in the Immigration Act of 1924. Following that ruling,

Hideko and Tetsuo could not be admitted as "children born to non-quota immigrants returning from a temporary absence." Her attorney was prepared to appeal the adverse decisions, and according to daughter Hideko years later, the lawyer succeeded because he had "connections to Washington, D.C."[68] Miyono Nojima and her two children were finally landed on February 3, 1933, after being detained on Angel Island for over two months.

Life after Angel Island

Although the Japanese were the second largest group to be processed through Angel Island, unlike the Chinese, they left no poems on the barrack walls and few stories of their detention experiences to their children, probably because their stay at Angel Island was so much shorter. Only a dozen of the sixty-two Japanese inscriptions found on the barrack walls by a research team of scholars in 2003 were carved by Japanese immigrants, basically to mark their time at Angel Island. For examples: "Miyamoto from Hiroshima Prefecture, year 43 (1910)" and "Fourteen years old, Kubota Noboru from Hiroshima Prefecture, 1936." One wall inscription, "Miyata Akemi," found in one of the small rooms occupied by Japanese women during the early years of the station's operation, is the only writing we have of a female detainee. All of the other Japanese inscriptions were written by prisoners of war and civilians repatriating to Japan during the World War II period.[69] In 1976, when Goso "Karl" Yoneda (he had changed his first name to Karl in honor of Karl Marx) returned to Angel Island for a visit, he did not see any Japanese poems on the barrack walls, only slogans. "Down with American imperialism, Down with Japanese imperialism, Long Live Communism" most likely had been written by communist deportees waiting to leave for the Soviet Union in 1932, and "Smash America and England, Japanese Army will land here soon" by Japanese prisoners of war during World War II.[70]

The chapter about Angel Island in Yoneda's autobiography remains the only extant detailed account by a Japanese detainee. As he concluded in that chapter, "If I learned any lesson from my two-month detention, it was that I had to *ganbaru* and *gaman*, I had to keep at it and persevere."[71] It was a lesson that many Japanese detainees at Angel Island learned well, not realizing that their detention ordeal was just the beginning of more hardships to come. American racism, compounded by the failures of diplomacy between Japan and the United States, made it more difficult for them to become American success stories despite years of hard work. Ultimately, their lives were disrupted and their faith in America shaken when 110,000 Japanese Americans were forcibly removed from the West Coast and confined in U.S. internment camps after the Japanese attack on Pearl Harbor.

The parallels between Angel Island detention and Japanese American internment are stark. Both involved the U.S. practice of segregating and confining "undesirable" people behind barbed wire based on American racism and skepticism that Asians could ever be loyal Americans and/ or Americans at all. Both places were characterized by overcrowded living conditions in army-like barracks, poor food, and unjust treatment of detainees as criminals who were considered "guilty until proven innocent." The physical discomforts and mental anguish experienced by Angel Island detainees and Japanese American internees are strikingly similar. Many of the Japanese poems written by *issei* in the internment camps echo the same sentiments of homesickness, despair, and resistance found in the Chinese poems on the barrack walls of Angel Island.[72]

After leaving Angel Island, Yoneda went on to become a labor organizer, longshoreman, and member of the Communist Party. He participated in many protests and strikes, for which he was beaten, arrested, and jailed. After one severe beating in 1931, he was rescued by Elaine Black of the International Labor Defense group. They fell in love and as interracial marriage between whites and Asians was prohibited in the state of California, the two were married in Seattle, Washington. During World War II, they were imprisoned in the Manzanar internment camp with their two-year-old son Tommy. Aside from suffering dust storms, extreme temperatures, and shabby living conditions, they had to contend with physical and mental harassment from pro-Japan *kibei* in the camps. Wanting to fight Japanese militarism and fascism, Karl volunteered for the U.S. Military Intelligence and served with distinction in the China-Burma-India campaign. After the war, Yoneda tried poultry farming for ten years before returning to longshoring and labor organizing. He remained active in the antiwar, labor, and redress movements until he died in 1999 at the age of 92.

Many picture brides like Shizu Hayakawa and Iyo Tsutsui, who had immigrated to America in pursuit of a rich and happy life, had their dreams dashed by racial discrimination and internment during World War II. Shizu worked for seventeen years as a live-in maid for an Italian American family in order to support her family in Japan and her husband, who became an invalid ten years after they married. Her workdays were arduous, long, and lonely. "When there is no time for one to talk to other Japanese people and your husband doesn't talk much, you become lonely and sad," she said. Things got worse after Japan attacked Pearl Harbor. The couple was imprisoned at the Heart Mountain internment camps in the Wyoming desert. Like many other *issei* evacuees, Shizu dealt with feelings of pain and anger with *gaman*. When the war ended, she chose to return to California, where she ran a successful catering business.[73]

Iyo Tsutsui found that life as a sharecropper's wife in Stockton, California, was nothing but hard work. She was initially shocked by the primitive living conditions, but quickly learned to adjust. Her workdays were endless. Aside from working in the fields growing beans and onions, she also cooked and washed for the field hands, and raised six children. After many years of hard work, the Tsutsuis finally saved enough money to purchase thirty-one acres of farmland under their *nisei* daughter's name. But all was lost when World War II led to their incarceration at the camps in Rohwer, Arkansas. Tragically, their married daughter died while giving birth in Manzanar. When they returned to farm in California after the war, they found that all of their farm equipment and household valuables had been stolen. Nevertheless, with *gaman,* they resumed farming with two of their children. Iyo never lost faith in America. She became a naturalized U.S. citizen as soon as Japanese aliens were allowed to do so under the McCarran-Walter Act of 1952.[74]

Most *kibei* like Jiro "Dick" Kobashigawa and Masayuki "Jim" Ariki, upon their release from Angel Island, went straight to work as farm laborers. Dick had once dreamed of becoming a pilot in the United States, but that dream was never fulfilled. He lost his job as a fruit stand grocer right after the Pearl Harbor attack. Soon, he found himself behind barbed wire at the Santa Anita Assembly Center. Labor was scarce during the war years, and Dick got out of camp by volunteering to work in Idaho harvesting sugar beets. It was backbreaking work and the Idaho winters were bitterly cold. Quite fortuitously, while in Idaho he met and married Sumiye Kogiso, a *nisei* whose family was on work furlough from the Minidoka Relocation Center. After the war, the couple spent two years helping Sumiye's parents resume farming in Oregon. Then they decided to move to Los Angeles with their three children to start anew. Dick's business as a gardener eventually paid off and he was able to buy a home, support his children through college, and travel around the country and to Japan with Sumiye.[75]

The time he spent locked up on Angel Island would leave a bitter taste in Jim Ariki's mind, not because of America's racist immigration policies but because of his parents' rejection. "Even at that age, I was thinking to myself, you see those stray cats over there at Angel Island, until they get old enough to catch mice themselves, their parents will always catch one and bring it back to them. My parents knew I never worked a day in my life, but they still tossed me away like that. That's when I decided, no matter what happens, I am never going back to Japan to see them." When Jim found out that his sister and brother-in-law in San Francisco did not want him around either, he resolved to strike out on his own. For the next two years he worked as a migrant farmhand, harvesting fruit at one orchard or another until he made enough spending money to go have a good time. "All the Japanese got to know us and they use to call us *mika bobu*, which means you're only good for three days." This lifestyle would have probably continued had he not met his wife Asako Tsuboi while picking grapes in Ivanhoe, California. They married, had a son, and settled down in Lindsay, California, when World War II disrupted their lives.

The family was interned at the internment camp in Poston, Arizona. Jim opted to leave camp and resettle in Denver, Colorado, where he found work in an ice plant. "They were short of workers, so they didn't have any choice but to hire us," he recalled. After the war Jim moved back to California with his family, had three more children, and spent the next forty years growing mushrooms on five acres of land in Gilroy, which he was able to purchase once the Alien Land Laws were repealed in 1956. As he resolved, he never saw or spoke to his parents again after his ordeal at Angel Island. But he did return to Angel Island for a visit in 2000. "I never thought I would be seeing the place again," he said, "because it was not a happy memory. I was worried all the time I was there and there was nobody for me to talk to."[76]

As for Miyono Nojima, who spent a total of eight months locked up on Angel Island—the longest detention for a Japanese immigrant, she was finally able to join her husband in Elko, Nevada, where she worked for many years in the family laundry. Because she was not living on the West Coast, she was spared relocation and incarceration during World War II. But her three daughters, who had married and were living in California at the time, were not. It was a sad time when she went to visit her daughter at the Topaz internment camp. According to her granddaughter Betty Kawamoto, "I was

Miyono Nojima visiting her family at the Topaz internment camp in 1942. From left to right, back row: Yuri Maruyama, Irene Kawamoto, Bruce Kawamoto, Miyono Nojima, Kimi Maruyama. Front row: Helen, Morris, and Betty Kawamoto. (Courtesy of Helen Kawamoto Migaki.)

always struck by the fact that my grandmother, who was not an American citizen, was free, while all of us who were American-born were behind barbed wire."[77] After her husband Fukujiro passed away, Miyono continued to run their laundry business. She lived out the rest of her days with her daughters in Chicago and San Francisco until she died at the age of 101. Throughout her life, she never spoke about Angel Island to her children or grandchildren. The details of her agonizing ordeal on Angel Island came to light only when her immigration case file was found at the National Archives. Miyono Nojima had suffered in silence, but in the last analysis, she, like many other Angel Island detainees, persevered and triumphed. They were able to overcome discrimination and go on to build a new life in America for themselves and for the next generation.

Although many Japanese detainees found Angel Island to be a prison and a place that instilled "agony, anguish and anxiety" in them, still their stays were short and very few were turned away. It was not so for the 8,000 South Asian laborers, students, and expatriates who came through Angel Island before the Barred Zone Act of 1917 put a stop to their immigration. Of all the immigrant groups, South Asians had the highest rate of rejection. Even though the Asian exclusion laws did not apply to them, without a strong country like Japan to protect them and a resourceful ethnic organization like JAA to assist them, many South Asian immigrants experienced undue hardships at Angel Island as they tried to overcome the many "obstacles" and "blockades" thrown in their way.

Sikh immigrants on Angel Island, c. 1916. (Courtesy of California State Parks, 2010.)

CHAPTER FOUR

"OBSTACLES THIS WAY, BLOCKADES THAT WAY"

SOUTH ASIAN IMMIGRANTS, U.S. EXCLUSION,
AND THE GADAR MOVEMENT

IN 1928, Vaishno Das Bagai, a thirty-nine-year-old father of three from Peshawar, in present-day Pakistan, took his own life in an apartment in San Jose, California. He had entered the United States through Angel Island thirteen years earlier with his wife Kala and three young sons, Brij, Madan, and Ram. Bagai, a longtime supporter of India's freedom and independence from Great Britain, had been eager to raise his children in the United States. He believed that America would be a place of freedom, education, and opportunity for his family. After being detained on Angel Island for a few days, the Bagais were admitted into the country. Vaishno relished his new life in the United States. He wore American suits, spoke English fluently, and adopted Western manners. He bought a home, ran an import business and general store, and became involved in the San Francisco-based Gadar (Rebellion) Party organized by South Asian immigrants to revolt against British rule on the Indian subcontinent. In 1921, Vaishno applied for and became a naturalized U.S. citizen by the federal court in San Francisco.

But thirteen years after his arrival in the United States, Bagai had become bitterly disappointed in his adopted homeland. South Asian immigrants experienced harassment and discriminatory treatment on and off Angel Island. Fellow Indian nationalists were placed under government surveillance, arrested, and deported from the United States. Alien land laws in California and other western states prohibited Asian immigrants from owning land or property. And a 1923 Supreme Court case had stripped

South Asian immigrant and U.S. Army veteran Bhagat Singh Thind of his naturalized citizenship on the grounds that South Asians were not white and thus not eligible to be naturalized under the country's laws.[1]

As a result, Vaishno Das Bagai and other South Asians who had become naturalized citizens were also denaturalized. U.S. officials tried to confiscate Bagai's naturalization certificate. Without the protection of U.S. citizenship, Bagai was subject to California's alien land laws. He was forced to liquidate his property, including his San Francisco-based general store. The final insult came when the U.S. government refused to grant him a U.S. passport to visit friends and relatives in India in 1928. They suggested that he reapply for a British passport, but having once renounced his British citizenship in the name of Indian nationalism, Bagai refused to reclassify himself as a British subject. Feeling trapped and betrayed, he committed suicide by gas poisoning in 1928. He left one letter to his family and another to the *San Francisco Examiner* explaining that he had taken his own life in protest. "I came to America thinking, dreaming and hoping to make this land my home...and tried to give my children the best American education....But now they come and say to me I am no longer an American citizen," he wrote. "Now what am I? What have I made of myself and my children? We cannot exercise our rights. Humility and insults, who is responsible for all this? Me and the American government. Obstacles this way, blockades that way, and bridges burnt behind."[2]

Like Vaishno Das Bagai, many South Asians experienced "obstacles" in their daily lives in the United States during the early twentieth century. This pattern of discrimination and hardship often began at the immigration station on Angel Island. From 1910 to 1940, an estimated 8,000 immigrants from the Indian subcontinent passed through the immigration station.[3] South Asians had been in North America since the turn of the century, but an increase in their immigration to the United States coincided with the opening of the Angel Island Immigration Station. They landed in a city that was embroiled in debate over Asian immigration. Chinese, Japanese, and Korean laborers had already been restricted through the Chinese exclusion laws and the Gentlemen's Agreement, but there was no law that specifically excluded South Asians. They became the next target of anti-Asian activists and immigration restrictionists.

Vaishno Das Bagai, c. 1910.
(Courtesy of Rani Bagai.)

The controversy over South Asian immigration put the new station and its officers to the test. Pressured by the Asiatic Exclusion League (AEL), Angel Island officials instituted an informal system of South Asian exclusion. Because San Francisco was the most important port of entry for South Asians coming to the United States in the early twentieth century, the events on Angel Island helped to shape the debate over South Asian immigration across the nation, and support for South Asian exclusion grew nationally. Eventually, South Asians were barred from the United States by the Immigration Act of 1917.[4]

South Asians had the highest rejection rate of all immigrants passing through the immigration station during its thirty-year history (see Appendix, Table 3). Unlike other immigrant groups, they had neither strong ethnic organizations (like the Chinese, Japanese, Russians, and Koreans) nor a strong home government (like the Japanese) to counter harsh restriction measures. Because of their support for Indian nationalism, South Asians already in the country also came under more scrutiny by Angel Island officials who cooperated with U.S., Canadian, and British officials intent on limiting the growing strength of the nationalist Gadar Party. Many immigrants made it into the country, including farmers, students, artisans, families, and political activists, but as the tragic story of Vaishno Das Bagai illustrates, Angel Island's discriminatory immigration policies and surveillance of political activists would shape South Asian Americans' lives long after they left the immigration station.

Punjabi Immigrants

South Asian immigration to the United States during the late nineteenth and early twentieth centuries was a direct consequence of the upheavals resulting from British colonialism on the Indian subcontinent. In the Punjab province of present-day India and Pakistan, new roads, railroads, and irrigation canals were quickly built in the name of colonial development. Local farmlands were transformed to support a cash crop economy that benefited Great Britain rather than the local population. Punjabis bore the brunt of heavy taxes to finance these projects, and many families fell into poverty and indebtedness. They also suffered heavily from a population explosion, droughts, famines, and severe epidemics. By the mid-nineteenth century, the Punjab—once known as the breadbasket of India—was overcrowded and could not yield sufficient crops to make farming profitable.

Many Punjabis looked abroad for opportunity. Some joined the British Army and served throughout the British Empire. Steamship companies, labor recruiters, and immigrants already in North America also promoted a culture of migration. Flyers, labor agents, and newspaper articles touted "opportunities of fortune-making." Lured by promises of employment and quick money, many South Asian farmers journeyed across the Pacific.

Modern transportation, including railroads and trans-Pacific steamships, made migration abroad more accessible than ever before. But passage to North America was expensive, much more costly for South Asians than it was for Chinese, Japanese, and Koreans. Immigrants borrowed money, often by mortgaging their homesteads, to pay for their passage. The route to North America was also longer for Punjabis. They needed to first board a train from their villages in the Punjab and travel to the port city of Calcutta, in Bengal. They then boarded a steamer for Hong Kong. From there, they could buy passage on a steamship to Vancouver, San Francisco, Manila, Singapore, Shanghai, Yokohama, and other parts of the world.[5]

By the early twentieth century, political unrest and massive discontent with British colonialism had set the stage for an unprecedented migration of South Asians to North America. By 1910, the U.S. census found over 4,700 South Asians in California, Washington, New York, and Oregon. This "decided increase" in South Asian immigration into the United States alarmed American officials. In 1911, H. A. Millis, the superintendent of the U.S. Immigration Commission, identified South Asian immigration as "the most recent problem of Asiatic immigration."[6]

South Asians in North America were a diverse group of Sikh, Muslim, and Hindu students, farmers, and former colonial soldiers from British India. The vast majority came from six Punjabi districts: Jullundur, Hoshiarpur, Gurdaspur, Ludhiana, Ferozepur, and Amritsar. Most were single, young men in their early twenties who had been independent farmers in their native villages. Those who were married often left their wives and children at home, for passage to North America was expensive and many migrants intended to return home. A considerable number of South Asian immigrants had been away from their homes for years, migrating throughout the British Empire before landing in the United States. Inder Singh, Argen Singh, and Siroop Singh, for example, arrived in San Francisco on September 22, 1913, after serving in both the British Army in India and in the Shanghai Municipal Police. Others were return immigrants who shuttled transnationally between India and the United States. Some immigrated with family members or came to join friends or family already on the West Coast. A few women and children came, but they were rare.[7]

The newcomers found jobs in the lumber mills, rope factories, and railroad camps in California and the Pacific Northwest or became farmhands in California's booming agricultural industry. Both Chinese and Japanese laborers—long the primary pool of farmworkers in California agriculture—had been excluded by the time that South Asians arrived in large numbers. Most settled in the Sacramento, Imperial, and San Joaquin valleys and found work in the state's orchards, vineyards, and sugar beet fields. The labor that they performed was, in the words of the U.S. Immigration Commission, the "roughest, most unskilled work" that whites shunned. They led a nomadic and hard existence, often migrating from ranch to ranch and working for the lowest wages.[8]

The "Hindu Invasion" and the Politics of Immigration on Angel Island

By the early 1900s, South Asians had become the latest targets of American immigration restriction campaigns. Exclusionists charged that South Asians were racially unassimilable laborers who competed unfairly with white workers and sent their money home. They argued that South Asians had inferior living standards and were threats to the existing racial order. Religious Sikhs were especially targeted, with one Washington newspaper describing them as "dirty and gaunt and with a roll of pagan dry-goods wrapped around [their] head[s]." South Asians were labeled "Hindus" or "Hindoos," in an effort to distinguish them from American Indians. The term "East Indian" was also used, but "Hindu," a misnomer that ignored the great religious diversity among the immigrants and the fact that the majority were actually Sikh, became a highly pejorative term commonly used by the media and government. South Asians were characterized as the least assimilable of all the Asian immigrants. As the *San Francisco Chronicle* explained in 1928, "certain races are excluded because their minds and manners of living are different from ours. That applies to Hindus even more than to Chinese or Japanese."[9] South Asians were also suspected for their nationalist political activity and their involvement in the Gadar Party. Many Americans were convinced that South Asian immigration represented the latest "yellow peril" of dangerous "Orientals" threatening the United States. Repeating earlier arguments made against Japanese immigrants and anticipating similar charges that they would make against Filipino immigrants, nativists argued that the present case of South Asians was the worst and most dangerous, since it compounded the Asian "problem" already in North America, and because it involved political subversives.[10]

A new phase of the movement against the so-called Hindu invasion coincided with an upsurge in activism by the Asiatic Exclusion League and the opening of the Angel Island Immigration Station. The local media in San Francisco played an important role in publicizing the new immigrant threat with sensationalist stories that identified "Hindu Cheap Labor" as a "Menace to Prosperity of the Coast." Newspapers also kept their readers updated on the arrival of new South Asian immigrants to San Francisco. Reporters were on hand to record the arrival of the *Manchuria* on January 31, 1910, which brought a group of 191 South Asians to the city. When over a hundred more arrived at the port just a few days later, the *San Francisco Call* declared that it was time to "Turn Back the Hindu Invasion." These alarmist articles were accompanied by illustrated cartoons and photographs detailing just how this "invasion" looked. When 136 "East Indians" arrived in San Francisco

"Undesirable Citizens"

San Francisco newspapers published sensational stories about South Asian immigration and bolstered the campaign to exclude South Asians from the United States. Illustrated cartoons of South Asians, such as this one which appeared in the *San Francisco Daily News* on June 28, 1910, often portrayed them as being subhuman, impoverished, bug-infested, and racially inassimilable laborers who would flood into the Pacific Coast with the assistance of greedy industrialists. (*San Francisco Daily News.*)

on the *Chiyo Maru* on February 3, 1910, photographers profiled the "turbaned dark men" who were "picturesque" and exotic. The accompanying text emphasized that the "influx of fortune hunting Hindu hordes" was a threat. Another photograph showed a crowd of South Asian men with their belongings on the dock after debarking from the *Chiyo Maru*. The photographs, with their exotic subjects, confirmed the article's headline message that the "Hindoos" were "not suited to Western Civilization."[11]

The statistics kept by the Angel Island office also added to exclusionists' alarm. While ninety-seven South Asians had been admitted in January 1910, 377 were allowed into the country during the next month. Only forty-seven were admitted in March, but by April 1910, San Francisco Commissioner of Immigration Hart Hyatt North reported that "the Hindus are coming here at the rate of eighty to 100 a week." Since the AEL was opposed to any South Asian immigration, these numbers sent exclusion advocates into a frenzy. By the spring and fall of 1910, San Francisco newspapers claimed that the "Hindu Horde" had grown so big that there were now a suspected 10,000 in California. The *San Francisco Call* explained that the immigrants came from the Punjab, where there were "starving millions waiting [for] the chance to follow their countrymen to the land of gold." "Uncle Sam's Domain" was quickly becoming "Sikh's Mecca," it complained.[12]

Hart Hyatt North found himself at the center of the AEL's new campaign to exclude South Asians. He treated South Asians like other immigrant groups and processed them under the general immigration laws, but this attitude was at odds with the beliefs of exclusionists and other Angel Island inspectors who were convinced that the government should actively restrict South Asian immigration whenever possible. For anti-Asian activists, the "likely to become a public charge" (LPC) clause of the general immigration laws provided a cover for racial exclusion. They reasoned that so much race prejudice existed against the "Hindu" that they would encounter difficulty finding work and become public charges. The "Hindus" might as well be excluded from the beginning.[13]

Typical was the sentiment of Immigrant Inspector Frank H. Ainsworth, who explained to the commissioner-general of immigration in Washington, D.C., that "these Hindoos are highly unassimilable," and that there were "many communities in which they are not wanted." Because of this prejudice, Ainsworth continued, "the time will come when it will be impossible for them to find employment in any capacity. Then we shall have the spectacle of a large vagabond population in our midst with no fixed place of abode and no substantial occupation."[14] He advocated an official immigration policy of exclusion, but Angel Island's Commissioner North rejected this position. South Asians might not be desirable citizens, he conceded, but "no government official has a right to refuse entrance to this country to any man entitled under the law to land." He also believed that most of the men arriving in San Francisco were legally admissible. If South Asians were to be legally excluded, then the United States needed to pass a general Asian exclusion law, North argued.[15]

The AEL lashed back and nicknamed the commissioner "Sahib North." With the full support of the San Francisco press, it initiated a campaign to remove North from office. The AEL and local newspapers argued that the "horde of Hindus [are] here to enjoy welcome extended by Hart North." Exclusion leaders also took their case to North's superiors in Washington, D.C., to complain that North was "not in harmony with public sentiment in California nor is he enforcing the law without fear or favor." A petition with 1,800 signatures called for North's removal. In October, North was suspended from his duties.[16]

Interrogations, Examinations, and Exclusion on Angel Island

After North's departure, immigration officials on Angel Island acted quickly to institute an informal system of South Asian exclusion. The number of South Asians admitted into the country dropped dramatically. In September, while North was in office, immigration officials debarred 46 percent of all South Asian applicants for admission. The next month, while North was fighting for his career, immigration officials denied entry to 181 out of 184 South Asian applicants, or 98 percent. By December, none of the fourteen South Asian applicants were admitted, and in April of 1911, the AEL reported satisfactorily that only eleven South Asians had been admitted in the past five months.[17]

Supported by immigration officials in Washington, D.C., Angel Island immigrant inspectors sought to find any and all grounds to exclude South Asians who arrived at the immigration station. First came the medical examinations. Like Chinese immigrants, South Asians were suspected of carrying contagious diseases that were dangerous to the American public. In August 1910, Dr. M. W. Glover, the chief medical officer of the U.S. Public Health and Marine Hospital Service on Angel Island, discovered hookworm in 65 percent of the South Asian immigrants applying for admission. Hookworm, which causes anemia, was listed as a "dangerous and contagious disease" that could result in automatic exclusion. Following the discovery, all South Asian passengers were examined for hookworm at the Angel Island hospital. Those found with the disease were denied entry if they could not pay for the treatment and required hospital stay. These costs were high and sometimes exceeded what immigrants were able to pay. Treatment for hookworm required a $50 deposit. Treatment for trachoma, an ailment for which South Asians were commonly excluded, could be as high as $300. If applicants did not have the funds for treatment, their only recourse was to accept exclusion and return home.[18]

In addition, a routine physical examination was used to determine if individuals possessed "physical or mental defects," such as hernias, heart ailments, poor eyesight, and deformities that could affect the alien's ability to earn a living. In 1910, for example, immigration officials denied three applicants because of physical deficiencies that they believed would prevent them from making a living. Indur Singh, age twenty-six, was certified as having a "poor physique" and thus unable to perform manual labor. Similarly, Bella, age twenty-eight, presented "a very poor physical appearance," and was "weak and emaciated looking," and Judda, age twenty-five, had an "impediment in his walk."[19]

There is no doubt that immigration officials used the medical examinations, including the very subjective "physical or mental defect" examination, to aggressively bar South Asians. Supporters of Asian exclusion specifically celebrated the medical testing of South Asians as a way to "stem the tide from India" that could further restrict immigration from China as well. As one California newspaper put it, "the hookworm is doing for California what Immigration Commissioner Hart North failed to do." Government statistics prove the newspaper's point. From 1910 to 1920, 28 percent of all South Asian applicants were barred because they were found to be mentally or physically deficient or to have contagious diseases.[20]

Twenty-one year old Hazara Singh "Janda" arrived at the Angel Island Immigration Station in 1913 and witnessed the severity of medical exclusions first hand. Singh applied for admission into the United States as a student planning to focus on mechanical engineering at the University of California at Berkeley. He brought $90 in gold and assured inspectors that his father would be able to support him in his studies. The inspectors were impressed by Singh's appearance, and he was admitted into the country after nine days in detention on Angel Island. Nearly ninety years after Hazara Singh arrived on Angel Island, his great-grandnieces, sisters Harjit K. Gosal and Hardeep K. Gosal, researched and wrote their family history. They found that while Singh was ultimately successful in getting admitted into the country, his time on Angel Island, and specifically the harsh treatment that immigrants received at the hospital, left a strong impression on him:

> Hazara Singh "Janda" arrived [at] Angel Island's immigration station on September 1, 1913 on the ship *Manchuria*. He left his mother country of India, his two sons, and his wife with the dream of creating a life for them in America. The voyage lasted about three months, and they encountered many relentless storms. Many people regretted leaving their homelands and others tried to remain hopeful despite the ill conditions on a ship with virtually no medical assistance.
>
> While he was still living, he told our father and some of his family about the hardships of his voyage. He often described the barracks where he and his fellow counterparts were kept when they first arrived as "horse stable-like." Their treatment was severe. These immigrants went through full medical examinations, and if they had any ailment which could not be cured at that time, such as trachoma, they were actually turned away. If it was a problem that was easily treatable, they were kept in [the hospital] for longer periods of time until they recovered.[21]

If they passed the medical examination, South Asian immigrants then went before a Board of Special Inquiry to answer questions regarding their legal right to enter the country. As was the case with other immigrant groups, South Asians from elite class backgrounds with diplomatic or other high-powered connections were admitted easily. Twenty-two-year-old Bhupendra Nath Ray, for example, applied for admission on December 17, 1910, as a student heading to the University of California at Berkeley. A letter from the American consul general at Calcutta personally vouched for him and his "fitness for admission to the United States." He also brought with him $125 in cash and stated that his father, a retired engineer, would be sending him $30–$50 a month for living expenses. The board unanimously agreed to admit him after asking just a few questions.[22]

Vaishno Das Bagai, his wife Kala, and their three young sons also impressed immigration officials. The Bagais, who arrived in San Francisco

Brij, Kala, Ram, Vaishno, and Madan Bagai, c. 1920–1921. (Courtesy of Rani Bagai.)

in September 1915 on the steamship *Korea*, were not like typical South Asian immigrants of the time. Vaishno was a well-educated man from an upper-class family in Peshawar rather than a farmer like most other South Asian immigrant men. The Bagais also migrated as a family and stood out from the mostly male immigrants. The sight of South Asian women in San Francisco was such a rare occurrence that Kala Bagai's arrival at the port was covered by a San Francisco newspaper with a photograph of Kala and her son, Ram. The article claimed that Kala Bagai was the "first Hindu woman to enter the city in ten years" and focused on the diamond nose ring that she wore. The Bagais spent a few days in detention upon their arrival because the immigration station was closed for the weekend. Immigration officials questioned Vaishno about why he had come and how he would support his family. They were immediately much less suspicious after Vaishno showed them that he had brought $25,000 with him. Almost seventy years after her arrival in the United States, Kala Bagai recounted her time on Angel Island to her children and grandchildren:

> Why did we come to America? The Gadar movement wanted to take the British out of India. Mr. Bagai was in that movement. He said, "I don't want to stay in this slave country, I want to go to America where there is no slavery."
>
> He got ready to come to America. His folks told him "don't take your wife and children." He says, supposing I go to America, I leave my wife here, and then after a few years, I come back and I may not like her. Because I might like American people there. That's why I am going to take her along and my children. That's how we all came together in America.
>
> 1915 we came. It happened to be Saturday, noon. And the boat people said, "you cannot leave today, Saturday and Sunday. Monday, the office will be open, then you can go." So they put me separate with the two little boys. Brij was with his father. I couldn't speak one word of English. When the eating time came, they said "Chow, chow, chow," so I understood that means to eat. So I went over there. I didn't like the food at all.

But I saw that they were selling some fruits, so I bought some fruits. But I did not know how much money to give. So I took the money and put it in my hand…and let him take whatever he wants. The third day, we left the [station], because we had plenty of money. There was no question of money. But they wanted to see. And I had all the jewelry on.[23]

With so much cash on hand to show immigration officials, the Bagais were readily admitted into the country. Because of their class status, they likely would not have been detained at all had they arrived in San Francisco during normal weekday business hours.

The case of Karam Singh, who applied for admission in September 1913, also illustrates how immigrants who could demonstrate financial stability, good character, and knowledge of English were treated more favorably than others. Like many other South Asian immigrants, Singh had already lived and worked in many other places before applying for admission into the United States. He had owned a liquor shop and worked as an inspector for the Shanghai Tramway Company for three years and as a watchman in a Manila timber yard for several months before applying for admission into the United States. On Angel Island, he impressed the immigrant inspector examining him who noted that Singh spoke "considerable English and appears to be far above the average in intelligence. He does not have the appearance of a laboring man and states positively that he will not accept such employment." The inspector concluded: "I do not think there is much likelihood of his becoming a public charge." Singh was admitted into the United States shortly thereafter.[24]

Karam Singh, 1913. (Scan by Vincent Chin. National Archives, Pacific Regional Branch.)

But immigrants such as the Bagais and Karam Singh were exceptions rather than the rule. The vast majority of South Asian applicants on Angel Island were farmers or laborers who were vulnerable to the informal system of exclusion that had been endorsed by the Asiatic Exclusion League and supported by immigration officials in Washington. Because the definition and context of the "likely to become a public charge" status was so vague and subjective, excluding South Asians under this category was very effective. For example, officials used a broad range of interrogation tools to establish any cause for LPC exclusion. These included grilling applicants about their financial status, prospective employment, ability to understand English, and whether they had relatives already in the United States who could come to their assistance in times of need.[25]

Immigrant inspectors cast the LPC exclusion clause so widely that they applied it to some cases that clearly did not fit the criteria. Such was the case of Robindra Nag, a twenty-three-year-old medical student who arrived in San Francisco on June 22, 1914. Nag came from a very affluent and powerful family in Calcutta and had the documents to prove it. His father was a magistrate and one brother was a lawyer. He brought with him a letter of introduction from the Calcutta YMCA that confirmed that the Nag family was "most respectable." He had connections to the San Francisco YMCA and an aunt came to the island to confirm his status as a student. Still, immigrant inspectors drilled Nag on any intention he had to "engage in any kind of manual labor in this country." Nag was clearly offended. "Certainly not," he replied. "I am a student here and my father will engage expenses. It will shock him; it will shock my parents. No one in our family ever worked; has ever engaged in manual labor; my uncle is a district judge." Nag was admitted into the United States after three days in detention.[26]

Immigration officials also used their own assessments of the local Bay Area labor market to categorize South Asians as LPC. It became standard procedure for immigration officials to record in their preliminary examinations of South Asians that the applicant was "the usual type of laborer" and was thus excludable because there was "no demand for this class at the present time." When Abdool Karim Khan, Nam Khan, and Sube Khan applied for admission in 1915, for example, Angel Island inspectors asked immigration service field agents to investigate labor conditions in the immigrants' intended destinations. Word came back from Fresno, where Abdool Karim Khan wanted to work, that there was an excess of applications for farm labor from "Hindus." The masses of unemployed white Americans in the state of California, immigration officials pointedly explained, should be hired first.[27]

Samuel Backus, who replaced Hart Hyatt North as commissioner of immigration in San Francisco, also cited discriminatory state legislation, such as the 1913 California Alien Land Law, which prohibited "aliens ineligible to citizenship" from owning land in California, as a reason that South Asians should be excluded. With such laws in place, Backus reasoned, South Asians would never be able to become financially successful and would thus end up as public charges. Backus used this rationale to rule against Sunder Singh, an applicant for admission in 1913 who wished to purchase farmland in California to become a grower. "But the [alien land] law of California prohibits him from owning land, so that part of his plan in any event cannot be put in operation," Backus concluded. He also explained that whites found South Asians so "undesirable" and "unreliable" that the immigrants would have difficulty finding employment, Singh was denied entry. In 1915, the Supreme Court ruled in *Gegiow v. Uhl* that immigration officials could not use local labor conditions to exclude immigrants from the United States, and the court ruling helped to stop such discriminatory practices against South Asian immigrants on Angel Island.[28]

Angel Island officials also used other class-based laws to deny admission to South Asians, such as the prohibition on contract labor in the United States. When Bela Singh answered questions during his hearing on Angel Island in 1912, he faced immigrant inspectors who were seemingly determined to prove that he was a contract laborer coming to the United States in violation of the law. "At whose solicitation, if any, are you coming to the United States?" Inspector Will Swasey demanded. When Singh responded that he came of his own accord, Swasey asked the question in a more roundabout way. "Do you know of any particular employment you can get?" "I will find out my countrymen, and they will find work for me," Singh replied. In the interrogations of other South Asians, inspectors were more blunt: "Have you been promised any work?" "Were any inducements offered you to come to the United States by any one in particular?"[29]

Under such strict interpretations of the law, South Asian immigrants found themselves in a bind. If they claimed to have no specific employment strategy, such as Bela Singh, they were judged to be persons "likely to become a public charge." On the other hand, those who had specific knowledge about an employer were suspected of being contract laborers or even labor recruiters. Immigrant Inspector Swasey pressed Lakha Singh to identify his job prospects. "Do you know of any place where you can get employment?" he asked. When Singh replied, "I will find my countrymen, and they will find work for me," Swasey pushed him to provide concrete evidence that Singh had "assurance" that this would actually happen. When Singh replied that he had heard from an acquaintance that work was easily found, Swasey then tried to establish that Singh was actually coming in as a contract laborer.[30]

The U.S. government went even further in its campaign to restrict South Asian immigration. Immigration officials were instructed to compensate for the lack of federal laws specifically mandating the restriction of South Asians by looking for *any* grounds for exclusion. As Commissioner-General of Immigration Daniel Keefe explained in 1913, if South Asian applicants were "not found to belong to some of the definitely excluded classes such as paupers, criminals, or contagiously diseased, [then] ground for exclusion was found either in the fact that they were persons of poor physique...or likely to become public charges." Government surgeons would then "render certificates to that effect."[31]

With such policies in place, Jogesh C. Misrow, an official "Hindustani interpreter" for the U.S. Bureau of Immigration at the port of Seattle, observed in 1915 that "virtual exclusion is the practice now, and the severe enforcement of the existing law has achieved the very end sought through [racial] exclusion measures." Government statistics prove Misrow's point. From 1910 to 1920, 61 percent of all applicants barred from the country were denied entry on the grounds that they were LPC. Another 28 percent were barred for medical reasons. Three percent of all exclusions were ordered because the applicant was believed to be a contract laborer. Another 3 percent of debarments were based on the belief that the applicants were polygamists.[32]

Statistics from the immigration service also illustrate how the aggressive application of general immigration laws to South Asians was more effective than both the use of race-based policies for other Asian immigrant groups and general immigration laws for non-Asians. From 1910 to 1932, 8,055 South Asians applied for admission into the United States; 2,020, or 25 percent, were debarred. Exclusion rates were highest prior to the passage of the 1917 Immigration Act. From 1911 to 1915, 54.6 percent of all South Asian applicants for admission were barred from the country. This is higher than the rate of exclusion for Chinese (9.1 percent) and Japanese (1.9 percent), both of whom were restricted by ethnic-specific restriction policies during the same years. The exclusion rate for South Asians is also higher than that for groups like Mexicans (8.1 percent) and Russians (2.6 percent), who were covered under the general immigration laws only. Rejection rates lowered significantly in later years (8.1 percent from 1916–1920), mostly because after 1917, South Asians were officially excluded as a group by immigration law and fewer immigrants attempted to come at all.[33]

The U.S. government was also active in deporting South Asians who were already in the country. From 1908 to 1920, 249 South Asians were deported from the United States. Over 31 percent were deported on the grounds that they were likely to become public charges. Another 43 percent were deported because they had entered the country without proper inspection. Many of these individuals came as sailors and stayed in the country after their shore leaves had ended. Eleven percent were deported for coming from the Asiatic Barred Zone after 1917, and another 11 percent were deported on various other grounds, such as crime, disease, and being a contract laborer.[34]

The informal policies of South Asian exclusion practiced on Angel Island resulted in two significant changes. As the number of immigrants rejected at U.S. ports began to return home, word of their unsuccessful journeys spread and discouraged prospective immigrants from trying to enter the United States. When 1,000 Punjabis returned to Hong Kong from San Francisco in August 1910, a Calcutta newspaper carried details of the strict medical examinations, long detentions, and exclusion rulings at the Angel Island Immigration Station. Upon reading this article, the U.S. consul in Calcutta applauded the efforts of immigration officials in San Francisco and explained to the U.S. secretary of state that if immigration officials continued to enforce a policy of exclusion, "it will not be long until there will be no more attempts on the part of Indians to override the policy of the U.S."[35]

Another effect of the strict enforcement policies in San Francisco was that South Asians were diverted to other ports of entry. Many were admitted through New York, and Bureau of Immigration intelligence reported that there were large numbers of South Asians in Cuba and Panama "ready to invade the Southern States through the Gulf ports of entry should it appear at all likely that they could gain admission." An inspector in Jacksonville, Florida, reported in 1913 that the "Hindoos" in Cuba were investigating ways to enter through that state as well.[36]

An increasing number of South Asians also sought to enter the United States mainland by first traveling to Hawaii or the Philippines, locales that immigration officials described as unguarded borders of or side doors to the United States. As W. C. Hopkinson, the "Hindu Interpreter" for the U.S. Immigration Service in Vancouver, explained, entry via the Philippines remained an attractive option. American immigration officials stationed in the Philippines were seen as more lax than their counterparts on the U.S. mainland. Also, it was believed that "Hindus [who] have landed in the Philippine Islands have practically free admission to the continental territory of the U.S." A loophole in the Immigration Act of 1907 allowed immigrants who entered American possessions like the Philippines to obtain certificates allowing them to go on to the mainland without a second examination by immigration officials.[37]

In July 1911, immigration officials in Manila warned that 6,000–7,000 South Asians already in the Philippines planned to gain admission into the United States through San Francisco. Immigration officials acted quickly to find a way to "stem the tide of undesirable immigration through this newly-found 'back-door' entrance." In December 1911, the Bureau of Immigration began requiring proof of examination and admission to the Philippines of all aliens seeking admission into the mainland United States. They also encouraged immigration officials in the Philippines to enforce the laws in the strictest manner possible so as to cut off the migration at its source and prevent "a large part of the Hindu immigration to those Islands."[38]

Nevertheless, South Asian migration via the Philippines continued for a few more years. When Anthony Caminetti, a California politician and long-term opponent of Asian immigration, became the new commissioner-general of immigration in June 1913, he used the power of the federal government to ask all steamship lines to voluntarily stop carrying

South Asian laborers as passengers. Most of the large and small steamship companies obliged, and almost immediately, ticketing agents enforced the informal agreement and refused to sell tickets to any South Asian laborer. In addition, the immigration service also revised its own regulations to end the practice of admitting immigrants coming from the Philippines without a second examination at a mainland port. Thereafter, all immigrants were required to demonstrate that they were not a "member of the excluded classes or likely to become a public charge if [they] proceeded thence to the mainland." These efforts finally closed back-door immigration from the Philippines, and the U.S. government moved one step closer to total South Asian exclusion.[39]

These aggressive exclusion tactics accounted for the high rejection rates for South Asians applying for admission into the country. Compared to other immigrant groups, South Asians faced a number of additional obstacles that made them vulnerable to restriction. There was little public outcry against their exclusion. As economist and immigration expert H. A. Millis explained in 1912, the procedures on Angel Island were met "with almost unanimous approval on the Pacific coast, where the Hindus are regarded as the least desirable, or, better, the most undesirable, of all the eastern Asiatic races which have come to share our soil." The 1911 U.S. Immigration Commission went even further and claimed that South Asians were "universally regarded as the least desirable race of immigrants thus far admitted to the United States." Given the fact that the commission had just studied thirty-nine immigrant groups in the United States, placing South Asians at the bottom of the heap was significant. The commission recommended that an understanding be reached with the British government to prevent "East Indian laborers" from coming to the United States.[40]

There were a variety of ethnic organizations that fulfilled the community's religious, social, and political needs. But unlike the Chinese, Japanese, Korean, and Russian immigrant communities, South Asians did not have a strong group that advocated on behalf of immigrants detained on Angel Island. In 1912, the Sikh community established the first gurdwara, or worship center, in Stockton. It served as a meeting place and social center for Sikhs in the United States. Many immigrants applying for admission mentioned that their first stop in America would be the Sikh temple where they could find work and locate relatives. But compared to the very active role that other ethnic organizations like the Chinese Six Companies, the Japanese Association of America, the Korean National Association, or the Hebrew Immigrant Aid Society played on behalf of immigrant detainees, the Sikh gurdwara in Stockton gave only limited assistance. In a few cases, the temple helped find witnesses to testify on behalf of immigrant cases or paid for detainees' medical treatment at the immigration station, but it did not hire attorneys or play a larger advocacy role.[41]

South Asians could not rely upon the diplomats of their home country to come to their defense either. The British government refused to intervene in the restriction efforts of the Canadian and American governments. Indeed, British officials were silent during all of the U.S. congressional efforts to restrict South Asian immigration, and the British ambassador refused to aid South Asian immigrants trying to oppose the exclusion bill. In fact, since Great Britain was becoming increasingly concerned with the Indian nationalist movement brewing among South Asians in the United States, British officials unofficially supported U.S. exclusion measures through secret channels and agents. Such tacit support for exclusion on the part of Great Britain contrasted sharply with the vehement opposition to Japanese exclusion communicated by the Japanese government. Consequently, unlike Japanese immigrants, South Asians were largely unable to prevent both the institutionalization of de facto exclusion policies on Angel Island and the passage of further exclusion laws in the United States.[42]

South Asian immigrants were not completely powerless, however. Those who continued to come through San Francisco and Angel Island learned to rely upon family members and friends already in America. In 1913, Neva Singh came to join a brother who had been working in California for twelve years. When he was threatened with exclusion, his brother sent money to release him on bond while the case was being determined on Angel Island. Similarly, Mangal Singh's brother, a six-year resident of Oregon, provided bail money and traveled down to San Francisco to hear the outcome of the case.[43]

Battan Singh, who came in 1913 to join a cousin working in Visalia, also relied upon his relative to gain admission into the country. At Singh's first hearing, inspectors recommended that he be denied entry into the country. They found him to have a "very poor physique" and argued that he presented no evidence that he was a property owner or had "resources of any kind anywhere." They were convinced "beyond any doubt that there is every probability of his becoming a public charge." Attar Singh, Battan's cousin, came forward to respond to these charges. He offered a prepared affidavit claiming that he regularly employed twenty-five men, and if his cousin were released, he would "take him down to the ranch and give him permanent employment there at a living wage. I usually pay $2.25 per day to my men." Battan Singh was admitted.[44]

As in the case of other immigrant groups, social workers and missionaries also lent assistance to South Asians on Angel Island. In her daily work at the immigration station, missionary Katharine Maurer attended to the various needs of South Asian immigrants. For example, when four men found themselves without warm clothes to withstand the foggy San Francisco weather, they asked Maurer for help. "We have got only working coat and pantaloon, which are not quite sufficient in such cold weather," they wrote. Maurer also handed out the Christian Bible to a group of Sikh men, who, she reported, "sat in groups absorbed in the Book." Maurer recorded visits with Natio, a famine victim from the Punjab region who was brought to the United States by missionaries and detained for two weeks in 1916. She happily reported that he made friends with a group of Korean and Russian Christian boys and enjoyed the Sunday services held at the immigration station.[45]

While social workers and missionaries like Maurer eased the detentions of many South Asians, still others faced immigrant inspectors and detention with little assistance. South Asian detention rates on Angel Island changed over the years. In 1910, at the height of the controversy over South Asian immigration, at least 1,714 South Asians were detained at the immigration station; 718, or 42 percent, were detained for eight to fourteen days, and 879, or 51 percent, were excluded and sent home. After 1917 and 1924, fewer South Asians applied for admission into the country due to the restrictive laws. Those who did continue to come were more likely to be members of the exempt classes. If they were detained, it was usually for a short period of time. Statistics from 1928 to 1940 indicate that 72 percent of South Asian detainees spent less than one week at the immigration station. The longest recorded detention of a South Asian immigrant on Angel Island was five months. Banta Singh arrived on May 29, 1935, as a visitor. He had studied electrical engineering at a school in Kansas City, and his father lived in Marysville, California. Banta was found to be afflicted with hookworm, and the Board of Special Inquiry did not believe that he sought to enter the United States for a temporary stay. Attorney Joseph Fallon requested that Banta be admitted with a $500 bond, but the request was denied by both the immigration service and the U.S. District Court. He was deported on October 31, 1935.[46]

Tara Singh may have been detained on the immigration station for even longer than Banta. Although there is no official record of him in the government's records, Singh carved two inscriptions into the walls of the men's barracks in Gurmukhi script used by Punjabi Sikhs. One was found on the side of a column in a second-floor room and is pictured on the next page:

One hundred days
Tara Singh
Sur Singh Village
Lahore District

Another carving by Singh appeared in a neighboring room and alludes to his long sojourn:

Tara Singh, Lahore
...nine months and...

Carving by Tara Singh in 1936, found in a second-floor room of the detention barracks building. (Courtesy of Architectural Resources Group.)

Kanta Chandra Gupta (second from left) and her five siblings arrived on Angel Island in 1910. Mahesh Chandra, who later married Kala Bagai, is in the back row, far right. (Courtesy of Liana Gupta Belloni.)

.... jail.
Tara Singh
19 June 1936[47]

Like Singh, Kanta Chandra Gupta, who arrived at the immigration station at the age of eleven, expressed similar feelings of imprisonment and frustration. Orphaned and fleeing an uncaring uncle, Gupta with her four brothers and sister arrived in San Francisco on July 2, 1910. The fourth of July holiday weekend delayed the business of immigrant inspections, and the children were placed in detention. Hospital staff suspected the family of being infected with tuberculosis, and their clothes and belongings were disinfected. The siblings were terrified that they would be separated from each other, and sadness and anxiety washed over them as they stared out of the grated windows of the detention barracks. Gupta recalled thinking that she and her family were "so close but, so far" from their new lives in America. The family was finally admitted into the country after a few days in detention and settled in San Francisco.[48]

Angel Island and the Gadar Movement

Kanta Chandra's and Tara Singh's frustrations about their detentions on Angel Island mirrored the growing discontent of many South Asians in the United States. They resented the discrimination they faced on a daily basis and the refusal of the British government to come to their defense. Like Korean immigrants who formed the Korean National Association to overthrow Japanese colonialism in their homeland, South Asians in North America became politically active in the cause of Indian independence. The presence of charismatic Indian nationalist leaders in North America turned a fledgling movement into a growing political force that alarmed British, Canadian, and American officials. By 1910, the United States had replaced Canada as the main site for organizing and promoting Indian nationalism, and political activists found receptive audiences in South Asian immigrant workers. In 1913, the loosely organized Hindustanee Association, which had branches up and down the coast of the United States and Canada, reorganized itself as the Gadar Party.

For many South Asians, the Gadar movement represented hope not only for an independent India but also for equal treatment in the United States and Canada. Gadar leader Gobind Behari Lal explained to South Asian farmers in Davis, California, that "it was no use to talk about the Asiatic Exclusion Act, immigration, and citizenship. They had to strike at the British because they were responsible for the way Indians were being treated in America." This rationale struck a chord in many of the farmers and laborers that Lal and other leaders met. The immigrants made donations, and a movement was born. Within a short period of time, a majority of South Asians along the West Coast subscribed to the revolutionary Gadar ideology.[49]

The Angel Island Immigration Station played a significant role in the development of the Gadar Party. Many Indian nationalists who were involved in the movement first entered the country as students through Angel Island. Highly educated and in possession of the right documentation and sufficient funds to support themselves, these students faced few hurdles to their admission into the country. But as their nationalist activities increased, some came under government surveillance.

Kartar Singh Sarabha was one of the Gadar leaders who came to America through Angel Island. He arrived in San Francisco on July 28, 1912, and was placed in detention while immigration officials investigated his case. In his interrogation, Singh told the Board of Special Inquiry that he could read and write English and that his intention was to study electrical engineering at the University of California at Berkeley. While immigration officials suspected that Singh might become a public charge, the $100 in cash that Singh brought with him swayed their opinion and he was admitted after three days. While a student at Berkeley, Singh, a Sikh, worked closely with Gobind Behari Lal and Har Dayal, both Hindus, to found the Gadar movement on the West Coast. Singh traveled among the farmers to talk about the Gadar cause and was known for his passionate speeches, his poetry, and his ability to fire up a crowd. He was also largely responsible for the printing operation of the *Gadar* newspaper. Printed in both Urdu, a major language in North India, and in Gurumukhi, the Punjabi script, the newspaper circulated throughout South Asian immigrant communities in the Americas, Europe, and East and Southeast Asia. Its goal was to rally the South Asian diaspora to the cause of Indian independence and to define a positive, collective identity among the immigrants as "nationalists."

After World War I broke out, the Gadar Party urged all nationalists to return to India to work toward the overthrow of the British. Thousands of immigrants-turned-revolutionaries returned to India carrying their own weapons and ready for armed revolt. The largest group of sixty men left San Francisco on the steamship *Korea* on August 29, 1914. Kartar Singh Sarabha was among them and reached Calcutta in November 1914. An uprising was planned for February 21, 1915, but before the nationalists could carry out their plans, Singh Sarabha and others were arrested by government authorities and tried for their role in the planned revolt. A series of three conspiracy trials took place in Lahore in 1915. Hundreds of individuals were sentenced to death, given life prison sentences, or sent to prison for shorter terms. Singh Sarabha was one of those sentenced to death and was executed at the age of eighteen. In the hours before his death, he wrote one last poem titled "On the Way to the Gallows," in which he offered to sacrifice his life to "Mother India." "I am a servant of Indians. India belongs to me," he proclaimed.[50]

Sohon Lal Pathak arrived in San Francisco in April 1913. The Angel Island immigrant inspector noted that Pathak was "of good appearance, spoke good English, and passed the medical examination." Pathak was admitted. He joined the Gadar Party in San Francisco and helped run its newspaper. During World War I, Pathak joined many other nationalists and returned to Asia, where he rallied Indian troops stationed in Burma to the nationalist cause. The British began a manhunt for Pathak and captured him in Burma. Pathak was defiant to the end and was hanged at the age of thirty-three.[51]

As South Asian farmers, laborers, and students joined the Gadar Party in the United States, Har Dayal and other Gadar Party leaders attracted the attention of British, Canadian, and American immigration authorities. The British government hoped that U.S. officials would view the Indian nationalists as dangerous and work to suppress Indian revolutionary publications coming out of San Francisco. Officials on Angel Island became central players in an international government surveillance network. Commissioner-General of Immigration Anthony Caminetti agreed to collect information on Indian nationalists beginning in 1914. He instructed immigrant inspectors to record detailed information on South Asian immigrants and their families, including their father's last name, their religion, address in India, and address of their nearest relative in India. He sent these records to both U.S. politicians trying to pass exclusion measures on South Asians and secretly to the British.[52]

Evidence of this international surveillance is apparent in the Angel Island immigration files. In May 1914, Muhammad Manlavie

Kartar Singh

Gurdit Singh

Kanshi Ram

Amir Chand

Rahmat Ali Shah

Sohan Lal

V. G. Pingle

Jiwan Singh

Jagat Singh

Kehar Singh

The above are among the 400 who have been hanged during 1915 and 1916.

Kartar Singh and Sohon Lal Pathak entered the United States through Angel Island as students. They became Gadar Party activists and returned to India and Burma in an effort to end British rule on the Indian subcontinent. They were both captured and executed by the British government. ("India's Heroes," *Hindustan Gadar* newspaper, 1916. Courtesy of the Bancroft Library, University of California, Berkeley.)

Baraktullah, a forty-nine-year-old language professor from South Asia, arrived on Angel Island from Tokyo. A Muslim, Baraktullah advocated unity among Muslims and Hindus in the name of Indian independence. As a professor at the University of Tokyo, he had published a staunchly anti-British newspaper, the *Islamic Fraternity*, which came to the attention of both British and Japanese authorities. He was fired from the university and sought new venues for his political activism in San Francisco. Immigration officials had already been alerted to his potentially dangerous activities prior to his arrival at the immigration station. His file includes a warning from Canadian immigration officials that he was a "prominent anti-British agitator, having traveled about in the United States, England, and Japan, for a number of years, advocating the formation of societies and leagues looking to the overthrow of the British Government in India." In spite of these allegations, Baraktullah was admitted into the country, and he eventually managed the Urdu edition of *Gadar*.[53]

One of the most prominent and charismatic leaders of the Gadar Party was Har Dayal, a well-educated Hindu from the Punjab region, who arrived in California in 1911. He taught philosophy at Stanford University and worked with South Asian immigrants on the West Coast to help spread the cause of Indian nationalism. He traveled to farms, lumber mills, and railroad camps to lecture about the injustices of British colonialism. Like Muhammad Manlavie Baraktullah, Dayal also came to the attention of Canadian and American officials. In January 1913, Canadian agent W. C. Hopkinson, a spy hired by the U.S., Canadian, and British governments, began trailing Dayal around the Bay Area. The British Embassy considered Dayal to be "a dangerous agitator." By May, Angel Island officials had officially joined in the surveillance of Dayal. Inspector Frank Ainsworth kept track of Dayal's visits to students and reported back to Hopkinson. In the fall, San Francisco Commissioner of Immigration Samuel Backus also began to investigate Dayal and reported to his superiors that Dayal had begun to gain the support of white citizens in the Bay Area. Angel Island officials advised Hopkinson on how a deportation charge could be effectively levied against Dayal. The arrest had to happen within three years of Dayal's initial admission into the country; he had to be known as a revolutionist or anarchist at the time of landing; and there needed to be local evidence that he belonged to a revolutionary society.

HAR DYAL, former Stanford University professor, political prisoner of the United States Government, whose hearing was held at Angel Island yesterday.

Har Dayal's activities in the winter of 1914 caused even more concern among American and British officials. On January 19, 1914, Dayal appeared in a San Francisco court requesting an application for U.S. citizenship, a status that would protect him from deportation. And in February 1914, he appeared as part of a delegation of South Asians who traveled to Washington, D.C., to protest against congressional bills introduced by three California representatives to exclude South Asians. Commissioner Backus, Commissioner-General of Immigration Caminetti, and British Embassy officials all agreed that it was time to deport Dayal because of his great influence among South Asian immigrants in the United States. A British Embassy complaint was made to U.S. authorities, and the warrant for his arrest was issued on charges of being an anarchist, a member of an excluded class, and for advocating the overthrow of the United States government or all governments by force. Dayal's

Coverage of Har Dayal's deportation hearing on Angel Island in the *San Francisco Chronicle*, March 27, 1914. (Photograph: *San Francisco Chronicle*.)

arrest on March 25 while attending a socialist meeting, made front-page news in the San Francisco papers.[54]

On March 26, 1914, Har Dayal boarded the ferry to the Angel Island Immigration Station for his deportation hearing. More than 200 South Asians gathered at the pier in San Francisco to lend Dayal moral support. The interrogation lasted three hours. No attorney was allowed, but a transcript was kept, making the Dayal case one of the first full records of a political interrogation conducted by federal officials. Immigrant inspectors led by Frank Ainsworth asked Dayal about his revolutionary ideas, and Dayal confirmed his contention that "the British Empire is sucking the life blood of millions of people in Ireland, India, and Egypt." But he stated that violence was not the answer. Rather, literary propaganda was the proper strategy. Immigrant inspectors sought out Dayal's views on a number of different subjects. They tried to link him to known anarchist Emma Goldman (he did not know her) and asked him to provide names of other South Asian students involved in the nationalist movement (he refused).

Finally, the interrogation came to the essential points. To the officials' accusation that Dayal was "using this city or country as a base from which to spread your propaganda of education among Hindus advocating the overthrow of the British government in India," Dayal simply answered, "Yes, that is why I am here. If I cannot do it here, I will go to some other country." But to the deportable offense that he was an anarchist, Dayal emphatically answered, "No." He asserted that his calls for armed revolt in India did not mean that he supported individual acts of anarchism. He also pointed out that rising up against an oppressive regime had a proud tradition of support in the United States. When Dayal left Angel Island, he gave a number of statements to the press. The *San Francisco Examiner* captured his defiant tone: "It is the despicable pro-British subservience of the United States government at present that is responsible for my arrest. The Democratic administration is licking the boots of England."[55]

Two days later, Dayal was freed on $1,000 bail, largely provided by members of the San Francisco radical movement. Commissioner-General of Immigration Caminetti had to admit that the United States had no legal jurisdiction for deporting Dayal. After his release, Dayal left for Switzerland and Germany, where he worked covertly with the remaining members of the Gadar Party and the German government to arrange for the shipment of arms to India for an uprising against the British. In what became known as the "Hindu-German Conspiracy," a large number of Gadarites as well as the diplomatic staff of the German consulate were arrested in San Francisco beginning in March 1917 and were charged with mounting a military expedition in violation of United States neutrality. The resulting six-month trial cost $3 million and became the longest and most expensive trial in American history to that date. Twenty-nine defendants were found guilty and served prison sentences. At the end of World War I, Dayal's views changed drastically and he aligned himself with the British Empire on the grounds that India was not yet ready for self-rule. He died in 1939 while on a lecture tour of the United States. Supporters of India's freedom from British colonial rule would have to wait until after World War Two to achieve their goals.[56]

Closing the Gate: Immigration after the 1917 and 1924 Immigration Laws

The sensationalist deportation hearing of Har Dayal on Angel Island and the government's claims that Indian nationalists like him were dangerous to the United States contributed to the growing South Asian exclusion movement. Despite the effective use of general immigration laws to institutionalize an informal system of racial exclusion, opponents of South Asian immigration remained convinced that a specific exclusion law was the only permanent solution to the "Hindu problem." South Asians were not only undesirable aliens and economic competitors, but, as the Dayal case demonstrated, they were politically dangerous subversives as well. After much debate, Congress passed a comprehensive immigration law in 1917 that expanded the number of excludable classes. It also provided an effective opportunity to finally exclude South Asians. The so-called Asiatic Barred Zone, which officially excluded "inhabitants of most of China, all of India, Burma, Siam, and the Malay states, part of Russia, all of Arabia and Afghanistan, most of the Polynesian Islands, and all of the East Indian Islands," closed the final loophole on Asian immigration. Since Chinese and Japanese laborers were already excluded by separate laws and agreements, the main group affected were South Asians. The informal exclusion policies created and practiced by immigration officials on Angel Island, in effect, became ratified when Congress passed the act.[57]

The 1917 Immigration Act accelerated the decline in South Asian immigration, but it did not end it altogether. Like the Chinese Exclusion Act and the Gentlemen's Agreement, it contained a critical class component that allowed the most elite to apply for admission: travelers, students, teachers, merchants, and immigrants who held various professional occupations. Immigrants who were returning after a "temporary absence" to an "unrelinquished United States domicile of seven consecutive years" were also eligible for entry, but they required special consideration by the attorney general.[58] In addition, the Immigration Act of 1924, which prohibited the entry of all Asian immigrants, allowed certain exempt classes, or "non-quota immigrants" such as students, ministers, and visitors "for business or pleasure," to apply for admission into the country on a temporary basis. Returning residents could also apply for readmission into the country. The numbers of South Asians coming under these categories were never large. From 1910 to 1920, 2,082 South Asians were admitted into the country; 1,886 were allowed in during the following decade. In 1940, the total South Asian population in the United States was just over 2,400.[59]

The new immigration laws dramatically changed the types of South Asian immigrants arriving at Angel Island after 1917 and their experiences there. The new immigrants usually came with educational and financial resources. There were a few more women in this group, and the immigrants came from all over India rather than mostly from the Punjab region. The 1924 immigration act had moved the bulk of immigrant screening to consular officials abroad who were given the power to grant visas to prospective applicants. Individuals still had to pass inspection at ports of entry, but if they arrived with a proper visa, they were more likely to gain entry than their pre-1924 counterparts. The "temporary" nature of their migration also led to less scrutiny by immigration officials. Most immigrants simply needed to submit their documentation and did not undergo interrogations. Many were admitted on the day of their arrival.[60]

South Asian students who could produce bona fide documentation of admission to a college were admitted fairly easily, for example. It helped if applicants provided additional documentation testifying to their class background or personal character as well. In 1926, Rasheed Nazar Mehomed Futehally brought with him a telegram from the School of Engineering in Milwaukee, as well as a letter of introduction from W. H. Stallings, the International Secretary of the YMCA in Berkeley, California, that noted Futehelly's "high class family" background and his family wealth. He was admitted on the day of his arrival after only a primary inspection.[61]

While prescreened South Asian students and other professionals faced an easier admission process on Angel Island under the 1917 and 1924 immigration acts, immigration officials continued to target other South Asians applying for admission. "Geographical exclusion" accounted for the majority of South Asian exclusions after 1917, but the general immigration laws were also used as a tool to deny entry. The literacy requirement, for example, placed South Asian women at a disadvantage because they were less likely to have had formal education than their male counterparts. In 1923, Kartar Singh, a South Asian woman, applied for admission into the country with her brother. Both claimed to be travelers, an exempt class under the 1917 act. While Kartar's brother passed the literacy test easily, Kartar, who admitted that she had not had "any education," only "home training," did not. Over several days at the immigration station, she was presented with a card containing words in the "Hindu, Punjab, and Afghan languages," but she was unable to read it. Immigrant inspectors then presented her with two "exhibits" that included "Hindu characters," and then later, books in her native Gurmukhi dialect. Unable to read any part of the exhibits or the books, she was barred from entering

Eighteen-year-old Leelabati Guhuthakurta and her twin sister Seeta from Bengal applied for admission as students in 1934 and came prepared with the proper documentation. They brought admission letters from Glendale Junior College in Glendale, California, as well as a letter of introduction from their uncle, the Reverend Swami Paramananda, founder and head of the Ananda-Ashrama in La Crescenta, CA, a respected nonsectarian place of worship founded in 1909. Reverend Paramananda offered letters from prominent white acquaintances as additional evidence of his own standing in his local southern California community. Leelabati and Seeta Guhuthakurta were landed on the same day as their arrival in San Francisco without having to go to Angel Island at all (Files 34194/1–2 [Leelabati Guha Thakurta] and 34194/1–3 [Seeta Guha Thakurta], IACF, SF. (Scan by Vincent Chin. National Archives, Pacific Regional Branch.)

the country. Kartar Singh appealed and was eventually granted temporary admission into the country as a traveler.[62]

Immigration officials also closely scrutinized those claiming to be returning residents, the largest group to be affected by the 1917 act, and used subjective standards to determine who could reenter the country. For example, Abdulla Khan returned to San Francisco in 1917 after a brief visit abroad and was taken to Angel Island for his interrogation. Although Khan carried documentation proving that he had been a legal resident in the United States in 1913, immigration officials refused to grant him the status of returning resident because he did not demonstrate proof of seven years of consecutive residency. It was ruled that Khan did not belong to any of the exempt classes in the Immigration Act of 1917 either. Therefore, the interrogation focused on his class status and his work as a laborer in a sawmill in Tacoma, Washington. When Khan's answers indicated that he was an ordinary laborer who operated the ripsaw and the planer in the mill, immigration officials ruled that he was excluded as a laborer from the barred zone.[63]

The next year, Ardjan Singh applied for readmission into the country as a returning resident. To document his prior residence in the United States, he presented a letter of recommendation from his former employer indicating that he had resided and worked continuously in the United States for eight years. With such evidence, Singh was ostensibly eligible for entry under the Immigration Act of 1917 as a returning immigrant who had left the country on a temporary absence. But immigration officials were seemingly bent on finding any grounds to exclude Singh. They questioned whether his five-year absence from the country really qualified as a "temporary absence." Singh explained that his absence from the United States had been caused by the disruption in travel due to the world war. He had not been able to return to the United States, but instead, had been forced to work in Asia. Immigration officials on Angel Island were not convinced and denied Singh reentry into the country. He appealed, but the commissioner-general of immigration was not sympathetic either. With no established definition of "temporary absence" in the law, the commissioner-general subjectively ruled that Singh's claim of five-year "temporary absence" from the United States" was both "illogical" and "ridiculous."[64]

Returning residents who came prepared with extensive documentation had better chances. Like Chinese Americans applying for reentry into the country, South Asian residents who could rely upon white Americans to vouch for their status and respectability were looked upon with favor by Angel Island officials. Raj Singh, an applicant for reentry in 1923 sent a telegram to Thomas Brown, his former employer in Fresno asking for help: "Am here at Immigration Station Angel Island need you as witness covering previous residence." Brown arrived at Angel Island two days later and testified that he had known Singh since 1915. When officials told Brown that they needed proof of Singh's seven years' residence in the United States, he returned to Fresno and then brought three white men to the Fresno immigration office to testify that Singh had lived there from 1915 to 1922. Brown's efforts paid off. Singh was readmitted into the country. Cases like Raj Singh's were rare, however, and the government's efforts to exclude both new and returning South Asians from the United States continued to be effective throughout the immigration station's history.[65]

Life after Angel Island

The treatment that South Asians encountered on Angel Island reflected larger patterns of discrimination against the entire South Asian community in America. Profiles of South Asians who made it off Angel Island reveal humiliation and tragedy, but also perseverance. Kartar Singh Sarabha, the student and Gadar activist, became extremely disillusioned and disappointed in the United States. Believing that America was a free and equal nation, he was shocked and humiliated when he heard himself being called a "damn Hindu" by whites. He blamed not only American racism but also the helpless, enslaved status of his homeland of India. The discrimination he felt in the United States made him even more determined to fight for Indian independence."[66]

Vaishno Das Bagai's wife Kala struggled with the everyday tasks of learning English, shopping, and caring for her three young boys. The Bagais also faced overt discrimination from their neighbors after they bought a home in Berkeley, California. When they pulled up to their new neighborhood with all of their belongings on moving day, they found that the neighbors had locked up the house so that the Bagais could not move in. "All of our luggage and everything was loaded on the trucks," recounted Kala Bagai. "I told Mr. Bagai 'I don't want to live in this neighborhood. I don't want to live in this house, because they might hurt my children, and I don't want it.' He agreed. We paid for the house and they locked the doors? No." After Vaishno's death, Kala focused on raising her children and saw them off to college. She also married again. Her husband, Mahesh Chandra, was a family friend in San Francisco who had also entered the United States through Angel Island.[67]

Hazara Singh, who had been admitted as a student in 1913, also ended up raising a family in the United States. He settled in Biggs, California, just north of Yuba City, a major settling point for immigrants from the Punjab. It is unclear what happened to his plans of studying mechanical engineering. He became a laborer, working on the railroads and farms to make a living and to send money to his family in India. His hope of bringing his wife and two sons to the United States ended when he learned that all three had died in India. Singh remained alone in the United States for nearly two more decades. There were few South Asian women, and antimiscegenation laws, which stayed on the books in California until 1948, prohibited

Madan, Brij, Kala, and Ram Bagai in 1933. (Courtesy of Rani Bagai.)

intermarriage between whites and nonwhites. In the 1940s, Hazara Singh married Gloria Melendez, a local woman from Gridley, California. At the time, there were many marriages between Punjabi men and local women, many of whom were Mexican. These families became part of a growing number of Punjabi-Mexican couples who formed vibrant biethnic communities. Hazara Singh saved enough money to buy his first ranch from a Japanese immigrant who, during World War II, was likely being forced to an internment camp. Over many years, Singh gradually acquired almost 400 acres of land. He also assisted many of his relatives who arrived in the United States in the 1960s. Gloria and Hazara had eleven children and are survived by a large family that settled in Yuba City.[68]

Kanta Chandra and her five siblings made it through Angel Island, but the family of six struggled through hard years after their arrival. They picked fruit for a living and slept in the orchards at night. Despite the hardships, they strove to survive and succeed. Both Kanta and her sister Prabha attended school. As a high school student in 1916, Kanta became the first South Asian woman to begin the process of applying for U.S. citizenship. She later married and had children. After her husband died, Gupta became a chiropractor, a profession with few women and even fewer South Asian women practitioners at the time. She also spoke and wrote passionately about women's education and Indian independence as a Gadar Party activist. Her brother, Mahesh, was also active in the Gadar Party and later married Kala Bagai.[69]

During World War II, American attitudes changed toward South Asian immigration due to both international and domestic events. South Asians in the United States lobbied politicians to revise U.S. immigration laws and to build support for Indian independence. In addition, India became an important ally in the United States' war effort. The Indian Army successfully halted the progress of the Japanese in both Central Asia and the Pacific. In 1946, the Luce-Celler Bill amended the Immigration Act of 1917 to allow South Asians to apply for admission to the United States under existing quotas. They could also become naturalized U.S. citizens.[70] The law, which President Harry Truman signed in July, was meant to signal an end to racial discrimination in the United States. The quota for India, which won its independence from Great Britain in 1947, however, was only 100 persons a year. Indeed, South Asian immigration to the United States would not occur on a significant scale until the 1965 act abolished all racial discrimination in immigration law. Although these changes came too late for Vaishno Das Bagai, Kala, Brij and Ram received their own U.S. citizenship after the Luce-Cellar Bill was passed.

Korean immigrants began arriving at the Angel Island Immigration Station at the same time that the controversy over South Asian immigration was at its peak. Like South Asians, they too were a colonized people. As

Japanese subjects, Korean immigrants were hampered by both the Japanese government, which refused to issue passports to Koreans, and by the U.S. government and its Asian exclusion laws. Many Koreans who were fleeing Japanese colonialism in their homeland found loopholes in these restrictions. Unlike South Asians, they were admitted into the country more readily because of their class status and the effective diplomacy and support of the Korean National Association. In the end, while South Asians had the highest rejection rate of all immigrant groups on Angel Island, Koreans had an easier time seeking refuge in America.

Three-year-old Rose Paik (Pok Yun Sun) with her mother Anna Yim (Im So See) and stepsister Pok Kyang Whan on the rooftop of the administration building, 1914. (Courtesy of USC Korean American Digital Archive.)

CHAPTER FIVE

"A PEOPLE WITHOUT A COUNTRY"

KOREAN REFUGEE STUDENTS AND PICTURE BRIDES

ON JULY 9, 1913, six Korean young men, claiming to be students, arrived on the *Mongolia* from Shanghai and were taken to Angel Island for inspection. They had come without passports or student documents. Japan had annexed Korea in 1910, but they all refused to acknowledge Japan's sovereignty over Korea. When asked by Inspector William Chadney why he was not a subject of Japan, being a native of Korea, twenty-two-year-old Cho Hin answered, "I left Korea [for China] before Japan annexed Korea, and so, I am not a subject of Japan." The immigrant inspector was not satisfied with his answer. "Of what country *are* you a subject? Are you a man without a country?" Cho had to agree, "I am now a man without a country." Complicating matters, all six men were found to have hookworm, for which they were debarred from entering the country. They would spend a week in the hospital and three more weeks in the same barracks as the Japanese and South Asian men while awaiting the outcome of their appeals. With the help of the Korean National Association (KNA), which was founded in 1909 to support national independence and protect the interests of Koreans overseas, the men were admitted on August 5, 1913. They became the first test case of U.S. immigration policy toward Korean refugee students.[1]

Another 1,000 Koreans would seek admission through the port of San Francisco during the next three decades—mostly young men claiming to be students, but also picture brides, wives, and children of alien residents. Fleeing a harsh life under Japanese colonial rule, they were the lucky ones to have found a way to America. To circumvent the Japanese government's ban on Korean emigration, they had had to steal across the northern Korean border into Manchuria, make their way to Shanghai under disguise to avoid detection by the Japanese police, and from there, wait to book passage on an American steamer going to San Francisco. Upon reaching their destination, they had to find a way to pass the test of both the Asian exclusion and the general immigration laws before they could be admitted into the country. The difficult journey and the many obstacles thrown in their way by both the Japanese and the U.S. governments explain why so few Koreans immigrated to America between 1910 and 1940.

Yet despite their small numbers, the Korean experience at Angel Island is worth examining in depth. It offers us a unique view of how "a people without a country," with the support of a strong organization like the KNA, found a way to transcend American policies of racial exclusion.[2] For a short period of time, Korean immigrants at Angel Island were treated with more leniency than the other Asian groups, Japanese included. As Woo Myong-won, a Korean picture bride who came in 1914, attested, "I was able to get ashore without immigration papers because the United States government knew of the harsh Japanese rule, and we were permitted off [the ship] as students. They were especially good to Koreans."[3] Although the Japanese consulate complained repeatedly that Koreans without Japanese passports should not be allowed into the country, immigration officials were directed by their superiors in Washington, D.C., to give Korean applicants "every proper consideration" and to admit them as long as they met the general provisions of the immigration laws.[4] This leniency toward Korean immigrants was influenced by the perception that their status as students and housewives did not pose a threat to American labor and by the State Department's willingness to deal with the KNA instead of Japan over matters of concern to Koreans in America.

Forced to Leave the Homeland

Known as the Hermit Kingdom, the Korean peninsula—located at the strategic crossroads of China, Japan, and Russia—had been in isolation for over two and a half centuries after repeated invasions from its neighbors. In 1876 Japan succeeded in forcing Korea to sign the Treaty of Kanghwa, opening three seaports to trade, ending Chinese suzerainty over Korea, and granting Japan extraterritorial rights to exploit the country's rich natural resources. Other Western nations, including the United States, Great Britain, Germany, Russia, Italy, and France, soon followed suit. A period of international rivalry for control of Korea ensued, with Japan claiming victory after it defeated China in the Sino-Japanese War of 1895 and Russia in the Russo-Japanese War of 1905. As a rising Asian world power,

Japan was able to declare Korea its protectorate in 1905 and formally annexed it in 1910. Although the United States had signed the Treaty of Amity and Commerce with Korea in 1882, promising to protect Korea against hostilities from another nation, it failed to do so. That was because President Theodore Roosevelt had signed the secret Taft-Katsura Treaty with Japan in 1905, whereby America would recognize Japanese hegemony over Korea in exchange for Japan's noninterference in U.S. affairs in the Philippines.[5]

Life for the Korean people deteriorated rapidly after Korea became a semi-colony of Japan and the West and after the Yi Dynasty succumbed to corruption and chaos. The penetration of foreign capitalism linked Korean farmers to the international market and a cash economy, thereby causing the agricultural economy and native handicraft industries to collapse. Laden with heavy taxes, many Korean farmers were forced off their lands. Unemployment and starvation mounted as a cholera epidemic followed by a drought, flood, and locust plague each took its toll in 1901–02. It was at this juncture that Hawaii's sugar planters, facing a labor shortage and wanting to counteract the militancy of Japanese workers, took advantage of the 1882 Treaty and began recruiting laborers from Korea through the assistance of U.S. foreign minister Horace Allen and businessman David Deshler. Convinced by Allen that allowing Koreans to emigrate to Hawaii would alleviate poverty and starvation in Korea and improve relations between Korea and the United States, King Kojong signed an edict to establish the Department of Emigration and gave Deshler permission to recruit and assist "free laborers" interested in going to Hawaii. It was his bank that advanced the necessary travel funds and his ships that transported the workers from Korea to Japan for passage to Hawaii.

Despite the enticement of good wages—fifteen dollars a month, five times what a laborer in Korea earned at the time—free housing, medical care, and schooling for the children, there were few takers from a population unaccustomed to traveling far from home. But by then, Christianity had taken a foothold in Korea, and American missionaries were able to persuade their converts to go to Hawaii—a Christian land, they were told, where they would be free of political and religious persecution and where they could better their condition. Consequently, 40 percent of the Korean emigrants to Hawaii were Christians. Others signed on out of economic desperation. Kim Sung-jin, who, along with her family, was recruited to Hawaii in 1905, recalled, "There was a famine and people all around were desperate to get where we could find something to eat or find a job so we could buy food to eat." She added emphatically, "There was no way we could have survived in Korea."[6]

From December 1902 to November 1905, when Japan successfully pressured the Korean government to ban emigration, some 7,400 farmers, laborers, artisans, and former soldiers from seaports and towns all over Korea left for Honolulu. Another 1,000 Korean emigrants were duped by a British agent into signing four-year contracts that sent them to Mexico's Yucatan peninsula, where they were put to hard labor on the spiny henequen plantations.[7] Word got back to Korea that they were being treated like slaves and worked to death. According to one report, the poor immigrants were spending the day in the thorny fields, sweating under the burning sun and cracking whips of Mexican foremen, and the nights nursing their thorn-pricked wounds in the mud huts. "Often they envied the life of the dogs in the house of plantation owners.... Those who were unable to work for a prolonged period, regardless of sickness from malnutrition or snake bites in the hut, would be abandoned in the wilderness and left to their own fate."[8] This tragic news gave the Korean government further cause to terminate all emigration.

Working and living conditions on the Hawaiian plantations were not optimal either. The free housing turned out to be dilapidated shacks without running water in overcrowded camps. The long hours and back-breaking work of cutting cane in a subtropical climate were more than most Korean laborers could bear. Stories were told of how young boys, women, and men, "with their fair hands blistered, faces and arms torn and scratched by the cane leaf stickers would sit between rows of cane and weep like children."[9] Many left plantation work within a year or two to work in the canneries, to grow rice and coffee, or to start small businesses like laundries, retail shops, and boardinghouses in the cities. At least 1,000 Koreans returned to Korea, while another 2,000 moved to the U.S. mainland for better-paying jobs in mining, railroad construction, and farming. But that window of opportunity was short-lived. On March 14, 1907, President Theodore Roosevelt issued Executive Order 589, which prohibited Japanese and Korean laborers holding passports for Hawaii, Mexico, and Canada from entering the continental United States.[10] The executive order would later stop the Korean "slaves" in Mexico from getting to Hawaii via the port of San Francisco.

After Japan annexed Korea in 1910, new policies were instituted to facilitate Japanese land purchases and Japanese import-export trade as increased numbers of Japanese farmers and businessmen began settling in Korea. In an effort to subjugate the Korean people and extinguish any seeds of rebellion, the new administration also disbanded the Korean Army, made Japanese the official language in the schools, shut down newspapers, prohibited public assemblies, and issued passports to only a select few. An essay written by a refugee student and published in *Sinhan Minbo* (*New Korea* newspaper) explained how political repression, cultural oppression, and economic duress in Korea had driven many of them to leave their beloved homeland:

To the Incoming Students: Are We Crazy to Come Here?

Remember why we could not study in our homeland? It was because the Japanese government closed all the private schools and forced all the public schools to teach in Japanese and about the glory of Japan. Why did we stop teaching in our homeland? It was because the Japanese principals humiliated and degraded all Korean teachers. Why did we give up our government positions? It was because we could not stand the fact that Japanese held all the high positions and we were forced to pander to them. Why couldn't we conduct business in the homeland? It was because the enemy held all the money and power and made it impossible for us to open businesses. Why couldn't we farm? It was because we could not produce enough to make a living. No, we are not crazy for leaving our homeland and crossing the Pacific Ocean to be free of our Japanese enemy. So let us not live a crazy life but study hard and uphold the honor of being Korean students.[11]

Despite the Japanese clampdown on Korean emigration, between 1910 and 1918, 541 refugee students and 115 picture brides fled their homeland for America by way of Manchuria, Shanghai, or Europe. Approximately 80 percent arrived at the port of San Francisco without passports. They claimed that they were not Japanese subjects because they had left Korea before annexation and were thus exempted from the passport requirement. Moreover, all insisted they were not of the laboring class in order to bypass President Roosevelt's executive order and Rule 11, which was issued on February 24, 1913, to prohibit alien laborers holding passports to other countries from entering the continental United States when deemed detrimental to labor conditions therein.[12] Their average length of stay at Angel Island was one week. Less than 5 percent of the Korean applicants were excluded and deported.[13] Some, like Whang Sa Sun and his wife Chang Tai Sun, who arrived on April 22, 1913, did not even have to go to Angel Island.

Whang Sa Sun was born in Uiju, Pyongan Province (North Korea) in 1885, the sixth of eight children. He attended missionary schools and graduated from Soongsil College. Whang was working as a high school teacher when he got involved in the national independence movement. He and his wife were both members of the anti-Japanese Sinminhoe (New People's Society) and narrowly escaped capture and torture by the Japanese police before fleeing to Manchuria. As Whang told his granddaughter Gail sixty years later, the couple had to disguise themselves as Russian refugees and cross the half-frozen Yalu River in the dead of winter to get out of the country. From Manchuria they made their way by train to Shanghai, where they boarded the *Mongolia* for America. This time they

Chang Tai Sun (left) and Whang Sa Sun with their children Elizabeth and Paul in 1917. (Courtesy of Gail Whang Desmond.)

wore Chinese clothes and pretended to be Chinese from Pokgun Province whenever they were stopped by the Japanese secret police. The steamship made three stops in Japan and one in Honolulu before the Whangs finally landed in San Francisco.[14]

"When I left Korea, I felt like a free man," Whang told his granddaughter. "At that time the Japanese military government persecuted the people, especially the young students and took them to jail. I wanted to come to America, a free country. Also, my brother was living in America." His brother Whang Sa Yong had immigrated to Hawaii in 1904 as a student and was active in the Korean independence movement there. He helped to prepare the way for his brother and sister-in-law's admittance to the United States by asking David Lee, KNA president, to vouch for them. According to the ship's passenger list, the couple was traveling second class and coming as a "clergyman" and "housewife." Those reasons, combined with Lee's sponsorship, were probably why they were landed from the ship instead of Angel Island.

The couple settled in San Francisco, where they had three children and became deeply involved in the Korean Methodist Church and the Korean National Association. "During that period," Whang explained, "the American people didn't respect the Asian people. I wanted some postal or factory work, but they wouldn't give it to me." Whang ended up opening a tailoring and cleaning shop on the outskirts of Chinatown to supplement his meager salary as a preacher. He was able to rent the store only by telling the white landlord that he was half-Russian. In 1928, he became the minister of the Korean Methodist Church, where he served until he retired in 1942. Although Whang Sa Sun was not detained on Angel Island himself, he often made trips there to testify on behalf of other immigrants. He assisted hundreds of students and political refugees with housing and job referrals, and he worked tirelessly to raise funds for the Korean Provisional Government and Army in Shanghai. Twice a widower, Whang died in 1974 at the age of eighty-nine. "He was a man of integrity and high ideals," wrote historian Bong Youn Choy. "He gave no attention to his own personal gain or glory, but always concerned himself with the welfare and interests of others."[15]

The Korean National Association

By the time the Angel Island Immigration Station opened for business in 1910, there were at least 1,000 Koreans residing in the continental United States.[16] A handful had come directly from Korea as students, ginseng merchants, and political exiles in the late nineteenth century. The majority were plantation workers who had remigrated from Hawaii to California and the western states, taking whatever jobs they could find on the railroads, in the canneries and mines, and on farms. Lumped with the Chinese and Japanese, Koreans were subjected to the same kinds of racial taunting, hostilities, and discrimination in the job market, housing, education, and public facilities. They could not own land, marry whites, or become naturalized U.S. citizens. In defense, Korean immigrants employed a strategy of racial accommodation. They walked away from jobs and situations where they were unwanted, worked harder to prove themselves when hired, and acculturated to Western ways. It was not long before they found their economic niche as tenant farmers growing rice, sugar beets, fruits, and vegetables, or as small shopkeepers in the cities.[17]

Although a small and scattered population, Koreans formed a cohesive community, united in their goals of mutual aid and national independence through the Korean churches, the Korean National Association, and by extension, KNA's weekly newspaper *Sinhan Minbo*. According to historian Hyung June Moon, it was because of their lonely existence in a hostile land, combined with the political situation in their homeland, that a strong bond of ethnic solidarity and mutual respect developed in the Korean community. "Each looked upon another Korean as a brother or a sister and the *esprit de corps* was admirable; 'all for one, and one for all' seemed to be the slogan." This meant not only sticking up for one another but also making sure that no one's behavior reflected poorly on the group's reputation as hardworking, law-abiding "puritans."[18]

This strong sense of Korean solidarity was transnational in nature and practice. The KNA, with regional headquarters in the U.S. mainland, Hawaii, Siberia, and Manchuria, provided the structure and leadership to mobilize support for national independence and to aid all Koreans living overseas. In the absence of a home government or consulate to protect them, the Korean community relied on the KNA to speak for them, defend their rights, and facilitate their entry into the United States. This was how the KNA got involved in the first test case of Korean transients on Angel Island. It all started when the organization heard about the plight of the 1,000 Korean "slaves" in Yucatan, Mexico, who, having completed their four-year contracts, were now free but destitute and caught in the middle of the Mexican revolution. The KNA dispatched two representatives, Whang Sa Yong and Pang Wha Joong, to investigate and set up a relief program and

KNA chapter there. Concluding that Hawaii offered them the best chance for survival, the organization got the Hawaiian Sugar Plantation Association to guarantee the Koreans jobs, raised over $9,000 to cover their travel expenses, and was in the process of securing entry permits for them from the U.S. government when four Korean leaders in Mexico jumped the gun and decided to board a ship in Manzanillo and head for Hawaii.[19]

When the ship stopped in San Francisco en route to Honolulu on September 19, 1911, the four men were, according to their legal counsel, "arrested on board the steamship 'City of Panama' and forcibly detained" on Angel Island. Appearing before the Board of Special Inquiry (BSI) chaired by Inspector Frank Ainsworth, all four showed passports issued by the Korean government in 1906 for business and traveling purposes in Mexico. They also held ship tickets that indicated Honolulu as their final destination. Upon questioning, they claimed they had never worked as laborers in Mexico and that they were going to Honolulu to explore business prospects. However, they had only $75 among the four of them and no proof for their claims of additional financial resources in Mexico. The BSI did not take long to decide against granting them transit privileges according to Executive Order 589. Moreover, the board believed that the applicants had limited funds and were likely to become public charges (LPC) if admitted to the United States. Commissioner of Immigration Samuel Backus concurred with the board's decision to deport them directly to Mexico, adding that the four men represented the advance guard of the Korean colony in Mexico, and if admitted, their cases would set a precedent whereby other Japanese and Korean laborers in Mexico would likewise seek admission to the United States.[20]

The Korean National Association assisted with the appeal process. In a letter addressed to the secretary of commerce and labor, legal representative Chauncey St. John argued that his clients were young, vigorous men capable of earning a living, that they had expended a great deal of money on the trip but still had savings in Mexico, and that they were not seeking to enter the United States but to reach the Hawaiian Islands. "The order to deport them to Mexico direct is an exhibition of unscrupulous tyranny," he concluded. The appeal was denied and the four men were deported on November 13, 1911. They had been detained on Angel Island for close to two months. Their failed attempt to pass through San Francisco en route to Hawaii put an end to KNA's plans to rescue the rest of the Korean "slaves" in Mexico. Funds collected for their passage to Hawaii were all returned to the donors. It was a hard lesson for the young organization to bear, but one that they learned well as they devised new strategies to help other Korean immigrants gain entry. Leading the way was David Lee, who became KNA's president in 1913.

Patriot, minister, interpreter, editor, community leader—these were the many roles that David Dae Wei Lee juggled and brought into play as he helped hundreds of Korean refugee students fleeing Japanese persecution make it through the immigration gateway and beyond. Born in Kang Suh, near the northern province of Pyongan, in 1878, Lee studied the Chinese classics and received his religious training at Soongsil College before immigrating to the United States as a student in 1903. In 1913, he became the first Korean to graduate from the University of California, Berkeley, and from the San Francisco Theological Seminary in 1918. He was simultaneously pastor of the Korean Methodist Church (1911–1928), port missionary and interpreter at the Angel Island Immigration Station (1913–1918), president of the Korean National Association (1913–15, 1917–19), and editor of the *Sinhan Minbo*. In these roles, Lee is credited with inventing the Korean typesetting machine, starting the Korean language school at his church, keeping nationalism alive in the Korean American community, and resolving immigration and political issues as they arose. Immigration officials at the Angel Island station came to regard him as a man of integrity and honor and to rely on his opinion and assurances to help them reach decisions on the Korean applicants. In case after case, he vouched for the immigrants' status as students with financial resources, guaranteed that they would not become public charges, paid for their medical treatment, or posted bonds to secure their release.[21]

David Dae Wei Lee in 1915. Lee devoted his life to serving his faith, his country, and the Korean American community at a great cost to his health and family. He died of exhaustion and tuberculosis in 1928 at the age of fifty, leaving his wife and four children in poverty. In 1995, in recognition of his contributions to the nationalist cause, the Korean government awarded him the Independence Medal. Ten years later, his remains were exhumed and reburied in the National Cemetery for Patriots in Dae Jun, Korea. (Courtesy of San Francisco Korean United Methodist Church.)

Since its founding in 1909, the Korean National Association had been working on regaining national independence while asserting their political identity as Koreans in America, and not Japanese subjects. In this regard they knew it was important that they secure diplomatic recognition from the United States. Immediately after Japan annexed Korea, the organization passed a resolution to declare the annexation null and void. The KNA also sent a message to all nations that had diplomatic relations with Korea, requesting that "In all diplomatic relations, the Korean National Association shall represent Koreans, and in all public events the national flag shall be displayed and the national anthem be sung as before." Presumably, the United States and Great Britain acknowledged receipt of the message but did not comment.[22] Then on June 25, 1913, attacks on Koreans in Hemet, California, presented the organization with the golden opportunity they had been seeking.

It all started when eleven Korean farm workers in Riverside, California, were recruited to Hemet by a white rancher to help harvest a bumper crop of apricots. Prior to their arrival, town citizens had already demonstrated their anti-Japanese feelings in urging the California state legislature to pass the Alien Land Law. When the Koreans arrived in Hemet on the train at midnight, they were confronted by a hostile crowd of unemployed white workers, who mistaking them for Japanese laborers, threatened them with physical violence if they did not immediately "beat it." The Korean workers boarded the next train out of there. Hearing of the expulsion and considering Koreans to be Japanese subjects, Japanese Ambassador Sutemi Chinda immediately ordered an investigation. The Koreans were more upset by the Japanese Embassy's interference in their affairs than they were by the racial hostilities of the white workers. Meanwhile, Secretary of State William Jennings Bryan, who was trying to mollify Japan's anger over the Alien Land Law, was fearful that the Hemet incident might further damage U.S.-Japan relations if not handled properly. He too ordered an investigation. Soon after, the Korean laborers, on their own, settled the indemnity matter with the white rancher to their satisfaction. But the KNA, seeing an opportunity to remove Koreans from Japanese control by establishing their own diplomatic identity with the State Department, gave David Lee the go-ahead to send the following telegram:

To the Honorable William Jennings Bryan, Secretary of State:

I have the honor to inform you of the recent expulsion of Korean laborers from Hemet, California, and to address you concerning the Japanese Consulate General's demand for indemnity. We, the Koreans in America, are not Japanese subjects, for we left Korea before the annexation of Korea by Japan, and we will never submit to her as long as the sun remains in the heavens.

The intervention of the Japanese Consulate-General in Korean matters is illegal, so I have the honor of requesting you to discontinue the discussion of this case with the Japanese government representatives. If there is any financial question between the Koreans and the persons who expelled our laborers, we will settle it without Japanese interference.[23]

Upon receiving the telegram, Secretary of State Bryan, who was opposed to Japanese colonial rule in Korea, saw a solution to his problem with Japan. On July 2, he announced to the Associated Press that the Koreans in America were not Japanese subjects and "therefore, United States official functions should, henceforth, deal directly with the Korean

National Association on all matters concerning Koreans." By doing so, he was able to avoid dealing with Japan over the Hemet affair in addition to the Alien Land Law. As far as the Korean National Association was concerned, Bryan's public announcement made them the unofficial diplomatic representative of all Koreans in America. It was exactly the authority they needed to influence decisions on political and immigration matters of concern to the Korean community.[24]

Refugee Students and Freedom Fighters

Two weeks after the Hemet incident, the six Korean young men arrived on the *Mongolia* from Shanghai without passports and with limited funds. According to the *Sinhan Minbo*, four of them were freedom fighters who had been arrested by the Japanese police and tortured before they made their escape.[25] They were immediately taken to Angel Island for further investigation. Three days later, they were called before a Board of Special Inquiry by Inspector Frank Ainsworth with David Lee serving as the interpreter. Each applicant was asked a series of questions to determine their eligibility for admission. Seemingly aware of the consequences of their responses, they each gave similar answers to that of fellow applicant Yin Chi Ham:

Q. Of what country are you a citizen? A. Korea.
Q. Are you a subject of the Emperor of Japan? A. No. I left Korea five years ago and stayed in China for five years, and never went back to Korea since the Japanese annexation of Korea.
Q. What is your father's occupation? A. My father established a big farm in China—more than ten acres. And he is in charge of a Korean school there.
Q. What income does he derive from this ranch? A. Seven thousand dollars gold yearly income generally.
Q. Have you any documentary evidence to show that you have been studying up to the time you left China to come to the United States? A. I left my documents at my home in China, because I passed through Japanese ports and was afraid they would be seized by the Japanese authorities.
Q. Why did you not secure a passport before leaving China to come to the United States? A. I can tell you the truth. It is impossible for a Korean student to get a passport anywhere. The Japanese government would never grant a passport to a Korean, so I never asked for it.
Q. What school will you enter in the United States? A. I don't know, but when I land in San Francisco, I will follow the advice of my friends and attend a certain medical school.

Q. Who will support you in the United States while attending school? A. My father will send me money within a few weeks.[26]

The board decided to exclude all six applicants for having hookworm and in the case of Cho Hin, who came with the least money—$30, for being LPC. With the help of David Lee, they appealed the decisions and applied for hospital treatment. Commissioner Samuel Backus was at a loss as to whether to grant them treatment or not since they had come without passports and had provided no evidence that they had the financial resources to pursue an education in America. He wrote the commissioner-general of immigration in Washington, D.C., for instructions.

Meanwhile, David Lee, in his capacity as KNA president, wrote a letter of appeal to the secretary of labor on behalf of the students, asking that they be granted medical treatment. He assured the secretary that the students were sons of wealthy parents who were capable of supporting their education in America. He also made a point of saying that the students were neither Japanese nor Chinese, but Korean. As proof, Lee enclosed a newspaper article with the headline, "Hemet's Korean Incident Closed by Bryan's Order: Secretary Is Informed Fruit Pickers Expelled from California Town Were Not Subjects of Japan." It was his way of reminding the immigration authorities that Koreans who left their native land before annexation should not be regarded as subjects of Japan, and thus should not be required to carry Japanese passports.

Unbeknown to Backus or Lee, American Consul General Amos Weder had written a letter to the secretary of state on February 22, 1913, regarding these same Korean students who had applied for passports at his office. He confirmed their student status and recommended that they be given special consideration:

> These young men are of attractive personality, unquestionably of the student class; some have means to support themselves while prosecuting their studies, others have friends who vouch for their support, including foreigners in the United States; and finally, they have an ardent desire to go to the land which they regard as friendly to them; they feel strongly against Japan. Their going would be to the advantage of the United States as well as fulfill their own ambitions.[27]

The American consulate had been unable to grant these students passports because they were legally not Chinese, but Japanese subjects, and were thus required to get their passports from the Japanese consulate. But as he pointed out in his letter, the Japanese foreign office had repeatedly refused to issue passports to Koreans. He concluded his letter by asking "if their alliance to Japan is such that no way remains for them to secure admission to the United States except by consent of the Tokyo foreign office, which is denied?"

The State Department referred the question to the Department of Labor. In response, Secretary of Labor William Wilson took the following position:

It is true, of course, that if these Koreans should come to a port of the United States from China and not present a passport, the provisions of the President's proclamation of March 14, 1907, and of rule 11 of the immigration rules would not technically apply to them, and probably the United States immigration officials would be obliged to admit them if it were shown that they were students and that in every respect they were admissible under the general provisions of the law. But, in this Department's judgment, it would not be in the interest of good administration (and probably you might think it objectionable from an international point of view) to offer the best encouragement to subjects of Japan living abroad to migrate to this country without subjecting themselves to the regulations regarding immigration that the Japanese Government has undertaken to enforce partly at the request of the United States Government.[28]

Both the secretary of labor and the commissioner-general of immigration decided to authorize hospital treatment for the six refugee students, and a second hearing was held in which David Lee as KNA president and George McCune, previously president of the Presbyterian College of Korea, were allowed to testify. Lee offered to cover the cost of their medical treatment as well as guarantee their stay in the United States while McCune confirmed that all of the applicants were Christians and students from well-to-do families. He also offered to sponsor Chung In Kooa, one of the students he knew well. In the end, although the students could not provide any documentary proof of their student and financial status, they were all admitted to the country a month after their arrival.

At the end of that fiscal year, Commissioner-General of Immigration Anthony Caminetti, a strong opponent of Asian immigration, noted the new "movement of Koreans to the United States" in his annual report. There had been sixty-seven Korean applicants that year as compared to twelve the previous year, he wrote. Thirty-seven were students who came on American vessels from Shanghai. None would admit to the status of laborer and most stated they had left Korea before annexation and therefore were not subjects of Japan. "The movement has not reached a serious volume at present, but inquiries now coming to us would indicate that it may soon become so large as to require the bureau's special attention," he warned.[29]

The ease with which Koreans were being admitted through the port of San Francisco annoyed the Japanese government, and the Japanese consul general in Shanghai began to apply pressure on the United States to abide by the Gentlemen's Agreement—in essence, to stop admitting Koreans without Japanese passports. According to a series of letters from the American consul in Shanghai to the secretary of state, Japanese officials were aware that, on average, twenty Koreans per month were fleeing to America by way of China, often with the help of American missionaries in Korea and China. To avoid detection by the Japanese secret police, the Koreans were known to disguise themselves as Chinese citizens and book passage only on American vessels. As pointed out in one letter, the Japanese resented the fact that Koreans "inimical to the Japanese government" could enter the United States so easily while Japanese citizens were debarred.[30]

In response to the objections raised by the Japanese consul general, Assistant Secretary of Labor Louis F. Post sided with the Korean students. In his letter to the secretary of state, he wrote:

> Koreans of the student class cannot be excluded from the United States merely because they have managed to leave Korea without obtaining passports from the Japanese government. The Immigration Service is doing all that it can, within the scope of the law and regulations, to prevent these practices; but when Koreans applying for admission are clearly entitled under the law to land at a United States port, of course no other action can be taken than to admit them.[31]

A liberal at heart, Post served as assistant secretary of labor from 1913 to 1921. He made his views on immigration known at a meeting of the American Political Science Association in 1915. He believed in the ideals of human freedom and equality irrespective of race or nationality, distrusted the administrative power of the Immigration Bureau, and disapproved of restrictive immigration policies.[32]

But as Koreans without passports continued to arrive from Shanghai and pressure from the Japanese government mounted, the Bureau of Immigration chose to differ with Post and began closing the gate on Korean immigration. On October 21, 1914, Acting Commissioner-General F. H. Larned issued a directive to the ports of Seattle, San Francisco, and Honolulu, calling their attention to the large numbers of Koreans who were embarking for the United States in Shanghai on American vessels to evade the passport requirements of the Japanese government. "In the interest of good administration," he told them, "this evasion of the regulations should be discouraged to the fullest extent possible, and the Bureau desires that such applicants shall be carefully inspected under the Immigration Act [of 1907] in every instance."[33]

Immigrant inspectors at the Angel Island station began to get tough with the newly arrived Korean students, demanding that they provide documentary evidence of their student status and financial situation. In the case of eight refugee students who arrived on August 21, 1914, from Shanghai on the *Korea*, each carrying exactly $50, they were all debarred as LPC for lacking any proof of their student status and any relatives in America to assist them. Lee pleaded with Commissioner Backus to admit them with KNA's guarantee, since they had arrived under the same circumstances as previous Korean students who had been allowed to land. "I am satisfied with the Board's decision to no longer admit people with such conditions," he wrote, "but they must give me time to prevent other students from leaving Shanghai for America unless they are well fitted to land." At the rehearing, the board badgered Lee with questions about the Korean National Association's financial situation after he agreed to post $500 bonds for each of the students. But in the end, all of the students were admitted, having spent only five days in detention.[34]

True to his word, Lee cabled Shanghai and ran an article in the *Sinhan Minbo*, which in part said:

> We hope incoming students will read and follow the guidelines written by the KNA. The fact that the San Francisco Immigration Station admitted more than 180 fellow Koreans in the past two years indicates that Koreans are being treated fairly. There are no words that can comfort those students who come to this country with high hopes and then are forced to return home without ever stepping foot on the hills of the Golden Gate. Please prepare well to meet all the requirements before the trip.[35]

From then on, KNA guidelines for incoming students and picture brides were published regularly in the *Sinhan Minbo*, specifying which documents and how much money they needed to bring. They also offered practical advice as to what to avoid. "For those students coming from China, please land in San Francisco rather than New York, where landing presents many problems to Koreans."[36]

There is no doubt that the Korean National Association was heavily involved in helping refugee students immigrate to the United States from Shanghai. The American consul in Shanghai reported in September of 1915 that a local agent of an American steamship company told him David Lee often ordered transportation for the Korean passengers. In addition, he said, Lee provided them with $50 to meet immigration requirements when they landed in San Francisco.[37] These charges were confirmed on November 6, 1916, when Immigrant Inspector Jackson Milligan caught a Hawaii KNA courier passing envelopes of money addressed to four Korean students aboard the *Ecuador*, which had stopped in Honolulu on its way to

San Francisco. Upon investigation, all four students insisted that their relatives had sent them the money through the KNA, but Inspector Milligan saw the delivery of funds as proof of previous charges made by Hawaiian Korean interpreter John Woo, that KNA was providing "show money" to incoming Korean immigrants. In his memorandum to the inspector in Honolulu, Milligan also wrote, "Interpreter Woo reports that it is common knowledge among the Koreans here that the official Korean interpreter at San Francisco receives a salary from the Korean National Association as well as from the Immigration Service for his work, and that he tells only so much in regard to these boys as is necessary in connection with their admission."[38] These charges would later damage the chances of the twenty-five Korean students from entering the country as well as tarnish the reputations of David Lee and the KNA.

According to the immigration case files of the *Ecuador* students, we know that Lee was not allowed to serve as their interpreter but was replaced by C. D. Morris, who had been a missionary in Korea. All of the applicants had come without passports and documents to prove their student status. In an attempt to assess their educational backgrounds, the board tested their math, English, and knowledge of history and geography. One failed the math test, another failed the history test, and only two of the students could speak English. Three students had no money at all, claiming that they had spent it all in Shanghai while waiting to secure passage on an American ship. They and the four students who had been given money by the KNA in Honolulu were grilled about their financial situation. Relatives and family friends who stepped forward to sponsor them, some apparently at the request of the Korean National Association, were cross-examined about their finances and relationship to the applicants. When David Lee appeared as a witness and sponsor on behalf of Pyun Pong Chick, whose father he knew well, Lee was questioned about his overall income and family expenses, and was told, "How will you support a wife, four children and yourself, and care for this boy, from the salary of $62.50 a month, at the present time when the cost of living is so high?" Following that remark, he was asked if he knew whether the KNA was funneling money to incoming Korean students at the port of Honolulu. Lee denied knowing anything about it. Commissioner Edward White, who had previously defended Lee as a man of integrity and honor, declined to do so this time.[39]

Except for Kiel In Young, who had three strong letters of recommendation and was admitted twelve days after his arrival, the other ten students were excluded and ordered deported. Nine of them were deemed LPC on the grounds that they had limited funds, no relatives or credible sponsors in the United States to assist them, and no profession or trade by which to earn a living if it became necessary. Lee Hong Nai, whose "hands show signs of labor," was excluded as a laborer in violation of the passport regulations (Rule 11). Three of the students who had received funds through the KNA were additionally charged with coming as immigrants "assisted by others" in violation of the Immigration Act of 1907. The students were detained on Angel Island for two months while Frank Ainsworth, now employed by the KNA as its legal counsel, filed appeals on their behalf. He argued that Koreans had a right to transmit money through the KNA if they so chose, that their families, not the KNA, had paid for their passage, and that no Korean had been known to be a public charge. "Is the Board not unduly apprehensive in its duty to keep Asiatic laborers out of the United States?" he wrote. This last statement is ironic coming from Ainsworth, who had recently sided with the Asiatic Exclusion League against South Asian immigration. With World War I raging in Europe and refugees fleeing to America in droves, Ainsworth also employed the refugee argument in his appeal without realizing that Congress, which was considering new immigration legislation at this time, had European refugees, not Asian refugees, in mind.[40]

> In the opinion of counsel this alien as others of his class should be considered not as the usual immigrant but more in that spirit which prompted Congress to write in the Immigration Law that political refugees should not be barred for political reasons if otherwise admissible. The Koreans may well be called the Belgians of the Orient. Their country has been occupied by a stronger power and their rulers deposed. Many have been forced to leave their native country. Those who left Korea before the Japanese occupation are veritable people without a country and Secretary of State Bryan according to the public press about July 1, 1913 announced that as such they would not be regarded as Japanese subjects.

Commissioner White, however, felt differently. He recommended that exclusion be sustained in all the cases, citing the Immigration Bureau's directive in each instance: "Attention is invited to Bureau letter No. 53260/91 of October 21, 1914, wherein the conditions referred to are identical with this alien's case, coming without a passport and embarking for the United States upon a vessel of American registry."

We may never know for sure who was telling the truth or what these students were thinking while detained on Angel Island except for the following letter that we found in Kim Chin Young's file. At his BSI hearing on December 4, 1916, he told Inspector James Lawler that he was twenty-one years old, born in Korea, single, a student, and heading to live with his brother-in-law Han Chang Ho, a farmer in Manteca, California. When asked why he had no money with him, he explained that he had plenty when he left home over six years ago, but spent it all while waiting for a ship in Shanghai. He added, "It was hard for my father to send me money to Shanghai, as the Japanese searched all the letters and it puts them under suspicion." The next day, when his brother-in-law showed up as a witness, he brought Kim $100 and said he would be willing to support him until the family could send more money from Korea. As was the common practice for Chinese applicants, Han and Kim were grilled about their family backgrounds in order to verify their relationship. Upon cross-examination, some major discrepancies emerged. Han said his wife was still in Korea and that they had no children. Kim, based on sporadic letters he had received from his family in Korea, said he thought his sister had immigrated to America three years ago and that the couple had a son. The board used the discrepancies as a further reason to exclude Kim. With the help of Ainsworth and the KNA, he appealed. While waiting for the outcome, he sent the following letter, sincere and desperate in tone, to the commissioner of immigration. It was translated by C. D. Morris.

To the Chief Immigration Officer:

I am a Korean who is in trouble, and wishing to come to America have suffered much during the last six years. I went to Southern Manchuria, where fearing arrest from the Japanese, even when eating, if they come near I had to flee. With God's help I have been able to cross the Pacific Ocean. If the Koreans go to Manchuria the Japanese arrest them and cause them much suffering. Therefore I have had to leave my parents and those I hold dear and travel hither and thither not knowing what it was best to do. Mr. Morris, who is interpreting, knows the condition of our people. America has pitied the Koreans and has received them although they had no passports. We know that we have not been able to keep the law in many ways and feel much ashamed.

Again I wish to speak of my condition. I came to America wishing to study the manufacturing of machinery. If one of you who is employed will take me to his home for three months, I will furnish my board and school expenses. After that money will come from my home. I have one hundred dollars to take with me now, so I hope that one of you will send me to a school where I can study English. There is one kind of work which I know how to do thoroughly. That is how to make leather shoes like the Americans wear. I trust that you will pity me and grant that I may stay here and study. If we have disobeyed the laws of America, we can understand why we should be sent back, but I do not see that I have broken the law and so trust that you will carefully think over my case again.

When I was examined my answers did not agree with my brother-in-law's and so you thought that he was not my brother-in-law, but he truly is my sister's husband. My brother-in-law and my first cousin (mother's sister's son) are both here in America so that there is no concern about money for my support, before money comes from my home in Korea. Therefore will not one of you take me for three months and prove me as to whether I am what I claim to be? I trust that you will call me once more for examination.

(Signed) Kim Chin Young

No one stepped forward to take Kim up on his offer. He was not called back for examination but deported with the others.[41]

Despite this first major setback with the *Ecuador* students, David Lee and the KNA remained involved in immigration matters on Angel Island, but they were not as influential in helping Koreans land. As the word got out that they were no longer welcomed in America, fewer Koreans immigrated. In late 1915, Commissioner White proudly wrote Commissioner-General of Immigration Caminetti, "I can assure the [Japanese] Consul that for some months past the provisions of Rule 11 have been strictly enforced with apparently effective result, as the applications for admission of this class of aliens have been generally decreasing, and for the past couple of months no applications for admission have been made."[42]

Then on July 26, 1917, the secretary of state and secretary of labor issued a joint order that put a stop to Korean immigration altogether. Passed as a war measure to protect the country from foreign agents and spies, the joint order required that all entering aliens carry passports visaed by a U.S. consul. When fourteen more Korean students arrived without passports aboard the *Columbia* from Shanghai on November 9, 1917, David Lee was back on the job as the Korean interpreter, but he was not able to help them gain entry. This time, the students came armed with strong letters of recommendation and student documents. Some even had relatives in America willing to assist them. Immigration officials believed them to be bona fide students but excluded all of them for "not being in possession of a passport properly visaed, as now required."[43]

In his appeal on behalf of the students, Frank Ainsworth argued that students coming from China were not required to have passports, but this point was soon discounted in a telegram from the Immigration Bureau that stated, "Exempt Section Six Chinese, all others should carry passports." Playing on the patriotic fervor

Kim Ok Yun's passport photo, 1926. (Scan by Vincent Chin. National Archives, Pacific Regional Branch.)

of a country at war, Ainsworth reminded the U.S. government that Koreans were political refugees no different from "those Hungarians like Lajos Kossuth [or] those patriotic Poles like Tadeusz Kosciuszko who, after their countries were captured by a stronger nation, fled to the United States where they were welcomed." In fact, he added, these Koreans may be safely admitted as "alien friends and not alien enemies," because they had all agreed in writing to join the U.S. armed forces if so required. This time, Commissioner White recommended that the department sustain all of the appeals, but the secretary of labor, for unknown reasons, would only admit eight of the fourteen students.

Korean students stopped coming after 1918 because of the new passport requirements. Not until Congress passed the Immigration Act of 1924, which barred all Asian immigrants but exempted students with proper documents and a visa from the American consulate, were 300 more Korean students, men and women, able to come. Among them were Kim Ok Yun in 1926 and Choi Kyung Sik in 1925.

When Kim Ok Yun arrived in San Francisco from Shanghai on the *President Pierce*, she came armed with a Section Six student visa issued by the American consulate at Shanghai and a letter of acceptance from the San Francisco National Training School. The visa indicated that she was a graduate of the Yei Sin Baptist Missionary School in Masan, Korea, and a naturalized Chinese citizen. According to her sister Shinn Kang-ae, who had immigrated as a picture bride in 1914 and was living in San Francisco's Chinatown at the time, Ok Yun had been an undercover agent in the anti-Japanese resistance movement in Korea.

> In 1919, she was in the Mansei movement,[44] and the Japanese would not give her a passport, so during the night she disguised herself as an old Chinese woman and escaped to China. My sister prepared for English and studied in China for three years before coming to the U.S. She had a Chinese passport. She dressed as a Chinese and passed undetected when the Japanese officials went aboard the ship to rout out the Koreans. When she arrived, the immigration authorities locked her up for one week. They said she had something inside sick and we had to make a $100 deposit.[45]

Ok Yum was found to have hookworm. After a brief interview, the BSI decided to admit her as a bona fide student on the condition that she be treated for the hookworm. The Korean National Association deposited $100 for her medical treatment and she was subsequently cured and released from the island twelve days later. For the next seven years, Ok Yum lived with her sister's family in Chinatown while she attended college. She did not dare seek employment or engage in any political activities for fear of jeopardizing her good standing as a foreign student. Upon graduating in 1933, she returned to her hometown in Korea, where she taught at a girls' school and rejoined the

Choi Kyung Sik's passport photo, 1925. (Scan by Eddie Wong. National Archives, Pacific Regional Branch.)

political movement for independence. Relatives in America never heard from her again and suspect that she may have been killed by the Japanese secret police because of her political activities.[46]

Unlike Kim Ok Yun, Choi Kyung Sik took a different route. He was able to secure a Japanese passport and an immigration visa from the American consulate in Korea before embarking from Yokohama on the *Taiyo Maru* for San Francisco. According to his immigration file, Kyung Sik graduated from Chosen Christian College with a degree in literature in 1924 and had been accepted as a student by De Pauw University in Greencastle, Indiana. His file also contained a letter in Korean signed by a relative and the mayor of Seoul certifying that 9,000 yen ($4,500) had been set aside for his education in America. Noting that "applicant speaks English fairly well, seems to be a bright young boy, is no doubt of student class," the Board of Special Inquiry landed him the next day.[47] From a poem that Kyung Sik composed and that was published in the *Sinhan Minbo* on April 30, 1925, we know that he did not enjoy his one-night stay at the immigration station.

A Night at the Immigration Station
by Choi Kyung Sik
Translated by Jikyung Hwang and Charles Egan[48]

Why are my hands,
Exhausted from crossing a vast ocean,
Now holding iron bars?
The rain cries out and wakes me up
Because it pities me.
Angel Island, sleeping tight,
No matter whether you hear this song or not,
It is the complaint of a foreign guest
Whose whole heart is burning.

Even though it's said America is wonderful,
How pathetic it has made me.
If my mother knew about this,
How shocked she would be.

This border created by rascals—
When can it be broken?
I hope people all over the world
Will become brothers soon.

April 3rd
Written on a rainy night at the immigration station on Angel Island,
    San Francisco, America.

Like Choi Kyung Sik, most of the Korean students who came to America after 1924 applied for their visas as Japanese subjects from the U.S. consulate in Seoul and were released from Angel Island within a day or two after they passed the immigrant inspection. Although there was less need for the Korean National Association to get involved in these cases, the organization continued to send a representative to greet each new arrival and to offer its services, such as paying for medical treatment, transmitting letters and money, and contacting witnesses and colleges to confirm a student's status. After the students were admitted, the KNA continued to assist them with housing, part-time employment, financial aid, and legal advice. In these ways, the KNA made it possible for many Koreans to land and succeed in America.[49]

In truth, as immigrant inspectors suspected, most of the refugee students who came before 1924 could not count on their families in Korea to support them in America. Rather, most had to take part-time jobs as gardeners, dishwashers, houseboys, and farmworkers. Their limited English and need to work made it difficult for them to keep up with their schooling. Only 20 percent of them graduated from college, but many opted to stay in America rather than return to an unstable country. In contrast, 65 percent of the Korean students who came after 1924 graduated from college, many at the doctoral degree level, because they were both academically and financially better prepared than the earlier wave of students. Although immigration authorities were quite diligent about enforcing the law that students not work and that they leave the country when they finished their studies, quite a few students overstayed their visas and remained in America. Those who returned to Korea were able to put their education to good use and help rebuild the country after independence from Japan was won in August 1945.[50]

Unlike the Chinese detainees, the Koreans left no poems on the barrack walls of Angel Island. But periodically poems were published in the *Sinhan Minbo*. Many of the poems dwelled on the trials and tribulations of immigrant life in America. A few, like Choi Kyung Sik's poem and the following poem, focused specifically on the Angel Island experience. Written under the pen name of Cloud, "Angel Island" was published on August 8, 1929.

Angel Island
by Cloud
Translated by Jikyung Hwang and Charles
Egan[51]

Angel Island, Angel Island, all the people said,
So I thought it would be like heaven.
Yet when the iron gate locks with a clang—
It feels like hell.

You, the masses of people
Who are wriggling in this steel-barred prison,
You have a home, you have a country.
So what is the reason for this sorrow?
It must be a hungry belly
That causes this Karma.

The only Korean inscription found at the immigration station appears on a column on the second floor of the detention barracks. The words, "Ryu in-bal, ku-wol-ryug-il," are written in Korean Hangul and Chinese characters, giving the person's name and the date: Rhew In-Bal, September 6, 1923. Translated by Hyong-gyu Rhew. (Courtesy of Architectural Resources Group.)

Picture Brides and Families

There were so few women among the early Korean immigrants to America that in 1910, the Korean male to female ratio was 6 to 1 in Hawaii, and 9 to 1 on the U.S. mainland. The scarcity of Korean women posed a problem for the single men who wanted to marry and stay in America rather than return to an unstable country under Japanese colonial rule. A small percentage of the men chose to intermarry with local women. Many others, learning from the example of the Japanese, took advantage of U.S. immigration policies and the Korean custom of arranged marriage to send for picture brides from Korea. Although the Japanese government had put a stop to Korean emigration, they were willing to let women out of the country as a way to calm political passions among overseas Koreans. For Korean women who were eager to go to the fabled land of gold and freedom, the picture bride route was their only way out.[52]

From 1910 until 1920, when the "Ladies Agreement" put an end to picture bride migration from both Japan and Korea, over 1,000 Korean women chose this route—951 immigrated to Hawaii and 115 to the U.S. mainland. Ranging in age from fourteen to twenty-five, the women were generally better educated and younger than their husbands by a decade or two. Most of the picture brides who went to Hawaii were from the southern part of Korea near Youngnam, while those who went to the U.S.

mainland via China were from the northern provinces of Pyongan and Hwanghae. Similar to the Japanese practice, a matchmaker or relative was engaged to help the groom in America find a bride in his hometown. Family backgrounds were investigated, and photographs and letters were exchanged. When the time came for the bride to leave for America, the groom sent the necessary travel funds to the bride. If she was leaving legally according to Japanese regulations, she would have been issued a Japanese passport. With that in hand, she traveled by boat to Yokohama, where she had to pass a physical examination before boarding a Japanese steamship for America. Those unable to secure a Japanese passport for one reason or another often left by way of China, much like the refugee students, and booked passage on an American steamship in Shanghai. Some of the young women were so brazen and desperate to get to America that they sought out the services of a matchmaker on their own.[53] Among the small number of Korean picture brides who came through Angel Island were nineteen-year-old Shinn Kang-ae in 1914 and eighteen-year-old Kim Suk-eun in 1913.

Ever since she heard about "the wonderful land of freedom" from American missionaries in Korea, Shinn Kang-ae had dreamed of someday sailing to America to continue her education. "At that time, Japan controlled Korea and I did not want to study under them, they were so cruel." A family friend in San Francisco recommended Shinn Han to her as a good man to marry. Han had immigrated to Hawaii in 1903 to work on the sugar plantations. After two years of hard labor, he had saved enough money to move to the mainland, where he started a dry cleaning business in San Francisco. Kang-ae's mother and older brother approved of the marriage and made all the necessary arrangements on her behalf, including securing a Japanese passport. Her brother, who was a tailor, had a Western suit made for Kang-ae to wear on the trip, and he accompanied her to Yokohama. There they stayed at a Korean inn for a short period while waiting for the results of her physical examination and for passage to the United States.[54]

After the ship docked in San Francisco, the first person to come on board to greet Kang-ae was none other than David Lee. "He was *kungminhoe* [KNA] president, and he could get a pass and go aboard," she explained. Lee kindly escorted her to Angel Island, where Kang-ae went through the physical examination and interview "with no problem" and promptly returned by ferry to San Francisco. She likely breezed through the interview because she had a Japanese passport and Lee was there to vouch for her. Kang-ae found her fiancé Han anxiously waiting for her at the San Francisco dock. When her daughter Sonia asked what her first impression of him was, she replied, "He wasn't too bad looking, much like the photograph. I knew he was going to be my husband. I didn't know about love, but I believe he is nice man." After all, didn't he send her a Korean-

Shinn Han (left), daughter Sonia, Shinn Kang-ae, and son Daye in 1917. (Courtesy of USC Korean American Digital Archive.)

English book, *Learning English without a Teacher*, to prepare her for life in America? "Your papa always good to me." A week later, abiding by U.S.immigration law, Kang-ae, dressed in a white gown and veil, and Han, in a rented black tuxedo, were married at the Korean Methodist Church (see photo on page 202). The couple settled in San Francisco's Chinatown, where Han ran a successful barbershop and Kang-ae worked as a seamstress at a garment factory while raising a family of four children.

Compared to Shinn Kang-ai, Kim Suk-eun had a hard time coming to America as a picture bride. A daughter of a wealthy businessman, Suk-eun grew up in the North, resenting the Japanese occupation. "The Japanese controlled education, and Koreans were forced to learn, use and speak Japanese," she said. "Day by day, no more freedom—that's why I wanted to leave Korea, and the only route was as a picture bride." Her girlfriends in America as well as political leader Ahn Chang-ho,[55] who was a friend of her father, recommended Kim Hong Kyun to her as a prospective husband. He was a thirty-two-year-old farmer in Sacramento, California. "Really, I didn't want to marry, but I did wish to get to America," she told Sonia Sunoo in an interview years later. But her parents were dead set against the marriage. "To go to America for an education is OK to them, but not as a picture bride," she explained. "My parents said, 'You go marry over there, and something go wrong, don't tell family. You go drown in the ocean.' I was so angry with them that I did not write to them for ten years after I arrived in America."[56]

Because she could not secure a passport from the Japanese officials, Suk-eun decided to escape across the Yalu River at night and make her way to Shanghai, where she booked passage with money that her fiancé had sent her. Disguised in a Chinese gown, she boarded the ship and hid from the Japanese authorities in the steerage room with two other picture brides—most likely Chang Kyung Ai and Lee Che Hyun, who were later detained on Angel Island with her. "I was very frightened," she recalled, "but I was lucky because I had money to bribe working people to keep quiet about me." The three women slept and ate in the steerage room. "I paid for my meals on the ship," Suk-eun said. "I was sometimes served Chinese food, sometimes American. I didn't like any of it, but I was hungry, so I had to eat it." After making one stop in Hawaii for a week, the ship arrived in San Francisco on August 2, and Suk-eun was married on August 24.

No mention was made of Angel Island in her interview with Sunoo, but according to their immigration records, Kim Suk-eun, Chang Kyung Ai, and Lee Che Hyun were all taken to Angel Island for further examination upon their arrival in San Francisco. After Suk-eun passed the physical examination, she was called to appear before the BSI with Lee acting as the interpreter. It was a brief interview during which she was asked fourteen questions about her background and reasons for coming to the United States. Kim Hong Kyun, who was there to claim her as his bride, was asked fifteen questions about his immigration status and financial situation. Satisfied that as a grocer with $1,000 in the bank and $120 in cash with him, he would be able to provide for her, the board admitted Suk-eun on the proviso that the couple be married according to American custom.[57]

Whereas passports, photographs, and proof of engagement were asked of the Japanese brides, the same was not required of Suk-eun and other Korean brides. When asked why she did not have any documentary evidence of her engagement, Suk-eun replied, "I stayed in China for many

Three newly married couples pose in front of the Korean Methodist Church at 1123 Bush Street in San Francisco. Shinn Han and Shinn Kang-ae are the couple in the middle; Whang Sa Sun is standing in the back row to the left of the church building; Whang Sa Yong is standing in the second row to the right of the man waving his hat; and the Reverend David Lee is standing in the back row to the right of Whang Sa Song. (Courtesy of USC Korean American Digital Archive.)

years and was unable to bring it with me." Aware of the plight of Korean refugees, the board seemed satisfied with her response, just as they were with Lee Che Hun's response as to why she did not have a passport, "I came from Shanghai." None of the three picture brides were even asked if they had any "show money." In contrast, the Korean male students who had also come without documentation were grilled about their nationality, family background, financial situation, and status as students. Suk-eun had also said she was a student before coming to America, but the BSI did not ask her for any proof. Instead, Inspector William Chadney made a point of noting in her file, "Applicant has the appearance of a student." The board was apparently only interested in stopping Korean laborers from entering the country. On the whole, immigration officials at the Angel Island station were more lenient with the Korean women than the men. The women were detained on Angel Island for no more than three days while the men were detained for five days to a month.

As agreed, Suk-en did marry Kim Hong Kyun in a wedding officiated by the Reverend David Lee, a week after she was landed. But her marriage did not turn out to be a happy one. She did not like being a farmer's wife.

> Soon after my arrival and marriage to Mr. Kim, I knew that an education could not be realized. Finding a job would be an impossibility. The depth of my despair and disappointment was greater than imaginable. I felt bitter that my husband was much older than what his picture revealed. I had been deceived. It was very difficult for me, under the circumstances to face the realities of my fate.
>
> I married Mr. Kim, took care of him and our four children, and kept house. This is my story and my secret which I am revealing for the first time, even to my own children. I am just a picture bride, married and that's all.

Suk-en was not alone in finding herself trapped in an unhappy marriage with her ambitions dashed. The *Sinhan Minbo* reported on other brides who had broken off their engagements and wives who had taken the initiative to file for divorce, an action that was extremely uncommon at that time.[58] One long article, "On Understanding Marriage by Photo Exchange," acknowledged that an arranged marriage was not the ideal way to get married, but for Koreans in America, there was no other way. The unsigned article went on to attribute the problem in these marriages to class incompatibility and self-disillusion. To the prospective groom, the article recommended that he be honest with himself and select a bride of equal or less stature to him in order to avoid being humiliated.

> Many of you in America are laborers who cannot even write a letter by yourselves, yet you are carrying around the photographs of women

who are middle school graduates, dreaming of which one to pick! Don't be a fool! Those educated Korean women who have been desperate to leave Korea since annexation will not treat you mere laborers with respect. It is best for students to choose students, teachers to choose teachers, and laborers to choose sincere women from the countryside.

To the prospective bride, the writer urged her not to be presumptuous or greedy, but to honor her commitment to the marriage.

How foolish you are as a homemaker if you think that you are better than your husband, who is laboring outside, just because of a little bit of education. Only the mature and truly learned person can recognize and respect the value of manual labor. Treating your husband with disrespect indicates that you have not learned anything. If you want happiness in life, you must treat your husband with love and respect.[59]

Many of the Korean men were married, but their wives were in Korea, and although the Japanese government was willing to issue passports to them, this was easier said than done. According to a letter that David Lee wrote to the Angel Island commissioner of immigration in his role as KNA president, such passports were impossible for Koreans to obtain at any price. Yet, as many as 200 men, all of whom had come to the United States before the annexation of Korea, wanted to bring their wives to America. In his letter Lee addressed two concerns Americans had about Asian women. He assured the commissioner that "there is not any single Korean woman in America who lived immoral lives, while there are good many other Oriental nationalities have trouble with it." Moreover, he wrote, "No Korean in America will permit his wife to work for a living." Written after the new passport and visa requirements were issued on July 26, 1917, the letter asked the commissioner to admit Korean wives and "engaged brides" without passports when they came from a country outside of Japanese dominion.[60] It was a good faith effort by Lee and the Korean National Association to help reunite couples, establish family life, and stabilize the Korean community, but to no avail. The commissioner's hands were tied by the joint order requiring visaed passports. Even Assistant Secretary of Labor Post could not help them. In reply to the secretary of state's request for clarification on the matter, he wrote, "Since those instructions [General Instructions 565 from the joint order] became operative in the Orient, it will not be possible for a Korean to land at a port of the United States unless he holds a passport obtained and approved in the manner specified by said regulations."[61]

Im So See was one of the few Korean wives lucky enough to secure a Japanese passport to immigrate to the United States with her stepdaughter Pok Kyong Whan, stepson Pok Tong Khan, and daughter Pok Yun Sun (see photo on page 176). Arriving in San Francisco from Yokohama on March 12, 1914, the family was taken to Angel Island for the physical examination and interrogation. So See told the Board of Special Inquiry through interpreter Lee that she had married Pok Kyung Soo, a widower with two children, five years ago in Seoul, and that they were going to join him in Idaho, where she planned to "keep house" and send the children to school. When asked if she had ever tried to come to the United States before, she replied, "No, it took us about 12 months to get our passport to come here now." When asked why it took so long, stepdaughter Kyong Whan explained, "The government takes a census and we had to wait until they found our names on the census and we had to be examined physically, and that took about 12 months." As other Korean immigrants had testified before, such delays in issuing passports were common and intended to discourage Korean applicants. But evidently, the Pok family persisted.[62]

Compared to the brief interviews of Korean picture brides and grooms, the interrogation of wives and husbands proved more difficult. Pok Tong Khan was asked over forty questions about his immigration and financial status. He told the board that he first immigrated to Hawaii in 1905, then to San Francisco a year later. His answers regarding his first wife's death and his remarriage in 1910 aligned with those of his wife Im So See. But the board was not convinced that he actually owned a house and farmed on nine acres of leased land near Boise. They decided to defer the case and detain the family on Angel Island until evidence could be produced. Only after they received a telegram from the postmaster in Mountain Home, Idaho, stating that "Park Kyung Soo fully able to support family, owns town lot, has leased small farm," did they admit Soo See and stepson Tong Khan on March 23, eleven days after their arrival. Because Kyong Whan had hookworm and Yun Sun had the measles, the two girls had to stay at the hospital for treatment and were not admitted until April 6. Still, they had all managed to pass the double test of proving their family relationships and Park's qualifications to sponsor and support them—no mean feat in order to enter through the Angel Island gateway to America.

Meung-son and Rose Paik on their wedding day in 1929. (Courtesy of USC Korean American Digital Archive.)

Sixty years later, Rose Paik (Pok Yun Sun) would explain why the family chose to come to America: "Japan took over and we were able to get away." She said her father was a bartender in Idaho at the time and the family initially farmed in Oregon. When Rose was almost fourteen, her mother died in childbirth. Soon after, the family moved back to Idaho to farm, growing beans, corn, potatoes, and strawberries. "In a farm family," Rose told Sunoo, "we all had to work, work, work! I was used to driving horses and pitching hay." When she turned seventeen, Rose agreed to an arranged marriage with Paik Meung-son, a farmer's son. The couple farmed in Utah for about seven years and then decided to move to Los Angeles, where Meung worked as a salesman for a Korean canned food company and where they raised a family of six children.[63]

Some Koreans, unable to obtain a Japanese passport and unable to immigrate to the United States without one after 1918 resorted to using Chinese passports. This was how Lyang Hong, who had come to the United States as a student via China in 1916, was able to send for his wife and daughter. The plan was quite ingenious and complicated because as Chinese subjects, they came under the Chinese Exclusion Act, which unlike the Gentlemen's Agreement, prohibited family members of laborers from immigrating to the United States. Lyang had to become a merchant in order to send for his family. That the plan worked—both wife and child were admitted a week after their arrival—attests to the excellent groundwork laid by Lyang as well as the assistance of relatives in Shanghai, friends and witnesses in San Francisco, and legal counsel Frank Ainsworth.[64]

On October 25, 1922, Pak Sum Oi arrived in San Francisco on the *Nile* from Shanghai, accompanied by her eight-year-old daughter Lyang Ai Shun. Upon questioning by a Board of Special Inquiry with Frank Kim as the interpreter, she claimed to be of the Korean race but a citizen of China through naturalization. She could read and write Korean, had about $50, and was going to her husband Lyang Hong. When asked what she expected to do in this country, if admitted, she replied, "Keep house."

Lyang Hong then appeared for questioning. He told the board that he was part owner of a ginseng shop in San Francisco and that he too was a naturalized citizen of China, at which point he produced the family's certificate of naturalization. The board, realizing that the case would have to be handled under the provisions of the Chinese Exclusion Act, had evidently never heard such a case before.

Q: How did you know it was possible for you to be naturalized as a Chinese citizen, and still be a resident of this country? A: I couldn't get a passport without that paper and had to become a Chinese citizen.

Q: But how did you know you could get this certificate of naturalization without going to China yourself and appear before the proper authorities? A: My brother wrote, telling me in order to get permission to come forward, I would have to be a Chinese citizen and I wrote him to do the necessary to make me a Chinese citizen and he did so, sending me the papers.

Q: Did your brother tell you it was possible for you to become a naturalized citizen of China, even though you were over in this country at the time?
A: Yes, my brother wrote me to that effect.

Still, Lyang had to prove to the immigration officials that Sum Oi and Ai Shun were indeed his wife and daughter and that he had been a merchant for at least one year prior to their application for admission. Within a few days, he satisfactorily established his merchantile status by the testimony of two credible white witnesses. He also produced his bank book showing $1,000 in savings and his firm's account books showing that he became a partner of Lyang and Chang Company on November 1, 1921. Lyang also asked Whang Sa Sun, who was present at his wedding in Korea, to come to Angel Island and testify to that effect. Finally, he got Frank Ainsworth to file all the necessary affidavits with the case. All this work paid off. Even though Lyang was six days short of being a merchant for one year preceding the application for his family's admission, Inspector Joseph Strand recommended the applicants be admitted as wife and daughter of a domiciled merchant.

Lyang Hong's son, Donald Lyang doubts that his father was ever a ginseng merchant. He remembers his father telling him that he was beaten up and thrown in jail by the Japanese for protesting. After he got to America, "he was a cook for awhile and he worked in the quicksilver mines, rice fields, and fruit orchards, taking whatever jobs he could find. It took him six years before he had enough money to bring my mother and sister over." Soon after, Lyang Hong got a position as a janitor and gardener for the Standard Oil Company in Coalinga, California. It was a good job and the family was provided with subsidized housing. Lyang remained with the company for twenty-seven years until he retired. True to her word, Sum Oi stayed home and raised a family of two boys and two girls. "We were the only Koreans in town," recalled Donald, "so my mother was pretty lonely in Coalinga. As far as social life went, there wasn't very much for my mother except when we visited Koreans in Reedley, Dinuba, and Delano." She passed away in 1938. His father, on the other hand, was active in the KNA and read the *Sinhan Minbo* faithfully to stay informed of developments in Korea and the Korean community. Lyang Hong lived long enough to see Donald return home alive from the Korean War, graduate from college, and become a successful manufacturing engineer and commercial property owner.[65]

Many other Korean immigrant families were not so fortunate. According to Paul Whang, the eldest child of the Reverend Whang Sa Sun, "As early as I can remember, it was a tough life for my parents. My father was deeply involved in the church and independence movement, while running a dry cleaning shop. His church pay wasn't much. They struggled." The family lived in the back of the shop and Paul recalled making weekly trips to a bathhouse in Chinatown because they did not have a bathtub. In 1939, Paul earned his teaching credentials from San Francisco State College, but "because of my color, they closed the door in my face," he said. Instead, he took a job at the Angel Island Immigration Station as a "messenger servant" for the hospital. Present when the fire broke out and destroyed the administration building in 1940, Paul served as a key witness in the investigation.[66] He left the immigration service to join the navy as a pharmacist at the start of World War II. After opportunities opened up for Asian Americans in the 1950s, Paul passed the San Francisco civil service exam for playground director and devoted thirty years of his life serving the recreational needs of Chinatown.[67]

Sonia Shinn Sunoo, the eldest child of Shinn Han and Kang-ae, had a similar story to tell. According to her book, *Korean Picture Brides*, her mother came to a rude awakening about America, "the wonderful land of the free," on her wedding night. Her husband Han had prepared comfortable living quarters for her behind his pressing parlor business, which happened to be in a white neighborhood.

> In the quiet of the night, a crashing sound of shattering glass awakened them. Vandals had thrown a rock through the plate glass window. Shards of glass flew everywhere. My mother, petrified with fear, stood by trembling and bewildered. She watched Papa board up the window and sweep the debris. He explained, "It would be useless to seek police assistance. This is a white man's world, and the less we bother, the better."[68]

For the next few years, the couple struggled to make ends meet. Han held two or three part-time jobs while Kang-ae ran the cleaning business and took care of their four children. There was no time for her to fulfill her dream of getting an education. Even after the family moved to Chinatown, where Han operated a five-chair barbershop, Kang-ae continued to work long hours in a sewing factory to help support the family. She eventually saved enough money to purchase a forty-room hotel, which became well known among Korean merchant seamen as Shinn Halmoni or Grandma Shinn's Kearny [Street] Hotel. She retired in comfort and lived to be eighty-eight years old.

Like Paul Whang, Sonia Sunoo grew up in the sheltered environment of San Francisco's Chinatown and was encouraged by her parents to pursue higher education. But upon graduating from San Francisco State College with a B.A. degree in English and biology, she was told it would be useless for her to go on to graduate school since the public schools in California did not hire Orientals. "What a shock it was that the first college graduate in the family would experience such discrimination," she wrote. Instead, she accepted a scholarship to the College of Cosmetology and with her parents' support, opened "Sonia's Korean Beauty Salon" on the outskirts of Chinatown. After she married political scientist Harold Sunoo and had two children, Sonia devoted many years of her life to teaching early childhood education and collecting oral histories of early Korean immigrants. She co-authored *Korea Kaleidoscope: Oral Histories* with Harold Sunoo in 1982 and wrote *Korean Picture Brides: A Collection of Oral Histories* in 2002.

As difficult as their lives were after Angel Island, Koreans were spared the pain and agony of internment during World War II. Even though Korea was legally a part of the Japanese Empire, the U.S. Department of Justice chose to recognize Koreans as an independent entity and ruled in January 1942 that they did not need to register as "enemy aliens." But like Japanese immigrants, Koreans had to wait until 1952 before they could resume immigration to the United States and become eligible for U.S. citizenship. In contrast, Russian and Jewish immigrants fleeing religious and political persecution at the same time as the Koreans were treated more leniently at Angel Island because of their race, nationality, and ethnic network of support in America. For them, Angel Island proved to be an open gateway to the Promised Land.

Deaconess Katharine Maurer (center) surrounded by a large group of immigrants from Russia and Central Europe in the multipurpose room of the administration building. (Courtesy of California State Parks, 2010.)

CHAPTER SIX

IN SEARCH OF FREEDOM AND OPPORTUNITY

RUSSIANS AND JEWS IN THE PROMISED LAND

THE ARRIVAL OF TWENTY-FIVE RUSSIAN STUDENTS FROM HARBIN, Manchuria, on August 29, 1922, made the front page of the *San Francisco Daily News*. Russia had fallen under Bolshevik control and Americans were fearful of communists infiltrating the country. Speaking for the group in English was twenty-five-year-old Nadia Shapiro: "We are without a country. We do not belong to the old regime and we do not want to join the Bolshevik Party, so what can we do? In America we hope to study journalism and learn your ways of government so we can take it back to our people." The students were immediately taken to the Angel Island Immigration Station for further investigation to determine if "this is the only reason they are here."[1] The Russian Revolution and increased political radicalism in the United States had put immigration officials on alert to stop alien radicals from entering the country. Their fears were unfounded as far as these White Russians (anti-Bolsheviks) were concerned. After an overnight stay on Angel Island, the students quickly passed the medical and immigration inspections and were formally admitted to the country.

Their experiences at the immigration station contrasted greatly with that of the Korean refugee students and other Asian immigrants who were given thorough physical examinations, interrogated for hours, and detained for weeks until a final decision was made. Admittedly, the Russian students came with proper visas, sufficient money, and the sponsorship of the YMCA, but more important, they were (white) Europeans and thus subjected to a different set of immigration laws and policies. The same could also be said of the other 8,000 Russians and Jews who passed through Angel Island between 1910 and 1940.[2] The most diverse of all the immigrant groups at the immigration station, they included Jews, Baptists, Molokans, and Mennonites who were fleeing religious persecution and military service; farmers, laborers, and tradesmen seeking better economic opportunities; soldiers, aristocrats, professionals, and intellectuals escaping political persecution under the new Soviet regime; and Jewish refugees seeking a safe haven from Nazism. For them, class, nationality, and political convictions, but not race, were the main criteria for exclusion.

Although immigrants from Russia were not subjected to the same race-based immigration restrictions as Asians, they could be rejected under the general immigration laws for being physically or mentally unfit, persons likely to become a public charge (LPC), contract laborers, immoral, illiterate, or political radicals. The most common cause for their exclusion was the LPC clause because many of them arrived as refugees with little or no money. Hundreds were detained for weeks at the immigration station while they appealed exclusion decisions. But with so many ethnic and religious organizations willing to assist them, their appeals seldom failed. Many of the new arrivals were scrutinized for their political views, but few were actually deported. Those coming in the early 1920s, after Congress passed the quota laws, found their nationality to be a liability. They experienced the longest detentions of all. But based on available immigration records, the average stay for the Russians and Jews on Angel Island was two to three days, and less than 2 percent were deported. This compares favorably to all the other nationalities with the exception of the Japanese.[3] Overall, the Russian and Jewish experiences on Angel Island were very similar if not better than those of their counterparts on Ellis Island, where their rejection rate was almost twice as high. For the overwhelming majority who were coming to escape religious or political persecution, Angel Island was truly a gateway to the promised land of freedom and opportunity. But for those few who were turned away or detained for weeks while awaiting decisions on their appeals, Angel Island was "a vale of tears."[4]

Fleeing Religious and Political Persecution

When Tsar Alexander III ascended the throne in 1881, the Russian Empire stretched across eleven time zones from the Baltic Sea to the Pacific Ocean. It was the largest country in the world and home to 150 million people of diverse ethnic backgrounds, including Ukrainians, Belorussians, Lithuanians, Poles, Jews, and Germans. It was also a developing country comprised of poor peasants and a growing population of underpaid industrial workers. Little emigration had taken place under the liberal reign of the tsar's father Alexander II. Peasants seeking land and better economic opportunities found them by migrating to Siberia. With the new reign, however, came new policies that discriminated against non-Orthodox and non-Russian peoples, spurring the exodus of millions of citizens over the next fifty years. While most left for reasons of religious and political persecution, some also emigrated to escape military service and improve their economic circumstances.[5]

Hardest hit were the Jewish people who had been confined to living in the Pale of Settlement (western border region of Russia) and subjected to anti-Semitic laws since the late eighteenth century. Alexander III rigorously added even more restrictions that reduced the Jews to poverty. Forced to live within the Pale's overcrowded cities, they were heavily taxed and prohibited from leasing land, engaging in certain trades, and receiving higher education. Worst of all were the pogroms in which Jewish homes and villages were sacked and burned, and thousands of Jews were massacred by Russian soldiers and peasants. Between 1880 and 1914, an estimated 3.2 million people left Russia for the United States, arriving primarily on the East Coast. Nearly half (1.6 million) were Jews. The majority settled in New York City, Boston, and Philadelphia, where they found work in the garment industry and mercantile trades, and established strong communities. Many would later help family and relatives in Russia immigrate to America, especially during the war years.[6]

Russian immigration through the West Coast was smaller and began later than on the East Coast. Russian fur traders and missionaries had first come to Alaska and the West Coast as part of the Russian Empire's eastward expansion in the eighteenth century, but the first large migration of Russians to California did not occur until 1904–12. That is when 5,000 Molokans came to settle in Los Angeles. Religious sectarians and pacifists, the Molokans had endured exile to the Transcaucasian region before embarking on a clandestine journey to America after the tsar had banned all emigration except for Poles and Jews. Most entered at the ports of New York, Montreal, and Galveston, but at least 300 came via Panama and thus ended up at the port of San Francisco. In 1905, twenty-seven Molokans became the first Russian immigrants to spend any time on Angel Island after they were found to be infected with trachoma and had to stay at the island's quarantine station for medical treatment.[7]

Other Russians traveled directly across the Pacific from Siberia, which became an important stepping stone to the United States in the early twentieth century. By 1910, close to half a million Russians were living in the vast lands of Siberia, including peasants, political exiles, religious dissenters, and former soldiers. They had been brought east by the massive 6,000-mile Trans-Siberian Railway which ran from Moscow to Vladivostok and connected the western part of the country to Siberia and the Russian Far East. Many had come from Ukraine and Central Russia, lured by the promise of free land by the tsar or the prospect of jobs on the railroad and in the mines. The building of the Russian-sponsored

Chinese Eastern Railway across Manchuria and a booming economy from the Russo-Japanese War also drew many Russians to Harbin and the surrounding area for jobs. However, once the war ended and the railroad was completed, many became unemployed.[8] Some 2,000 Russian workers, answering the call of labor recruiters, immigrated to Hawaii between 1909 and 1912. Among them were Anton and Evdokia Samborisky.

Evdokia had been raised as a Baptist in the town of Odessa. Repeated attacks by Cossacks on her family for refusing to follow the Russian Orthodox Church forced them to move to Omsk, Siberia, where her father found work as a railroad mechanic and where they could worship in peace. But in 1905, Evdokia's father got in trouble for plotting against the government. The family was forced to move again, this time 150 miles away to the village of Khristianovka, where families were being offered fifteen acres of land for every son they had as part of a state-sanctioned settlement policy—never mind that it was 40 degrees below zero for nine months of the year and that the village was sparsely populated. It was there that Evdokia met and married Anton Samborisky, a handsome Pole who had just retired from the Russian Navy, and gave birth to their daughter Evgenia. That same year Evdokia remembered finding on the kitchen table a "wondrous" letter postmarked from America, a place that her mother had always described as "heaven where it never snows and everyone has money." To them, America sounded like the Promised Land. Wanting to leave Siberia for greener pastures, Anton struck a deal with a labor recruiter to go work on the sugar plantations in Hawaii. The problem was how to leave Russia when the tsar's ban on emigration was still in place.[9]

Three days later, the couple stole away with six other Russian families on the Trans-Siberian Railway for Vladivostok and made their way to Harbin. From there the families rode in mule-drawn wagons for nine days, eating stale bread and eggs they bought along the road. A premature baby born during the trip died. Everyone was told to burn their identification papers before crossing the Amur River to Dairen. For over a week they hid in a chicken house before being smuggled aboard a ship bound for Kobe. The crossing was rough and Evdokia recalled being given red onions to deal with her seasickness. After stopping in Kobe for three days, they boarded the *Siberia Maru* for Hawaii. In exchange for their passage, Anton worked for three months harvesting sugar cane for low wages before moving to Hilo, where he found work as a house painter. In 1916, the family finally made it to San Francisco and the Promised Land.

With the advent of World War I, the Russian Empire began to slide into political, economic, and military chaos. Millions of people were caught up in the bloodshed and devastation of a war that the Russian Army was too ill equipped to win. In 1915 alone, two million Russians were killed, wounded, or captured. By 1917, there were six million starving refugees on the move throughout the country.[10] As travel across the Atlantic diminished drastically, many who wanted to leave war-torn Russia took the eastern route via Siberia and Manchuria to Japan, then across the Pacific to the West Coast. While Ellis Island processed fewer European immigrants at this time, the arrivals at Angel Island increased significantly. Among them were Jews fleeing the fighting at the eastern front or evading conscription altogether. Solomon Levin, who arrived in San Francisco in May 1916, wept as he told a newspaper reporter the following story about his experiences in the trenches outside Warsaw that had brought him to America.

> I was not afraid of the war. I was eager to go because I thought with oth-
> ers of my race that it would mean our emancipation. We were all eager
> to fight and went into the trenches singing. And then the little spites of
> the Russians made themselves felt in many ways. We, the Jews, were
> their servants and we had no choice but to do as they told us. When one
> is killed in the trenches the officers do not question if the bullet comes
> from a German rifle or from a gun held by a comrade. Even this we
> could bear for the prospect of freedom from future torture. But when
> they made our regiment, the one with the greatest number of Jews, the
> one made up of residents of the Pale of Settlement, leave the shelter of
> the trenches and enter the open field to deflect the fire of the Germans
> and Austrians, to be killed without a chance to escape, I ran away.[11]

Somehow, Levin escaped death on the battlefield and found himself in a Hong Kong hospital when he regained consciousness. With the help of relatives in Denver, Colorado, he was able to purchase passage on a ship bound for San Francisco.

War weariness and a failing economy marked by unemployment, rising prices, and food shortages led discontented workers, peasants, and soldiers to force the collapse of the tsarist autocracy in March of 1917. This was followed by a second revolution in November led by the Bolsheviks, which succeeded in overthrowing the Provisional Government in Petrograd. Soon after, a civil war broke out between the White Army and the Red Army that lasted until 1921. The Bolsheviks were victorious and in late 1922, they established the Soviet Union. By then, over 2 million people had fled Russia for neighboring European countries and China, with approximately 30,000 settling in the United States. Many Russian refugees who came through Angel Island in the 1920s were escaping the Bolshevik reign of terror against the old order, including the clergy, landowners, military officers, government officials, and the intelligentsia who represented "bourgeois" values in general. Traveling through Siberia, they encountered civil war and atrocities committed by both Red and White armies. Typhus and looting added to the danger; hunger, cold, and travel by cattle cars on unreliable trains compounded their misery.[12] Among them was Nadia Shapiro, who had come with the group of students in 1922.

Nadia Shapiro at the time of her immigration to the United States in 1922. (Courtesy of Hoover Institution Archives, Stanford University.)

Born in a small town near Kiev, Ukraine, Nadia was only eight months old when her family moved to Irkutsk, Siberia. There her father practiced law and Nadia received her formal education. When the civil war reached Siberia in 1918, her family was living in Blagoveschensk while Nadia was attending a women's college in Moscow. Responding to a frantic message from home, she set out with some classmates on a thirteen-day journey by cattle car through Russia. Nadia arrived home safely, only to witness Bolshevik troops storm the city and defeat the town militia and local Cossacks. As she described the ordeal, 3,000 people were butchered in the streets before nightfall, 30,000 escaped into the hills, and 8,000, including her family, fled the country. Dodging the Red Army's fire of rifles and machine guns, they crossed the frozen Amur River by sled and on foot into Manchuria.[13]

Her family resettled in Harbin, a city teeming with Russian refugees all vying for scarce work, food, and shelter. Nadia's father was fortunate to secure the position of city attorney and she found work as a journalist for a Russian daily newspaper. But in 1922, seeing no future for herself as a writer in Harbin and unwilling to return to her country while it was under Bolshevik control, Nadia decided to go to America with the help of the YMCA. "I had high hopes, two hundred dollars and a fondness for the Stars and Stripes that had always spelled security in turbulent lands," she wrote.[14]

Mennonite farmers in Siberia, who found the Soviet policies of land reform and attacks against their religious beliefs and way of life unbearable, also fled to America at this time. Nick Friesen was sixteen years old when his family of six arrived in San Francisco from Siberia by way of Harbin and Kobe in 1929. They were Dutch Mennonites, who for 400 years had been on the move, seeking religious freedom, military exemption, and good farmland. As he tells it, his people first migrated from Prussia to Ukraine to farm at the invitation of Catherine the Great in 1789. "She gave them land and many privileges. They would not have to pay taxes, learn Russian, or serve in the army, and they could run their own schools and churches." The Mennonites were good farmers, hardworking and thrifty, and they became quite prosperous. But when Mennonites came under attack during the 1905 revolution, several thousand families, including the Friesens, decided to move to the southwest region of Siberia to farm. Nick's father John Friesen bought 250 acres of pastureland in the Omsk area and within three years became a successful wheat farmer. By 1919, Friesen's estate was worth 60,000 rubles of gold. But all was lost

Nick Friesen on board the *Tenyo Maru* that brought him from Kobe to San Francisco in 1929. (Courtesy of Nick Friesen.)

when the Soviet regime came to power and instituted forced collectives and tax policies that targeted wealthy farmers like Friesen. Compounding their problems were repeated raids by the Red Army and bandits that cleaned them out of their grain, livestock, equipment, and food. "We had to leave to save our lives," said Nick.[15]

Unable to secure passports from the Soviet government in Moscow to leave the country, the Friesens stole across the frozen Amur River in the middle of winter in four sleds, under constant fear of being discovered and machine gunned by the Soviet border patrol. Then followed a 500-mile bus ride through the Manchurian mountains with an eye open for bandits. By bribing the Chinese authorities, the family finally made it to Harbin, where they waited eight months for visas to the United States. As Nick described their time in Harbin: "Sparse meals, hard beds on the floor, battles with insects, long hours of work, waiting, waiting, waiting, and praying." Thanks to the help of the Mennonite Central Committee in America, special arrangements were made through Secretary of Labor James Davis to permit small groups of Russian Mennonites into the country as skilled farmers.

To get to Kobe, Nick remembers taking a train from Harbin to Pusan, Korea, then a boat to Shenasaki, Japan, and from there a train to Kobe. The voyage across the ocean took eighteen days, with brief stops in Yokohama and Honolulu. "We were traveling the cheapest we could, way down in the bottom," he said. "But I never slept down in the hold. I slept on deck." Being young and adventurous, he enjoyed socializing with the other passengers. He distinctly remembers one African American couple who were professional roller skaters returning from a tour in Japan. They befriended him and taught him to count from 1 to 100 in English. What Nick disliked the most about the trip was the food that they were served in steerage—lots of cooked eggs and fish, but he always remembered the excitement of seeing San Francisco for the first time as their ship pulled into the Golden Gate. All he could say was, "Ah, freedom at last."

Passing the Medical Exam

Before any of the passengers were allowed off the ship to start their new lives in America, they had to pass the immigrant inspection to prove they were physically fit and legally admissible. Third-class and steerage passengers, which accounted for most of the Russian and Jewish refugees, were ferried to Angel Island for the medical and immigrant inspections. Even someone as well known as Alexandra Tolstoy, the daughter of writer Leo Tolstoy, was forced to comply with the regulations. She had escaped political persecution in the USSR by going to Japan and from there had found a way to come to America. Out of economic necessity, she had traveled in third class with her secretary Olga Kristyanovich and Olga's sixteen-year-old daughter Maria. Tolstoy's initial reaction was, "We were indignant. Why such unfairness? Why are they sending us to that island when they let the first- and second-class passengers go directly ashore?" When told that everyone coming from Japan by third class had to be inspected for parasitic diseases, she immediately detected the class bias but not the race bias behind the policy when she asked, "But why would worms not dare to make the acquaintance of rich people, but instead prefer to live with third-class passengers?"[16]

Nadia Shapiro and her fellow students all breezed through the inspections in a day. According to her account of the medical exam, they were given more deference and leniency by the medical staff than the Asian applicants. While waiting to be examined, the students noticed that whereas the doctor had expertly everted one Japanese immigrant's eyelid to check for trachoma, used a stethoscope to listen to the breathing of another, and pulled some aside for further examination, when it came to their turn and the doctor was told they were White Russians, "he lost some of his brusqueness." He directed his assistant to take their pulses "while he slowly passed in front of them, not touching anyone but peering into their eyes for possible symptoms of trachoma. 'Okay,' he said to the powers following him. 'They're all right.' And he was gone."[17] The cursory exam was more like the "six-second line inspection" given to new arrivals at Ellis Island. So brief was the physical exam for Nick Friesen that he could not even recall any details, although H. P. Isaak, a Mennonite from Harbin who came six months after Friesen, wrote in his memoirs, "We had to disrobe, with the exception of our shorts. Then we were inspected, tapped, and listened to by two men, who, we presumed, were doctors."[18] It is no wonder that few Russians or Jews ever complained about the medical exam as the Chinese did.

Shapiro and Isaak made no mention of a stool examination because by then, it was only required of passengers who had lived in an Asian country for a considerable period of time. Alexandra Tolstoy, Olga Kristyanovich, and daughter Maria were not so fortunate. According to Tolstoy's memoirs, when a nurse brought in three chamber pots, Maria squealed at her mother, "Mama, but I don't need it.... What are they going to do, hold us here the whole day? My stomach is never going to work."[19] Although they all eventually passed the stool test, Tolstoy failed the vision test and had to later convince the Board of Special Inquiry (BSI) that her poor eyesight had never prevented her from making a living as a writer and lecturer.

Unlike Asian immigrants, very few Russians were diagnosed with contagious diseases such as trachoma, hookworm, or tuberculosis, which usually meant deportation without appeal. Some were barred for medical conditions that might impair their ability to earn a living, such as a hernia, heart disease, senility, varicose veins, and defective vision. But in almost all cases, applicants found ways to successfully appeal their exclusions. Of all the immigrant groups on Angel Island, they had the best resources of support, including the Russian consulate, churches, ethnic organizations, and immigrant aid societies. In 1918, when Victoria Bogush arrived from Poland with her five children to join her husband, a farmer in New Hampshire, she was rejected for trachoma. Because her children were considered her dependents, they were all subsequently excluded as LPC cases. No appeal was possible for trachoma, but Bogush was allowed to appeal the LPC charges. Two days later, the Russian consulate wrote a letter inquiring about her case and stating that the Polish Society of San Francisco would be willing to take care of the family should they be allowed to land. She was not released. Ten days later, a letter came from the law firm, Cobleigh and Theriault, ascertaining that their client Stefan Bogues (Bogush's husband) was "owner of considerable property and a responsible citizen in every way." The attorney made a point of saying, "This is rather an extreme case as this poor woman has struggled from the Western part of Russia, clear across Siberia, through Japan, and is now in California with her five children. It is a case which calls for unusual attention." This letter must have helped. A week later, Victoria Bogush was "medically released" and the entire family was admitted into the country.[20]

In another inadmissible case involving a contagious disease, Nikolai Simonovich, an engineer from Harbin, was excluded for having advanced pulmonary tuberculosis when he arrived in December 1930. His wife Tatiana, considered his dependent, was excluded as LPC, even though she was sure she could find work in America. After all, she had previously worked as a clothing designer. But the assumption then was that women would become public liabilities without the support of their men. Nikolai could not appeal the board's decision to exclude him, but the couple retained a lawyer to appeal Tatiana's exclusion. Soon after, a telegram of support for their admission arrived from the Ukrainian Russian Civic Center in Los Angeles, simply stating that Nicholas Simonovich had been "commander of Kolchak White Army during World War," that "he will be a loyal and valuable immigrant," and that "his return to China will mean death." It would take another two months of deliberation, but in the end, the couple was granted temporary admission for six months under bond. After a number of extensions, they were admitted for permanent residence in 1933.[21]

For those who were denied entry because of physical defects that put them at risk of becoming public charges, their class status or access to economic assistance were crucial factors in their appeals. In many cases, they were admitted if they could post a $500 public charge bond. Elia Elterman, a fifty-four-year-old widower traveling with two teenage children, was initially excluded because, in the words of Inspector Robert Sherrard, "he is undersized, emaciated, frail looking, quite hard of hearing and badly deformed [hunchback]...and has the appearance of belonging to the poorer of the Russian laboring classes." But he had four older sons in Boston quite capable of supporting him. With the help of the Hebrew Immigrant Aid Society (HIAS), the sons posted a $1,000 bond and their father and two siblings were finally released after being detained on Angel Island for two months. David Janzen, one of the Mennonites from Harbin, was excluded for having a hernia, although he testified that it never stopped him from doing hard labor as a farmer in Russia. He spent close to a month locked up on Angel Island while waiting for a decision on his appeal. The secretary of labor, noting that his physical defect could be remedied by an operation, recommended admission upon the filing of a $500 bond. Janzen had arrived penniless after exhausting all his funds in his long journey from Russia. Fortunately, he had the backing of the local Mennonite Church, whose members were willing to post a bond on his behalf. Haim Maber, a Russian war veteran who was also excluded for a physical defect—both of his legs had been amputated due to war injuries—was not so fortunate. He was in transit to Argentina and told the board that he had a sister and a job in a shoe factory waiting for him there. But he had insufficient funds to reach his final destination and evidently no local relative or organization to come to his aid. Maber was deported after being detained on Angel Island for one month.[22]

Excluded for Being LPC

The lack of any legal definition as to who might be considered "likely to become a public charge" resulted in inspectors having great latitude to exclude "undesirable aliens" for a variety of economic and social reasons. In a 1910 directive to all port commissioners, Commissioner-General of Immigration Daniel Keefe instructed them to require every alien to prove "clearly and beyond a doubt" that he would not become a burden to society because of his occupation, physical condition, or lack of funds. In the case of a woman or minor child, they needed to have a sponsor who was willing and able to support them. Keefe was known to favor immigration restrictions. He advocated for the strict interpretation of all immigration laws in order to exclude South Asian immigrants. He also sought to restrict Jews who were coming to the United States in great numbers.[23]

Commissioner of Immigration William Williams at Ellis Island evidently shared the low opinion of the "new immigrants" held by Keefe and other nativists. Many of the newer Southern and Eastern European immigrants, he wrote in his 1911 annual report, were from "backward races," had "very low standards of living, possess filthy habits, and are of an ignorance which passes belief."[24] In an effort to keep out these "low grade immigrants," Williams began to require all newcomers to have at least $25 plus a ticket to their final destination. Caught off guard, many Jewish immigrants were excluded and deported as a result. HIAS successfully challenged the $25 rule in court by arguing that it was an extra-legal means of exclusion. Taking the cue from Keefe's directive, Williams then began to use "poor physique" as a reason to reject Jewish applicants. Almost immediately, their exclusion rates shot up, with more than two-thirds of the exclusions attributed to Williams's strict enforcement of the LPC law."[25]

Judging by their remarks and dealings with refugees from Russia, immigrant inspectors at Angel Island evidently did not share the views of Williams or the nativist movement. Nor was there any evidence of anti-Semitism in their treatment of Jews. Instead, they often demonstrated empathy that facilitated the admission of immigrants from Russia. This was especially true of individuals who were fleeing religious persecution. Although there was no refugee policy in place at the time, Angel Island immigrant inspectors abided by President Woodrow Wilson's intentions to keep the United States open as a political asylum for residents of European countries at war.[26] During hearings, inspectors would ask leading questions such as, "Did you leave Russia because of religious persecution? Do you feel you would be persecuted in any manner if you returned to Russia?" These kinds of questions were rarely asked of Korean or Mexican refugees who were also fleeing war conditions or political persecution at home. On the contrary, immigration officials repeatedly questioned the credibility of Korean refugee students and their witnesses who promised them jobs, but tended to take the word of their Russian counterparts at face value. Written comments such as, "The applicant testified in a very frank and ready manner and the Board believes his statements are true," appeared more often in the Russian case files than in the Asian ones.

If the experiences of Russian immigrants on Angel Island were different from those of their compatriots arriving on Ellis Island, they were also different from what Asian immigrants encountered at the Angel Island immigration station. For example, Angel Island immigration officials found no reason to distrust the (white) Russian, German, and Yiddish interpreters as they did the Chinese interpreters. In fact, it was not unusual for the board to call upon white witnesses to help translate when an official interpreter was unavailable. Certain inspectors were tough in raising objections to their admittance on the grounds that the local job market was dismal, but never that the Russian or Jewish person's ethnic background would make it difficult for him to find work, as they sometimes reasoned in the cases of South Asian and African persons. As long as someone credible stepped forward with a job offer, that was often good enough for the board to dismiss the LPC charges.

The earliest arrivals from Russia, mainly young men looking for work, did not even have to wait for a job offer before being admitted. Take, for example, a group of eleven men who, upon arrival in May 1913, were all deemed LPC and detained on Angel Island for further questioning. They were each asked a total of twenty questions about their occupations, finances, political convictions, and reasons for coming to the United States. Most were farmers or laborers originally from the Caucasus area of the Russian Empire. Six had resided in Siberia for a few years prior to leaving for America. All had Russian passports and at least $50. When asked why he was coming to America at this time, thirty-three-year-old Nikolai Dudieff, who had left his wife and son in Russia, replied, "I had bad crops in Russia for the last two years, and I heard that I could get here more wages and have a better life, so I came here." Unlike the Asian LPC cases, these applicants were not asked to produce witnesses testifying to their good character or likelihood of finding work. They were not required to submit written documentation of their finances either. Satisfied by the testimony of the applicants alone, the board unanimously admitted all Russian immigrants within a day of their arrival.[27] Army deserters were treated just as leniently. Aleksei Chakashoff, a shoemaker coming to join a cousin in San Francisco, was detained on Angel Island for three days as an LPC case. He was only asked nine questions at his hearing. The BSI dwelled on why he had deserted, to which he replied, "It is very hard work and the food and clothing is very poor and they don't pay anything." No one had to testify on his behalf, not even the cousin who supposedly sent him the passage money to come from Yokohama.[28]

The LPC clause was more stringently enforced against women and children who came without their husbands and fathers. When a party of eight Russian Baptists from Harbin, consisting of machinist Andry Hudoshenekoff and his wife Maria; widow Daria Kalandrina and her eight-year-old son; Alexandra Okulova and her two young children; and Anesia Chegerova, a twenty-three-year-old student, arrived in May 1913, they had a hard time convincing the inspectors that they would not become public charges. All said they had received letters from a friend named Mr. Derek, encouraging them to come to America, "a good country where they could make a good living." Nothing was said about religious persecution as a factor until Evdocem Derek himself came to Angel Island to testify. A twenty-six-year-old shoemaker from Russia, he had been in

A group of Russian men
pose in the recreational
yard outside their
barracks, c.1915. The
hospital building is
behind them. (Courtesy
of California State Parks,
2010.)

the United States for only four months but said he had a good job working as a drill machinist at Union Iron Works, making $2.25 a day. When
asked why he had written friends in Harbin to come to America, he said,
"I come here to this country—free country; I belong to the Baptists, and
all the time we make service, free; in my country over there all the time
closed up the churches; make good living too, in America. I find it good
and send letter to come to America." He and N. E. Varonaeff, the pastor of
the Russian Baptist Church, who testified on the same day, told the board
that they could provide jobs and housing for the party.[29]

The BSI decided to admit the Hudoshenekoffs but exclude the rest of the
group on grounds that they had little money, no relatives in the country,
could not speak English, and would have difficulty finding employment
in San Francisco. Moreover, Commissioner Samuel Backus argued, "this
office feels exceedingly reluctant in encouraging the migration of single
women or women with children and without husbands, who have no
close relatives in this country to assist them." The party appealed and with
the support of the American Baptist community, retained the law firm of
McGowan and Worley to represent them. Letters came from the YMCA
and the First Baptist Church of San Francisco, offering to furnish bonds
that they would not become public charges. But what convinced the board
members to change their minds was the testimony of Emelian Noshkin,
who owned 5,000 acres of land in Delmar, Sonoma County. He had arrived
in the United States a year earlier with his wife and eleven children. He told
Inspector Will Swasey that he bought the land in Delmar for $250,000 to
establish a colony for Russian Baptists. The farm had fifty-six people, including thirteen women and sixteen children, all working or attending school.
Noshkin offered to take the new arrivals to the ranch and find employment
for them. Convinced that the immigrants would be well taken care of by
their own people, the board decided to admit them under bond.[30]

Jewish Immigration and Hebrew Aid Societies

Large numbers of Russian, Polish, and Lithuanian Jews began arriving at Angel Island in 1915. They were mainly men who had left their homes to escape the turmoil of war and military duty. For most of them, it had been a long, arduous, and expensive journey as they made their way across Siberia to Harbin or Shanghai, and from there to Japan to board a ship to Seattle or San Francisco. Simon Yankell Sinelnikoff, a farmer who had left his wife and two young children in Cherikoff to come to America, told Inspector James Lawler that he started out with 600 rubles but spent it all on a false passport, bribing border guards, and paying a guide to help him cross the Russian border to Harbin. By the time he arrived in America, he was penniless.[31] Others in a similar predicament explained that they had lost time and run out of money because of unexpected delays in China or Japan. They easily fell into the LPC category upon arrival and were detained on Angel Island until they could prove otherwise. For many of them, having the staunch support of the Hebrew aid societies made a significant difference in the outcome of their cases.

When fifteen Russians, all single men between the ages of seventeen and thirty, arrived in San Francisco in April 1915, ten of them (one Russian and eight Jews) were deemed LPC and taken to Angel Island for questioning. It helped that they all showed strong physiques, had good job skills (house painter, cap maker, engineer, machinist, farmer), and were well dressed. But more important, Josef Brachmann of the Hebrew Relief and Jewish Shelter, came to Angel Island to testify on their behalf. He apparently did not know any of them personally but was willing to provide them with housing and help them find work. He told Inspector Weiss that the Jewish Shelter had a membership of 1,500 and the support of many wealthy Jewish people in San Francisco. "We always take steps to see that Jewish boys obtain work and do not become beggars." The board evidently trusted him, as all the men were released in his care within a day of their arrival.[32]

Other Russian Jews who came later that year had a rougher time as the local unemployment rate rose and the welcome mat wore thin. They were generally asked more questions about their backgrounds and financial status and detained on Angel Island for longer periods of time than Russian gentiles—nineteen days on average compared to the latter group's ten days. Their longer stay was partly due to the backlog of cases and the increased numbers of appeals as more Jews were excluded. The average detention time for Jewish applicants on appeal was six weeks.[33] As they did in the cases of South Asian and Mexican immigrants, immigrant inspectors often cited the local unemployment situation as a reason to reject applicants. Whereas before they would have landed a Jewish LPC case if someone came along with a job offer, the boards now dismissed such offers on the grounds that they were not made in good faith but on the basis of racial bonds. Moreover, as Commissioner of Immigration Samuel Backus argued in one case, "There are great numbers of persons unemployed who are doubtless fully qualified to fill the position offered, and to whom the opportunity should, in all justice, be first extended."[34]

Fortunately for the Jewish immigrants who were having trouble getting landed, they had the rich resources of the Hebrew Immigrant Aid Society at their disposal. Founded in 1885 to facilitate the lawful entry of Jewish immigrants into the United States at Ellis Island, HIAS opened a Pacific Coast Branch in San Francisco in May 1915 to accommodate the increased traffic of Jews coming across the Pacific to America. Similar to the important roles played by the Japanese Association of America and Korean National Association at Angel Island, HIAS extended a variety of services to the detainees. Once when seventeen Jews refused to eat the non-kosher food served them in the dining hall during Passover Week, the organization provided them with matzo and proper food to eat in their detention quarters.[35] The organization went to great effort to help contact relatives through the Yiddish press and to find sponsors willing to provide Jewish immigrants with jobs or post bonds on their behalf. Most important, HIAS attorneys had an excellent track record of filing and winning legal appeals on exclusion cases. Of the 321 Russian Jews who arrived in San Francisco between April and December of 1915, twenty-seven appeals were filed and sustained. Of the 364 arrivals in 1916, twenty-one were assisted with appeals and all were landed except for one.[36] This success rate can be attributed to the groundwork laid by the organization's lawyers, especially Simon Wolff. Not only was he well connected in Washington, but he was also very effective in filing legal briefs. HIAS credited him with preventing the deportation of over 100,000 Jewish immigrants at all ports of entry during his many years of service.[37]

Take, for example, the case of Lebe Schneeveis, who arrived in San Francisco from Yokohama in September 1915 without a cent to his name. He told the BSI at his hearing that he was born in Petrograd, was twenty-nine years old, unmarried, and a carpenter by trade. When asked why he was coming to the United States at this time, he replied, "I served seven months in the Russian army, and after that in view of the way the Jews have been treated in Russia, I decided to not stay with the army any longer, and made my escape [via] Siberia." Although the board noted that Schneeveis appeared healthy and of good physique, he had no money, no friends or relatives in America to assist him, and there was no demand for his trade in the vicinity. The BSI voted unanimously to exclude him as an LPC case. William Traube, HIAS representative on Angel Island, quickly got Louis Brown, who owned a wood carving business in San Francisco, to offer Schneeveis a job as a wood polisher. The board, however, did not believe the offer was "made in good faith" and decided to stand by their earlier decision to exclude him. Their decision was supported by Commissioner Backus, who, in his summary report to the Washington bureau, wrote, "While this office is fully cognizant of the hardships and possible danger to life incident to his deportation, it feels that proper consideration of the present number of unemployed available in this vicinity would seem to warrant the disregard of [job] offers of this character [from a stranger and at the solicitation of HIAS]."[38]

In HIAS's appeal to the secretary of labor on behalf of Schneeveis, the attorney made the usual argument that the appellant was a man of good physique and intelligence who would make a "splendid citizen," that he was a good carpenter capable of making an honest living, and that the exclusion order was unwarranted since businessman Louis Brown and HIAS were willing to guarantee the appellant. The secretary of labor sustained the appeal, possibly because the U.S. Supreme Court had just ruled in *Gegiow v. Uhl* that the Bureau of Immigration could not base admission on labor market conditions that had no relation to an alien's personal qualifications.[39] Schneeveis was landed under bond after being detained on Angel Island for six weeks. The organization's work did not end there. Six months later, when asked by the immigration service to locate Lebe Schneeveis, Traube had to admit that the alien had disappeared. The organization forfeited the $500 bond money. This case was an exceptional one; most other times, HIAS was able to show that their charges were gainfully employed and thereby have the bonds canceled.

Excluded for Illiteracy

Jewish women and children who were fleeing the war in Russia began arriving in 1917–18 to join family members mainly on the East Coast. With transatlantic travel greatly reduced because of the war, they had to travel east across Russia to Harbin and then to Yokohama. Many ran out of funds before reaching their destination because of unforeseen delays and the depreciation of the ruble after Tsar Nicholas II abdicated in March 1917. According to HIAS reports, thousands of Jewish women and children were stranded in Vladivostok, Harbin, and Yokohama without food or shelter. "Conditions appalling, sickness, want, heavy demands" was how Samuel Mason, manager and director of HIAS, described the situation. The organization immediately sent funds and staff to provide Jewish refugees with housing, food, clothing, and medical care. HIAS also helped many of the refugees contact relatives in America to make arrangements to complete their journey to America.[40]

Their arrival in America coincided with the passage of the Immigration Act of 1917, legislation intended to curb the new immigration from Europe and exclude South Asians. The literacy clause in the new law required all immigrants sixteen and older to pass a literacy test. Those fleeing religious persecution were exempt from the test, as were immediate family members of alien residents in the United States. Nevertheless, the literacy requirement made it much harder for Jewish women like Brucha Punchik and Zlota Schneider to enter the country.

Brucha Punchik, who came with her sister, Mrs. Machla Reiss, in December 1917, was initially excluded for failing the literacy test, but she was later also diagnosed with hearing and mental deficiencies. As Punchik explained to the board, she was normal and could read and write until her "accident" three years earlier. "The Jews of my native village were being driven out by the Cossacks," she said. "They were burning up the houses and I was thrown to the ground by an explosion and lost my senses." Her sister claimed that Punchik had attended Hebrew School for six months and was able to read and write in Yiddish prior to the accident. But when Inspector Swasey asked if it was on account of religious persecution or their safety that the Russian Cossacks had driven them out of their hometown, Mrs. Reiss replied, "We were robbed and driven out by the Cossacks with whips in order to keep us from falling into the hands of the Germans." Without realizing it, she had lost her sister's chance to be exempted from the literacy requirement on the basis of religious persecution. The board unanimously ordered Punchik deported as an illiterate.[41]

Harry Wolff, HIAS's attorney in San Francisco, immediately filed an appeal on her behalf. He argued that his client had been brutally driven out of her country by reason of her religious convictions as a Jew, and as a result, had been temporarily deprived of her ability to read fluently. In conclusion, he wrote, "it would be a gross injustice and act of inhumanity to order this applicant returned to Russia, inasmuch as it appears from the testimony that she was driven out under most strenuous circumstances." The appeal was sustained and Punchik was paroled for the duration of the war to the Hebrew Immigrant Aid Society. Two years later, according to a memo in her file, "her condition had improved steadily," and she held a job that paid $10 a week.

Twenty-three-year-old Zlota Schneider was caught in a worse situation when she arrived in October 1917. Not only was she illiterate but she also had no money. Claiming that she was single and had been self-supporting as a dressmaker since she was fourteen, Schneider explained that her uncle in America had sent her sufficient funds to join him in Philadelphia. But unexpected delays in Harbin for five weeks and in Yokohama for another six weeks had caused her to use up all her money. Fortunately, the Hebrew Immigrant Aid Society in Yokohama had been willing to provide her with free housing and to lend her passage money to come as far as San Francisco. "Were you disturbed at all in your home country on account of your race, being a Hebrew, or on account of your religion?" she was asked. "No, never molested in my home town by any authorities," she replied. Inspector Swasey tried to prompt her further, "Are you seeking admission to the United States to avoid any religious persecution in your native country?" But Schneider replied, "No, I am not seeking admission for that reason." Based on her testimony, the board ordered her deported as an illiterate, as an LPC case (she had no funds, no sponsor, and she had accepted charity in Yokohama), and as an assisted immigrant (her passage was paid for by HIAS).[42]

The Hebrew Immigrant Aid Society came to her defense and filed an appeal. This time, no mention was made of religious persecution since Schneider had made no such claim during her interrogation. Instead, attorney Harry Wolff submitted three affidavits of support from family members in Philadelphia, including Schneider's husband, Solomon Schmukler, a tailor who immigrated to the United States four years earlier. As the wife of an alien resident, Schneider should have been exempted from the literacy test. The case was reopened and Schneider was asked to explain why she had lied about her marital status. She explained that because her marriage had not been performed by a Russian priest or civil authority, the Russian government had refused to give her a marriage certificate. Without one, she was not able to get a passport to leave the country as a married woman, so she decided to claim she was a single woman. The BSI, however, was unforgiving. In view of the fact that she had made false statements before, they chose not to believe that she had a husband in the United States and affirmed their decision to reject her on the same grounds as before. The secretary of labor ultimately ruled in Schneider's favor, and she was admitted under bond for the duration of the war. By then, she had been detained on Angel Island for three months. It would take another two years before the Bureau of Immigration was convinced that she was indeed the wife of Solomon Schmuckler, at which time Acting Commissioner-General of Immigration Alfred Hampton canceled her bond and authorized her outright landing.

Excluded and Deported for Radicalism

As a series of labor strikes and bomb attacks broke out in the United States in 1916 and 1917, employer and patriotic groups were quick to blame foreign radicals for influencing American workers with Bolshevik ideas. Playing on American fears during the war, nativists were able to persuade Congress to tighten immigration restrictions against alien radicals. While the Immigration Act of 1903 specifically excluded and deported anarchists and any alien who advocated the overthrow by force of the U.S. government within three years after their entry, the Immigration Act of 1917 excluded any alien who belonged to a revolutionary organization. Further legislation in 1918 called for the deportation of aliens who *at any time* after admission were found advocating radical beliefs.

The Red Scare of 1919 that erupted after World War I ended was an attempt by the federal government to root out and deport foreign radicals already in the country. Coordinated by Commissioner-General of Immigration Anthony Caminetti and Attorney General A. Mitchell Palmer, federal agents and local police forces raided the offices of the Industrial Workers of the World (IWW), the Union of Russian Workers, the Communist Party, and other "subversive" organizations. Thousands of suspected radicals were arrested and prosecuted without regard for due process of law. The Bureau of Immigration ordered close to 3,000 aliens deported across the nation, but Louis F. Post, assistant secretary of labor, ruled that most of the warrants were illegal and in the end endorsed the deportation of only 556 radical aliens.[43]

San Francisco inspectors were just as guilty of prejudicial arrests and judgments. Even before the Red Scare, they had been involved in the surveillance of South Asian nationalists. During the year of the Palmer raids, Commissioner of Immigration Edward White issued thirty-nine warrants of arrest for aliens of the radical class. Five men were eventually deported, including Fredrick Harold Berger, a Russian immigrant who had been in the United States for less than five years. He was initially arrested for drunkenness in Fresno, California, but when the U.S. marshal found an IWW card on him, he was turned over to the immigration authorities. During his hearing, Berger admitted to being a Bolshevik sympathizer, a syndicalist since he was thirteen, and an IWW member. But when asked if he was an anarchist, he replied, "I do not believe in murdering or in other acts of violence but I believe in the principles of anarchy as an ideal principle, the brotherhood of all the world, no nations or governments." Berger was arrested under warrant by the immigration service and taken to Angel Island for a second hearing, at which time Inspector Swasey tried unsuccessfully to charge him with the more serious offense of advocating the overthrow by force of the U.S. government. Commissioner-General of Immigration Caminetti issued a warrant for his deportation in April 1918, but it took the Department of Labor twenty months of deliberation before Berger was finally deported to Russia for daring to advocate anarchy. By then, he had spent a year incarcerated on Angel Island, four months in the San Francisco county jail, and another six months on Ellis Island.[44]

A few months after the Bolsheviks stormed the Winter Palace in Petrograd in November of 1917, immigration officials at all U.S. ports of entry were instructed by the State Department to send them monthly lists of all new Russian arrivals.[45] From then on, all Russian immigrants were suspected of being Bolshevik agents and closely scrutinized by immigrant inspectors, even someone like music composer Sergei Prokofiev. He had left Russia for America at the start of the civil war to pursue new sights and new audiences for his music. As he wrote in his diary: "To go to America, of course! Here it is becoming sour—there, life is in full swing; here, slaughter and wildness—there, cultural life; here, pathetic concerts in Kislovodsk, there, New York and Chicago." It took him all of four months to travel across Siberia by train, to procure visas for Japan and the United States, and to book passage to Hawaii. By then, the ruble had lost half of its value and his funds were almost depleted. Then to his chagrin, he was not permitted to land when his ship arrived in San Francisco. Instead, he was sent to Angel Island with five Chinese and all those traveling from Russia—twenty passengers in total. He suspected that the United States might have gotten word that the Russian government was preparing to declare a defensive war against the Allies and were thus looking for spies among them.[46]

Prokofiev was confined in the hospital for two nights while he waited impatiently to be called for the interrogation. The door to his room, however, was not locked and he was allowed to stroll the grounds between the hospital and the immigration compound. When his turn came, "They asked me a number of questions, necessary and unnecessary things, but several of them were outright masterpieces," he wrote in his diary.

Q. Do you sympathize with the Allies in the war? A. I do.
Q. Do you sympathize with the Bolsheviks? A. No.
Q. Why? A. Because they took my money.
Q. Were you ever at their meetings? A. I was.
Q. Did they talk well? A. Yes, but not logically.
Q. Are you a member of a political party? A. No.
Q. Why? A. Because I consider that an artist should be outside of politics.
Q. Have you ever been in jail? A. Yes, in yours.

More than likely the immigrant inspectors took his sarcastic replies in stride. Shortly after the interrogation, Prokofiev was admitted into the country, thanks in no small part to the Russian consulate in San Francisco and the fact that his baggage of papers and music sheets had not turned up any incriminating evidence. He never forgot his vexing entry into the United States and his unpleasant "exile" to the island.

More than a decade after Prokofiev's troublesome encounter with immigration authorities at Angel Island, Alexandra Tolstoy had a similar experience. Although she was originally detained for having "defective vision, which might affect her ability to earn a living," the investigation quickly turned to her political views. "Why, if you are so opposed to Bolshevism, you lived freely in Soviet Russia for twelve years and the Bolsheviks never touched you?" she was asked. For two hours, Tolstoy explained how she had been arrested five times and how Lenin had helped her by issuing a decree to keep the Tolstoy institutions free of anti-religious propaganda. "If I were not here, I would be in prison in Russia,"

Alexandra Tolstoy writing in her study in Newton Square, Pennsylvania, 1933. In 1939, Alexandra Tolstoy co-founded the Tolstoy Foundation in America, which helped thousands of European refugees resettle in the United States. She became a U.S. citizen in 1941, lectured widely in defense of human rights, and never returned to Russia. (Courtesy of Bettmann/Corbis.)

she told them. "The Reds do not leave you alone. Your conscience just keeps pulling until you cannot go on any longer." When asked if she planned to become a U.S. citizen—a question that was never asked of Asian immigrants since they were ineligible—Tolstoy hesitated before replying she would in five years if the Bolsheviks were still in power. She was evidently quite persuasive, for Chairman Joseph Strand summarized her case as follows: "I am satisfied from her statements that she is anti-Bolshevik and that she would, if admitted, become a loyal citizen of this country. I therefore move her outright admission."[47]

Refugee Students, Bolsheviks, or Cheap Labor?

Thousands of college-age soldiers and students like Nadia Shapiro found themselves stranded in Harbin at the end of the civil war. Their education had been interrupted by eight years of war and the prospects of finding a good university or securing employment in the area appeared dim. Out of sympathy for the refugee students and concern for the future development of Russia, a group of local businessmen and expatriates formed the Harbin Committee Rendering Aid to Russian Students to help those who wanted to continue their education in the United States. Their hope was that the students, once trained in industry, agriculture, and the sciences, would return to help rebuild Russia. The United States was selected over other countries because of its proximity to Harbin and the understanding that the students would be permitted to work there while they attended college. The Harbin Committee, through its Students' Bureau, provided information about conditions in America, organized the students into groups, and arranged for their group visas and transportation. It also worked closely with the Harbin branch of the YMCA to ensure that the Russian students would be met and assisted by the local YMCA upon their arrival. In this way, the Harbin Committee was able to help 450 students immigrate to the United States from 1921 to 1923.[48]

When Nadia Shapiro's group arrived in San Francisco on August 29, 1922, newspaper reporters were there to greet them. But there was also Agent N. M. Hess, a Federal Bureau of Investigation (FBI) agent assigned to cover incoming passengers from Asia. He immediately took note of the group of Russian students who he suspected were political radicals disguised as students. He proceeded to investigate their backgrounds with Nadia serving as his interpreter. As Hess later reported to J. Edgar Hoover, then deputy head of the FBI, he observed that the students did not speak English and "were not of a particularly intelligent type," so he asked which universities they planned to attend. The students told him that they had been instructed to report to George Martin Day, foreign student secretary of the YMCA at the University of California, Berkeley, and that he would see that "they were admitted into the country."[49]

Agent Hess decided he had better interview George Day next, especially after he learned that Day had spent eight years in Russia attending college while working for the YMCA. From the interview, Hess learned that the American consulate in Harbin had been working closely with the YMCA in issuing group visas to the "so-called students." Day also told him that because the students came with limited funds and lacked English proficiency, 90 percent of them had to first work and learn English before they could enter college, and only 25 percent were enrolled in universities at the time. In essence, the so-called students were being landed on a "good faith" basis and there was no one keeping track of their whereabouts after they had been admitted into the country. According to Day's account of the interview, Hess asked, "How are we to know but that Lenin and Trotsky are sending a lot of Bolshevik propagandists over here under the guise of students, for this is a mighty easy way for them to get into this country." In defense of the Russian students, Day told Agent Hess that he was confident that they were anti-Bolsheviks and bona fide students. "Give me a year and I'll promise that the majority of these Russians will be in universities, colleges, or technical schools."[50] But his words fell on deaf ears.

Even before Agent Hess came on the scene, Immigrant Inspector Strand had already expressed his suspicions to Commissioner Edward White that the Russian students were really coming to work, not to study. But because they came with the proper documents, had the support of

As YMCA foreign students secretary at UC Berkeley from 1921 to 1923, George Martin Day (center) helped many Russian students prepare for college and adjust to life in America. (Courtesy of Hoover Institution Archives, Stanford University.)

the YMCA, and appeared "well nourished, fairly intelligent, and apparently respectable," he had no reason to reject them. When asked by Hess whether he thought any of the Russians in question were even potential students, Strand replied that they were being admitted on good faith only, that they had no relatives in the country or sources of income, and that "they were purely cheap labor entering the country under the guise of 'students' and might become public charges at any time." Unfortunately, he added, under the current immigration regulations, it was impossible to disbar or deport them unless it could be proven at a later date that they had indeed become public charges. In his report to Hoover, Hess joined Strand in recommending that all students desiring to come to the United States to study be required to apply for a visa as individuals based on his or her own merits. "The practice of visaing groups of passports for entry into this country permits the abuse of passport regulations and the entry of [dangerous] people who otherwise would not be admitted."[51]

Already disturbed by the large numbers of immigrants coming from Southern and Eastern Europe at a time when nativists were clamoring for more immigration restrictions, Commissioner-General of Immigration William Husband was now concerned with the possibility of alien radicals entering the country under the guise of students. He believed that another way to stop the Russian influx was by excluding the students as "aliens whose passage has been paid for by, or who have been assisted to come by, an association." The secretary of state got involved and directed the U.S. consul in Harbin to take steps "to discourage the migration of these aliens if it is found they are coming here contrary to the spirit of the Immigration Act." On March 8, 1923, Consul G. C. Hanson, who sympathized with the plight of the Russian students and who firmly believed that American trade interests would be advanced when the students returned to Russia, submitted his report. Although the committee gave financial assistance to some students, he wrote, "it does not appear that they were induced to undertake the journey to America." Hanson also assured the State Department that both the Harbin Committee and his office had been very careful about investigating each applicant's political views, character, and references before allowing them to proceed to the United States. Moreover, the U.S. consul announced, he would not be able to issue any more visas after March 1923 because the Russian quota for the fiscal year had been exhausted.[52] So ultimately, it was the Quota Act of 1921, which limited the total number of annual admissions and placed quotas on Southern and Eastern European immigration, that helped solve the problem of the Russian students.

Locked Out by the Quota Laws

When the *Shinyo Maru* arrived in San Francisco on July 15, 1923, with 128 Russians, including twenty-three students from Harbin, all were excluded because Russia's quota for July—5,363—had already been exhausted. Up to that point, Russian immigration had been slow because of the civil war and prolonged fighting in the Russian Far East, and the quota law had not posed a serious obstacle. But the arrival of 526 Russian refugees from the Philippines on July 2 had helped to deplete that month's quota. The refugees had fled Vladivostok eight months previously in twenty Russian naval vessels when the city fell to the Red Army. Eleven of the ships made it to the Philippines in early 1923. President Warren G. Harding welcomed the refugees to the United States under the terms of the quota law and they were transported from Manila on the *U.S.S. Merritt* with the help of the American Red Cross. Upon arrival at San Francisco, the passengers were taken to Fort McDowell on Angel Island, where they were housed and processed. Consequently, ninety-seven Russians from the *Shinyo Maru* were excluded and had to spend three months locked up on Angel Island waiting for the results of their appeals.[53]

In their first appeal, the students from Harbin protested their pending deportations and asked to be exempted from the 1921 quota act. "We are not adventurers that come to make money," they wrote. "Please don't mix us up with the common immigrants that have filled the immigration quota.... We ask you to consider us only as students [with the] exclusive aim to continue our education."[54] Commissioner John D. Nagle forwarded the letter along with the students' files to the Bureau of Immigration in Washington, but to no avail. The secretary of state had already ruled in May that the Russian students were to be regarded as immigrants migrating for permanent residence, since it was believed that many worked as laborers instead of attending college.

The students, along with some fifty other Russian detainees slated for deportation, next tried petitioning the federal court for writs of habeas corpus to question the legality of their detention. In refusing them admittance Judge John Patridge said, "It has been the experience of this court

A group of Russian students from Harbin waiting to be processed in the registry room at the Angel Island Immigration Station. The photograph is from the collection of Michael Hrenoff (fourth from the far right). (Courtesy of Maria Sakovich.)

that the melting pot does not always melt. Too many aliens are brought to the country who cannot always be infused into our life. The time when America was considered as a refuge of the oppressed from all the world has passed and, for that reason, Congress passed the law limiting immigration."[55] Out of desperation, fifteen Russian immigrants took Commissioner Nagle up on his offer to be deported to Yokohama and return in time to be admitted under the October quota.[56]

Meanwhile, the Russian students stayed "behind bars" on Angel Island, not knowing when they might be released. In an article in the *Russkii Golos*, a weekly newspaper published in Harbin, Vasily Troitsky described their "desperate situation" to friends back home. As the following excerpts show, however, the students enjoyed more privileges and were better treated than their Asian counterparts on the island.

We have before us a veil of grates that they put on the doors, windows and even in the small garden where we are permitted to go for a walk twice a week. The fence of that garden is surrounded by barbed wire, although during the entire existence of the immigration station nobody tried to escape from here. We Russians have three rooms for 50 people. In one, we sleep on beds, and in the other, we spend our spare time. The days pass very monotonously. We get up at 9:00 A.M. and breakfast at 9:50, have lunch at 12:00 and dinner at 4:00 P.M. They feed us well, better than on the steamer.

At 11:00 visitors are permitted to call on us, which is a great pleasure and when they leave at 2:00 we hurry to know from each other the last news concerning our release, which sometime are good and at others bad. When the news is good we all begin to feel better, hoping we will soon be released. Yesterday we organized a farewell concert [consisting of Russian music, songs, and dances]. We ordered candies, sweets in the City, and made out a program after receiving permission from the authorities. We invited the administration and all white people who were kept in the immigration station and began the concert in the dining room at 8:00 P.M....

On August 18th, the eve of St. Nikolas Day, Father [Vladimir] Sakovich, at our request, conducted prayer service and the dull rooms of the immigration building warbled with songs of the Russian church service sung by the Students' Chorus. Many days have passed since that time and we have organized three plays by Chekhov and put on some other small shows. All this, of course, cannot kill the mood we are in at the immigration station. We spend our evening in playing chess and checkers, in singing, organizing competitions, reading and thus forget for awhile ourselves and our troubles.[57]

The article ended with a poem by student Nicolas Masloff. The sentiments expressed in the poem echo those found in the Chinese poems.

In a country free, humane and honorable,
Where liberty flourishes and all men are brothers,
We sit behind bars and watch with anguish
The sea, mountain and the azure ebb-tide.
We sit and grieve for our great steppes,
For the green forests where the nightingale sings,
For the Russian soul, so simple and clear to us,
For the glory and power of former Russia.

Oh, the fate of the Russian emigrant is very bitter,
He sees much trouble if he leaves without precautions.
He will come to Angel Island to sit behind bars,
And the guard's eye will watch after him.
He will curse immigration, Angel Island, and
Remember the League, the League of Nations,[58]
And will send it all to the devil.

Finally, word came from the Department of Labor in early October that sixty-four of the Russians who had been detained on Angel Island since July were to be released temporarily until November 1, when they would be admitted under that month's quota. According to the *San Francisco Chronicle*, their release was due to the earthquake that devastated Japan on September 1, 1923. "All sailed from Yokohama and the Government does not care to return them to that port in its destroyed state."[59] The students were so overjoyed by the news that they tried to carry Commissioner Nagle, who weighed over 200 pounds, on their shoulders. Only one of the students, Vladimir Borisoff, was denied entry because his passage had been paid for by a theatrical company in Harbin, making him an "assisted immigrant" and inadmissible in the eyes of the immigration officials. Separated from his fiancée who had come with him from Russia, he promptly went on a hunger strike in protest. In the end, he was not deported. There were, however, twenty-nine Russian refugees who were deported to Yokohama, despite their pleas to the American public for help.

> We cannot help feeling that the order for our deportation came through a mistake; that a liberty-loving people could not refuse us shelter under their protecting flag. Could the land that promised us shelter send us back to the dungeon and the firing squad? Our lives are in your hands, for to send us back is to send us to our death. We appeal to you in the name of all that is humane to revise the decision of your immigration officials.[60]

Although the Quota Act of 1921 succeeded in reducing the immigration of Southern and Eastern Europeans from 75 percent of total immigration in 1914 to 31 percent in 1923, anti-immigrant nativists were still not satisfied. Arguing that the inferior breed of new immigrants threatened America's racial foundation, political stability, and economic prosperity, they continued to clamor for a restriction law that would erect even more barriers to their immigration. Congress responded with the Immigration Act of 1924," which caused the Russian quota to plummet from 24,405 in 1921 to 2,248 in 1924.[61]

Arriving after the 1924 Act

The Immigration Act of 1924 transferred the screening of applicants abroad to the American consulates rather than at the ports of entry. Both the new restrictions and the new screening process immediately reduced the numbers of immigrants admitted into the country at San Francisco by 50 percent, from 16,263 in 1923/24 to 8,170 in 1924/25 (see Appendix, Table 1). Moreover, the 1924 act gave the responsibility for coordinating the distribution of quotas to the consulates, thus reducing delays and the possibility of exclusion at the port of entry. The new process was a vast improvement, as consular staff were quite diligent about investigating an applicant's medical, political, and economic background before issuing them a visa.

Most of the Russians immigrating at this time were fleeing the new Soviet regime and the political and economic instability in Harbin caused by the overpopulation of refugees and the Japanese occupation of Manchuria in 1931–32.[62] Many well-to-do Russians were coming as quota immigrants to join family in America; others came as temporary nonimmigrants to visit, attend college, or do business. The majority were admitted to the country after primary inspection aboard the ship. However, anyone with a questionable status, insufficient funds, or a medical problem was still required to go to Angel Island for inspection. Very few were detained for more than a day or two. Quite a few were able to post bonds to gain admittance to the country.

During the global depression of the 1930s, immigration officials were ever more diligent about enforcing the LPC law. Most of the Russians detained on Angel Island were there because they had a medical condition that might prevent them from earning a living. For example, Girsh Leibovich Agranovich, a Jewish merchant from Harbin, was deemed LPC because he had Parkinson's disease, even though he made a point of saying, "I am not figuring on working. I am going to live with my family [in New York]." He had come with $225 in cash and had the sponsorship of his son, a civil engineer, and two brothers-in-law who were in the fur business. Their combined assets were worth $198,480.60, according to the affidavit of support. Still, two members of the board were not satisfied and voted to abide by their earlier decision to reject him on LPC grounds. Agranovich appealed and was detained on Angel Island for six weeks before the secretary of labor granted him temporary landing under a $500 bond.[63]

Regardless of their economic standing, many elderly immigrants like Pavla Georgievna Alexandrova, who was seventy-two years old in 1939, were excluded for "Senility, Class B, which may affect ability to earn a living." Coming to join her daughter and son-in-law who were civil servants in Washington, D.C., Alexandrova had no intention of seeking employment, but she had lost the affidavit of support from her daughter and had only $60 in cash, not quite enough for a train ticket to Washington. Father Vasili Shaposhnikov of the Russian Orthodox Church Abroad came to her rescue and was able to contact her family in Washington. Only upon receiving telegrams attesting to her family's guarantee of support plus the purchase of a train ticket on her behalf was Alexandrova admitted into the country.[64]

Even though the Russian Mennonites immigrated to the United States during the Depression, they had an easy time at Angel Island because Secretary of Labor James Davis had personally granted them "preferred quota" status as skilled farmers. They were processed through the immigration station within a day or two. One exception was seventy-three-year-old Jacob Neufeld, his wife Helena, and their nine children. When they first arrived on Angel Island, they marveled at the bountiful meal at dinner and the kindness of Mrs. Schurat, a missionary worker who provided all of them with a change of clothing. But after three days of interrogating every member of the family and their sponsors, a niece and nephew in California, the board decided to exclude the family "as paupers, as persons whose passage was paid for with the money of another, to-wit, a religious society known as the Mennonites, and as persons likely to become public

"Down the Russian Steppes to America" was the headline that appeared with this photograph of the Neufeld family in the *San Francisco Examiner* on October 16, 1930. From left to right: Father Jacob, Mother Helena, Jake, John, Helen, Henry, Frank, Bill, Dave, Abe, and Herman. (Courtesy of the Bancroft Library, University of California, Berkley.)

charges." Inspector Strand also cited the Depression and Jacob Neufeld's poor vision, age, and senility as reasons for their exclusion. Upon hearing the news, two of the older boys blurted, "Japan will not permit us to stay there; there is nothing doing in China; and they would not let us remain in Russia, they would shoot us there." As reported in the *The Mennonite* newspaper, "The result was that the old gentleman fainted and had to be carried out of the room and the rest of the family set up a lamentation that might be heard for a block."[65]

Members of the Mennonite Brethren Church in Shafter, located in central California, immediately sprang into action when they heard the news. They personally met with Commissioner Edward Haff at the immigration station and wrote an appeal to the secretary of labor, offering to post a public charge bond on behalf of the family. They also prevailed upon their representatives in Congress to send telegrams of support to the secretary of labor. Their efforts and political connections evidently paid off. After being detained on Angel Island for three weeks, the Neufelds were admitted into the country under a $1,000 bond. But their dealings with the Immigration and Naturalization Service (INS) did not end there.

During the next five years, the family never failed to report to INS every six months to say that the three oldest boys were working as farm laborers, the children were attending school, and they had not received any public assistance. In 1933, they were even able to buy a ranch in

The Mennonites were pacifists, but the Neufeld boys (from left to right) Frank, John, Jake, Bill, Dave and Abe "were so proud of the fact that they had been allowed to come into this country that they all volunteered to serve in World War II," said Herbert Neufeld, the youngest son in the family. (Courtesy of Herbert Neufeld.)

Madera. But despite their pleas for the INS to cancel the $1,000 bond so that they could return the money to a nephew, Immigrant Inspector Borstandt would only recommend that it be reduced to $500, since the family was still in debt for the ranch and to the Mennonite Church for their passage to America. Out of desperation, Helena Neufeld wrote First Lady Eleanor Roosevelt a letter explaining their problem and asking her for help. "I always say to my children, 'If in trouble, go to your mother; she will tell you what to do!' Would you, mother of this land, help us so that the bond should be returned? Perhaps, this is possible, so that the people who had been charitable need not starve?" While there is no official record of a response from Mrs. Roosevelt, the bond was canceled three months after Helena wrote the letter.

Fleeing Nazi Persecution

In 1938, after Germany invaded Austria and Czechoslovakia and turned to state sanctioned pogroms to drive the Jews out of the country,140,000 German and Austrian Jews fled their homelands to find refuge in Western Europe, China, and abroad. An estimated 24,000 took the eastward route by sea from Italy to Shanghai, where no visas were required for entry, or by land across Siberia to Harbin and Japan. From there, some 3,000 refugees crossed the Pacific and reached their final destinations in the United States, Canada, Australia, and Palestine, while the remaining 21,000 stayed in Shanghai until the end of the war.[66]

Based on ship passenger lists and the BSI registry, we know that at least 500 Jewish refugees made it to San Francisco from Shanghai and Yokohama in 1939 and 1940. Many had been forced to take indirect routes, staying for months in another European country, Shanghai, or Japan while waiting for their visas to the United States. Applying for the visa itself had been a long ordeal, given staff shortages, the quota laws, stringent enforcement of financial requirements, and the anti-Semitism at some American consulates.[67] The majority of refugees were admitted into the country after primary inspection aboard the ship. About 25 percent were detained on Angel Island for BSI questioning, usually because they had insufficient funds to get to their final destination or because they lacked proof of financial support from a relative in the United States. Among them were Elfriede "Alice" Edelstein and her mother, Hilda Edelstein.

Born in Vienna, Austria, the only child in a middle-class Jewish family, Alice Edelstein led a comfortable life until the Nazis annexed Austria in 1938. Then began the pogroms, mass arrests, confinement into ghettos, confiscation of Jewish properties and businesses, and the barring of Jews from professional practice and public service. "I wasn't allowed to go to school anymore," Alice recalled. "My father had a very profitable lumber business and they just took it away from him. And then he left." Close to 100,000 Jews fled Austria by the end of 1939, including Alice's father, Marcel Edelstein. As she explained, "It was important for him to get out of the country because they were rounding up all the men, and he only had enough money to get one visa to Santo Domingo [in the Dominican Republic]." Before he left, Marcel looked up every "Edelstein" in the phone directories of every major American city and wrote them to sponsor his wife and daughter. One family in Milwaukee agreed to help and sent affidavits to that effect. Then began the long wait for a visa from the American consulate, for the 1924 quota act allowed only 785 Austrians to immigrate to the United States per year.[68]

By the time Hilda and Alice secured their visas and were ready to leave in July of 1940, Italy had entered the war and the Mediterranean Sea route was closed to them. They decided to escape by land to the Pacific. They took the Trans-Siberian Railway from Moscow to Vladivostok with only six dollars in cash and a limited amount of luggage. The train ride took close to four weeks. "It was a tedious journey but I was so glad to get out of there," explained Alice. From Vladivostok they took a ship to Kobe. There they joined 100 other Jewish refugees from Nazi Germany on the *Rakuyo Maru*, which brought them to San Francisco. Alice recalled she had a "horrible" time on her voyage across the Pacific. "They gave us fish at every meal and I was seasick every minute of the way." By the time the ship arrived at its final destination, Alice had lost twenty pounds. "We landed in San Francisco and they had a push-cart there with grapes," she said. "They were five cents a pound! I couldn't believe it, so many grapes for five cents."

Because they had no money to pay for their train tickets to Milwaukee, Alice and Hilda Edelstein were detained at the immigrant station for three days until their sponsor sent funds to them through the Council of Jewish Women in San Francisco. "The women working there were extremely kind to me," Alice said. "They were shocked at my weight because all my

Alice Steiner as a teenager in Vienna. (Courtesy of Nora Steiner Mealy.)

clothes hung on me after I lost twenty pounds. So they saw to it that I ate. We had oatmeal and lots of milk at every breakfast—absolutely horrible! I don't remember what else I ate, but [being lactose intolerant] I did not eat that oatmeal." Her stay on Angel Island was so short that Alice did not even notice the overcrowded and makeshift conditions at the immigration station due to the fire that had destroyed the administration building two weeks before she arrived.

Overall, the immigration officials at Angel Island were more sympathetic and lenient toward the Jewish refugees than with most other LPC cases. Szymon Zuckerman, a businessman who arrived with only $5, was initially excluded as an LPC case. But the board voted unanimously to admit him after he explained, "I came here on account of persecution over in Poland through the Germans." A witness also confirmed the wealthy background of Zuckerman's sponsor in New York. "Though he has very little funds of his own at the present time, as he is a refugee, I am satisfied that he will not become a public charge if admitted," wrote Inspector Earl Cushing in the summary report.[69]

Even those with medical problems were allowed to land within a few days. Alfred and Klara Marill came on the same ship as Hilda and Alice Edelstein. They were excluded and detained on Angel Island for three days because together they had only $25. Moreover, Alfred, an attorney and musician, was certified as having speech and vision impediments as well as bronchitis, while his wife Klara, a milliner, was afflicted with varicose veins and defective vision. But they had three affidavits of support from relatives in New York. In spite of their medical conditions, they were landed as soon as their relatives sent them $400 via the Hebrew Immigrant Aid Society. Similarly, Arthur Muller, a grain merchant who was excluded on LPC grounds because he had a double hernia and a deformed leg, was admitted within two days of his arrival after his sister and wealthy brother-in-law came to Angel Island to testify on his behalf.[70]

In another case, Isaak Adler, who once owned a shoe store in Vienna, and his wife Mathilde were held overnight in April 1940 because they were "Suspected LPC." They had come from Shanghai with only $22 and were on their way to New York to live with their daughter. As Isaak explained to the BSI, "On account of being a Hebrew, I was put in a concentration camp, and there we had to stay until we found a free way out. And the only free way was to Shanghai." Because the Nazis allowed them to take finished goods but no money, Isaak had his wife and daughter buy themselves two expensive fur coats worth over $2,000 to bring to America. The inspectors, impressed with their "prepossessing appearance" and story, voted unanimously to admit them into the country. "They have the usual history of Hebrew immigrants having been deprived of their property and sent to a concentration camp in Austria, after which they were permitted to go to Shanghai, China," wrote Inspector Garcia in the summary report. "However, they apparently salvaged a little of their assets by turning them into valuable furs which their daughter in New York now holds," he added.[71]

Hans Singer had a similar story to tell. He was in a concentration camp in Dachau, Germany, for five weeks. His wife gained his release by buying him a ticket for Shanghai, "the only place that welcomed Jews." He stayed there for over a year, waiting for a visa to the United States, where he had siblings living in Pittsburgh. However, they had recently arrived from Nazi Germany themselves and did not have the financial resources to sponsor him. His brother Carl was able to get his employer Joseph Levy to submit an affidavit of support on his behalf. Although Hans Singer tried to assure the immigration officials that he planned to start his own business so that he would not take work away from another laborer, they still denied him landing on LPC grounds. The board cited the high unemployment rate and the fact that the sponsor was not related to the applicant and therefore had no legal obligation to support him. Singer appealed the decision and was detained on Angel Island for six weeks—the longest detention time for a Jewish refugee in 1939–40. He was finally admitted into the country after Levy posted a $500 public charge bond on his behalf.[72]

Alice Edelstein and the other Jewish refugees were lucky to have gotten out of Central Europe and to have made it to America before the Nazi and U.S. governments closed the gates on them in 1941. In an effort to stop the infiltration of Nazi spies into the country, the U.S. State Department directed American consulates to stop issuing visas to refugees with close relatives in occupied European countries after July 1, 1941. Three months later, the Nazis barred all legal exits from their territories and began sending Jews to the death camps.[73]

Remembering Angel Island

After their short delay on Angel Island, Hilda and Alice Edelstein took the train to Milwaukee, where they found work as a housekeeper and as a cashier at a Jewish bakery. In 1946, Alice married Harry Steiner and the two moved to Detroit, where he worked as an engineer and she as a bookkeeper. They had three children and decided to settle down in Oakland, California, after visiting relatives in the area. According to their daughter Nora, they chose to move to the area because Alice always thought of Angel Island and San Francisco Bay as the most beautiful place on earth. "She was always grateful to have gotten out of Vienna and land at Angel Island." In an interview before she died in 2008, Alice Steiner said as much: "I was lucky all the way. A great part of my family who were older all died in the Holocaust, and I miss them. But, you know, that's the way it was."[74]

When asked what Angel Island meant to him, Nick Friesen, still alert and spry at ninety-five, replied, "We were so happy to finally be in the United States, Angel Island represents freedom and nothing but happy memories for me." His father John Friesen, who had come earlier to raise travel funds for the Mennonites in Harbin, met the family at the San Francisco pier after they were released from the island. Nick remembers they were driven directly to Reedley in central California, stopping only for dinner at a Chinese restaurant in Merced. They arrived late Saturday night, attended church on Sunday, and started work on Monday, picking figs for 40 cents an hour. "Jobs were hard to come by because of the Depression, but we were just glad that we were in a free country," he said. Nick started out as a truck driver for a fruit packer, but ended up farming in Reedley for over thirty years while raising a family of four children. Widowed at sixty-two, he remarried at the age of eighty-five to Mary Krueger, a German Mennonite from British Columbia. Every five years since 1980, Nick has faithfully attended the "Harbiners reunion" to commemorate their deliverance from Soviet tyranny.[75]

As for Nadia Shapiro, who came to study journalism in 1922, she was able to put her writing and multilingual skills to good use. She worked as a feature writer for the *San Francisco Examiner* from 1923 to 1932, as a research editor for the Works Progress Administration during the Depression, and as a translator for the U.S. Office of Censorship and Central Intelligence Agency during and after the war. Nadia became a U.S. citizen in 1928 and never returned to Russia. Her memories of Angel Island can be found in the first chapter of an unfinished novel about "the adventures, romantic and otherwise, of Russians who have found a refuge in America." The following excerpt describes a group of students' first reactions to being locked up in the immigration barracks on Angel Island:

> Standing by the barred windows, they looked over the sun-spangled waters of the Golden Gate, alive with white ferry-boats, and the honey-brown coast range of California which framed the turquoise water. Sunlight poured its warm gold on a tiny pier not fifty yards beyond their windows where men, free to come and go, were boarding a white motor launch. By pressing their faces to the wire, they could look from their second-floor windows upon the garden below, with the Stars and Stripes floating from a pole surrounded by palms. That was the World Outside.[76]

Although his parents Jacob and Helena Neufeld were ill treated at Angel Island, Herbert Neufeld said they were "absolutely thrilled" when they were finally granted permission to enter the country, so thrilled that his mother named him Herbert after the president when he was born a few months later. "Angel Island represented the gateway to heaven to my family—all the freedom, luxury, and privileges that come with being a citizen of this country," he explained. "They were just so happy that God had answered their prayers and brought them here."[77] So too were the other 8,000 immigrants from Russia, who like the Steiners and Neufelds, had fled religious and political persecution by going east across the Pacific to the Promised Land.

Like many coming from Russia, Mexicans also fled political turmoil and persecution, and *el norte* promised refuge. Also like Russian immigrants, Mexicans were not subjected to specific race-based immigration restrictions that regulated Asian immigration. They too were mostly measured for admission on the basis of the general immigration laws. But unlike Russians, Mexican immigrants became increasingly identified as an immigrant "problem" to be solved along the same lines as the "Asiatic invasions" from China, Japan, South Asia, and the Philippines.

Mexican refugees sitting on a dock in Southern California under the guard of U.S. soldiers, 1913. (© San Diego Historical Society.)

CHAPTER SEVEN

EL NORTE

MEXICAN IMMIGRANTS ON ANGEL ISLAND

ON FEBRUARY 20, 1916, brothers Juan, Frederico, Fortunato, and Antonio Cesana arrived on Angel Island from Mexico on a small steam schooner. Coming to join their brothers Eustrofio and Henuevo in San Jose, California, the brothers were among the many Mexicans fleeing the chaos, violence, and destruction of revolutionary Mexico. "The revolution is paralyzing everything, that is the reason I left," Antonio told immigrant inspectors during his immigration hearing. Brother Eustrofio elaborated even further: "the revolution took everything away from them down there." Their only chance for survival was in *el norte*.[1]

Between 1900 and 1930, one and a half million Mexicans migrated north to the United States. The vast majority came across the U.S.-Mexico border and entered the country through one of the border checkpoints at Nogales and Douglas, Arizona; Calexico, California; and Brownsville and Laredo, Texas. The Júarez-El Paso border crossing was the main point of entry for Mexicans on their way to California. But at least 400 came, like the Cesana brothers, by the sea and Angel Island. Entering the United States through San Francisco was especially common during the Mexican Revolution, because the ocean passage was a safer route than entry across the land border.[2]

Most Mexicans coming to the United States during this time were male laborers heading to rural areas in the American Southwest. The Mexicans arriving on Angel Island, however, were different. They were a demographically and occupationally diverse group that included men, women, children, merchants, skilled and unskilled laborers, and domestic servants. Similar to their Russian counterparts on Angel Island, they came as refugees, to reunite with family, or for work. The majority came from 1913–20 during the peak years of the Mexican Revolution. Some were entering the United States for the first time; others had been in the country before. Like other immigrant groups on Angel Island, Mexicans sought new lives in the United States. But their experiences both at the immigration station and in the United States were also unique. Unlike Asians, Mexicans faced no immigration laws specifically barring their entry into the United States. In fact, U.S. immigration policy facilitated the movement of Mexican migrant laborers northward, and immigration officials only selectively applied the general immigration laws to them. But Mexicans were not treated the same as European immigrants either. While Europeans were generally valued as potential Americans, Mexicans were mostly valued for providing temporary labor. The lax regulation of Mexican migration was thus not evenly applied across all Mexican migrants. Immigration policies privileged male laborers or members of the middle and upper classes who would not be financial liabilities to the United States. On Angel Island, Mexicans who could not demonstrate their value as laborers or who were otherwise seen as moral and economic risks were kept out. As American anxiety grew over the unprecedented number of Mexicans entering and staying in the United States during the 1920s, characterizations of Mexican immigrants as a racially inferior foreign invasion became dominant in national immigration debates. In addition, the regulation of Mexican immigration became more restrictive, especially at the border, but also on Angel Island. These efforts signaled a shift in American attitudes that would place Mexicans at the center of American immigration debates in both the twentieth and twenty-first centuries.

El Norte: Mexican Migration to the United States

In 1946, writer and activist Carey McWilliams mused that Mexicans in the United States were "not really immigrants; they belong to the Southwest." After all, McWilliams continued, much of the American West—including Angel Island—had belonged to Mexico until the U.S.-Mexico War ended in 1848. After the U.S. victory, Mexicans became outsiders in their own land seemingly overnight, but the movement of Mexicans to the United States (and back to Mexico) continued. In 1900, there were 103,393 Mexican-born residents in the United States, most of them residing in Arizona or Texas. Migration to California increased dramatically from 1900 to 1930, especially during the 1920s. Mexicans accounted for over 11 percent of the total legal immigration to the United States during that decade alone. In addition, an estimated 100,000 individuals entered without inspection from Mexico per year during the same period. By

1928, there were two million Mexicans in the United States, with 82 percent residing in Arizona, California, New Mexico, and Texas.[3]

A combination of factors on both sides of the U.S.-Mexican border facilitated this great migration northward. In the United States, the southwestern economy was expanding at an accelerated rate as railroad construction began to link the West to the rest of the nation. Railroad and other labor contractors ran a highly organized and large-scale labor recruiting business that brought Mexican laborers to railroad construction sites, mines, farms, and factories. In California, Mexicans filled a serious chronic immigrant labor shortage caused by the Asian exclusion laws and the Immigration Acts of 1917, 1921, and 1924. During the 1920s, Mexicans were the largest ethnic group of farmworkers in California's citrus, walnut, melon, grape, lettuce, sugar beet, and cotton fields, helping the state become the largest producer of fruits and vegetables in the West by 1929.[4]

In Mexico, dramatic economic and political changes beginning under the reign of President Porfirio Díaz (1876–1911) and continuing through the Mexican Revolution (1910–20) also contributed to the mass migration of Mexicans abroad. Porfirian economic policy focused on modernization and Westernization, explicitly favoring foreign (especially U.S.) investment at the expense of Mexican farmers and workers who were left impoverished and landless. The country experienced rapid, but very unequal, growth fueled by agricultural and mineral exports to the United States and European countries. Uncertain economic conditions became much more pronounced at the end of Díaz's era. Widespread drought and hunger also ravaged the land from 1905 to 1907.[5]

Although Díaz was reelected to a seventh term in 1910 at the age of eighty, the growing social and economic inequality in the country gave rise to an anti-reelectionist movement led by Francisco I. Madero. A wealthy liberal reformer from the northern state of Coahuila, Madero unsuccessfully challenged Díaz in the fixed elections of 1910, and when defeated, declared the Díaz election null and void. An armed revolt began, and uprisings in key states defeated the federal troops. Díaz resigned in May 1911, and the first phase of the revolution ended, but peace and stability did not follow. Instead, Mexico entered a decade-long struggle for military and political control. In February 1913, Madero was overthrown and later assassinated. A succession of leaders and warring factions vied for power over the next several years, setting in motion another round of violence as guerilla armies and more formal armies fought around the country. In 1920, a nonviolent phase of the revolution began under the leadership of Alvaro Obregon.[6]

The revolution shook the foundations of Mexican society. One-tenth of the country's population perished during the decade of war. Warring factions ravaged towns throughout the country and destroyed farmland and railroads. Much of the countryside experienced continuous armed

Mexican refugee mother Matilde Martinez and children, 1914. (San Francisco History Center, San Francisco Public Library.)

rebellion. The violence greatly disrupted the Mexican economy, and inflation and unemployment rose. Mexicans from both ends of the socioeconomic and political spectrum—*campesinos* (farmworkers) and *hacendados* (rich agriculturalists)—fled from persecution, and the country's economic challenges and political instability forced even greater numbers of Mexicans abroad in search of survival.[7]

The large migration of Mexicans northward was facilitated by policies on both sides of the U.S.-Mexico border. Mexico promoted migration to the United States as a way of managing a dramatic population growth. The remittances that Mexicans in the United States sent back home also sustained the Mexican economy. President Venustiano Carranza (1917–20) even provided transportation costs for Mexicans wanting to work in the United States, and his successors in the post-revolutionary era continued to allow mass migration northward.[8]

The U.S. government's lax enforcement of immigration policies at the U.S.-Mexico border also made possible the mass migration of Mexicans northward throughout the early twentieth century. Unlike the strict controls established for other immigrant groups, especially Asians, a deliberate policy of "benign neglect" was practiced when it came to Mexicans. The U.S.-Mexico border was largely unregulated, which also contributed to the increase in Mexican migration. Before 1924, there were only sixty Bureau of Immigration agents regularly stationed along the entire 2,000-mile length of the U.S.-Mexican border stretching from the Pacific Ocean to the Gulf of Mexico. Even after the government increased its surveillance of the borders, agents were mostly concerned with stopping Asians and Europeans from entering without inspection, and the Border Patrol only selectively applied immigration laws to Mexican migrants. Mexicans faced long lines and rude immigration officials, but many federal immigration policies that were mostly designed to regulate European or Asian migration, such as the law barring migrants who were "likely to become public charges" (LPC), were circumvented or ignored for Mexicans in order to meet the labor demands of southwestern employers. Even the literacy test and the head tax provisions of the Immigration Act of 1917 that were more directed toward Mexican migration were largely ignored at the border. Some U.S. policies even facilitated the entrance of Mexican laborers into the country. From 1917 to 1921, an admissions contract program provided temporary entrance visas to workers to fill the labor shortage caused by World War I. The majority of these visas went to Mexicans. The literacy test and the ban on contract laborers for Mexicans were also suspended.[9]

Until the 1920s, Mexican male laborers routinely crossed the border to work during the agricultural season, then returned south for a few months or longer, and then remigrated north again. The idea of the "northern pass," or an unregulated border crossing into the United States became common for generations of Mexicans. Mexican families were thus highly transnational, with some members working and living in the United States while others remained in Mexico. This circular cross-border migration suited both southwestern employers who wanted a steady stream of laborers, and nativists, who found the temporary Mexican laborer less threatening than other immigrant groups who stayed to settle in the country.[10]

Most Mexicans in the United States during the early twentieth century were male laborers. An estimated 90 percent were farmworkers. Women emigrated alone only in the rarest cases. Daughters were expected to remain at home until they married. As husbands and fathers became more established in the United States, they began to send for their wives and children to join them up north. The number of Mexican women in the United States increased, but overall, their numbers were small.[11]

A more diverse array of Mexicans applied for admission into the United States through Angel Island. Many applicants were middle class, with a large proportion of women and children. While many came for work, others came as refugees fleeing the chaos, persecution, and economic instability of the Mexican revolution. The Flores family, for example, had enjoyed a comfortable existence on their ranch in Mazatlán prior to the revolution. But as the revolutionary fighting reached their city, their crops suffered. "Last year there was nothing at all on the ranch," twenty-year-old Rosa Flores explained to immigrant inspectors on March 3, 1914. "We had ten cows, [but] the revolutionaries used them for food." Rosa's father, a supporter of the Constitutionalist faction, became so afraid for his own safety that he fled Mazatlán and sent his daughters to the United States to join their cousin in San Francisco. Also fleeing Mazatlán was twenty-year-old seamstress Elena Rendon, who applied for admission into the United States in June 1914. "There is war at Mazatlán now between the Constitutionalists and the government troops," she explained. "I am leaving...on account of the conditions there." Elena hoped to join her sister in Portland and find work as a servant to a wealthy Portland family. Moses Galcono resorted to stowing away on a steamer heading up north to San Francisco for his own personal safety. As he told immigration officials in August 1913, "[the] Revolution [is] down there and they grab everybody for soldiers. I don't care to be a soldier."[12]

An immediate fear of persecution caused Maria Lopez to flee Mexico with her infant son Miguel in 1919. Her husband, a military paymaster for revolutionary leader Venustiano Carranza, had been brutally murdered in front of her and their son in a barn outside of Guadalajara. While he lay dying, Maria fought off the attackers, but as her grandson Michael explained, "she knew she had to leave" to keep her family safe. Maria fled with Miguel and caught a boat leaving the country. "She took a boat because she realized that there was less of a chance of [meeting] bandits or people that would bring her harm. She wanted to get *out* of Mexico...she did not want to be traveling *through* it," explained Michael. Maria had not planned on going to San Francisco, specifically, but that is where the steamship was heading, and she leaped at the chance to escape. By the time they arrived at the Angel Island Immigration Station, both she and her son were sick. Miguel had whooping cough and was quarantined at the station hospital. Maria was pregnant with twins and was not in prime physical condition. Immigration officials ordered the two to be returned to Mexico, but Maria refused to go back to a country where her family would be in danger. According to family lore, she told a guard that she needed the best lawyer she could get to help her challenge the deportation order. The guard jokingly told her to write to President Woodrow Wilson. Maria followed his instructions and wrote to the president. A telegram came back from First Lady Edith Wilson urging immigration officials to allow Maria and Miguel into the country, and they were admitted soon thereafter.[13]

The intervention by a first lady into the immigration affairs of the country would have been very rare, and no immigration records survive to document any correspondence by Mrs. Wilson on behalf of the Lopezes. But the U.S. government did act broadly on behalf of other refugees fleeing revolutionary Mexico. At least two times during the revolutionary period, the American consulate in Mazatlán chartered transport ships to bring American citizens and their Mexican spouses and children north to San Francisco for safety. Angela and Santiago Vasques arrived on the U.S. Army Transport *Buford* in October 1913, a trip that had been arranged by the U.S. consulate in Mazatlán and the Red Cross. On another trip

After fleeing the violence of revolutionary Mexico with her son Miguel, Maria Lopez was admitted into the United States, married Joe Gargiulo, and settled in San Rafael, CA. They opened a Mexican restaurant and had three children together. This photograph of the Gargiulo family was taken in 1933. Top row, left to right: Maria Urzua (Lopez) Gargiulo, Giosue (Joe) Gargiulo, Miguel (Michael) Angelo Lopez. Bottom row, left to right: Rose Maria Gargiulo, Frank Albert Gargiulo, Joe David Gargiulo. (Courtesy of Michael Lopez.)

in February 1914, Maria Gonzales explained that the American consul in Mazatlán had "furnished" passage for herself and to "all foreigners upon application." "Why did you leave down there?" asked one of the immigrant inspectors. "No use for me to stay. Fighting there," she explained. "You came here as a refugee?" asked an inspector. "Yes," replied Gonzales. The U.S. government's recognition of Mexicans as refugees is significant. Although the United States did not formally begin to regulate refugee migration until World War II, the case of Mexicans and other refugees fleeing persecution in their homelands signals an early acknowledgment by U.S. officials of refugee status as a cause for admission into the country.[14]

Mexicans like Gonzales most likely chose to enter the United States by sea rather than cross the land border for safety reasons. During the Mexican Revolution, regular travel routes along the railroads became increasingly dangerous. The sea route was safer and more convenient for those already living along or near the Mexican coast.[15] Most Mexicans who applied for admission through San Francisco were born in the coastal states of Jalisco and Sinaloa and traveled from West Coast ports, such as Mazatlán, Manzanillo, Salina Cruz, and Acapulco. Steamship lines, like the Pacific Mail Steamship Company (PMSS), made regular stops at these ports as they traveled between Central America and North America in the late nineteenth and early twentieth centuries. Other Mexicans traveled on freight steamers or found more creative strategies. The Artesiros family, for example, arrived on the freighter *Erna*. Humberto Pequeros signed on as a cabin boy on the *Prince Waldemar* in order to get to San Francisco in 1915. Herman Lupio worked aboard the *Citriana* as a fireman, and Moses Galcono and Jesus Morales entered as stowaways.[16]

Passenger records from the PMSS indicate that the majority of Mexicans (76 percent) coming by steamship to San Francisco traveled in third class or steerage, while 24 percent came in first class.[17] Although most Mexicans traveled in third class, they were not necessarily without financial resources. Steamship travel was expensive, especially during the revolutionary years. In 1914, Tito Araica told immigrant inspectors that it cost him a total of $173.30 in Mexican dollars to travel by steamer from Guadalajara in the middle of the country to Colima, Manzanillo, and finally, to San Francisco. The steamship fare alone was $151.50.[18]

Testimony and evidence given by Mexicans on Angel Island indicate that many of the migrants applying for admission came from middle-class backgrounds, with at least a record of gainful employment, well-placed connections, some savings, and even property in their names. Forty-six-year-old Parcenta Herrera and her twenty-two-year-old nephew arrived on the *Peru* on September 15, 1914, from Mazatlán and claimed to have "considerable property" estimated at $500 in Mexico, for example. Merchant and property owner Tito Araica came later that year and brought $2,000 with him to the United States. His plan was to join his brother, a jeweler and watchmaker, in Daly City, California. The sons of wealthy or well-connected politicians or military officers also came into the country through Angel Island. Fifteen-year-old Bernardo Fregoso was sent to study in the United States by his father, an architect in Colima, Mexico. Humberto Pequeros, the thirteen-year-old son of a former general in the army, arrived in San Francisco in November of 1915. Two years later, Arturo De Cima, the son of the former U.S. consul in Mazatlán, arrived on Angel Island and was examined and admitted that day.[19]

Middle-class and elite Mexicans, like this son of a Mexican colonel (left), with another young man, faced few obstacles entering the country through Angel Island. (General Commission on Archives and History, United Methodist Church, Drew University.)

Domestic servants in the employ of wealthy Americans represented another group of Mexicans who made the journey by sea to the United States. Twenty-year-old Maria Mayin and two friends arrived at Angel Island on January 22, 1914, destined to join the Sullivan and O'Brien families in Los Angeles. John Sullivan, a self-described "old timer in California" involved in the "colonization" business in Colima, Mexico, came to the island to vouch for the girls. He claimed that he and his wife had "unusually good conditions for taking care of them. We have a separate house for servants and we probably would be able to give them more than they ever had before," he told immigration officials.[20]

John Sullivan may have lived up to his promise of giving Mayin and her friends "unusually good conditions," but the reality of domestic servant exploitation was clear in other cases involving Mexicans who were detained on Angel Island. They were often abandoned at the whim of their employers when delays in their processing caused inconvenience or required extra financial cost. For example, forty-eight-year-old Maria Salvador, a cook for Mrs. Rosa Rica de Beltran of Los Angeles, arrived in 1914 with her employer. A routine medical examination found that Salvador had hookworm. Because the medical treatment would delay Salvador and inconvenience the Beltrans' travel plans, they abandoned her on the island and she was deported back to Mexico. Fourteen-year-Margarita Gonzalez came as a "nurse girl" for the baby of her employer Mr. S. M. Ochoa in September of 1916. When Commissioner of Immigration Edward White informed Mrs. Ochoa that under U.S. immigration laws, Gonzalez had to attend school until she was sixteen and that she would only be admitted under bond (requiring an extra financial cost from the Ochoas), Mrs. Ochoa refused and told the immigration officials to send Gonzalez back to Mexico.[21]

One of the largest groups of Mexicans applying for admission through Angel Island were those joining relatives already working and living in northern California. Fifteen-year-old Bernardo Fregoso arrived on the *City of Para* in November 1914 to join his aunt and uncle, who were both U.S. citizens. He was detained for five days and then admitted. Forty-six-year-old Parcenta Herrera and her nephew traveled from Mazatlán to join Herrera's two sons and two sisters working in San Francisco. They were detained for four days before being admitted into the country. And twenty-year-old seamstress Rosa Flores sought to be reunited with her cousin and aunt and uncle, who had been in San Francisco for eleven years. She was detained for four days before being admitted into the country.[22]

Los Autoridades (The Authorities): Mexican Immigration Cases

As they did with other immigrants, immigration officials on Angel Island applied the nation's immigration laws in order to admit able-bodied, respectable, and self-sufficient immigrants while excluding others who posed economic, racial, or moral risks to the nation. Mexicans' encounters with *los autoridades* mirrored those of other immigrants at the immigration station. Some had minimal contact and were readily admitted into the country. Others found the experience humiliating and confusing. Like other new arrivals at the immigration station, Mexicans had to undergo the routine medical examination and pass the government's tests for fitness and disease. Those who received clean bills of health were then brought before immigration officials who considered their right to enter the United States. There are few records that document the medical examinations of Mexican immigrants on Angel Island in detail. But individual cases indicate that Mexicans were tested for loathsome and contagious diseases that were grounds for exclusion. From 1910 to 1920, 9 percent of Mexicans applying for admission at all U.S. ports of entry were denied on medical grounds.[23]

Because only the general immigration laws applied to Mexicans, their immigration hearings were very different in tone and intensity from those involving Asian immigrants. In particular, Mexican migrants were not subject to the same degree of institutionalized suspicion that characterized the processing of Asian immigrants on the island. For example, immigration service regulations forbade Chinese applicants claiming U.S. citizenship by birth from calling fellow Chinese as witnesses since it was believed that they were untrustworthy and would lie on behalf of the applicant. Mexicans claiming U.S. citizenship, however, faced no such hurdles or policies. Eleven-year-old Felix Herrera, for example, was admitted as a returning U.S. citizen on the basis of short statements given by his Mexican-born aunts and brothers living in San Francisco. They all testified that Herrera was born on Minna Street in the city. In comparison to the hours of detailed questioning of Chinese witnesses in similar cases, Herrera's relatives were asked a total of five questions each. There is no indication that Herrera had to produce a birth certificate or any other documentation of his native status during his hearing. Still, immigration officials had no doubts about the veracity of their claims, which were automatically accepted as "conclusive" evidence regarding Herrera's birth in the United States. He was admitted into the country after four days of detention.[24]

In addition, there was not nearly the same type of government manpower devoted to Mexican immigration business as there was to Asian immigration. In some cases, Chinese inspectors were even assigned to investigate matters relating to Mexican cases. This lack of staff reflected both the smaller numbers of Mexican migrants on Angel Island and the lower priority that the U.S. government placed on regulating Mexican migration at the nation's seaports.[25]

While Mexican immigration regulation on Angel Island was not as rigorous as it was for Asians, it still differed from the processing of Mexicans at the U.S.-Mexico border. Angel Island immigration officials did not institutionalize a policy of "benign neglect" toward Mexican immigrants like their counterparts along the U.S.-Mexico border. Like European and other non-Asian immigrants, Mexicans were still subjected to a wide range of general immigration laws that sifted immigrants according to fitness, self-sufficiency, class status, respectability, and morality. Some were detained, but their rates of detention were more similar to those of European immigrants. Most first-class passengers from Mexico were admitted from the steamship. Twenty-five percent of applicants were detained for only one day. The remaining immigrants traveling by third class spent an average of two days detained at the immigration station, with a few spending only a few hours and one spending sixty-two days.[26]

Class Privilege and Middle-Class Mexicans

Like middle-class and elite immigrants of all backgrounds arriving on Angel Island, Mexicans who could demonstrate appropriate wealth or class standing or who had powerful connections on the mainland fared much better than their working-class counterparts. When fifteen-year-old Bernardo Fregoso, arrived on the *City of Para* on November 5, 1914, from Mazatlán, for example, his relatives were ready to lend credibility to the student's application for admission. His uncle, Michael Herrera, a U.S. citizen who worked in a paint factory, came to the island to testify on his behalf and told immigration officials that Bernardo would live with him and his wife and that they would be responsible for his care. To demonstrate that they were readily able to do this, Hererra showed immigration officials the deed to his property, indicating a house and land worth $1,800. Bernardo was detained for five days and then landed. Similarly, when ten-year-old Bonifacio Magana and his mother were called for their hearing before the Board of Special Inquiry on Angel Island, his father, Felipe, a cigar maker in San Francisco, came prepared with evidence of his employment and good standing in the community. He brought his membership card to the cigar maker's union and a letter from his employer, Frankel Gerdts & Co., located on Clay Street in San Francisco. The letter vouched for his good character and status as a "steady and industrious workman." Felipe also presented receipts showing that he regularly paid his rent on a flat on Mason Street. The family was admitted.[27]

Families like the Maganas and Herreras were smart to bring evidence of their wealth or class membership to the immigration station. These documents helped boost the claim of applicants that they would not become public charges. Powerful mainland connections were also useful. Arriving in March of 1910, Mr. Artesiros, a barber, his wife, and their infant son were excluded on the grounds that they had no financial resources and were likely to become public charges. The case was deferred until Father Sarda, the woman's uncle and "a prominent Catholic divine of Oakland," was able to travel to the island a few days later. Sarda's testimony convinced the board that the family would not become public charges. They were landed on that same day.[28]

Middle-class dress, appearance, and decorum also helped distinguish applicants and increased their chances of admission. Christina Alonso, an orphan traveling with her aunt in 1918, impressed immigration officials because she was "well dressed; very bright and shows signs of having been well cared for; she speaks, reads, and writes English." The board noted that the aunt had only $75, but other factors made the immigration officials confident that neither the girl nor the aunt would end up as public charges. The aunt brought glowing recommendations from former employers, and she had, the board concluded, "every appearance of being a woman able to make a living for herself and child." The two were detained for four days and then allowed to enter the country.[29]

In contrast to middle-class immigrants, Mexicans who arrived penniless or who appeared poorly dressed did not fare as well in their interactions with immigrant inspectors. Jesus Morales, for example, arrived on the island as a stowaway on the *Grace Dollar* in April 1915. He was a single laborer who had been in the United States before. His parents were also in the United States. Although he had been admitted into the country at Nogales a few years earlier, this time, immigration officials were unwilling to readmit him. "How much money have you?" immigration officials asked Morales. "Not one cent," he answered. Morales was quickly excluded as likely to become a public charge. Adolpho Cisneros, an applicant for admission in 1917, was, according to the Board of Special Inquiry, "very poorly dressed, his clothes being uncleanly in appearance." Cisneros' poor appearance was interpreted as evidence that he was indeed poor and would likely remain poor in the future. He was ordered excluded under the LPC clause of the general immigration laws. Cases like those of Morales and Cisneros were common. From 1910 to 1920, 47 percent of Mexicans applying for admission at all U.S. ports of entry were denied under the LPC clause. From 1920 to 1930, the rate was 29 percent.[30]

In a few cases where class status was unclear, immigration officials ordered special investigations of applicants' financial status to help determine whether they were at risk of becoming public charges. This was a common procedure with other immigrant groups as well. When Maria Gonzales, wife of naturalized American citizen Ruben Clemens, arrived as a refugee on a U.S. transport ship in February of 1914, the final decision on her case was deferred until immigration officials could determine if Clemens could support his wife and child as he claimed. "Do you know anything about this man's financial condition?" they asked Charles J. O'Connor, a Red Cross official who had helped organize the transportation of Gonzales and other refugees from Mexico. "Yes, he is just barely making a living. I was out there yesterday and I saw the little flat he has fixed up for his wife. He is poor but he is making it go." Officers later concluded that Mr. and Mrs. Clemens appeared to be "good, honest, industrious people," and the family was reunited in the United States.[31]

"Respectable" Mexican Women

Just as class privilege paved the way for middle-class Mexican immigrants to enter the country, gender also played a role in facilitating the entry of Mexican men versus women. Like other immigrant groups, Mexican women were held to different standards under U.S. immigration policy than their male counterparts. American immigration laws placed a higher premium on the migration of Mexican men over women, because southwestern employers

While some immigration laws, including the literacy test, were ignored along the U.S.-Mexico border, they were enforced on Angel Island and disproportionately affected Mexican women. Cecilia Tapia was excluded as an illiterate in 1917. (Scan by Vincent Chin. National Archives, Pacific Regional Branch.)

wanted a ready pool of Mexican male migrant laborers. The U.S. government's lax enforcement of Mexican immigration at the U.S.-Mexico border facilitated this movement of male laborers into the country. At the same time, Mexican women and children had less value as laborers, and American immigration law enforcement was not as lenient with them. Single Mexican women and women traveling alone were disproportionately scrutinized as economic and moral risks and were excluded as illiterates, persons likely to become public charges, or as persons with suspect morals.[32]

The ways in which the literacy test was applied to Mexican migrant women on Angel Island, for example, illustrates how immigration regulation differed both by place and by gender. At the U.S.-Mexico border checkpoints, the literacy test was often ignored in the government's lax enforcement policy that facilitated the entrance of Mexican laborers into the United States and into American industries. The same was not true for Mexican women applying for admission through Angel Island. When nineteen-year-old Cecilia Tapia applied for admission at Angel Island on March 18, 1917, she was scrutinized and detained for her inability to read and write in any language. Tapia arrived in San Francisco with an American passport from the American consulate in Salina Cruz. Although the American consul noted that Tapia could neither read nor write, he suggested admission anyway. He reported that Tapia had a brother and sister in San Francisco who were in "easy circumstances" and were prepared to give a bond on the applicant until she had learned to read. During her hearing before the Board of Special Inquiry on March 19, Tapia testified that she had attended school for only three months when she was nine years old. She could write her name and read a few letters, but she failed to read the standardized literacy test in Spanish offered by the officials. The board noted that the applicant was in good health, was bright and intelligent, and neatly dressed. Her sister, who came to the island to testify, also "impressed the Board very favorably." Nonetheless, immigration officials disagreed with the American consul's recommendation to admit

Tapia. The board excluded her as an illiterate and she was returned to Mexico.[33]

Other aspects of the general immigration laws, including the LPC clause, were also aggressively applied to Mexican women applying for admission through Angel Island. Like all immigrant women, unaccompanied Mexican women almost always had to have a hearing before a Board of Special Inquiry. They were judged according to how well they fit middle-class standards of female respectability. This included being virtuous and moral, as well as dependent upon a husband or father who could support them. Cases that exemplified this version of female domesticity and respectability were often approved for admission. For example, when twenty-seven-year-old Maria Cabezud and her four young children arrived at the immigration station from Jalisco on the *Newport* on May 14, 1915, their right to enter the country rested completely on husband Joaquin's employment status and his ability to support his family. Joaquin had entered the United States three years earlier through El Paso and had been working as a clothes ironer for H. Gomez & Company in Madera, California. He had recently gone into the tailoring business for himself and regularly sent $15 per month to Maria and the children in Jalisco. Maria testified that the family was able to live comfortably on these wages and had never had to depend on charity. The reason they were all coming to the United States was so that the children could receive an American education. During his interview with immigration officers, Joaquin told them that his business was worth $500 or $600. He brought evidence of $430 in bank savings, and he showed them another $180 in cash that he brought to the station. The family made a good impression on immigration officials. They noted that Joaquin had "the appearance of respectability" and that he would "properly care for his wife and children; [who] also appear to be respectable." The family was detained for seven days while two of the Cabezud children were treated for scabies and then all were admitted into the country.[34]

While Maria Cabezud represented the type of female migrant—a wife and mother with a husband who could support her—that U.S. immigration officials were happy to admit, Angela Vasques did not. She came under immediate suspicion by immigration officials as soon as she arrived at the immigration station in December 1920. She claimed to be married to Santiago Vasques, who accompanied her, but the couple had no identification papers or marriage license to verify their relationship. They claimed that a fire in their hometown of Colima had destroyed all personal documents. The lack of records raised a red flag to immigration officials. Even more troubling was a tip from a fellow passenger that Angela was a "notorious prostitute" in the city of Tepic. Immigration officials convened a Board of Special Inquiry. "What were you doing previous to marriage?" they asked Angela. "I was not doing anything; only staying at home," she answered. "It is alleged that you practiced prostitution before coming to this country. Is that so?" they pressed. "No," she protested. "I was married when I was very young and am a worthy girl." The inspectors continued their accusations. "You have never had any sexual relations with any man except this man you claim to be your husband. Is that right?" "Yes," Angela answered. Not being completely satisfied with her answers, immigration officials then turned to her husband, Santiago. "Your wife was a woman of good character all the time?" they asked. "Yes, sir," Santiago answered. "You had no occasion to 'shake her' as the saying is?" they inquired, alluding to the possibility that Santiago was making money procuring sexual clients for Angela. "No, nothing like that!" Santiago protested. As this aggressive line of questioning indicates, immigration officials clearly suspected the Vasqueses of immoral behavior and false claims of marriage. Inconsistencies in their testimony led Inspector David Griffiths to believe that the couple was simply "concocting a story for the purpose of deceiving the immigration officers here." During a second hearing, both testified again under oath that Angela had never engaged in prostitution. Santiago brought evidence of good character from his former employer, the superintendent of the Southern Pacific Railway in Mexico. Immigration officials noted that the couple's claim that their papers were lost in a fire was "in large measure substantiated by [Santiago's] personal appearance which bears scars and disfigurations, indicating that he has been in a fire as stated." The fact that Santiago had been endorsed by the American consul at Mazatlán also certainly helped the case. Immigration officials remained doubtful, but the commissioner of immigration supported the decision to admit the couple. The two were "young, healthy persons of good appearance," reported the commissioner. "The woman flatly denies her alleged following of an immoral occupation, and whether it is true or not, the husband stands by his wife and takes responsibility for her proper conduct during their so-called marriage." After three and a half weeks of detention on the island, Angela and Santiago Vasques were admitted into the country.[35]

Maria Sanchez, an applicant for admission in December 1920, faced similar accusations of immorality as Angela Vasques. Traveling with her infant son, Jose, Sanchez had a complicated case in which accusations of prostitution and other immoral behavior were made against her. Sanchez hoped to start a new life with her mother, three sisters, and brother in San Francisco. However, her ex-lover and father of her child, identified only as Pedro, attempted to sabotage her flight to the United States. Pedro, who Sanchez claimed had a history of domestic abuse, wrote a letter to the immigration authorities on Angel Island while Sanchez was en route to the United States. The letter charged that Sanchez was a prostitute and was suffering from syphilis. Immigration officials questioned her intensively about her history with Pedro, any sexual relations she had had with other men, and her knowledge of carrying syphilis. During the six weeks of her detention, Sanchez's family came to the island and pledged to assist and support her and her baby and brought gifts to ease their suffering. In the end, immigration officials voted to exclude. They question if her relationship with Pedro and her illegitimate child constituted crimes of immorality under immigration law, but noted that her "conduct of low moral standard" made it plausible that she would "continue the same mode of living in this country" and that she would have difficulty supporting herself and her child. Immigration officials had accepted unsubstantiated evidence of immoral behavior as proof that she had indeed acted immorally in the past and that she would again continue to act immorally in the future. Sanchez appealed the decision. The commissioner of immigration noted that the case was a difficult one that "appeal[ed] strongly to the sympathies." He agreed with the decision, but conceded that he was not "unfavorable to their landing under bond." When evidence came in to the immigration service from the Associated Charities of San Francisco that Sanchez's relatives had been forced to accept food from the relief agency, Sanchez and her son were found to be persons likely to become public charges, and they were returned to Mexico.[36]

Simona Gonzales, a twenty-one-year-old servant from Mazatlán who applied for admission in June 1914, also came under immigration officials' suspicious gaze because she had had a child out of wedlock. They asked detailed questions about her sexual past and her relationship with the father of her child. "Were you ever married?" they asked Gonzales during her Board of Special Inquiry hearing. "I lived with my mother, and a man [Michael Foster] kept a store close by, and while my mother was gone, I stayed with him four night[s]. The child died two days after birth," she explained. "Do you consider this man Michael Foster your husband?" the inspecting officer asked. "No," Gonzales replied, "just a man I passed the time with." The board then turned to her employer, Rafael Maximin, for questioning. "Do you know anything about the moral character of this girl?" the officer asked Maximin. "Yes, I know. I know about that. I guess two and a half years ago, she had a baby," he replied. "You are still willing to take care of her?" the board asked. "Yes, she has no father, no mother, or anybody to look after her. We had her baby baptized in our church and the baby died in the church," he answered. Despite the fact that Maximin was a wealthy man who owned a store and a tortilla factory in San Francisco and was willing to take care of Gonzales, the board ordered her excluded and denied hospital treatment for hookworm. As Inspector Griffiths stated, Gonzales had admitted to committing "a misdemeanor involving moral turpitude prior to coming to the United States. I do not believe the woman is of good moral character."[37]

Inspectors were more lenient in the case of fifty-year-old Dolores Flores, whose adult son, born out of wedlock, was fully aware of and accepting of his mother's status. Moreover, Flores refused to be cowed by immigration officials' moral grandstanding during her examination. "How is it that you claim to be destined to your son and you claim never to have been married?" the inspecting officer demanded. "I did not need to get married to have a son," Flores retorted.[38]

Immigration officials' surveillance of migrant women's morality extended even to female witnesses who came to the island to testify on behalf of applicants in detention. When Sofia Jimenez appeared in March 1917 to testify on behalf of her son, for example, immigration officials asked questions regarding her own sexual relations with men after she admitted that she "never had a husband." "Did you ever live with any other man except [the father of your son?]" they asked. "Have you ever had any immoral relations with any other man?" The interrogator did demonstrate some respect for the witness and asked her if she minded being asked "questions along these lines in the presence of the alien," her son. She said no.[39]

Inspectors also tried to ensure that relatives already in the United States would exert good moral authority over incoming aliens. When eighteen-year-old Dolores Veco arrived in 1914 from Mazatlán, inspectors closely questioned her sister about how she would monitor Veco's behavior. "You will give this girl a home and take care of her?" they asked. "If she is willing to stay with me and be good," the sister answered. "If she don't, I don't want bad girls with me." This answer, with its ring of righteous morality, seemed to placate officers. Veco was admitted after three days of detention.[40]

Immigrant inspectors' vigilante examinations of Mexican women's sexuality and respectability resulted in high exclusion rates. From 1910 to 1930, more Mexican women were excluded for being suspected prostitutes than any other group of immigrants applying for admission at U.S. ports of entry.[41] In contrast to the close attention given to female migrants' sexual behavior and moral pasts, immigration officials paid only passing notice to cases where men's heterosexual activity strayed outside of the bounds of marriage. Fathers of illegitimate children, for example, were not treated with nearly the same scrutiny or censure as their female counterparts. Rather, the status of their illegitimate children was recorded solely as factual. George R. Paulson, an American citizen, desired to bring his illegitimate child born to a Mexican woman to the United States. When he applied for admission, the immigrant inspector questioning him did not pry or probe into his sexual past. His answer that "I was not married to this woman but she kept house for me" appeared sufficient enough. He and his child were landed after one day.[42]

The Mexican Immigration "Problem"

While class status and gender-based standards of respectability were consistently used to determine which Mexican migrants should enter the country and which ones should not, race increasingly entered into the equation as American anxiety over Mexican immigration grew. By the 1920s, an unprecedented number of Mexicans were entering the country, and more of them were staying to raise families. Americans began to question the soundness of the lax enforcement of immigration laws at the U.S.-Mexico border. Although Mexican immigration remained largely protected by agricultural and industrial employers through the 1920s, the chorus of growing anti-Mexican sentiment grew louder. Like Asian immigrants, Mexicans became increasingly described in racial terms. They were characterized as an ignorant "hybrid race" of Spanish and Indian origin, or "Indian peons" who were docile, indolent, and backward because of both their race and their Catholicism. Their only value was in providing the degraded agricultural labor that whites could not (or would not) perform. George P. Clemens, the head of the Los Angeles County Agricultural Department, explained that Mexicans (and Asians) possessed unique "crouching and bending habits" that whites did not possess. But their value diminished greatly during times of economic recession or when they moved out of the fields and into factories and industries where they competed with whites for employment. Then, Mexicans and Mexican Americans were seen as "foreign usurpers of American jobs."[43]

By the 1920s, anti-immigrant activists were lobbying for the restriction of Mexican immigration along the same lines as the successful campaigns to exclude Asian immigrants. The massive numbers of Mexican laborers, they argued, were a major menace to the Southwest. Major Frederick Russell Burnham warned that "our whole Southwest will be racially Mexican in three generations unless some similar restriction is placed upon them." V. S. McClatchy, editor of the *Sacramento Bee* and a leader of the earlier campaign to exclude Japanese migrants, warned that both the Filipino and Mexican "immigration problem[s]" were "major hardship[s] on the American people." The "wholesale introduction of Mexican peons," he claimed, presented California's "most serious problem" in the 1920s.[44]

The characterization of Mexicans as an undesirable, racially inferior immigrant invasion increasingly filtered into immigration officials' deliberations in Mexican cases on Angel Island. Inspectors routinely conflated persons of Mexican ancestry with being "poor" or having low intelligence. References to the "average Mexican," or individuals who were "poorly clad, not over intelligent, but evidently of the agricultural class" were common in immigration hearings. When they inspected Mexican applicants who were middle class in appearance or who displayed intelligence and respectability, they identified them as being exceptional for their race. When Luis Algarin arrived in San Francisco in late 1915, for example, he impressed immigration officials with his appearance. Both he and his brother, the inspecting officer reported, appear "to be far above the average Mexican" and seemed "industrious in their character."

The "fine" appearance and behavior of fifty-year-old seamstress Eutacia Losano also convinced immigration officials that she should be admitted in 1915. The Board of Special Inquiry found that she was "well dressed and answers questions intelligently. [She] appears to be of the better class of Mexican people." Losano was admitted after three days of detention.[45]

So-called average Mexicans faced increasing scrutiny as the regulation of Mexican immigration became more restrictive, especially at the border but also on Angel Island. General immigration laws—including the LPC provision—were used with more frequency and intensity to restrict Mexican immigration. Immigration officials looked for evidence of savings, property, or signs that the applicant could withstand the tough physical exertion required for manual labor. When thirty-six-year-old Catarino Lopez, his wife Esther Galarza, and their three children applied for admission in September 1913, Inspector William Chadney and the Board of Special Inquiry asked only a few cursory questions of Lopez before unanimously voting to exclude the entire family as likely to become public charges. Lopez had only $9, his wife was in a stage of advanced pregnancy, and two of his three children were found to be afflicted with hookworm. Commissioner of Immigration Samuel Backus concluded that neither Catarino nor Esther could secure jobs as laborers and support their growing family. "The aliens themselves present a very poor appearance, the father...is thin, scrawny-looking and not at all rugged; the mother is in delicate condition, expecting to be confined very shortly, and the children give very strong evidence of being illy nourished and poorly developed," reported the commissioner. The family's "poor," "scrawny," and "delicate" appearances were used as evidence of actual and future poverty. Inspector Chadney concluded that the Lopezes would "in a short while become public charges."

Esther Galarza Lopez and her children, including twins who were born at the Angel Island Immigration Station's hospital in 1913. (General Commission on Archives and History, United Methodist Church, Drew University.)

The family's Galarza relatives in Sacramento rallied to their defense. Catarino's brother-in-law Jose Castillo sent a handwritten note in English to the station in support of the Lopez family's application. Esther's brother Gustavo Galarza traveled to the station nine days after the family landed to testify on their behalf. He told immigration officials that he

Ernesto Galarza on burro, Sacramento, CA, 1916. (Courtesy of William D. Estrada.)

had a good job working in irrigation projects in Sacramento and had $69. The family sought assistance from the Sacramento-based newspaper *Catholic Herald* and the YWCA. While both organizations wrote letters of support for the family, neither made concrete promises to support them financially should they become public charges. The immigration service's deportation order remained in place. In the intervening months, Esther Galarza had entered the final weeks of pregnancy and was unable to travel. In October, she gave birth to twins, and on December 27, 1913, the entire Lopez family was deported back to Mexico.[46]

Chicano historian and activist Ernesto Galarza remembered the plight of the Lopez family well. Esther Galarza Lopez and Catarino Lopez were his aunt and uncle, and he recalled his visit to Angel Island and the family's struggles to help their relatives in his autobiography, *Barrio Boy*. The Galarzas had already tried to reunite with the Lopezes in the United States once before, but that attempt had failed. Ernesto was just eight years old when the Lopezes were detained. As a young boy, he did not understand the particularities of the case or the law's prohibition on LPC cases. But he did understand the feelings of helplessness and sadness in both families that resulted from the order to deny entry.

> With safer bearings of our own we were ready for another attempt at a family reunion. One had already failed. The Lopez's had left Jalco and reached Mazatlán but had returned to the village to await better times. Now the revolution was moving south again, making travel by rail to the United States unsafe. It was agreed that they would make the journey by sea to San Francisco.
>
> By the kitchen calendar we counted the days. On the last one Gustavo, my mother, José and I took the train for a trip that was a fiesta of smiles and anecdotes, and a great deal of reminiscing about our last days in Jalco when we had last seen our relatives. Together again we would be four men accustomed to *trabajo*, sufficient to support the women and the young.
>
> On the waterfront we boarded a launch that took us across the bay to Angel's Island where our kinfolk were in quarantine. The boat churned

up a heavy wake and seagulls swooped around us, squeaking. As she always did, my mother nodded her head this way and that, explaining the things or the people she was calling to my attention. I watched the pilot turn us smoothly alongside a wharf. A man in uniform took us through a building and out into an open courtyard from which we could see the city across the bay. A strong sea wind was blowing, cold and salty.

The Lopez family were standing at the far end of the yard: my aunt, slender and poised in long skirts and a shawl; don Catarino, in freshly washed work clothes, a coat and a felt hat which he held clamped down with one hand; Jesús, Catarino, and a younger brother wrapped in blankets. Huddled between them were two wicker baskets, each with a twin, born on the trip.

There was no laughter, no shouting for joy, no backslapping at the reunion. The excitement was inward and it came out only in the smiles and the formal, gentle *abrazos* all around. Following the cue of the adults I merely said: "How are you, Jesús? How are you, Catarino?" And they answered, "How are you, Ernesto?"

My cousins were shy and I just stood by them, staring at my relatives, one by one. My aunt and my mother were talking. Gustavo and José were listening to Don Catarino.

The women took our hands, the men carried the cribs and together we went inside the building. After a long wait the man in uniform joined us. An interpreter was with him.

The immigration officer, through the interpreter, was explaining. The Lopez's would not be allowed to enter the United States. There were papers on the desk in front of him. He explained the rules and the laws and the orders and they all made the same point: the family would be detained for a few days on the island and would then have to return to Mexico the way they had come.

So it was hello and good-bye in one afternoon. We left them by the wharf. From the launch we waved and lost them in our wake.

The trip back to Sacramento was like returning from a funeral. My uncles exchanged puzzled questions, bitter and despairing, anger and grief in their faces, staring out of the window to avoid looking at each other.

They paid little attention to my comments, caught up in their own distress. The man in uniform had merely shown us some papers but he had not told us why. He had not even said what would have to be done to bring our family back and take them home with us. I saw him vividly in my mind, ugly and menacing, and silently called him all the names I could think of, like *gringo pendejo*. But my secret revenge did not make me feel better as I tried to guess what Gustavo meant when he had said on the launch: "Es una injusticia." Our hopes had been denied and our joy had been turned to sadness by people we were powerless even to question.[47]

Many Mexican immigrants like the Lopezes were denied entry under the LPC clause. Those applying during economic recessions in the United States found it even harder to gain admission into the country. During these times, white Americans no longer recognized any value in Mexican labor, focusing instead on its threat. On Angel Island, immigration officials found it easier to justify excluding Mexicans on the perceived competitive threat they posed to (white) workers. Juan, Frederico, Antonio, and Fortunato Cesana, for example, were classified as "average" working-class Mexicans when they applied for admission in February 1916, a time when California was experiencing a war-related economic downturn. Given the fact that they were "not conversant with the English language" and that there was currently a "great number of unemployed in the vicinity of San Francisco and adjacent towns," the applicants were characterized as aliens who posed an economic threat to California workingmen and were ordered excluded under the LPC provision.

In the Board of Special Inquiry hearing, the immigration officers considered the brothers' case within the context of what they believed to be a Mexican immigration "problem." They discussed the dangers of Mexican immigration and the racial differences between Mexicans and whites. The chair of the board explained that it was "the experience of this office that our penal institutions are filled with persons from Mexico." Their "roving disposition...forced [them], perhaps, to commit crimes which has brought about their incarceration; and we continually in this office are investigating and deporting men of the same class as appear before the Board now." Linking Mexicanness with criminal behavior, the inspector continued, "there are more Mexican criminals in percentage than other aliens in this state." These arguments connected Mexican immigrants like the Cesana brothers to larger societal dangers that Mexicans allegedly posed to American society: economic competition with white workers and a growing crime rate. Race combined with economics to sustain the government's main argument that the brothers would be unable to find employment during the wartime recessed economy.

The brothers attempted to demonstrate that they were likely to find work and would not be public charges. But when Eustroforio's employer, H. C. Davey, president of the New Guadaloupe Mining Company of Santa Clara, came forward to testify that he and Eustroforio had discussed the possibility of the brothers working at the mine before they had left Mexico, the board ruled that the brothers were attempting to come into the country as contract laborers, another excludable offense. The brothers appealed the decision and hired attorney Arthur Shannon to present their case. Shannon's brief to the U.S. Department of Labor described how the brothers had had an "inherent longing to come to the United States" since they were children. He emphasized that the men were sober and industrious, young, "strong and able-bodied, ready and willing to work." The appeal was effective. After immigration officials had seemingly used all of the tools at their disposal to try to deny entry to the Cesana brothers, the commissioner of immigration reversed the decision to exclude, stating that the men were not in danger of becoming public charges. Juan, Fortunato, Frederico, and Antonio were landed on appeal.[48]

Angel Island versus the Border

The difficulties that the Cesana brothers faced on Angel Island reflected a national shift in American attitudes about unregulated Mexican migration between the 1910s and 1920s. A ready supply of migratory Mexican laborers was acceptable, even encouraged by the American people, as long as they did not compete with white workers. Ideally, they would work and then return home. But as soon as Mexican workers posed an economic threat and began to stay in the United States rather than go back to Mexico, their large numbers, their alleged racial inferiority, and their suspect morals were all interpreted as risks to the nation. By the 1920s, anti-immigrant activists began lobbying for the restriction of Mexican immigration. Unlike the case of Asian immigrants, Angel Island was not at the epicenter of these debates, and Mexican immigrants did not face the same kind of scrutiny at the immigration station as their Asian counterparts.

If the experiences of Mexicans on Angel Island were distinctive from those of Asians at the immigration station they were also quite different from those of other Mexicans entering the country by land across the U.S.-Mexico border. In particular, the processing of Mexican immigrants on Angel Island contrasted sharply with the procedures in place at the Júarez-El Paso border crossing, the main point of entry for Mexican immigrants. By the time the national debate over Mexican immigration was gaining momentum, only a very small number of Mexican immigrants were entering the United States through the immigration station on Angel Island. Large numbers of Mexicans did continue to use the entry points along the border during the 1920s, and correspondingly, the most intense campaigns to restrict Mexican immigration were centered in southern California and southwestern states like Texas and Arizona.

As a result of these campaigns, the regulation of Mexican immigration across the border became transformed from a casual and easy inspection—with perhaps a few questions asked by officials—to a tense and formal bureaucratic process that cast suspicion on all Mexicans. The chaotic nature of the Mexican Revolution, Mexican immigrants' attempts to evade paying the new U.S. head tax established in 1917, and an overall heightened government obsession with hygienic procedures and policing all contributed to this change at the border. After four fatal cases of typhus fever were reported in El Paso in 1917, border officials established procedures to place everybody entering the United States from Mexico under the strictest quarantine. The government assigned additional personnel to the site of the international bridge connecting the two countries and expanded its facilities for the inspection of aliens. Many of the new medical and inspection procedures had originated at the immigration station at Ellis Island and were followed on Angel Island as well. Upon arrival on the American side, immigration officials initially separated first-class from second-class immigrants. Those who appeared more wealthy were inspected briefly on the trains. By contrast, those who belonged to the laboring classes were subjected to sanitization, bathing, delousing, and a humiliating medical examination. Their clothing and baggage were fumigated.[49]

After receiving medical clearances, Mexican immigrants were then subjected to general immigration examinations to determine any mental or physical defects, and aliens were required to take a literacy test. Aliens who claimed marriage but were unable to produce documentation were then sent before a special Board of Inquiry. If the board decided that the marriage had not occurred, the couple could be excluded on grounds of "moral turpitude." Those who were not required to appear before the board had only to present their head tax receipts before being discharged. The rate of immigrant processing at the El Paso station was large. As many as 500 to 600 persons were detained for endless hours each day without benefit of drinking fountains or toilet facilities. Government officials examined an estimated 236 bodies per hour in El Paso, whereas physicians examined slightly over 350 bodies a day on Ellis Island.[50]

The changes at El Paso, combined with the government's rigorous new scrutiny of Mexican immigrants, signaled an enormous change in how the United States regulated Mexican immigration. The border became a highly contested line of demarcation separating the United States and Mexico. The El Paso border crossing became a site comparable to the immigration stations on Ellis Island and Angel Island. The same medical examinations and class-conscious and race-conscious procedures that had long been part of the routine inspections at these two seaport immigration stations were extended to the border.[51]

During the 1920s, the divisive debate over Mexican immigration continued. The quota provisions of the 1921 and 1924 immigration acts had not included countries in the Western Hemisphere, including Mexico. But beginning in 1926, immigration from Mexico became a primary target. Representative John C. Box, a Democrat from Texas, introduced a succession of bills seeking to amend the Quota Act to restrict Mexican immigration. Behind him stood an alliance of small farmers, progressives, labor unions, eugenicists, and racists. Although restrictionists were unsuccessful in their efforts to get legislation passed that set a quota on migration from Mexico, they did manage to bring about passage of the bill that created the Border Patrol in 1925, which more strictly enforced entry along the Mexican border. Beginning in August 1928, consular officers began to deny visas to most Mexicans seeking entry into the United States, basing their decisions on the grounds of illiteracy, the probability of becoming a public charge, or arrival as a contract laborer. The numbers are striking. Between 1923 and 1929, an average of 62,000 Mexicans a year legally entered the United States. After the changes went into effect, only 2,457 Mexicans legally entered the United States in 1930. After March 1930, all Mexican laborers, with the exception of those who had previously resided in the United States, were also unilaterally denied visas.[52]

A new chapter in the history of Mexican migration into the United States had begun. During the 1920s, Mexicans in the United States had been transformed from migratory workers who crossed the U.S.-Mexico border with ease to undocumented immigrants or "illegal aliens" in territory that had been part of Mexico less than a century before. During the Great Depression of the 1930s, Mexican immigrants were also targeted for repatriation like Filipinos, many of whom exited the country through Angel Island. Coercive repatriation programs forced approximately one million persons, or one-third of the Mexicans residing in the United States, to return to Mexico. In four Southern California counties (Los Angeles, San Bernadino, Riverside, and San Diego), one-quarter of the Mexican population left.[53]

Just like hundreds of thousands of other immigrants, Mexicans found Angel Island to be either an open door pointing the way to new lives in the United States or a closed gate forcing their return to Mexico. Unlike many Asian immigrants, they were not subjected to the same institutionalized suspicion or harsh exclusionary laws designed to keep them out of the country. But their experiences were different from those of European immigrants as well, especially after anti-Mexican sentiment increased in the 1920s and calls to restrict Mexican migration became more widespread. By the 1930s, the regulation of Mexican immigration would be most similar to that of Filipinos, who also lost the privilege of entering the United States with few restrictions and became targets of discriminatory immigration and repatriation laws.

Filipinos arriving in the United States, 1924. (Courtesy of Photographic Collections, Visual Communications.)

CHAPTER EIGHT

FROM "U.S. NATIONALS" TO "ALIENS"

FILIPINO MIGRATION AND REPATRIATION THROUGH
ANGEL ISLAND

IN THE FALL OF 1924, Rafael Magno left Santa, his native village in the province of Ilocos Sur and headed for the Philippine capital of Manila. There, he boarded an American steamship and sailed for Honolulu. As a "U.S. national" by virtue of the United States' colonization of the Philippines, Magno and the more than 150,000 Filipinos who migrated to Hawaii and the U.S. mainland in the early twentieth century could travel freely within the territorial domain of the United States. Neither immigration restrictions nor lengthy examinations and detentions on Angel Island applied to them. Instead, they were given cursory examinations on board their steamships and then were allowed to disembark. Magno worked on Hawaiian plantations for four years and got married on the island of Kauai before returning to the Philippines with his wife. But times were tough back home. In April of 1934, he borrowed 195 pesos from his father and brother to return to the United States. He and his second cousin traveled to San Francisco on the *President Hoover*. They were bound for Watsonville, California, where another cousin promised them work in the fields. Magno planned to stay in the United States for six years and then return home.[1]

U.S. immigration laws had changed since Magno had entered the country eleven years earlier. While he and his fellow passengers on the *President Hoover* had sailed from Manila to the United States, a new law had gone into effect. The Tydings-McDuffie Act of 1934 granted independence to the Philippines. But it also changed the status of Filipinos from "U.S.

273

nationals" to "aliens subject to the immigration laws of the U.S." The change in status was highly significant. U.S. nationals were colonial subjects who owed their allegiance to the United States and did not need passports or any documentation to enter the country. Aliens, or foreigners who were not citizens of the United States, however, did. Thus, when the *President Hoover* docked in San Francisco, all Filipinos on board the steamship were taken by ferry to the Angel Island Immigration Station for questioning by immigration officials.[2]

The cases of Magno and his fellow Filipino shipmates presented a legal quandary. They had sailed from Manila to the United States after the Tydings-McDuffie Act had been signed into law in the United States in March, but before the law had been accepted by the Philippine government in May. Filipino passengers on five other ships arrived in San Francisco under similar conditions. In total, 261 Filipinos would face questions about their legal status. Could they be considered under the old rules since they had been at sea when the law had gone into effect? Or would they automatically be excluded once they arrived in the United States? On May 16, Magno appeared before Inspectors Hanlen, Tomkins, and Oliver at the immigration station and answered their many questions about his work history, land holdings in the Philippines, family members in both the United States and the Philippines, earlier trips to the United States, and intention to stay in the country. Immigrant inspectors treated Magno as an alien rather than a U.S. national, and after finding that he was not in possession of a "valid Immigration visa or any other documents required by the immigration laws of this country," they denied him admission into the United States under the Tydings-McDuffie Act.[3]

The change in legal status had a great impact on both new Filipino migrants and returning residents. Prior to 1934, hardly any Filipinos spent time on Angel Island because of their colonial status as U.S. nationals. After 1934, when they were reclassified as aliens, immigration from the Philippines was limited to fifty persons per year, and Filipino immigration slowed to a trickle. Those Filipinos who did continue to come to the United States, including returning residents and U.S. citizens, were subjected to some of the same interrogations and detentions that applied to other Asian immigrants, and Filipinos began to be detained on Angel Island in more significant numbers.

Filipinos in the United States also became targets of government-sponsored repatriation programs after 1935 in which the Angel Island Immigration Station played a key role. Angel Island immigration officials were key architects and enforcers of the Filipino repatriation program, and the immigration station served as the detention center for repatriates on their way back to the Philippines.[4]

The number of Filipinos who were actually processed or detained on Angel Island was not large compared to other immigrant groups. But Angel Island's involvement in Filipino exclusion and repatriation reminds us of its larger role as a immigrant gateway into and out of the country. For some Filipinos, the Angel Island Immigration Station was an entry point to a better life in America; for others, it was also the last stop on a forced journey out of the country, a reminder of the legacy of American colonialism in the Philippines.

Coming to the "Land of Paradise"

The earliest Filipino migrants to the Americas came as sailors with the Manila galleon trade that carried Chinese luxury goods between Manila and Acapulco from 1565 to 1815. Some "Manilamen" settled near New Orleans. Large-scale Filipino migration to the United States was rooted in the American conquest of the Philippine Islands in 1898. The United States acquired the Philippine Islands, along with Puerto Rico and Guam, as a result of its victory in the Spanish American War in 1898. The United States had annexed Hawaii earlier that year and with its new possessions became an imperial power. Filipinos' colonial status distinguished them from other immigrants and shaped every aspect of their migration to and lives in the United States.

The conquest of the Philippines was violent, and resistance to American colonialism was strong in the islands. Nevertheless, American officials saw the U.S. role in the Philippines as one of "benevolent assimilation." As President William McKinley declared, it was the role of the United States to educate, civilize, and uplift Filipinos so that they could one day rule themselves. American colonialism in the Philippines brought American-style schools, the English language, American teachers, and an American-style public health system. American ideals, history, culture, and values were emphasized in the schools, and the generation of Filipinos who came of age during the early American colonial period came to view America as a "land of Paradise."[5]

At the same time, posters promoting immigration to the United States could be found all over the Philippines, and a culture of migration took root. Economic factors pushed an even larger number of Filipinos to seek opportunities abroad. American colonial policies led to increased poverty, tenancy, and landlessness. Families began to pool together what little savings they had to purchase tickets to the United States, and labor recruiters preyed upon desperate Filipinos with tales of quick money to be made in America. The U.S. government also established a "pensionado" program that brought elite Filipino students to American universities. It was hoped that these pensionados would return to the Philippines to complete the process of Americanization in the islands and to take up leadership positions in the Philippines.[6]

The majority of Filipinos who came to the United States before World War II came from the Ilocos, Pangasinan, and Tarlac regions on the island of Luzon. Many first went to Hawaii to work on the sugar plantations, where plantation owners sought labor competition for the largely Japanese workforce. Between 1907 and 1919, American recruiters from the Hawaiian Sugar Plantation Association brought over 24,000 Filipinos to Hawaii; from 1920 to 1929, another 48,000 followed.[7]

The migration was slower to the mainland United States. The first Filipinos to arrive in San Francisco were likely Filipino servants or stewards to U.S. navy officers. The 1920 census counted only 5,603 Filipinos on the mainland, many of them students. In the mid-1920s, the Dollar Steamship presidential liners began to offer affordable third-class passenger tickets from Manila to San Francisco, Los Angeles, and Seattle. From 1920 to 1929, more than 31,000 Filipinos arrived at California ports. Many had come from Honolulu, where they had worked as plantation laborers, a privilege denied to Japanese and Korean laborers who were prevented by law from entering the United States from Hawaii. By the late 1920s, the majority of Filipinos arriving on the U.S. mainland came directly from the Philippines rather than Hawaii, and in 1930, the population of Filipinos in the U.S. was 56,000. They were overwhelmingly young, single, male, and destined for farms in California's Central Valley or canneries in the Pacific Northwest and Alaska. The small numbers of married Filipino migrant men often left their wives and children behind while they worked in the United States, but most had other family members, including brothers, fathers, cousins, and uncles, already in the country. Women constituted less than 7 percent of the entire Filipino population in 1940.[8]

The trans-Pacific voyage between the Philippines and San Francisco took almost a month and was memorable mostly because of the rough travel conditions. The steamers typically made stops in Hong Kong and Tokyo, where additional passengers boarded. The next stop was Honolulu and then San Francisco or Los Angeles. Most Filipinos traveled in the steamers' crowded and unsanitary third-class section.[9]

Eliseo Felipe was twenty-one when he left his home in Laoag, Ilocos Norte to brave the long trans-Pacific voyage to the United States in 1933. He hoped to gain some of the wealth and opportunity that the steamship companies and labor recruiters promised. As a U.S. national, he did not have to go to the Angel Island Immigration Station for any inspection or interrogation.

We were a very poor family in the Philippines. My father was a farmer and a little bit of a carpenter and a goldsmith. He tried many

Eliseo Felipe, 1940. (Scan by Vincent Chin. National Archives, Pacific Regional Branch.)

jobs just to make a living. I just finished high school—ten years, from first grade up to high school. I cry when I think of my life because so many of my co-graduates were going to school then in Manila, and here I was back home in the old province. They were beginning to get a higher education than me, but what can I do? My father can't afford it.

I was a carpenter, farmer, and those kinds of jobs. I earned about 50 centavos a day, which is about 25 cents American money. Jobs like digging irrigation ditches. I felt kind of low compared to those who were getting a high education. So I was determined to see if I could come to the States.

There was an agent who recruited people to go to Hawaii. My brother and my uncles and so many of my relatives are already in Hawaii, so I asked the immigration officer if I could come to the States. And they said, yes!

The fare then was 190 pesos (or $64). So I was scared my father won't be able to find a way to give me extra money to come here. Thank goodness, he sold a little piece of land, I was so happy...

There I go, get into the boat. Man! It took about twenty-nine days. There were other cargo and animals down in the steerage. The waves were so wild, I was sick from Manila until I got to Hawaii. I could hardly eat anything. But it didn't bother me. I was determined. When we got to Hawaii, they asked everybody who wanted to get off in Hawaii to get off. So I said, my golly, I better go to America because I had my brother and uncle over here.

[There was no immigrant inspection in San Francisco.] I just got off the boat. It was like getting off the bus. There was someone from my hometown who came to the pier. He noticed me and he took me to his friend and relatives, where they live in San Francisco. I had about $3 left, but it didn't worry me at all. I don't know why, but I think someone was leading me to a good life.[10]

Filipinos landing at the port of San Francisco usually did not stay in the city for very long. While there was work to be found as doormen, janitors, or cooks in the hotels and restaurants in the city, most new arrivals headed out to the Central Valley to find agricultural work. Stockton became home to the largest Filipina/o community outside of the Philippines from the 1920s to the 1970s and was known as "Little Manila."[11]

Although they had been immersed in lessons about the "best of America" in the Philippines, once in the United States, Filipinos quickly learned about some of America's worst characteristics: exploitation of laborers and racial discrimination. Eighty percent of Filipinos in the United States became migratory laborers traveling among the major agricultural centers like Delano, Stockton, the San Fernando Valley, and the canneries in the Pacific Northwest and Alaska. Filipinos were the largest Asian immigrant migratory workforce in California during the late 1920s and 1930s. The Chinese, Japanese, and South Asian farm laborers who had come before them had all been excluded by federal immigration laws. Filipinos dominated the asparagus and lettuce industries, which required "stoop labor" to harvest the crops. Growers routinely claimed that the shorter stature of Filipinos and other Asians as well as Mexicans made them more physically suited than whites to the hard labor needed in these fields. In Salinas, Filipinos worked eight to ten hours a day, earning 15 cents an hour until 1933, when the wages were raised by 5 cents.[12]

Eliseo Felipe, who began working in Stockton soon after his arrival in 1933, explained that Filipinos followed the crops. His work took him from Stockton to Wyoming, Montana, and Utah. "I stayed in different camps because crops followed the different seasons. So when asparagus is over here, we are already done, getting ready for grapes. Then when the grapes is over, the tomatoes are ready to ripen up. We had to go where the

Filipino asparagus cutters in the 1920s. By the 1920s and 1930s, Filipinos made up the largest Asian immigrant work force in California agriculture. (Photograph by John Y. Billones. Courtesy of Filipino American National Historical Society, Stockton Chapter.)

job was. Name it, baby, I was there. I was not particular. I just wanted to work." Felipe was paid 19½ cents per hour when he first began working. The highest he received was about 25 cents, just before the start of World War II. Even as their wages increased, Filipinos remained among the most exploited laborers in the agricultural industry.[13]

Another "Asiatic Invasion" and the Anti-Filipino Movement

At first, Filipino migration to the mainland United States caused little opposition. Their numbers were still relatively small compared to other groups. As American colonial subjects, they were either ignored or praised as being "good citizens." But as their numbers began to steadily increase in the 1920s, they were increasingly seen as a "problem." No longer contained in a far-off American colony, Filipinos in America symbolized the inherent contradiction between American colonialism and benevolent assimilation policies in the Philippines, on the one hand, and Asian exclusion and domestic racism in the United States, on the other.[14] Especially during the Great Depression, Filipinos were increasingly described as undesirable Asians, another "Asiatic invasion" that was worse than the Chinese, Japanese, and South Asians who had already been successfully excluded by 1924. Repeating earlier anti-Asian arguments, nativists charged that the present case of Filipino immigration was truly the worst and most dangerous of the Asian immigration problems. Filipinos were portrayed as a "backward, uncivilized, wild and naked people" who had criminal tendencies and who would never make good U.S. citizens. V. S. McClatchy, editor of the *Sacramento Bee*, emphatically declared that the Filipino question was "equally important as the Japanese immigration problem." The growing number of Filipinos "swarming into the United States," he continued, "would lower citizenship standard[s], and if left unchecked...would lead to the destruction of the republic." California Congressman Richard J. Welch from San Francisco agreed and told the public in 1930 that Filipino immigration was "one of the gravest problems that has ever faced the people of the Pacific Coast." Both Welch and McCarthy supported an all-out ban on the new invasion.[15]

American labor organizations and other opponents of Filipino immigration demanded Filipino exclusion in the name of white workers' rights and living standards. Filipinos, they claimed, were an economic danger because they competed with a broad swath of American workers. "They take away jobs as chambermaids and housemaids from middle-aged women and jobs from elevator boys and leave able-bodied American seamen walking the streets, all because they, the Filipinos, will work for less," police judge George Steiger claimed in 1930. The charge of job competition masked a deep-rooted racial antagonism directed toward all Asians.

There were few native white migrant laborers in California agriculture in the 1920s. Filipinos mostly competed for jobs with Mexicans, Japanese, South Asians, and Koreans.[16]

In their opposition to Filipino immigration, eugenicists and nativists argued that Filipinos threatened the racial purity of white America. Ignoring the fact that Filipinos spoke English, were Christians, were educated in American schools, and were familiar with American popular culture, anti-Filipino forces charged that Filipino "little brown brothers" were completely unassimilable. But the primary complaint against them seemed to be that they upset the existing racial hierarchy between whites and nonwhites in the United States. Their flashy clothes, sexual relations with white women, and big cars challenged the myth of white supremacy in ways that other Asian immigrants had not. The sexual behavior of the largely male population particularly raised white fears of interracial mixing. V. S. McClatchy, who became chair of the California Joint Immigration Commission (a coalition of labor and nativist groups), complained that Filipinos were the "worst form of Orientals," because their interracial relationships brought about the "delinquency of young girls." In 1926, California's attorney general extended the state's antimiscegenation civil code to include Filipinos.[17]

Anti-Filipino violence escalated in the late 1920s and early 1930s. On New Year's Eve in 1926, white men went in search of Filipinos in Stockton's hotels and pool halls, and by the end of the night, eight men had been stabbed and beaten. Over the next few years, Filipinos were expelled from the Yakima Valley in Washington; Filipino laborers socializing with white women were attacked in Dinuba, California; and mobs attacked Filipinos in Exeter, Modesto, Turlock, and Reedley. In December 1929, a mob of 400 white men attacked a Filipino dance hall in Watsonville after a local newspaper published a photograph of a Filipino man and white teenage girl embracing. Even though the couple was engaged and had the blessings of the girl's family, the incident touched off many political pronouncements about the economic and moral threat that Filipino immigrants posed. Four days of rioting ensued after the attack on the dance hall, leaving many Filipinos beaten and one dead.[18]

Vigilante violence translated into legal discrimination against Filipinos as well. In January 1930, the Northern Monterey County Chamber of Commerce passed a number of anti-Filipino resolutions. In Stockton, hotels and landlords refused to rent to Filipinos. Police routinely arrested Filipinos at random or raided gambling halls. The violence and legal and extra-legal discrimination directed at Filipino migrants became so intense that writer Carlos Bulosan was moved to write that "it was a crime to be a Filipino in California." Labor and patriotic organizations, including the California Joint Immigration Committee, the American Federation of Labor, and the American Legion, made Filipino exclusion a central issue at their national meetings from 1927 to 1929. Paul Scharrenberg, secretary-treasurer of the California State Federation of Labor, testified before Congress that Filipino exclusion was necessary because they were cheap laborers who could not be assimilated, and their moral conduct caused "serious offense" to whites.[19]

The main obstacle to Filipino exclusion, however, was Filipinos' status as U.S. nationals, which allowed them to enter the country without restrictions. The first step, exclusionists agreed, was to try to change the legal status of Filipinos so that they could be legally excluded from the United States. Toward that end, Congressman Welch introduced legislation that would declare Filipinos "aliens." In the Senate, Senator Samuel M. Shortridge (R-CA) introduced a slightly different bill restricting Filipino immigration along the lines of the Chinese exclusion laws. Only students, visitors, merchants, government officials, families, or servants would be admissible. Both the Shortridge and Welch bills failed because, as U.S. nationals, Filipinos could not be subjected to immigration laws written for foreigners. Lawmakers began to recognize that Filipino exclusion could only be achieved through Philippine independence. California State Attorney General Ulysses S. Webb made the connection between the two explicit in congressional hearings in 1931. "We want exclusion of the Filipinos and independence would exclude them," he explained. "If independence were granted, that would make them automatically subject to the act of 1924 [which stipulated that no "alien ineligible to citizenship" would be admitted] and they would be excluded." For their part, Philippine nationalists, who struggled to free their country from the United States, were willing to trade independence for Filipino exclusion, and their support allowed for new legislation to be drafted and passed.[20]

The 1934 Tydings-McDuffie Act

The Tydings-McDuffie Act was signed into law in the United States on March 24, 1934. The act granted the Philippines commonwealth status and a promise of independence after a ten-year waiting period. Philippine nationalists referred to the bill as the "Philippine Commonwealth and Independence Law." The act established an important pathway toward independence, but it also maintained many facets of the colonial relationship with the United States. The new government established in the Philippines had to be acceptable and subject to the approval of the United States, and American exports to the islands would remain duty free. In terms of immigration, the Tydings-McDuffie Act finally fulfilled the goals of exclusionists. It classified the Philippines as a "separate country" and placed Filipino immigration under the general immigration laws, including the 1917 Immigration Act and the 1924 national origins quota system. The Philippines was allotted an annual quota of only fifty persons—the lowest quota the United States assigned to any country in the world. It placed Filipinos slightly above other Asians, like Chinese and Japanese, who were both barred from naturalization and entry into the United States under the 1924 act. But unlike Chinese and Japanese immigrants, who had been able to bring their wives and children over for some years, the Tydings-McDuffie Act cut Filipinos off from their families in the Philippines. The overall effect of the law was Filipino exclusion. The act also changed the status of Filipinos—both new immigrants and those already in the United States—from U.S. "nationals" to "aliens." They would thereafter be subjected to the same general immigration laws, examinations, interrogations, detentions, and deportations as other immigrants. Reclassified as aliens, Filipinos were also barred from becoming naturalized citizens, leasing or owning land, and receiving federal or state assistance.[21]

The six steamships heading for San Francisco when the Philippine Legislature approved the Tydings-McDuffie Act carried 261 Filipinos with uncertain legal status. They had left the Philippines as U.S. nationals but arrived in the United States as aliens. San Francisco immigration officials sent the following telegram on May 1, 1934, to the Immigration and Naturalization Service (INS) in Washington, D.C.: "Morning papers report Philippine legislature today accepted independence measure stop Steamer President Taft arrived seven forty this morning with seventy three Filipino passengers stop Request telegraphic instruction as to disposition to be made in their cases." Commissioner-General of Immigration Edward Shaugnessy wired back from Washington that day instructing Angel Island officers to parole the Filipino passengers to a "responsible person" while a final decision was made. On May 10, Commissioner of Immigration Edward Haff requested permission to employ Marcelino Revilla as an "emergency Philippine interpreter" to take care of the unprecedented number of arrivals from the Philippines.[22]

Filipino passengers arriving in San Francisco in the days after the Philippine Legislature accepted the Tydings-McDuffie Act were given a medical examination at the immigration station hospital. Most were able to go before a Board of Special Inquiry within a week or two of their arrival. They were then denied admission into the United States on the grounds that they were considered aliens subject to all immigration laws of the United States. Those without proper visas or who were suspected of being contract laborers, illiterate, or likely to become public charges were denied entry. Applicants were informed that they could appeal the exclusion decision to the secretary of labor, which all did. While waiting, the Tydings-McDuffie Filipinos were allowed to enter the country on parole after being photographed and fingerprinted.[23]

The "responsible person" to whom the Filipino passengers were paroled was Anne Clo Watson, executive secretary of the International Institute of San Francisco, a settlement house that had formerly been part of the

YWCA. Located in downtown San Francisco, the institute had a mission to protect and integrate "foreign born and racial groups into [American] civilization." It hoped that immigrants and their children would become Americanized, responsible citizens. The institute organized international bazaars and dances and offered English language and domestic skills courses for foreign-born women. It also became increasingly involved in the legal aspect of immigration, and staff members routinely gave legal advice in matters pertaining to citizenship, deportation, and family reunification. This work put International Institute officers in direct contact with local immigration officials.[24]

Immigration officials on Angel Island, supported by their superiors in the INS and the Department of Labor, asked the International Institute to take responsibility for the parole of the Filipino "boys." Over the next few weeks, the institute became responsible for all of the Filipinos in limbo. The parolees were allowed to travel to their desired destinations, but they were required to notify institute staff of their destination and any time they moved. Each parolee carried an addressed postal card. As Mrs. James Reed, president of the Institute's Board of Directors wrote in 1936, some of the cards were returned, but many were not.

There are signs that Filipinos arriving on Angel Island trusted and relied on institute employees for assistance and counsel, especially Eugenia de Estoita, the Filipino caseworker. When newly arrived Filipinos fell victim to mercenary taxi drivers, for example, they wrote to the International Institute with warnings to give to other Filipinos leaving Angel Island. "Thank God we arrived in Salinas yesterday," wrote Vicente Vigillia, Ricardo Ibarra, and Rufo Boromeo to de Estoita on May 18, 1934. "But let me tell you what a terrible thing happened to us on the way." A taxi driver charged exorbitant rates and refused to take the riders all the way to their requested destination. He even threatened them with a gun. "We want that all Filipinos coming out of Angel Island will not experience the same thing which happened to us," they explained. They included the identity of the driver, his state badge and license. Staff workers could not take any legal action against the taxi drivers, but they changed their methods of "getting the Filipino boys to their stations and protected them" as they left the island.[25]

The International Institute's role changed dramatically when the appeals of the Tydings-McDuffie Filipinos were dismissed and their exclusion from the United States was affirmed in February of 1935.[26] Of the 138 parolees under the institute's responsibility, only two were admitted on appeal and two others were still under consideration. Those who were successful in their appeals were individuals who could prove that they had been prior residents in the United States before the bill had been passed and had gone to the Philippines for temporary visits. The remaining 134 were ordered to return to the Philippines. When the Department of Labor called on the International Institute to let the parolees know that their permission to enter the United States had been permanently denied, institute employees leaped into action. They issued letters to the Filipino parolees at their last-known addresses instructing them to report to Angel Island for voluntary departure. If they did not, the letters warned, they would be subject to deportation. Notices were published in the main Filipino newspapers in San Francisco, Stockton, and Salinas. Announcements were made to Filipino groups. As Mrs. James Reed reported to the San Francisco commissioner, "the response to the effort was...very limited." Many of the parolees had either moved away as part of their lives as migratory laborers or deliberately went into hiding to avoid deportation. Reed promised that the institute would "stand ready to be of any service within our power," but that power was limited. It was up to the Department of Labor to fully apply the law in order to "accomplish the return of the boys to the Philippines."[27]

Angel Island officials looked for the missing men up and down California, across the United States, and even in the Philippines. Inspectors interviewed family members, neighbors, employers, Selective Service Board officers, and postmasters in their quest to find, arrest, and deport the Tydings-McDuffie Filipinos. The searches lasted years, and in most cases, the individuals were never found. In 1937, Inspector Earl Cushing traveled throughout the small towns and ranches around Watsonville, California, looking for Rafael Magno with no success. Almost ten years later, Inspector R. B. Jones was looking for Magno in San Francisco. Magno's file does not indicate that he was ever found.[28]

Marcelo Domingo's case reveals how the immigration service's zealous manhunts had repercussions for entire families and communities. In 1937, officials in the San Francisco office wrote to Domingo's mother in Ilocos Sur for his address. They conveniently provided a postage-paid envelope. The immigration service next tracked down Portonato Domingo, Marcelo's brother who resided in Pismo Beach, California. "I would like to know why your office need his present address?" Portonato asked. "This said brother of mine is already in some parts of the Atlantic coast to attend school, but I have not received a letter from him so far." Portonato promised to send his brother's address when he himself heard from him. The Angel Island office transferred the case to Los Angeles, where immigration officials called Portonato for an interview. When he failed to respond, immigration officers went looking for him and found him at a Japanese gambling house in Guadalupe in November 1937. As the officers approached his table, Portonato reached into his pocket and quickly handed a bundle of letters to a friend. But he was too late, and Inspector Millard Chaffin confiscated the letters. Portonato was brought in to the San Luis Obispo office, where he was questioned relentlessly about his brother's whereabouts and the contents of his letters, many of which were apparently written by Marcelo under an alias. By the end of the interview, Portonato was pledging, "I am willing to help and I want him to be back in the Islands....I will follow your instructions and try and locate him by letters and when I do I'll call you and we can then go and get him. It may take some time but I'll keep trying." In the months following the interview, Chaffin reported back to the Angel Island office that "continuous lookout" had been kept up for Marcelo, but that he had most likely moved on. The immigration service kept Marcelo Domingo's file active for almost ten years before suspending the deportation order in 1946 due to the lack of steamer service to the Philippines.[29]

Filipinos as "Aliens"

The impact of the Tydings-McDuffie Act on those hundreds of Filipinos who were at sea when the law went into effect had great consequences for people like Marcelo Domingo. For many, the government's decision to exclude and deport Filipinos who arrived after May 1, 1934, affected them for years afterward. By reclassifying Filipinos as "aliens" instead of "U.S. nationals," the Tydings-McDuffie Act completely transformed the ways in which both new Filipino immigrants and returning residents were inspected and admitted into or excluded from the country. Before 1934, there was no limit to the number of Filipinos who could migrate to Hawaii or the mainland United States. After 1934, Filipino migration was limited to fifty persons a year, and the few new immigrants admitted had to carry valid visas. Residents returning to the United States after temporary visits abroad could apply for reentry as "nonquota immigrants" under the Immigration Act of 1924, but they had to provide documentation of their employment and residential history in the United States. Both new and returning Filipinos were subjected to the same medical examinations and interrogations as other groups on Angel Island. As a result, an increasing number of Filipinos were detained at the immigration station. From 1928 to 1940, there were 583 Filipinos on Angel Island; 73 percent were held for less than one week.[30]

One of these was Ambrosia Galutera, a twenty-one-year-old English teacher from Bayombong, Nueva Vizcaya, and bride of Florentino Ravelo, a Filipino resident of the United States. Thirty-seven-year-old Ravelo had been in the United States since 1920. He had worked as a railroad laborer in Montana and then became a clerk in the U.S. Postal Service in Chicago, Illinois. The couple was married in Nueva Vizcaya, Philippines, on January 5, 1935, and sailed for the United States shortly thereafter. When they arrived in San Francisco, Florentino applied for readmission as a returning permanent resident. Ambrosia applied for admission under the new annual quota of fifty persons assigned to the Philippines. She was number seventeen.

The couple was taken to the Angel Island Immigration Station. Ambrosia possessed a valid visa, a baptismal certificate verifying her birth date, and record of her marriage to Florentino. But she needed to pass the medical examination, and immigration officials had to verify Florentino's claims of being a returning resident of the United States. Once at the immigration station, Ambrosia passed the medical examination. Like all other detainees, the couple was separated into the men's and women's areas of the detention barracks and were not allowed to see each other. This separation took Ambrosia by surprise and caused her great distress. Two days into their detention, Florentino and Ambrosia were interviewed separately by Inspector G. W. Heckert. Florentino gave details of his first arrival in the United States in June 1920, a trip to the Philippines and readmission into the United States in 1930, and his last departure for the Philippines in November 1934. He also verified his employment history and gave inspectors a letter from the postmaster of Chicago describing his good standing at the post office. Additionally, he included details about

Longtime U.S. resident Florentino Ravelo (right) and his wife, Ambrosia on the shipping dock in Manila before their departure to America on the *President Hoover*, January, 23, 1935. With them is Ambrosia's older brother Florentino Galutera. After arriving in San Francisco, the couple was detained at the immigration station on Angel Island for five days. (Courtesy of Estrella Ravelo Alamar.)

his income, his address in Chicago, his family members in the United States, and his marriage to Ambrosia. After five days, the couple was released.[31]

Like Florentino Ravelo, other Filipinos already living in the United States prepared documentation of their work history and financial assets before taking any trips abroad. Eliseo Felipe, who had first arrived in 1933, decided to return to the Philippines for a visit in January 1940. He had saved $700 for a roundtrip ticket and as a gift to his family in the Philippines. Before he left San Francisco, he made sure to fill out a notarized affidavit that gave his name, birthplace, age, address, employment, and amount of personal savings. While such documentation had not been necessary for Filipino migrants before 1934, they learned that after being reclassified as aliens, such affidavits were crucial in facilitating reentry. Felipe's affidavit also included evidence of his employment as a bellboy with the Apartment Investment Co. of San Francisco. His employer, D. H. Dexter, swore that the company would be "able to maintain and support" Felipe and that it would "agree and guarantee to re-employ" Felipe upon his return to the United States.

After five months in the Philippines, Felipe began the journey back to the United States. On May 7, 1940, he was inspected by the U.S. Public Health Service in Manila and cleared for departure. The next day he traveled third class on the *President McKinley* back to San Francisco. With his paperwork in order, Felipe was surprised to be stopped by immigration officials when he arrived there. During his first trip to the United States in 1933, he had simply disembarked. This time, he was taken to Angel Island. "They just took me. I don't even know why," he said years later.

On June 1, he appeared before Inspector Abraham Hemstreet for an interrogation. Hemstreet wanted to make sure that Felipe had not been repatriated by the United States, which would have made him ineligible to return to the country. He also verified that Felipe had financial resources and gainful employment. Felipe could point to the $20 he carried with him, the letter from his employer, the money in his Bank of America savings account, and his $1,500 in life insurance policies. His answers satisfied the inspector, and he was readmitted into the country after a two-day detention. His short time at the immigration station was not memorable. "It was just for a day or two days. Eat and sleep, that's all." Unlike Chinese immigrants, whose long detentions caused anguish and despair, Felipe did not worry about when he would be released or whether he would be kept at the immigration station for a long time. "All I was interested in was getting back to San Francisco. They asked me if I had been working in San Francisco, where I had been, and that's about it. Then they took me out and put me on a little boat for San Francisco. I was sure I hadn't done anything wrong."

Compared to other Asian immigrants, Eliseo Felipe's time on Angel Island was unremarkable except for the fact that his 1940 readmission differed so much from his 1933 arrival. Felipe had adjusted to the new requirements by securing the necessary documentation. Even with such records, he had still been detained. But Felipe's detention also reveals how Filipinos' changing legal status after 1934 translated into new experiences with immigration law on Angel Island. For Filipinos who had grown up hearing about the promise of the United States in the Philippines and for returning residents who had achieved some success in the United States, this change in status came as a shock. As Eliseo Felipe explained years later, "I still wonder, they didn't even tell me why they had to detain me over at Angel Island."[32]

Returning Filipino American citizens also faced delays reentering the country after the Tydings-McDuffie Act, and some were detained on Angel Island. Such was the case of Maria Natividad (Nattie) Gaitos Ellorin, a native-born citizen from Stockton, California, applying for readmission into the United States on May 15, 1940. To her surprise, she found herself a victim of both the new Tydings-McDuffie Act and an older gender-based law that affected the citizenship and immigration status of Asian American women who married Asian aliens. Nattie was married to Flaviano Ellorin, a U.S. resident of Filipino descent born in the Philippines. Under the Act, Flaviano had been reclassified as an alien. This in turn impacted Nattie's immigration and citizenship status, because under the Cable Act of 1922, any woman citizen who married an alien ineligible to citizenship "cease[d] to be a citizen of the United States." A 1925 Supreme Court decision had ruled that Filipinos, like other Asians, were ineligible for citizenship, and many Asian American women found themselves expatriated upon their marriage to foreign-born Asian men.[33]

Because there were so few American-born Filipinos in the United States at the time, Nattie Ellorin's case was unique, and when she appeared on Angel Island for readmission into the country, the inspectors did not know how to handle the case. At her Board of Special Inquiry hearing on May 16, 1940, they asked her: "Did anyone ever tell you or suggest to you that your marriage to Flaviano Ellorin might have some effect on your United States citizenship?" "No, no one ever said anything to me about it," she replied. Both she and Flaviano were interrogated in separate sessions and then put into detention in the separate men's and women's barracks. Both the separation and the uncertainty over her status caused distress. Years later, she told her daughter Joyce that she was "very scared and cried all night."[34]

Nattie and Flaviano Ellorin on their wedding day in 1930. (Courtesy of Joyce Ellorin.)

Nattie Ellorin was admitted back into the country the next day, but not as a U.S. citizen. Immigration officials determined that she "may have lost her United States citizenship," though they could not find any definitive legal or administrative ruling on a similar case. They decided to admit her as a "returning immigrant" and a citizen of the Philippine Islands by marriage. For Nattie Ellorin, both the Cable Act and the Tydings-McDuffie Act had placed the status of her U.S. citizenship in jeopardy.[35]

Even Filipino Americans whose citizenship status remained secure after the Tydings-McDuffie Act faced obstacles on Angel Island after 1934. Elisa Calloway was one of fourteen children of a Filipino mother and white American father who was a veteran of the Span-

Elisa Hawkins and her daughter, Lourdes, arrived on Angel Island on June 26, 1935. (Courtesy of Eliza Brooks.)

ish-American War. Her parents had met while her father was stationed in the Philippines during the American occupation. Later, he retired from military service but continued to work for the U.S. government in the Philippines as a civil servant. From an early age, Elisa heard wonderful stories about the United States from her father. Letters from her American aunts and uncles enthralled her with their descriptions of life in America, and her father talked about his dream that one of his children would be able to travel to the United States to get an education. When her older brother died tragically at the age of nineteen, Elisa took it upon herself to fulfill her father's dream. She graduated from the Philippines Normal School and taught elementary school for a year while she saved money to come to the United States. In 1927, the nineteen-year-old sailed with her older sister, Petra, who was engaged to an American soldier, and her younger brother, Dick. As children of a U.S. citizen, they entered the country as U.S. citizens with American passports. Their admission into the country went very smoothly, and they did not have to go to Angel Island. Elisa attended college in Chicago. There, she met and married Basilio Hawkins, a childhood acquaintance who had also grown up in the Philippines and was part of a club for mixed-race children of white American soldiers and Filipino women. Basilio had entered the United States on a U.S. Army Transport in 1924, had attended the University of Chicago, and eventually found work in the post office.

In 1934, Elisa Calloway Hawkins made a trip back to the Philippines with her daughter Lourdes to visit her ailing father. She stayed there for ten months, during which time the Tydings-McDuffie Act had been passed. When she applied for readmission into the United States, she and her daughter were subjected to the new procedures regulating Filipino migration and were sent to Angel Island. Immigration officials needed to verify her status and her claim that she had not been repatriated by the U.S. government, which would have made her ineligible to return. At the immigration station, she witnessed racial discrimination that she had not expected. "She just heard such glorious, wonderful tales from her father," her daughter Elisa Brooks explained, that she was surprised to see racial segregation at the immigration station and how there were separate dining rooms for Asian detainees and European detainees. The divisive race relations in California between whites and Chinese and Japanese immigrants also "really surprised her." After two days in detention, Elisa and Lourdes Hawkins were released and made their way back home to Chicago. She never mentioned her time on Angel Island to her children. As her daughter explained, she "just took it in stride and from there, she just moved on. It wasn't traumatic or anything."[36]

Although Filipino migration to the United States changed dramatically after 1934, the detentions for Filipinos on Angel Island were usually short and they did not cause as much distress or anguish as they did for Chinese detainees. Many Filipino detainees never talked about their detentions with their children. Others mentioned their time on Angel Island only in passing, or like Elisa Hawkins, "just moved on." For many Filipinos, the United States remained a place of opportunity. Educated about the promises of America from a young age in the Philippines, their experiences on Angel Island did little to shake their faith in the United States. Joyce Ellorin, the daughter of Nattie and Flaviano Ellorin, thinks that despite the traumatic stay at the station and the questioning of her mother's citizenship status, "Angel Island was one step closer to a better life than what they had in the islands."[37]

Angel Island and Filipino Repatriation

As the worldwide Great Depression ravaged the American economy, however, that "better life" that the Ellorins and other Filipinos sought became harder to achieve. Anti-Asian exclusionists applauded the fact that Filipinos were virtually now excluded from the United States, but they identified the more than 50,000 who remained in the country as a continuing problem. Racism, labor strife, and sexual anxiety continued to keep the "Filipino problem" alive. Congressional attempts to deport Filipinos from the United States began as early as 1933. These mirrored national efforts to deport immigrants in general, and deportation rates increased during the 1920s across all groups. From 1910 to 1918, an average of 2,750 immigrants were deported annually. In 1930, 16,631 immigrants were deported.[38]

In California, deportation efforts focused on Mexicans and Filipinos. When Filipino laborers began to fall into the ranks of the unemployed, politicians and others complained that they were becoming burdens to the state and recommended wholesale deportation. The Filipino Repatriation Act of July 10, 1935, stated that any Filipino born in the Philippines and living in the United States could apply for the "benefits" of repatriation to the Philippines at the expense of the United States. The bill also mandated that any repatriate would be barred from entering the United States ever again.[39]

Just as Americans had justified colonizing the Philippines through "benevolent assimilation," the ideology of benevolence characterized the Filipino repatriation program. Angel Island Commissioner Edward Cahill called repatriation "a Big Brotherly gesture of help and assistance to the Filipinos who have come to the United States and now find themselves in difficulties." Missionaries like Deaconess Katharine Maurer also viewed Filipino repatriation as "purely humanitarian in its purposes" and declared that the Filipino repatriates awaiting their passage home on Angel Island found the immigration station to be a "Grand Hotel." The International Institute even offered the assistance of its Filipino interpreters to the immigration service during the repatriation efforts. But others, such as the journalist Carey McWilliams, viewed repatriation as "a trick, and not a very clever trick, to get [Filipinos] out of this country." Government officials hoped that between 10,000 to 30,000 Filipinos, or nearly half the total Filipino population in the United States, would voluntarily leave the country under the repatriation program.[40]

As the port closest to the largest concentration of Filipinos in the United States, the Angel Island Immigration Station and its officials played key roles in the Filipino repatriation movement. It served as the detention center for Filipinos waiting to be returned to the Philippines, sometimes holding hundreds of repatriates in its barracks. Angel Island's Edward Cahill was also a major architect of the repatriation program and the leading force behind the government's vigilant enforcement efforts. He gave newspaper interviews and radio addresses throughout Northern California, and he dispatched Angel Island officers throughout the Central Valley to answer questions and to post notices about the program in local post offices, pool halls, and restaurants. He also closely monitored Filipino newspapers to determine how the program was being received in the community. He felt strongly that any "insidious opposition" to the program or any misconceptions about the motivation of the program needed to be "detected and counteracted" at once. He also advised politicians and other government officials on how the program should be enforced and publicized.[41]

Cahill paid close attention to public relations because he was sensitive to charges that the repatriation law was simply a massive deportation campaign in disguise. In public, he repeatedly assured Filipinos that departure was "purely a voluntary act" and that there was no compulsion on the part of the government. He instructed fellow officials in the immigration service that there must be "no record, either written or spoken" that the department tried to "coerce or force" the Filipinos to participate in repatriation. Cahill's correspondence reveals, however, that the "benevolence" of repatriation masked a race-based campaign to rid the country of as many Filipinos as possible. He wrote of the repatriation movement's benefit to another group, organized labor. And he frankly admitted that the repatriation act was really the "only remedy available" to the "Filipino Problem" in the United States. As he reminded his superiors in Washington, D.C., the Filipinos competed with white workingmen and brought crime, disease, and interracial hatred to American communities. Repatriation was "the most practical solution" for inassimilable aliens like the Filipinos, and it was a "genuine humanitarian program" that would allow Filipinos to live "normal lives in their own climate, among their own friends and families, with their own women."[42]

But Filipinos were suspicious of the law and confused about how it worked. Some were quite vocal in their opposition to the bill, finding it a direct manifestation of American colonialism in the Philippines. Pedro Buncan submitted his application to return home to the Philippines in June 1935, but he did so with bitterness for the policy and for the American role in promoting Filipino emigration in the first place. As he wrote to the secretary of labor:

> I admit with sincerity that the poor Filipinos made a great mistake of coming to the United States but this mistake lies to the white American insulting dogs. In the Philippine Public Schools we learn your Constitution and also the American Text books which contained the two rotten Phrases Equality and Freedom. These phrases lure the mind of the poor Filipino youths. We have come to the land of the Free and where the people are treated equal only to find ourselves without constitutional rights as accorded to other territories of the US. We . . . did not realize that our oriental origin barred us as human being in the eyes of the law of the white insulting dog. You would rather accept a European imegrant [sic] to become citizen even if he has numerous criminal records.[43]

Cahill's own visits to major Filipino communities in northern California confirmed his suspicion that Filipinos were "sour" on repatriation. The immigration service was soundly denounced at community meetings. Few Filipinos wanted to return home as poor as they had been when they left. Filipinos were also aware that the act had a catch—any individual who accepted these "benefits" was ineligible to return to the continental United States ever again unless he or she had permission from the secretary of labor.[44]

Despite Cahill's insistence that repatriation was not forced deportation, complaints from the field suggest that immigration officials acted otherwise. Filipino organizations complained that Filipinos who had not volunteered for repatriation had been picked up by the immigration authorities and held for deportation nonetheless. Angel Island Commissioner Cahill himself also worked closely with California prison authorities to facilitate the immediate repatriation of Filipino natives in prison once they had become eligible for parole or at the end of their sentence. Nearly a hundred Filipinos from state prisons, asylums, and hospitals were repatriated.[45]

As the repatriates sailed for home, more complaints of mistreatment were aired in the press. To diminish the cost of transporting the repatriates to the Philippines, the immigration service waited until there was a sizable number of passengers sailing before placing them on a steamship. Filipinos who arrived in San Francisco before the departure date were detained at the Angel Island Immigration Station, causing much bitterness and complaint. As the *Filipino Pioneer* reported on March 6, 1937, a group of ninety-nine repatriates was detained for three days on the island where conditions were miserable. Some families were separated, "mother from children and husband from wife." Families with small children found the confinement "almost unbearable." Some of the sick were not given proper food, and repatriates had to pay for hospitalization. The Filipinos complained that Angel Island officers treated them as if they were criminals or deportees. They referred to Angel Island as "Devil Island."[46]

On the ship, things were not much better. "We're like prisoners," a group of the repatriates claimed in a letter protesting their treatment. They demanded "American dishes, proper bedding, towels, and soaps," and respect from the ship crew. Things were made even worse on March 6 when the ship hit a tanker in San Francisco Bay and passengers were transferred to another steamship.[47]

Over the next few months, the Angel Island Immigration Station continued to play a role in the Filipino repatriation program. Katharine Maurer noted in May 1937 that "several Filipino repatriation groups, escorted by inspectors, departed from this port," including 200 who were delayed on the island due to the San Francisco seamen's strike. In February 1939, she reported that a group of 150 Filipino repatriates were at the station for several days prior to the sailing for Manila.[48]

The Filipino repatriation program lasted for three years without the results the U.S. government desired. The first boat of Filipino repatriates sailed for Manila in 1936. The last one sailed in 1939. In total, only 2,190 Filipinos returned to the Philippines out of 108,260 Filipinos residing in the entire United States. Edward Cahill admitted that the results were disappointing.[49]

The Wienke family was among the over 2,000 Filipino repatriates who left the United States during the 1930s. Ludwig and Carmen Wienke struggled to support their family of six in San Francisco and were led by social workers to believe that their only choice was to repatriate back to the Philippines. Ludwig, a naturalized American citizen of German descent, and Carmen, a biracial Philippine-born daughter of a U.S. Army soldier, had met while Ludwig served in the U.S. armed forces in the Philippines during World War I. They married in a Manila church in 1919 and had six children in the Philippines and one in San Francisco. In 1931, all of the Wienkes were living in California, but work was hard to find. Ludwig later told immigration officials on Angel Island that "jobs were very scarce and I had a pretty hard time securing employment." He found part-time work, but the family was forced to live on government assistance for eight months.

While the family was on relief, a social worker named Mrs. Wilbur came to visit their home. She told the Wienkes about the new U.S. government repatriation program that would send the family back to the Philippines. As Carmen Wienke described, "[She] made me make that application [for repatriation to the Philippines]. She came to the house and told me according to her record I was born with six children in the Philippine Islands, and I was on relief and for me to go and get repatriated back to the Philippine Islands. I didn't want to go back home. She gave me a week to [go to the immigration office and apply for repatriation]. Otherwise she said we would be cut off of all aid."

The situation was confusing and frightening. The family believed that through Ludwig's naturalization, they were all American citizens and thus could not be forced to leave the country. But "the visitor made me believe I was not a citizen and the children too," Carmen explained. Carmen did not check with immigration officials about the family's immigration status. "I was afraid," she later admitted. "My husband was sick and I had seven children to take care of. I didn't know anything about the whole thing. When you are on relief you just have to mind the visitor and go out or starve." After they had been cleared for repatriation, the Wienkes rushed to sell all of their belongings. They left San Francisco in June 1936.

Carmen soon began to question whether their repatriation had been justified. After the family arrived in Manila, she approached U.S. officials for clarification. Both the high commissioner of the Philippines and the American consul told her that if she was married to an American citizen, then she and her children were all American citizens. Ludwig eventually found steady work in a hardware store in Manila, but the global depression and civil unrest in the Philippines made life uncertain there. After three years in the Philippines, Ludwig and his eldest son, Edward, returned to San Francisco in April 1939 and were admitted as citizens of the United States. Ludwig got a job in the U.S. Army Transport Service. Edward enlisted in the Civilian Conservation Corps. They sent word to Carmen and the rest of the family to come back to the United States. When Carmen and her children arrived in San Francisco in August, however, they were refused admission on the grounds that they were not citizens but immigrants likely to become public charges. The youngest son Carl, a native-born citizen, was admitted, but remained with the family on Angel Island. The Wienkes' problem stemmed from two significant legal technicalities. Ludwig had become a naturalized U.S. citizen one day after a new naturalization law had been passed. The act of May 24, 1934, allowed for derivative citizenship to pass from a naturalized American to their children, but only after a period of five years' continuous residence in the United States. The Wienkes' previous residence in the United States had lasted four years and four months. Carmen could not claim U.S. citizenship through marriage, and although her father was a U.S. citizen and she might have inherited his citizenship status, her parents had not been formally married. Immigration officials used these two technicalities to exclude Carmen and her children.

The Wienkes hired well-known immigration lawyer Joseph P. Fallon, and Ludwig appealed directly to Secretary of Labor Frances Perkins. Perkins affirmed the decision to exclude, though she recognized the "distressing circumstances of the case." "To require the return of the children to the Philippine Islands would visit extraordinary hardship," she wrote. She recommended that the children be allowed to travel to Mexico, where Carmen had some relatives, while Ludwig applied again for the family's admission as nonquota immigrants. The Wienkes and their lawyer appealed the secretary's decision in the federal district court, but the judge ruled against them.

The Wienkes' plight reached a sympathetic newspaper audience. On February 29, 1940, the *San Francisco Call* published an editorial highlighting the injustice facing the Wienke family. Describing the Wienkes as a "good solid American famil[y]," the *Call* charged that "families of worthy citizens [are] barred from [the] U.S., while undesirable aliens are coddled. The immigration laws of this country either are cockeyed as they can be, or there is something radically wrong in the way they are administered." Nevertheless, the government's position remained unchanged. All Wienke children except American-born Carl were found to be aliens, and the family was deported on March 24, 1940.[50]

The Wienkes spent eight months in detention on Angel Island, most likely the longest detention for Filipino immigrants. We do not know how the family fared in the cramped detention barracks. But we do know that Carmen never stopped fighting for justice for her family. When immigration officers suggested that six-year-old Carl be separated from the family and go to the mainland under the care of the Social Service Bureau, Carmen insisted that the family stay together on the island. When immigration officials ruled against her family, Carmen staunchly maintained the justice of her position: "What I want to make clear is that under the laws of the Philippine Islands, [my children] are not Filipinos. The children belong in their own home....My children are Americans...and they have a right to come here any time."[51]

The Wienke family's deportation from the United States in 1940 is just one example of how Filipinos' changing legal status after 1934 affected their lives in the United States. Filipinos who had previously entered the country with minimal inspection were, after the Tydings-McDuffie Act passed, required to document their prior residence in the United States.

Eliseo Felipe with his family in 1951: Wife Vicki and daughters Gloria, Evelyn, and Vivian. (Courtesy of Evelyn Felipe.)

New immigrants had to obtain one of the fifty visas made available per year. Previously treated as U.S. nationals, Filipinos found themselves reclassified as aliens who were deportable and coerced into repatriation. By the mid-1930s, thousands of Filipinos were caught in the middle of the government's twin efforts of Filipino exclusion and repatriation. And although they were couched in colonial-era terms of "benevolence," U.S. policies demonstrated little compassion in real life.

World War II was a turning point for both the Philippines and Filipinos in the United States. As allies in the Pacific war, the Philippines and the United States fought Japanese forces together and the bonds of interracial brotherhood between Americans and Filipinos were emphasized in the media and by politicians. White attitudes toward Filipinos in America softened in tangible ways. The California attorney general reinterpreted the state's alien land laws prohibiting aliens ineligible to citizenship from owning or leasing land in order to allow Filipinos to buy farmland and become farmers.[52]

At the same time, Filipinos clamored to volunteer in the U.S. armed forces to help defend the Philippines and join the American fight against Japan. The First and Second Filipino Infantry Regiments were formed in 1942 to recognize the "intense loyalty and patriotism" of Filipinos in the United States. In California, 16,000, or 40 percent of the state's entire Filipino population, registered for the first draft, and 7,000 would eventually serve. One of those was Eliseo Felipe, the San Francisco apartment bellboy who had been surprised to be detained on Angel Island during his second trip to the United States in 1940. He became a naturalized U.S. citizen as part of a mass naturalization ceremony for soldiers and was sent to New Guinea and then to the Philippines during the war. He stayed in the military for the next twenty years and brought his wife and daughter to the United States in 1947 on an army ship. Other laws opened up wartime employment to Filipinos, and in 1946, Congress passed the Luce-Celler Act, which allowed Filipinos to become naturalized citizens. With the 1965 Immigration Act, migration from the Philippines opened up again, and over 660,000 Filipinos entered the United States in the next twenty years.[53]

The history of Filipino migration and repatriation through Angel Island reveals how much U.S. immigration policies had changed by the time the station closed in 1940. The United States government had excluded all Asian immigrants by diplomatic agreement, exclusion laws, barred zones, and discriminatory national quotas. Immigration from Southern and Eastern Europe was also severely restricted. The United States' historic welcome to all immigrants had ended. In its place was a highly regulated, complicated, and hierarchical system of immigration laws that favored some over others.

The Angel Island Immigration Station had changed as well. Originally built to process new arrivals on their way into the United States, it also became a detention center to facilitate the removal of undesirable immigrants already in the country. Filipinos would be the last large group to be processed through Angel Island. By the time they began arriving on the island either on their way into or out of the country, the immigration station's days were numbered. A fire destroyed the administration building on August 12, 1940, and the immigration station closed. Filipinos were among the 150 detainees who were transferred to the new immigrant detention facility in the city of San Francisco a few months later.

At midnight on August 12, 1940, a fire broke out. Caused by an overloaded circuit in the basement of the administration building, it almost led to the total destruction of the immigration station. Bellows of smoke rising over the administration building could be seen the next morning after firefighters battled through the night to contain the fire. (San Francisco History Center, San Francisco Public Library.)

CHAPTER NINE

SAVING ANGEL ISLAND

GUARD CLARENCE ZIEG had just started his work shift at midnight in the administration building when he noticed smoke "coming from what appeared to be the dining room where the women ate." He immediately ran for the fire alarm, smashed the glass, and turned on the alarm. With the help of two other guards, he started the evacuation, "giving a fire signal by word of mouth." They got all thirty-two Chinese, Japanese, and Russian women out first, and then worked on clearing the building of the 151 German crewmen from the scuttled liner *Columbus*. By then, the entire basement and dining room were engulfed in flames and the building filled with smoke.[1] Lee Puey You, who was asleep in the Chinese women's quarters at the time, remembered, "It was really bad—the flames and smoke. Everything was burnt in the women's barracks and we had to flee."[2] Within the next half hour, the guards had emptied out the detention barracks behind the administration building of 200 Asian immigrant men and twenty-three European men, who were waiting to be deported. Myron Wong, who was eleven years old at the time, recalled seeing a guard kick open their door to warn them of the fire. "Boy, we saw the sky lit up red, right on top of the roof. My brother and I were so scared; we quickly got some clothes on, grabbed some blankets, and ran outside."[3] Even under such dire circumstances, guards were told to keep all the inmates segregated by race and gender. The women were moved to the hospital, the Chinese men to the Army stables, the European men to the guard house, and the German crew to the quarantine station.

Guard William Fields was at the main switchboard in the administration building when he heard the fire alarm. He was able to reach both the San Francisco fireboat and Army fire department for help. Within fifteen minutes, two crews from the *Dennis T. Sullivan* fireboat, a company of soldiers from Fort McDowell, and the German crew from the *Columbus* were at the dock helping to bring the water hoses from the boat to the burning building. "It was quite an effort to get these lines all pulled in," said Captain Fred Smith of the San Francisco Fire Department. "I would put one of my experienced men on the line and there would be four or five Germans on it. Everyone worked in fine harmony. When the Germans got tired and we got tired, we had the soldiers working, and after a while the Germans came back again." When the water supply ran out, Captain Smith resorted to connecting the hose from the saltwater hydrant to his fireboat. The added pressure enabled the men to keep the hoses going longer. As Captain Smith remarked later, "But for their help, there would have been more damage done, because here to the east you have the hospital and on this end you have the Chinese quarters, and here was this fire, just like a cornucopia, and a lot of heat. If it had not been for the German crewmen and the Army, we would have lost the whole thing."[4]

Twelve hours later, billows of smoke could still be seen rising from the ruins, but the fire was under control. The administration building and the connecting stairway to the Chinese men's barracks were destroyed, but the detention building and hospital were saved. Soldiers had been stationed every ten feet outside the barracks ready to control the fire with wet sacks and to prevent any of the Chinese immigrants from returning to the building to retrieve their belongings. Many valuable immigration records that had been locked in a steel vault survived the fire. Although the German seamen and other detainees were able to drag some of the furniture and filing cabinets from the burning building, many documents and photographs were destroyed. Amazingly, only two people were injured or killed. Private Herman C. Schneider was fatally wounded when a wall collapsed on him.[5]

Following the fire, the twenty-three deportees were moved to the San Francisco county jail, and the immigrants and *Columbus* crew were moved to the hospital and quarantine station on the island. Portable army kitchens were set up on the grounds. According to Myron Wong, detainees were served meals in the exercise yard for a week until the kitchen was repaired. "They gave us a canteen of food to eat, just like in the Army," he said. "Then later they sent us back to the dormitories."[6] When an influx of Central European refugees arrived in San Francisco at the end of August, they had to be detained on the ship because of the crippled conditions on the island.

Given all the problems with the immigration facilities throughout its history, the government had no intention of rebuilding on Angel Island. Temporary quarters were found at a Salvation Army training center at 801 Silver Avenue in the city, and 150 Chinese, Filipinos, and Central

European refugees were transferred there on November 5, 1940.[7] The detention facility subsequently moved to Sharp Park, fifteen miles south of San Francisco, in spring 1942, and finally to the new immigration offices at 630 Sansome Street in 1944.

The fire closed down the immigration station on Angel Island and the site reverted to the U.S. Army on February 4, 1941. Renamed the North Garrison, it was used for processing and housing American troops, German and Japanese prisoners of war, and enemy aliens bound for inland camps. After the war, it served as an outgoing port for Japanese prisoners and repatriates, and as a processing center for returning troops. Angel Island was declared surplus property in July 1946 and turned over to the state of California. It formally became part of the state park system in 1963. For over twenty years, the immigration station had been unoccupied and abandoned, suffering neglect, vandalism, and decay. In 1968, the California State Parks decided to develop the immigration site for recreational use. The remains of the administration building and the wooden pier were removed, and the rest of the immigration buildings were slated for demolition. But thanks to the efforts of one park ranger and a group of Asian American activists who understood the historical significance of the buildings and the poems within, this did not happen.

Over the next forty years, community activists and descendants of Angel Island detainees recovered the history of immigration through Angel Island, successfully lobbied for National Historic Landmark status, secured funds to restore the site, and embarked on a massive preservation project. Their efforts have been guided by a commitment to preserve forgotten chapters in America's immigration history and connect them to issues of inequality in the past and present. While early campaigns

Room 105, the Chinese men's barracks on the first floor of the detention building, 1970s. Each pole could hold three tiers of bunk beds on each side. (Photo by Chris K. D. Huie.)

focused on preserving the history of Chinese detainees at Angel Island and building local and regional support for the site, later efforts sought to garner national recognition and support for preserving Angel Island as a symbol of America's multiracial history of immigration and as a site of conscience with national and international significance. Always in the background of Angel Island's history as an immigration station and transformation into an immigration museum has been its eastern counterpart Ellis Island, whose multimillion dollar restoration was completed in 1990 to great fanfare. Its celebratory story of American immigration continues to appeal to a broad cross-section of Americans. In contrast, the road to restoration for Angel Island has taken longer and proven more difficult. Its cautionary tale of exclusion and inclusion is just beginning to reach the same national audience for support.

Saving the Poetry, Stopping the Demolition

In May of 1970, Alexander Weiss had just started his new job as a seasonal park ranger on Angel Island when he came across the detention building in North Garrison for the first time. The area was "off limits" to the public and there was no electricity in the building. Stepping on creaking boards and broken glass, he entered the dark building with a flashlight and noticed Chinese calligraphy on the walls. "First I saw the deeply carved stuff and I said, wow! But then I looked around and shined my flashlight up and I could see that the entire walls were covered with calligraphy, and that was what blew me away. People had carved this stuff on every square inch of wall space, not just in this one room but all over." Although Weiss could not read the writing on the walls, he knew they were culturally and historically significant. His supervisor did not share his opinion. Weiss was told not to bother with the "bunch of graffiti" because the building was going to be torn down as part of the Master Plan to develop the site.[8]

Park ranger Alexander Weiss in 1980. (Photo by Connie Young Yu.)

When Weiss saw the employee cottages on the hillside deliberately set on fire for a fire training exercise, he decided it was time to act. He told George Araki, his biology professor at San Francisco State College, about the writings on the wall. Araki's mother had come through Angel Island as a picture bride, so he knew the historical significance of the place. After seeing the poems himself and learning that the building faced imminent demolition, Araki quickly got photographer Mak Takahashi to come out to the island with floodlights to photograph every inch of wall that had writing. "We wanted to at least have pictures of the poems in case they succeeded with their Master Plan," explained Weiss. Araki showed the photographs to faculty and students in the Asian American Studies Department, which had just been established after a five-month Third World Students' Strike, a movement to demand ethnic studies faculty and curriculum that would focus on the histories and contemporary issues of African Americans, Asian Americans, Chicanos, and Native Americans. College students and community activists began making field trips to Angel Island to see the poetry. "They were all young Asian American students whose parents and grandparents had come through Angel Island, but they had no idea of this history because their parents would not talk about it," recalled Weiss. "I told them they're going to burn it, so if you want to save it, write letters to the State Park Commission."

Years later, when asked why he was willing to risk his job to call attention to the poetry in the detention barracks, he replied, "Actually, I am also an immigrant, so I have an empathy with immigrants." Weiss was born in Vienna, Austria, and came to America as a Jewish refugee from the Holocaust in 1940 when he was four years old. "The Nazis came in 1938 and my father had to sign over all his property, his house, and his business just to get exit visas for my mother, myself, and my sister. We arrived with just five dollars in my father's pockets." This led Weiss to a lifetime of fighting persecution and oppression. As a college student, he volunteered as a Freedom Rider in Mississippi to help desegregate interstate buses in the South. "What was going on in the South was outrageous, like what happened in Europe. I wasn't going to be one of the good Germans that looked away," he said. He also helped to organize housing sit-ins in San Francisco for the Congress of Racial Equality. Weiss's strong convictions about fighting racial discrimination are evident in his response to people whenever they credit him for discovering the poems.

I didn't discover the poems. They had been there for years and other people knew they were there. But I'm proud of the fact that I was able to turn on the ignition and get the motor running so that people like Paul Chow could step on the gas and get the car to move to where it is today, a national historic landmark. We needed to save the immigration station to remind us of the tough times some immigrants had coming to this country. They were treated shabbily, but they actually made this country a better place. We don't have exclusion laws anymore, but we could have them in an instant tomorrow. It could easily happen to some other group of people. That's why we need memorials like concentration camps and Angel Island, so that we will learn from our past and not repeat the same mistakes.

Alexander Weiss's call to the Asian American community to take political action could not have come at a better time. The project to reclaim and restore Angel Island unfolded against a backdrop of Asian American activism around issues of social justice. The civil rights, antiwar, and Asian American movements in the 1960s had heightened second-generation Chinese and Japanese Americans' awareness of racism and sense of ethnic pride. Many Asian Americans were inspired to return to their roots and recover their history and dignity as people of color in America. For them, the effort to save Angel Island became synonymous with their larger political goal to confront the racism and exclusion Asians faced in America. As political activist Connie Young Yu explained, restoring the immigration station meant restoring dignity, honor, and freedom to the pioneering immigrants. Yu, whose grandmother had been detained on Angel Island in the 1920s, wrote that "the immigration barracks, with the expressions of suffering and struggle visible on the walls, is a fitting memorial to the courage and determination of our ancestors.... It would serve as a reminder of America's past discriminatory policies toward Asians, and strengthen our resolve to continue to oppose any return of racial exclusion laws and detention centers."[9]

Asian American journalist Chris Chow took a leading role in the early efforts to save and preserve the immigration station. He had first heard about the Angel Island poems from UC Berkeley professor Ronald Takaki at a meeting of the East Bay Asians for Community Action. When told that the barracks were soon to be torn down, the group was "aghast, outraged, and fired up to fight," recalled Chow. "I really felt it in my bones that this was a story that needed to be told, a historic landmark that needed to be saved, and a place consecrated by the blood, brains, and tears of my forebears that needed to be preserved." Chow soon headed a new group called the Ad-Hoc Committee to Save the Angel Island Detention Center. The organization's goal was to stop the demolition of the immigration barracks and preserve the poetry so that past injustices would not be repeated in the future. There was also talk about turning the site into a state historic landmark like Manzanar, the World War II internment camp for Japanese Americans located in southern California. The committee began spreading the news about Angel Island in the Asian American community and lobbying government officials to save the immigration station.[10]

California Assemblyman John Foran, whose district included San Francisco Chinatown, was the first to respond to the issue. He introduced House

Resolution No. 205, which established the China Cove Historical Advisory Citizen's Committee to study and make recommendations on how the state could best preserve the historical interpretation of the immigration station. Foran also asked Paul Chow, a civil engineer with the California Department of Transportation and an active member of the Chinese American Democratic Club, to help him put the committee together. Chow was willing to take on the task. His father, Chow Wan Gai, had been detained on Angel Island for six months in 1922, and like many other former detainees, had been too humiliated to ever talk about it. He first found out about Angel Island from his mother, after his teacher could not answer his question asking if the Chinese had landed on Plymouth Rock. Chow's mother told him, "Angel Island, shhhh!" The shroud of silence in his family history lifted after he visited Angel Island for the first time with his father. "He stood where his bunk had been and cried for twenty minutes. It was the first time I ever saw my father cry. He was seventy-four years old. And he asked me, 'Do you know what it feels like to be free to walk in and walk out of this place? Do you know what it is like not to talk of this for fifty years?'" At that moment, Chow realized how restoring the barracks could help legitimize the Chinese who had been degraded by American society. "This will give us our Valley Forge, our Statue of Liberty, and an eternal reminder that we do belong in America," he explained. This line would become one of his favorites for the next twenty-five years as he led the crusade to preserve and restore the Angel Island Immigration Station.[11]

At the first meeting of the China Cove Committee (later changed to the Angel Island Immigration Station Historical Advisory Committee, AIISHAC), Chris Chow was elected as chairman, Paul Chow as liaison to California State Parks, and Connie Young Yu, a writer and historian, as secretary. The committee's initial preservation efforts focused on saving the site and the poetry, recovering the history of Chinese detainees at the immigration station, and lobbying for state support. A number of community-based scholars, including Yu, engineer and historian Him Mark Lai, poet Genny Lim, and librarian Judy Yung, conducted historical research, interviewed former detainees, and collected and translated the Chinese poems into English. Chris Chow, Paul Chow, and Yu lobbied successfully for state funds, engaged in community outreach, and gave educational tours of the immigration site. Architect and historian Philip Choy lent his expertise to the preservation plans, working closely with Fong Chan, a structural engineer, and nine members of the University of California Asian Architectural Student Society to complete a structural analysis of the immigration barracks and a cost estimate of the needed repairs and improvements.[12] According to Chris Chow, all of this work was done on a volunteer basis and "in the spirit of third world liberation, community self-determination, and taking control of our own stories and images from the racial chauvinism of many white Americans."[13]

Room 105, the Chinese men's barracks, turned into an exhibit room, 1980s. (Courtesy of Architectural Resources Group.)

Refurbished women's quarters in the detention building, 1980s. (Photo by Daniel Quan.)

The hard work of many people to save the immigration station culminated in a commemorative ceremony on Angel Island attended by over 500 former detainees and their families on April 28, 1979. Restaurateur Victor "Trader Vic" Bergeron, who had employed many Chinese over the years, conceived and donated an eight-foot, 6,000-pound granite monument that was dedicated to the immigrant detainees. In the photo, California State Assemblyman John Foran presents Paul Chow with a California Legislative Resolution for the occasion while AIISHAC members Lawrence Jue and Connie Young Yu look on from the sideline. (Courtesy of the Angel Island Immigration Station Foundation.)

Tom Yip Jing, who was detained on Angel Island for two months in 1921, returned to Angel Island for the first time in 1979 to attend the ceremony with his daughter Judy Yung and wife Jew Law Ying. The inscription on the monument was chosen from among many entries in a couplet competition co-sponsored by AIISHAC and the *Chinese Times*. Translated into English, the winning couplet by Ngoot P. Chinn reads, "Leaving their homes and villages, they crossed the ocean only to endure confinement in these barracks. Conquering frontiers and barriers, they pioneered a new life by the Golden Gate." (Photo by Harry Jew.)

In January 1976, AIISHAC's "Report and Recommendations on Angel Island Immigration Station" brought together the extensive historical research to make bold claims about the national significance of Angel Island. It explicitly compared Angel Island to Ellis Island and other well-known and celebrated sites where American history had been made:

> Angel Island Immigration Station presents the first, the only, and the best opportunity to fully interpret the history of Asian immigration to the United States. This is our Plymouth Rock, our Valley Forge, our Alamo, our Statue of Liberty, our Lincoln Memorial all rolled into one.... In the same way that Ellis Island has been enshrined as a national monument to commemorate European immigration to America, Angel Island Immigration Station should be recognized and declared a National Historic Landmark.[14]

The report recommended full restoration of the immigration barracks, proper display of the wall inscriptions, and the construction of a center for lectures and exhibits. Soon after he received the report, Assemblyman Foran introduced a bill to appropriate $250,000 for major repairs in the detention building and preservation of the poetry. Thanks to the lobbying efforts of AIISHAC, the California Legislature approved the bill, and Governor Jerry Brown promptly signed it into law in July 1976. The immigration station was saved.

The long process of restoring the immigration barracks followed. Project architect Philip Choy took nine months to complete the drawings for stabilizing and restoring the building. To preserve the architectural and historical integrity of the place, his plans called for the same materials and techniques as were used in the original construction. He was also adamant that the historical treatment of the site should not gloss over the racial discrimination of the time. "None of this tourist stuff," he explained. He wanted the place to "reflect the experiences and feelings of the immigrants when they first came to the island, this so-called land of hope and freedom."[15] Special care was given to protect the writings on the walls. They were to be disassembled board-by-board for seismic bracing and later reassembled. Because of budget shortfalls and the need to meet fire and handicap access requirements, it took four years to complete all the repairs and seismic upgrades. Meanwhile, Joann Weiler and staff in the Office of Interpretive Services worked on the historical and interpretive research, and then took another year to design and install the exhibits with input from AIISHAC.[16]

Finally, in February 1983, the first floor of the immigration barracks was officially opened to the public as an interpretive center. Visitors were able to see for themselves the compelling poems on the walls, the re-created living quarters for the women, the bathroom where suicides were rumored to have occurred, and an orientation exhibit on the Angel Island immigration story. However, full restoration and interpretive work on the immigration station were far from complete. It would take another group of Angel Island descendants with the same passion and vision, but who possessed different political skills to finish the job.

Achieving National Historic Landmark Status

In an effort to keep the restoration project alive, Paul Chow founded the Angel Island Immigration Station Foundation (AIISF) in 1983. Its mission was clear: to be the community steward of the site, to create public awareness of its historical significance, and to complete the work of preserving and restoring the immigration station. Over the next two decades, new leadership and a professional staff turned many of these goals into realities. Key players included Daniel Quan, an architect and interpretive exhibit designer; Felicia Lowe, a broadcast journalist and the producer of *Carved in Silence*, a film about Chinese exclusion and detention on Angel Island; Kathy Lim Ko, a program developer and fund-raiser; and Katherine Toy, a secondary schoolteacher and program administrator. Driven by their personal family connections to Angel Island and their shared vision of its becoming a premiere destination site, they worked hard and long to bring Angel Island's history to a larger audience, build strategic partnerships with government agencies and national allies, secure additional state and federal funds, and reframe Angel Island as a central chapter in American history.

In 1993, AIISF decided to launch a national public awareness campaign to call attention to Angel Island's history and to expand the foundation's donor base. Daniel Quan was hired to design a traveling exhibit titled "Gateway to Gold Mountain" to bring the Angel Island story around the country. For

Over 600 people attended the National Historic Landmark celebration at Angel Island on May 16, 1998, to witness Brian O'Neill (right), superintendent of the Golden Gate National Recreation Area, bestow "the nation's highest recognition that can be given to any cultural resource in this country" on the U.S. Immigration Station at Angel Island. John Knott (left) receives the plaque on behalf of the California Department of Parks and Recreation. (Photo by Kenneth Lee, courtesy of the Angel Island Immigration Station Foundation.)

the next two years, he traveled with the exhibit across America, eventually ending up on Ellis Island and at the Smithsonian Museum. The exhibit provided AIISF with a platform for networking with legislators, public agencies, and community groups across the country, and thus laid the groundwork for the site to eventually attain federal recognition and funding. Quan took over the AIISF presidency in 1996 and sought to achieve National Historic Landmark status for the immigration station. The first application by California State Parks had been turned down in 1994, but thanks to Philip Choy, who rewrote the proposal, the National Register of Historic Places officially named the Angel Island Immigration Station a National Historic Landmark in December 1997. An exuberant Quan called the designation "a milestone in American history," as Angel Island was only the second Asian American site after Manzanar to receive this status. In his opinion, official recognition also meant that Angel Island was now an equal to Ellis Island.[17]

Soon after, Angel Island also received official project status under the Save America's Treasures (SAT) program run by the National Historic Trust for Historic Preservation and in 1999 it was named one of the Trust's "11 Most Endangered Historic Places," along with Ellis Island. "As one of the most powerful reminders of the Asian American immigration experience, the future of the Angel Island Immigration Station must be secured for the education and enlightenment of generations to come," Richard Moe, president of the National Trust, testified.[18] The prestigious designation drew the nation's attention once more to the importance of the Angel Island story and the urgency to preserve the immigration site. That fall, First Lady Hillary Rodham Clinton, who chaired the SAT preservation program, made a personal appearance at AIISF's fund-raising reception in San Francisco to lend her support. The following year, the foundation successfully applied for a $500,000 grant from SAT to preserve the Chinese poems at Angel Island. At the same time, they lobbied state legislators for support. Under California State Senator and President Pro Tem John Burton's leadership, $400,000 was included for Angel Island in an appropriations bill and $15 million was set aside for Angel Island in Proposition 12, a state bond measure dealing with clean air, water, and park initiatives that passed in 2000.

National Historic Landmark status and designation as an endangered historic place catapulted the immigration station into the national spotlight. It also allowed the foundation to tap into federal resources and funding, which Angel Island's status as a state park had prevented them from doing before. At the invitation of Senator Daniel Akaka of Hawaii, Angel Island became involved in preliminary plans to establish a West Coast Immigration Museum on the San Francisco waterfront as a counterpart to Ellis Island. The museum project never came to fruition, but AIISF was given $50,000 for a feasibility study, which allowed the organization to begin long-range planning. Felicia Lowe and Daniel Quan organized a series of visioning workshops, in which interpretive specialists, park and museum planners, historians, and creative thinkers were asked to help develop a new vision for the immigration site. Participants suggested broadening the history of Angel Island to include the experiences of other immigrants who entered from the Pacific. They also saw the possibilities of using the site to examine issues of immigration, race, culture, and class conflict in the past and present. It was hoped that visitors would be able to learn and reflect on all those who came through the site with empathy and compassion.[19] "Out of the workshops," explained Lowe, "came this wonderful document, a blueprint that gave a general sense of the possibilities of the Angel Island story."[20] The ideas from the workshop would become the guiding principles of the Master Plan to fully restore the site.

As the foundation pursued federal funding and a broader base of support, it sought to reframe Angel Island's immigration story as an American story of triumph and diversity, and not just a tragic story about Chinese exclusion and detention. Katherine Toy, who became AIISF's first executive director in 2000, successfully conveyed this message when she lobbied Congress for support. Appearing before the Subcommittee on National Parks, Recreation, and Public Lands, which was considering an appropriations bill for Angel Island, she said, "Angel Island and Ellis Island serve as bookends to the national story of immigration, not only in geography, but also in meaning and experience. While Angel Island Immigration Station represents a difficult chapter in our national history, it is ultimately a story of triumph and of the perseverance of immigrants to endure and establish new lives in this country."[21] Representative Lynn Woolsey (D-CA) and Senator Dianne Feinstein (D-CA), who introduced identical bills in the House and Senate, both emphasized that Angel Island contributed greatly to the understanding of our nation's rich and complex immigration history. "With over a million people being processed through the site," said Woolsey, "millions of Asian descendents nationwide are eager to see their roots in this country honored in the same way that we honor Ellis Island." Speaking in support of the bill, Representative Mark Souder (R-IN) remarked, "Compared to the $156 million support to restore Ellis Island, this restoration project is a bargain and of no less significance." He was adamant that the importance of the site and its contribution to U.S. history made its official status as part of the California State Parks system irrelevant. "Our Nation's history must be preserved regardless of official status."[22]

After two years of debating the issue, the Angel Island Immigration Station Restoration and Preservation Act, authorizing $15 million for Angel Island, was unanimously passed by Congress and signed into law by President George W. Bush in December 2005. Intense lobbying and reframing the Angel Island story as an American story that showed "the perseverance of the immigrant spirit and the diversity of a great nation" had won Congress over. With over $30 million committed from both government sources and the National Trust, the foundation was now ready to tackle restoration.

Restoring the Site, Building the Museum

The restoration process required intensive research of the immigration station's buildings, cultural artifacts, history, and grounds. Architectural Resources Group in San Francisco was brought in to study the three major historic structures on the site and to conduct a conservation study for the written inscriptions on the walls. The Olmstead Center for Landscape Preservation in Brookline, Massachusetts, was commissioned for a cultural landscape study of the site as a whole. And Daniel Quan Design was contracted to coordinate all three studies and direct a separate poetry translation and interpretation study. The detailed studies were completed within two years and recommendations were incorporated into the Master Plan, which was approved by the California State Parks in 2003. The plan called for rehabilitating the site in five phases at an estimated cost of $57.5 million dollars. The foundation was set to begin implementing Phase I, which involved preserving the poems, restoring the detention barracks, interpreting the administration building footprint, site landscaping, and upgrading of all site utilities.[23]

The restoration designs for the site and the detention barracks as well as a conservation plan for the poetry were completed in the next year. During this time photographs were taken of all the poems and inscriptions, wall segment by wall segment. Four Chinese scholars—Charles Egan, Wan Liu, Newton Liu, and Xing Chu Wang—mapped the locations of all the writings and artwork, as well as translated and interpreted them. Altogether, 187 Chinese poems, ninety-six Chinese inscriptions, sixty-two Japanese slogans and inscriptions, and ninety-four inscriptions in English, Punjabi, Russian, Korean, Spanish, Italian, and German were found. In addition, thirty-three carved images of animals, ships, and flags were recorded. Their exhaustive study helped to shed light on the diversity of people who were detained on Angel Island and to lend new meaning to the Chinese poems. Meanwhile, conservators did chemical analysis of the paint layers in each room and worked to recover poetry beneath the paint on the walls. To preserve and protect the poems, they carefully hand cleaned, stabilized, and repaired the wall surfaces, field-tested different ways of raking light on the poems for display purposes, and repaired and sealed the windows, doors, and ceilings.[24]

Once construction commenced in 2005, the detention building was closed to the public. For the next four years, construction crews worked on retrofitting the building, upgrading the infrastructure for essential services and drainage, and improving utilities and handicap accessibility. A series of terraces were created to convey the size, function, and importance of the administration building, and the covered stairway was rebuilt. Landscaping was done to replicate the look during the immigration period. Construction was slow and hampered by weather conditions, old and erroneous data, the discovery of Indian remains and artifacts, and a wildfire that burned the

Restored detention barracks with covered stairway and tables where the dining room once stood, 2009. (Photo by Vincent Chin.)

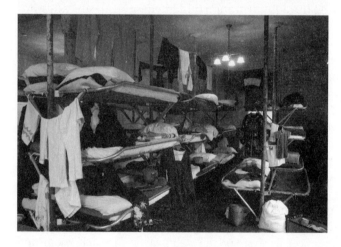

Exhibit of women's barracks showing personal effects. (Photo by Frank Jang.)

other half of the island's terrain in 2008. When completed, the detention barracks bore a strong resemblance to their 1920s façade. On the inside, bunk beds, furnishings, personal belongings, and an audio soundtrack were installed to re-create the crowded living quarters of the Chinese, Japanese, Russians, and a dozen other nationalities. Special lighting and audio kiosks enabled visitors to better view and appreciate the Chinese poems on the walls. To simulate the interrogation process, a granite table etched with questions asked of detainees along with certificates of identity was installed within the footprint of the former administration building. One half of the table was made of granite from the Sierra Nevada and the other half, granite from South China. Along the concrete risers, words such as loneliness, frustration, segregation, confinement, courage, and sacrifice were sandblasted into the surface to represent the different feelings of immigrants as they were processed through the immigration station. The overall effect was to give visitors a greater sense of the physical presence of the station, the power of the governing authority behind it, and the feelings of those it affected.[25]

Phase I of the restoration project was nearly completed and plans were under way for a grand reopening when state officials announced that because of a budget crisis, all operations were to be put on hold. Despite the fact that some of the exhibits were unfinished, the AIISF decided to go ahead with the event. On February 15, 2009, a cold and stormy day, over 1,500 people, including government dignitaries, park officials, former detainees, descendants of detainees, volunteers, and supporters, boarded the ferries and gathered under a white tent on Angel Island to celebrate the restoration and reopening of the immigration station. "Excuse me if I'm emotional during this ceremony," said a teary Kathy Lim Ko, president of the foundation. "There are many people who came before me in this thirty-plus-year effort and for them, I am sure they are more emotional than I am. But for me, having worked on this project for over ten years, today is literally a dream come true." After acknowledging pioneers Alexander Weiss, Paul Chow, and Philip Choy, and all the sponsors, funders, volunteers, board members, and staff who had helped to make the restoration project a success, she went on to offer a new and elevated vision of the restored immigration station.

> The immigration station is a site of conscience, about immigration past, present, and future. It is a place for reflection on the very personal immigration experience, but also on international relations and social justice. And it is a place of reconciliation for the wrongs that were done and the human rights that we must uphold. For this is part of our American experience, important enough to be designated by the Federal government as a National Historic Landmark, the highest distinction in the land bestowed to a place of national significance.[26]

In closing, Ko reminded the captive audience that much more work remained to be done. Plans were already under way to raise another $30 million to restore the hospital as an exhibit space and genealogy center, the power house as a visitor's center, and to rebuild the pier. "When we're all done," she promised, "Angel Island will be a premiere destination site."

The advocacy and preservation work of two groups of community activists and descendants of Angel Island detainees culminated in three important events: 1979, when the granite monument was dedicated to the immigrant detainees; 1997, when the Angel Island Immigration Station was officially designated a National Historic Landmark; and 2009, when the newly restored immigration site reopened. Angel Island's restoration efforts took much longer than Ellis Island's. The preservation histories of the two sites have also differed dramatically. Ellis Island's emphasis on the opportunities and liberties that European immigrants have enjoyed in America has appealed widely to American families, corporate sponsors, and local and federal governments. According to historian John Bodnar, Ellis Island reinvigorates "the view of American history as a steady succession of progress and uplift for ordinary people."[27] Angel Island's more complicated multiracial history of inclusion and exclusion recalls a different view of American history, one that calls attention to the tensions between American ideals and realities in the past as well as the present.

On the one hundredth anniversary of the Angel Island Immigration Station, this message finally reached a national audience in President Barack Obama's proclamation of January 21, 2010, as National Angel Island Day. After summarizing the immigrant experiences at Angel Island during "an unjust time in our history," the proclamation concluded as follows:

> If there is any vindication for the Angel Island immigrants who endured so many hardships, it is the success achieved by those who were allowed entry, and the many who, at long last, gained citizenship. They have contributed immeasurably to our Nation as leaders in every sector of American life. The children of Angel Island have seized the opportunities their ancestors saw from across an ocean. By demonstrating that all things are possible in America, this vibrant community has created a beacon of hope for future generations of immigrants.

EPILOGUE

THE LEGACY OF ANGEL ISLAND

ANGEL ISLAND was important in its own time, and it remains vitally significant today. One hundred years after the Angel Island Immigration Station opened its doors, the United States still struggles to resolve its contradictory relationship with immigration. Immigrants from around the world are once again coming to the United States in search of the American Dream, and America continues to celebrate its rich immigrant heritage. At the same time, the early years of the twenty-first century have been a time of increased anxiety over new immigration, and debates over immigration and race have continued to divide the country. In the most recent past, post-9/11 policies have treated immigration as a threat to national security and domestic unity, and congressional attempts to reform immigration laws failed resoundingly in 2007. In addition, the number of immigrant arrests and detentions has increased dramatically. Unlike a century ago, when immigrant detainees were housed in immigration stations like Angel Island, today's immigrants wait out the days, weeks, and months in isolated detention centers and county jails far from their families and communities. In both the ongoing debates over immigration and immigration reform, Angel Island's history continues to be timely and relevant.

Changes in Immigration Policy after 1940

Much has changed since the Angel Island Immigration Station closed its doors in 1940. Beginning during World War II, radical transformations in immigration law ended the era of Asian exclusion and liberalized immigration policy. Wartime alliances, foreign policy agendas, and an acute labor shortage led to the repeal of the laws excluding Chinese and South Asian immigrants and barring them and Filipino immigrants from naturalized citizenship. New policies also facilitated the mass migration of Mexicans into the country. From 1942 to 1964, an estimated 4.5 million *braceros*, temporary farmworkers and other laborers from Mexico, were admitted under the Bracero Program established by the U.S. and Mexican governments. New policies allowing for the admission of refugees were also put into place after World War II and during the 1950s. The 1952 Walter-McCarran Act reinforced the tough restrictions of the 1920s by maintaining the national origins quotas and put in place a new "Asia Pacific Triangle" race quota aimed at restricting Asian immigration into the United States. But it lifted the racial bar to citizenship, thus allowing Japanese and Korean Americans to become naturalized citizens. The United States government also continued to shift the burden of screening all prospective immigrants to American consular officials overseas. Instead of being inspected upon their arrival in the United States, prospective immigrants now apply for immigrant or nonimmigrant visas from American consuls overseas before their departure.[1]

In 1958, President John F. Kennedy ushered in a new era of public opinion about immigration. He hailed the United States as a "nation of immigrants" and argued that immigrants were the bedrock upon which the country had been built. After his assassination, the 1965 Immigration and Nationality Act was passed as part of President Lyndon B. Johnson's civil rights agenda. The act ended all formal discrimination in immigration law by abolishing the national origins quotas and creating a new set of preference categories based on family reunification and professional skills. With this law, Congress hoped to facilitate immigration from Europe, especially from countries like Italy, Greece, and Poland, which had the largest visa backlogs due to the old quota system. Lawmakers were given assurances that increased immigration from Asia, Africa, or Latin America would be unlikely under the new law. Indeed, a new 120,000 person numerical cap on immigration from the Western Hemisphere limited migration from Mexico for the first time, and overall limits on immigration were set with hemispheric and country-specific quotas.[2]

However, the 1965 act had a number of unintended consequences. Immigration to the United States remained high. Prior to 1965, the peak decade for immigration was 1911–20, when over 5.7 million immigrants entered the country. During the 1980s, a record 7.3 million immigrants came to the United States. The large numbers of European immigrants lawmakers expected never materialized; instead, immigration from Latin America and Asia increased dramatically. New immigrants from China, India, Korea, and the Philippines came as professionals or for family reunification. Since

1975, more than one million refugees have arrived from Vietnam, Cambodia, and Laos as a direct result of U.S. intervention in Southeast Asia. Immigration from Latin America also increased. By 2007, Latin American immigrants made up 54 percent of the total foreign-born population, while Asians were at 28 percent.[3]

By placing an annual cap on immigration from the Western Hemisphere, the 1965 Immigration Act also dramatically reduced the number of visas available to Mexican immigrants. As a consequence, undocumented immigration from Mexico increased beginning in the 1970s and set off a divisive debate that continues to this day. In the midst of a deep national recession, alarmists talked of the "loss of control" over the country's borders. Racialized metaphors of war like "invasion," "conquest," and "save our state" were commonly deployed to describe undocumented immigration from Mexico. The Immigration Reform and Control Act of 1986 (IRCA) attempted to "get tough with" undocumented immigrants and their employers, but lax enforcement and migrant adaptation have proven such provisions to be ineffectual. Instead, during the 1990s, the U.S. government turned to border patrol initiatives with military codenames like "Operation Gatekeeper" in San Diego, California, "Operation Rio Grande" in Brownsville, Texas, "Operation Safeguard" in Nogales, Arizona, and "Operation Hold the Line" in El Paso, Texas. From 1993 to 1996, the U.S. Congress increased funding for the Border Patrol by 102 percent. The U.S. Border Patrol arrested approximately one million individuals along the U.S.-Mexico border in the year 2000 alone. Still, undocumented immigrants continue to risk their lives to enter the country and to remain here. In 2007, the Census Bureau estimated that there were 11.6 million undocumented immigrants in the country. The majority is from Mexico, but Europeans, Asians, Africans, and other Latin Americans also comprise part of the undocumented population.[4]

Post 9/11 Immigration Policies

Following the terrorist attacks of September 11, 2001, the immigration debate shifted toward national security issues after the discovery that the plane hijackers were Muslim and Arab foreigners who had been legally admitted into the United States. Eleven days after the attacks, President George W. Bush created the Office of Homeland Security. Immigration regulation was placed under the jurisdiction of the newly created Department of Homeland Security (DHS) in 2003. Immigration and Customs Enforcement (ICE) took over the responsibility for border security and immigrant detention and deportation from the now defunct Immigration and Naturalization Service.[5]

Many new policies were put into place to track, control, detain, and deport immigrants suspected of terrorist activity or those deemed a potential threat to national security. A section in the "Patriot Act" passed in the House of Representatives in October of 2001 allowed the long-term detention of noncitizens without a hearing. The government detained between 1,500 and 2,000 people, mostly foreigners, under the justification that they were "suspected terrorists." Many of the detainees were held for months without access to legal counsel and some were even deported in secret, but none were charged with being involved in the September 11 attacks.[6]

Other initiatives increased the government's efforts to remove immigrants with existing deportation orders. In February 2002, the immigration service established the "Absconder Apprehension Initiative" to locate 314,000 foreign nationals who had ignored court orders to leave the country. While the initial focus of the program was on approximately 6,000 immigrants from countries identified as al Qaeda strongholds, the vast majority of immigrants affected have been Latin American. The program was also expanded to immigrants with temporary visas and even those who were in the process of completing the process for legal residency in the country. An estimated 7,500 noncitizens were screened by the government under this program. In addition, there has been an increase in the number of workplace raids for undocumented workers. A new policy was also put in place that required political asylum seekers to be detained while their cases were decided.

The antiterrorist policies have had a disproportionate impact on Middle Eastern and South Asian immigrants. The workplace enforcement and absconder policies have affected immigrants from Latin America, especially from Mexico. Today's deportees are disproportionately Latino; they make up 40 percent of those sentenced in federal courts, even though they are only about 13 percent of the adult population. But the new broad reach of post-9/11 immigration policies has impacted all immigrant communities, not just those suspected of terrorist links or undocumented entry. Deportation policies in general have become "harsher, less forgiving, and more insulated from judicial review."[7]

At the same time, the U.S. government has attempted to fix an immigration system that politicians and advocates from all sides agree is broken. A visa backlog prevents both low-skilled and highly skilled workers from entering the country to fill jobs at the same time that American employers continue to rely on immigrant labor. As a result, undocumented immigration has been on the rise. These immigrants are often forced to live in the shadows of American society where labor exploitation and criminal behavior remain hidden. Despite these problems, efforts to find federal solutions to fix the broken immigration system have failed in recent years.

Immigrant Detention in the Twenty-First Century

As a result of post-9/11 policies, immigrant detention rates have skyrocketed. In 1996, the U.S. government had a daily immigrant detention capacity of almost 8,300 beds. But from 2005 to 2008, the number of detainees held for deportation or waiting political asylum increased by 65 percent. Immigrant detention is the fastest growing form of incarceration in the country. In 2009, more than 32,000 people who were not American citizens were reportedly held in detention on any given day. ICE reported that more than 407,000 people had been detained by the federal government on immigration-related issues during 2008 alone. The numbers keep growing with each passing year as the U.S. government tightens its enforcement of immigration laws and seeks to arrest and deport undocumented and other immigrants.[8]

Compared to the volume of detainees at the Angel Island Immigration Station, the numbers of contemporary immigrant detainees are astounding. From 1913 to 1919, the years for which we have the best empirical data on detention, 20,471 individuals (just over 2,900 a year) were detained at the station or its hospital for more than one day, with an average stay of just over seven nights. Even at the busier Ellis Island station, the number of immigrant detentions was more than half of what it is today. In 1907, a peak year of immigration, there were 195,540 detentions, 62 percent of which were temporary, lasting no more than five days.[9]

Like those detained on Angel Island or Ellis Island, today's detainees are either waiting to be deported or are in the process of challenging their deportation. They include individuals who have been arrested on immigration-related charges or who have been convicted of a crime, including minor and immigration-related crimes, or who are seeking asylum. The government's new immigrant detention policies ensnare not only recent border-jumpers and convicted felons but also torture survivors, parents of U.S. citizen children, and long-term lawful permanent residents (persons with "green cards") with strong ties in local communities. According to the Human Rights Watch organization, 77 percent of recent legal immigrant deportees had been convicted for such nonviolent crimes as undocumented entry, immigration offenses, driving under the influence of alcohol, disorderly conduct, and even traffic violations. All detainees have already been punished for their crimes, but if they are found to be deportable, they will be banned from the United States for life regardless of family ties or length of residence. Many are in the process of getting their legitimate claims to remain in the United States approved. One example includes Tanveer Ahmad, a longtime New York City cabdriver who paid his taxes, applied for immigration visas, and was married twice to American women. His deportable offense was a fine for disorderly conduct in 1997, when he attempted to stop a robbery at the Houston gas station where he worked. He brandished a gun at the would-be robbers. The gun turned out to be unlicensed, and Ahmad was fined $200. When Ahmad and his wife failed their green card interview, Ahmad was left without a valid visa to remain in the country, and the disorderly conduct fine provided the government with enough justification to arrest him in 2005 and place him in detention.[10]

The U.S. government has not been prepared to handle the dramatic increase in the number of immigrant detainees or their diverse needs. As was the case on Angel Island, today's detainees include men, women, and children from different countries, with varying medical conditions and vastly different legal circumstances. Additionally, just as immigration officials scrambled to detain Chinese immigrants on passenger ships in the immediate days after the passage of the Chinese Exclusion Act of 1882, ICE officials have struggled to find enough facilities in which to hold the growing number of detainees. In the summer of 2007, for example, the government hastily built the Willacy Detention Center, a 2,000-bed detention center in Raymondville, Texas, in the remote southern tip of the Rio Grande Valley. Ringed by barbed wire, the $65 million windowless tent city is the nation's largest immigrant detention facility and houses up to 2,000 people ordered deported from the country.[11]

Even with facilities like those in Raymondville, the federal government does not operate enough detention centers on its own. With only twenty-two government-run facilities in operation in 2009, the government has largely outsourced immigrant detention to high-priced private contractors such as the Corrections Corporation of America. Sixty-seven percent of all immigrant detainees are housed in a rapidly growing patchwork of more than 350 county and state jails, profit-making prisons, and federal detention centers, where they are integrated with the rest of the prison population. Cities and counties have been eager to participate in the "immigrant gold rush," especially in light of the economic recession that began in 2008. The cost of detaining immigrants averages $95 a day, totaling tens of millions of dollars in expenditures in jails and other facilities across the nation. The federal government allotted $2.4 billion for immigrant detention in 2008 and 2009.[12]

The outsourcing of immigrant detention presents several problems. Unlike detainees on Angel Island, today's detainees are often housed with the general prison population, including violent criminals. Moreover, prison administrators often lack training and expertise in immigration law enforcement and do not have any authority over individual cases and immigration claims. Thus, detainees are given few details about the immigration charges made against them, their legal options, or how to communicate with the proper authorities. Unlike the Angel Island or Ellis Island immigration stations which were centrally located in big metropolitan areas and close to immigrant communities, families, and advocates, today's immigrant detention facilities are often located in deserts and industrial warehouse districts.[13]

Detainees are incarcerated for as long as it takes for the final decision to be rendered. Government records differ on the length of detention—from an average stay of thirty-seven days to ten months. The longest case was three and a half years, and other deportees might face indefinite detention if their home countries are unwilling to accept their return or do not have diplomatic relations with the United States. Today's detainees are confined for much longer periods than those on Angel Island and Ellis Island. On Ellis Island, most stayed only one night, awaiting money or the arrival of relatives. On Angel Island, nearly 60 percent of those who were detained stayed less than three days, while Chinese immigrants, who were 70 percent of the detainee population, had an average stay of two to three weeks.[14]

Government reports, congressional hearings, and media investigations criticizing the nation's current immigrant detention system sound eerily similar to those conducted in the early twentieth century when Chinese community leaders complained of overcrowding, unsanitary conditions, and harsh enforcement procedures on Angel Island. Current newspaper reports describe a ballooning immigrant detention system that functions with little oversight, accountability, or transparency. The *Washington Post* argues that immigrant detention occupies a "hidden world" where errors in medical care, poor administration, faulty record-keeping, and severe staff shortages seriously jeopardize due process and normal standards of American justice.[15]

Like on Angel Island, some of the loudest complaints about the current U.S. detention system relate to the poor conditions of the facilities in which immigrants are housed. At the hastily built Willacy Detention Center in Raymondville, Texas, detainees are housed in huge tents on concrete pads that hold 200 men or women divided into four "pods." Detainees are confined for twenty-three hours a day. The whole compound is surrounded by fourteen-foot-high chain-link fences looped with barbed wire. Tents are windowless and there are no partitions or doors that separate the five toilets, five sinks, five shower heads, and eating areas. According to a government investigation, there is often insufficient food, clothing, medical care, and access to telephones. The food quality in general is poor, and there are not enough eating utensils for all detainees, so some eat with their hands. Lights are kept on twenty-four hours a day. Some detention centers never allow detainees outdoor recreation; others let them out onto "tiny dirt patches" only once or twice a week. Young children were put behind razor wire at the T. Don Hutto Residential Center near Austin, Texas. At the federal detention center in San Pedro, California, conditions were so overcrowded that detainees staged a riot in August 2008.[16]

The poor conditions at immigrant detention facilities have continued in part because so much of what happens in the detention system is hidden from view. Detainees are not guaranteed free legal representation or access to judicial review, and as a consequence, only one in ten has an attorney who can lobby on behalf of the detainee for release, proper medical care, or a move to another facility to be closer to family. Individuals may ask for a review of their cases by an immigration judge, but many detainees do not realize that making such a request is possible. When reviews do happen, immigration judges order releases with bonds that are often too high for the detainees and their families to meet. "Detainees have less access to lawyers than convicted murderers in maximum-security prisons, and some have fewer comforts than al-Qaeda terrorism suspects held at Guantanamo Bay, Cuba," the *Washington Post* concluded.[17]

The poor conditions and management at immigrant detention centers have led to tragic results. Investigative reporters and researchers have sounded the alarm on a "massive crisis in detainee medical care." Physically sick and mentally ill detainees are housed in "overcrowded compounds" and "locked in a world of slow care, poor care and no care." Medical spending has not kept pace with the dramatic growth in the detainee population, and a huge shortage of medical doctors, nurses, and technicians compromises the already poor system. Moreover, staff have been neglectful or even dismissive of detainee medical complaints, and flawed medical judgments and administrative practices are routine occurrences. From 2003 to 2009, 104 immigrants died while in ICE custody. One was Jason Hiu Lui Ng, a U.S. resident originally from Hong Kong, who died in June 2008 after an aggressive form of cancer was left undiagnosed and untreated while he was in detention. Ng had entered the country sixteen years earlier and had overstayed his tourist visa. In the intervening years, he held steady employment, married a woman who was a U.S. citizen, and had two sons born in the United States. Despite numerous attempts to acquire a green card to stay in the country, Ng was found deportable for overstaying his visa and was placed in detention in three different facilities around New England. When he complained of severe pain, officials accused him of faking his condition and denied pleas for an independent medical evaluation.[18]

The high-profile media coverage of immigrant detainee deaths prompted the House of Representatives to conduct a hearing on the problem of immigrant detainee medical care in June 2008. Gloria Armendariz, wife of former detainee and Vietnam veteran Isaias Vasquez, testified about her husband's eighteen-month detention in Texas facilities. He had been arrested and slated for deportation in November of 2004 after being found in possession of marijuana. A long-time schizophrenic, Vasquez received inadequate medical attention after detention center staff took him off his medications. When he became disoriented and uncooperative, Vasquez was placed in solitary confinement and was gassed. He remained there for six or seven months, sometimes falling and hitting his head. Armendariz's complaints to detention staff were dismissed, and Vasquez became frail and undernourished. Eventually, DHS dismissed the case against Vasquez. He became a naturalized citizen in 2007 based on his military service. "Now he has good and bad days, but he still suffers from the treatment memories of [his detention]," his wife told Congress.[19]

Congressional representatives also heard about the case of Amina Mudey, a torture survivor from Somalia who spent five months in ICE custody while appealing for asylum. Soon after she arrived in shackles at the Elizabeth Detention Center in New Jersey in April, 2007, center doctors misdiagnosed her complaints about headaches and put her on a powerful antipsychotic drug that caused very serious side effects, such as convulsions, drooling, and lactation. All requests to see a medical doctor were denied or ignored for weeks. Only after her attorney threatened to file a federal lawsuit to force detention officials to transfer Mudey to a hospital did they comply.[20]

Congresswoman Zoe Lofgren did not mince words in her condemnation of current ICE practices. After citing government documents indicating that medical treatment was denied for serious conditions such as tuberculosis, pneumonia, bone fractures, head trauma, chest pain, and other serious complaints, Lofgren called ICE practices "inhuman" and argued that "ICE's policy may be designed to deny care and save money rather than to provide care and save lives."[21]

Angel Island and the Immigration Debate in the Twenty-First Century

The United States' controversial immigrant detention policies have been implemented at the same time that record numbers of immigrants continue to come to the country. The 2000 census revealed that the United States was accepting immigrants at a faster rate than at any other time since the 1850s. In 2007, there were over 37.5 million foreign-born residents, making up 12.5 percent of the American population.[22] Since 1965, the doors to the United States have been opened wider than at any other time since the late nineteenth century. Like the generations of newcomers before them, today's immigrants have chosen the United States because they want to reunite with family members already here and because they continue to believe in the economic opportunity and the freedom from political persecution that the United States has historically offered. They settle throughout the country, not just in big cities along the east and west coasts. They and their children are already transforming American society and culture, and through them, the United States continues to be a nation of immigrants.[23]

Americans in general still embrace the idea of welcoming newcomers from different parts of the world, even if the welcome may be warmer for some groups than for others. At the same time, Americans' ambivalence about immigration remains deeply ingrained in both public discourses and in immigration law. As in the past, they are still grappling with the questions of the first decades of the twentieth century: Who should be allowed in and who should be kept out? How can immigration policy best serve the nation? How should the country control suspicious activities among foreigners already in the United States? And at what risk to immigrant communities and cost to our own civil liberties? In short, can the United States be both a nation of immigrants and a gatekeeping nation?

Like the immigrant detainees on Angel Island, today's immigrants find themselves caught in these larger debates over immigration. In 2008, an anonymous immigrant likened their detention to being caged in a prison. "Whether I'm documented or not, I'm a human being," they told an interviewer. "I used to think birds in a cage were so pretty but no one should be deprived of freedom—no one should be caged."[24] Sometime during the thirty-year history of the Angel Island Immigration Station, another anonymous immigrant expressed similar frustrations in a carved poem found on the walls of the men's detention barracks:

In the last month of summer, I arrived in America on ship.
After crossing the ocean, the ship docked and I waited to go on shore.
Because of the records, the innocent was imprisoned in a wooden
    building.
Reflecting on the event, my heart is vexed and depressed.
I composed a poem to rid myself of sadness and worry...
As I record the cause of my situation, it really provokes my anger.
Sitting here, uselessly delayed for long years and months, I am like a
    pigeon in a cage.[25]

From its founding, the United States has benefited from the skills, ideas, capital, labor, creativity, and values that immigrants have brought to this country. Immigration is critical to our economy, families, and communities. It is also a central component of our national identity. As we continue to debate the role of immigration in twenty-first-century America, we would do well to remember the role that Angel Island has played in American immigration history.

For thousands of immigrants who were barred or deported from the United States, Angel Island was both a first and last stop on a forced journey back home: Filipino repatriates, Chinese laborers, women and workers from many different backgrounds. For many others, Angel Island was the stepping-stone to new lives and freedoms in America: Mexican and Russian refugee families who fled violence, chaos, and persecution in their homelands; Korean and South Asian nationalists who fought against the colonialism oppressing their homelands; Filipino laborers and Chinese paper sons who later served in the U.S. armed forces and earned the full benefits of U.S. citizenship; and Japanese picture brides and Chinese wives who were able to start families and broaden their own horizons as workers and homemakers. Over half a million people from eighty countries were processed through the immigration station on Angel Island, the majority of whom were detained for brief periods of time. For many of them—perhaps even most—America lived up to its promise of freedom and better economic opportunities, if not for themselves, then for their children and grandchildren.

America's contradictory relationship to immigration is written on the walls of Angel Island. We welcome the "huddled masses yearning to be free" at the same time that we unfairly detain and deport immigrants based on flawed immigration policies. Remembering both sides of this complex history helps us recognize what is still great about the United States and what remains to be done to fulfill America's promise as a nation of immigrants.

APPENDIX

Table 1: Arrivals and Departures at Port of San Francisco, 1910–1940

Year	ARRIVALS			DEPARTURES		
	Aliens	U.S. Citizens	Total	Aliens	U.S. Citizens	Total
1909/10	9,636	5,818	15,454	15,454	4,946	20,400
1910/11	9,095	4,249	13,344	13,344	5,892	19,236
1911/12	8,489	5,567	14,056	14,056	5,994	20,050
1912/13	9,201	5,909	15,110	15,110	5,699	20,809
1913/14	10,138	5,404	15,542	15,542	6,303	21,845
1914/15	14,426	6,168	20,594	20,594	5,514	26,108
1915/16	13,704	6,254	19,958	19,958	5,239	25,197
1916/17	12,484	5,082	17,566	17,566	5,418	22,984
1917/18	17,644	4,547	22,191	22,191	4,283	26,474
1918/19	18,568	5,299	23,867	23,867	5,358	29,225
1919/20	22,888	6,273	29,161	29,161	8,703	37,864
1920/21	22,751	7,402	30,153	30,153	8,574	38,727
1921/22	14,056	7,339	21,395	21,395	8,332	29,727
1922/23	14,348	6,885	21,233	21,233	7,531	28,764
1923/24	16,263	6,980	23,243	23,243	6,228	29,471
1924/25	8,170	5,589	13,759	13,759	6,252	20,011
1925/26	9,225	5,825	15,050	15,050	6,274	21,324
1926/27	19,347	8,065	27,412	27,412	7,389	34,801
1927/28	10,232	6,943	17,175	17,175	7,352	24,527
1928/29	10,420	7,530	17,950	17,950	7,318	25,268
1929/30	10,300	7,812	18,112	18,112	8,941	27,053
1930/31	7,878	7,921	15,799	15,799	7,500	23,299
1931/32	5,096	7,271	12,367	12,367	7,000	19,367
1932/33	4,129	5,933	10,062	NA	NA	NA
1933/34	4,965	7,185	12,150	NA	NA	NA
1934/35	6,727	8,299	15,026	NA	NA	NA
1935/36	6,768	9,858	16,626	NA	NA	NA
1936/37	6,309	9,907	16,216	6,995	9,862	16,857

(continued)

Table 1: Continued

Year	ARRIVALS			DEPARTURES		
	Aliens	U.S. Citizens	Total	Aliens	U.S. Citizens	Total
1937/38	6,418	8,763	15,181	15,181	8,642	23,823
1938/39	6,521	6,402	12,923	12,923	5,558	18,481
1939/40	5,167	6,627	11,794	7,329	6,409	13,738
Totals	341,363	209,106	550,469	482,919	182,511	665,430

Source: U.S. Dept. Commerce and Labor, *Annual Report of the Commissioner-General of Immigration*, 1910–1912; U.S. Dept. of Labor, *Annual Report of the Commissioner-General of Immigration*, 1913–1932; "San Francisco Discrict Reports," 1937–1940, File numbers 55957/819, 55989/719, 56013/619, 56054/519, Entry 9, RG 85, NARA, DC; U.S. Dept. of Justice, INS, "Report of Passenger Travel between the U.S. and Foreign Countries, by Ports as Specified," 1931 to 1940, and U.S. Dept. of Labor, INS, "U.S. Citizens Arriving from Foreign Countries," 1936–1940, courtesy of USCIS History Office and Library, U.S. Citizenship and Immigration Services, Dept. of Homeland Security; U.S. Congress, House, *Statistical Abstracts of the United States*, 1936.

Table 2: Angel Island Arrival Case Files by Birth Country

Birth Place	Arrivals	Birth Place	Arrivals
China	44,585	Panama	25
United States	13,354	Greece	22
Japan	8,620	Peru	19
Germany	401	Thailand	19
Russia	382	Malaysia	18
Philippine Islands	362	Sweden	18
Korea	360	Hungary	17
India	296	Denmark	16
Mexico	207	Tahiti	16
United Kingdom	198	West Indies	16
Australia	119	Norway	15
Spain	83	Portugal	14
Italy	57	Jamaica	13
Indonesia	50	Chile	12
El Salvador	46	Switzerland	12
Guatemala	45	Dominican Republic	11
Poland	42	Afghanistan	10
Canada	38	Columbia	10
Austria	36	French Indochina	10
France	33	Formosa	9
New Zealand	32	Argentina	8
Netherlands	29	Czechoslovakia	8
Nicaragua	28	Persia	8
Singapore	26	Belgium	6

Yugoslaiva	6	Ceylon	2
Finland	5	Lithuania	2
South Africa	5	Mauritius	2
Syria	5	Puerto Rico	2
Turkey	5	Surinam	2
Costa Rica	4	Arabia	1
Romania	4	Bulgaria	1
Samoa	4	Cape Verde	1
Venezuela	4	Ecuador	1
Armenia	3	Estonia	1
Borneo	3	Fiji	1
Iraq	3	Ghana	1
Latvia	3	Honduras	1
Alaska	2	Luxembourg	1
Brazil	2	Born at Sea	16
Burma	2	Unknown	196
Total			70,052

Source: Records of the Immigration and Naturalization Service, RG 85, Investigation Arrival Case Files, 1884–1944, National Archives, Pacific Regional Branch. This table is based on the reported birth country given in the Board of Special Inquiry case files of arrivals at the Angel Island Immigration Station from 1910 to 1940. USA includes people who were born in Hawaii. Although we estimate that 300,000 aliens were detained on Angel Island, we found only 70,052 case files at the National Archives. With the exception of the Chinese, the majority of immigrants were not interviewed by the board or were interviewed only briefly, and through the years, many files have been lost, destroyed, or consolidated into other types of INS files. Our gratitude to Bill Greene, Vincent Chin, Eddie Fung, and the many volunteers who helped compile the statistics for this table. Their names appear in the Acknowledgments.

Table 3: Alien Applicants for Admission to U.S. and Percent Debarred by Nationality, July 1, 1910–June 30, 1932

	TOTAL APPLICANTS						% DEBARRED					
FY Ending June 30,	1911–15	1916–20	1921–25	1926–30	1931–32	1911–32	1911–15	1916–20	1921–25	1926–30	1931–32	1911–32
Nationality												
African	51,926	54,549	62,638	21,120	4,848	195,081	2.95	3.94	4.77	8.21	5.80	4.45
Armenian	28,599	6,140	20,551	5,974	1,152	62,416	5.00	2.22	4.55	3.68	4.08	4.43
Bohemian, Czech	43,383	2,051	22,436	15,273	1,172	84,315	0.83	4.29	1.07	1.45	1.79	1.11
Bulgarian, Serbian, Montenegrin	58,768	8,563	17,141	7,329	1,736	93,537	6.66	5.79	3.73	5.39	3.34	5.88
Chinese	**25,027**	**65,892**	**75,677**	**43,267**	**14,309**	**224,172**	**9.12**	**2.13**	**4.65**	**5.11**	**3.20**	**4.41**
Croatian, Slovenian	135,272	2,562	25,846	9,398	2,237	175,315	1.67	5.04	2.28	3.83	2.82	1.94
Cuban	32,798	35,623	41,055	43,038	11,252	163,766	0.38	0.31	0.69	0.46	0.52	0.47
Dalmatian, Bosnian, Herzegovian	19,369	357	2,740	1,431	348	24,245	2.08	6.16	3.32	2.24	2.01	2.29
Dutch, Flemish	75,692	44,355	50,420	37,237	8,849	216,553	0.95	1.45	2.99	3.43	2.19	2.00
East Indian	**3,053**	**1,721**	**1,595**	**1,182**	**504**	**8,055**	**54.57**	**8.08**	**8.40**	**6.35**	**1.19**	**25.08**
English	428,194	262,647	457,160	399,488	89,813	1,637,302	1.92	2.62	3.30	3.74	3.43	2.94
Finnish	52,773	18,381	18,299	10,899	2,873	103,225	1.77	2.69	4.62	5.22	2.82	2.83
French	119,498	128,295	189,814	144,509	25,920	608,036	3.29	6.02	5.78	5.81	11.00	5.57
German	398,347	40,653	317,230	378,227	69,121	1,203,578	1.29	5.18	1.85	1.44	1.10	1.61
Greek	186,636	75,462	54,330	28,094	7,108	351,630	4.10	1.93	3.17	2.42	1.76	3.31
Hebrew	**463,606**	**61,440**	**301,705**	**79,467**	**15,082**	**921,300**	**1.77**	**3.65**	**2.25**	**4.71**	**4.77**	**2.36**
Irish	221,892	87,354	202,535	235,782	28,828	776,391	1.80	3.73	3.36	3.11	5.24	2.95
Italian (north)	193,592	31,161	75,109	37,265	9,109	346,236	1.32	1.82	1.92	2.90	2.51	1.70
Italian (south)	938,343	202,508	403,419	169,296	38,505	1,752,071	1.91	1.67	1.75	1.28	1.11	1.76

Nationality												
Japanese	52,986	73,223	59,147	37,471	13,526	236,353	1.88	1.46	0.98	0.82	0.93	1.30
Korean	483	775	599	466	143	2,466	4.56	7.23	1.34	5.15	1.40	4.54
Lithuanian	83,668	2,163	8,217	4,304	1,405	99,757	1.19	8.83	5.10	5.79	2.06	1.89
Magyar	135,726	2,052	34,577	15,375	4,334	192,064	1.13	6.87	1.97	6.73	4.45	1.87
Mexican	108,029	212,376	318,511	271,587	11,813	922,316	8.10	7.73	3.11	3.78	18.23	5.15
Pacific Islander	110	244	173	129	42	698	0.91	5.33	15.03	8.53	0.00	7.31
Polish	495,862	22,375	77,952	34,164	7,203	637,556	1.32	5.68	2.71	7.08	4.47	1.99
Portuguese	49,798	45,021	36,656	17,996	4,457	153,928	1.28	1.28	2.37	4.48	2.45	1.95
Rumanian	58,274	3,996	13,529	5,536	1,136	82,471	3.22	6.23	4.12	6.70	5.72	3.78
Russian	162,262	17,907	25,924	16,001	4,551	226,645	2.65	7.80	5.02	6.68	3.47	3.63
Ruthenian, Russniak	133,814	3,801	7,415	4,629	649	150,308	2.07	16.31	14.42	32.38	17.41	4.04
Scandinavian	235,291	103,663	185,161	146,617	26,583	697,315	0.92	1.13	2.15	2.76	1.24	1.68
Scotch	144,868	86,391	208,499	191,460	31,688	662,906	2.18	3.15	3.96	4.02	4.51	3.51
Slovak	110,027	6,275	56,175	15,574	4,549	192,600	0.96	1.00	1.34	7.75	3.14	1.67
Spanish	70,361	86,195	70,262	38,309	9,076	274,203	2.19	1.99	3.98	3.14	1.92	2.71
Spanish American	16,497	28,098	31,239	39,799	9,608	125,241	0.97	1.36	2.17	1.54	1.20	1.56
Syrian	36,832	7,844	14,384	6,879	1,767	67,706	7.90	5.51	6.23	5.32	6.57	6.97
Turkish	8,398	1,108	1,554	1,532	369	12,961	8.66	4.15	4.12	2.22	2.71	6.80
Welsh	15,823	6,032	11,628	12,866	2,171	48,520	1.83	2.70	4.89	4.57	3.82	3.49
West Indian	12,072	14,403	15,525	11,003	3,128	56,131	0.66	0.50	0.89	1.28	1.54	0.85
Other peoples	19,554	9,032	8,787	5,810	1,394	44,577	9.29	4.73	7.27	8.33	8.18	7.81
Total	5,427,503	1,862,688	3,525,614	2,545,783	472,358	13,833,946	2.13	3.36	2.94	3.36	3.56	2.78

Source: U.S. Dept. of Labor, *Annual Report of the Commissioner-General of Immigration*, 1927–1932. Data unavailable for specific ports and for the years 1933–1940. Nationalities in bold font had a significant presence on Angel Island. Compiled by Vincent Chin.

NOTES

ABBREVIATIONS

AR-CGI   Annual Reports of the Commissioner-General of
Immigration

CGI   Commissioner-General of Immigration

FOIA   Freedom of Information Act

IACF, SF   Investigation Arrival Case Files, San Francisco, Records
of the U.S. Immigration and Naturalization Service, RG
85, National Archives, Pacific Region, San Bruno, CA

IISF, IHRC   International Institute of San Francisco Records,
Immigration History Research Center, University of
Minnesota

INS COSCCF   Central Office Subject Correspondence and Case
Files, Entry 9, Records of the U.S. Immigration and
Naturalization Service, RG 85, National Archives,
Washington, DC

PMSS   Pacific Mail Steamship Company

NARA, DC   National Archives and Records Administration,
Washington, DC

NARA, PR   National Archives and Records Administration, Pacific
Regional Branch

SRR   Survey of Race Relations, Hoover Institution Archives,
Stanford University

A NOTE ON LANGUAGE AND TERMINOLOGY

1. For the definition of a nonquota immigrant, see section 4 of the
Immigration Act of 1924 (43 Stat. 153).
2. Donna Gabaccia analyzes the historical use of the terms *illegal
immigration* and *illegal immigrant* in "Great Migration Debates:
Keywords in Historical Perspective," Social Science Research Council,
"Border Battles: The U.S. Immigration Debates," July 28, 2006, http://
borderbattles.ssrc.org/Gabaccia/index.html (accessed October 9, 2009).
For a historical study of the origins of the "illegal alien" in American
law and society, see Mae Ngai's *Impossible Subjects*. On the use of the
term *undocumented immigrant*, see the press release by the National

Association of Hispanic Journalists, "NAHJ Urges News Media to Stop Using Dehumanizing Terms When Covering Immigration," www. nahj.org/nahjnews/articles/2006/March/immigrationcoverage.shtml (accessed September 25, 2009).

3. Sobredo, "From 'American Nationals,'" xvi; Ngai, *Impossible Subjects*, 100; Hing, *Defining America*, 44.

4. The authority to expel or deport aliens from the United States was first established in 1789 in the Alien and Sedition Acts (Act of June 25, 1798). Deportation policy reemerged and was actively enforced beginning in 1882 with the Chinese Exclusion Act and was expanded to contract laborers in 1888 and more broadly to other aliens, such as prostitutes and alien radicals who entered the country in violation of later immigration laws. On the growth of deportation policy in the late nineteenth and twentieth centuries, see Lee, *At America's Gates*, 43, and Hing, *Defining America*, 209–11. For a discussion of the INS role in "cleaning house" or deporting immigrants who had broken the law while residing in the United States, see Sakovich, "Angel Island Immigration Station Reconsidered."

5. On terminology, see "SAJA Stylebook for Covering South Asia & the South Asian Diaspora," South Asian Journalists Association, www.saja. org/stylebook.html#I (accessed January 9, 2008).

INTRODUCTION

1. New arrivals were processed in Montreal and Vancouver in Canada; on the East Coast in New York, Baltimore, Boston, Miami, and Philadelphia; along the Gulf Coast in Jacksonville, New Orleans, and Galveston; along the U.S.-Mexico border at El Paso; and on the West Coast at Portland, Port Townsend, San Diego, Los Angeles, Seattle, San Francisco; and in American territories like Honolulu and San Juan, Puerto Rico. The immigrant stations on the East Coast generally processed a larger number of arrivals than those on the West Coast. See Stolarik, *Forgotten Doors*.

2. File 10382/54 (Wong Chung Hong), IACF, SF.

3. See Appendix, Table 1.

4. Files 12904/4–6 to 4–10 (Lopez family), Case Files of Investigations Resulting in Warrant Proceedings, NARA, PR.

5. Files 12777/18–1 (An Chang Da), 12777/18–2 (Yin Chi Ham), 12777/18–3 (Chung In Kooa), 12777/18–4 (Cho Hin), 12777/18–5 (Lee Chang Soo), and 12777/18–6 (Kim Lyul), IACF, SF.

6. File A2 283 668, Alien Investigative Case File, Bureau of Citizenship and Immigration Services, FOIA Division, in possession of Kathy and David Ang; Kathy Ang, correspondence to authors, June 20, 2009.

7. Ivy Gidlow to Elsa Gidlow, January 20, 1929, Elsa Gidlow Papers, Gay and Lesbian Historical Society.

8. Act of March 3, 1875 (18 Stat. 477); Chinese Exclusion Act, Act of May 6, 1882 (22 Stat. 58). For more on the Page Law, see Peffer, "Forbidden Families." On the ways in which the Chinese exclusion laws set precedent in federal immigration regulation, see Lee, *At America's Gates*, 40–43. On the Supreme Court's rulings on the power of the federal government to

regulate immigration, see Salyer, *Laws Harsh as Tigers*. The 1893 Supreme Court case *Fong Yue Ting v. United States* ruled that immigration exclusion and expulsion were matters of civil, not criminal law. Markowitz, "Straddling the Civil-Criminal Divide," 298–304; and Kanstroom, *Deportation Nation*, 4.

9. Act of August 3, 1882, ch. 367 (22 Stat. 214); the Alien Contract Labor Law is also known as the Foran Act (23 Stat. 332); Immigration Act of 1891 (26 Stat. 1084); Immigration Act of 1903 (32 Stat. 1203); Immigration Act of 1907 (34 Stat. 898). For more on the Gentlemen's Agreement restricting Japanese laborers, see Chapter 3 of this volume.

10. Immigration Act of 1917 (39 Stat. 874). For more on the effects of the Immigration Act of 1917 on South Asians, see Chapter 4 of this volume.

11. The Quota Act of 1921 (42 Stat. 24) limited total annual admissions to 355,000 and restricted the number of aliens admitted annually to 3 percent of the foreign-born population of each nationality already residing in the United States in 1910. It particularly limited the immigration of Southern and Eastern European immigrants, whose populations had been much smaller in 1910. The Immigration Act of 1924 (43 Stat. 153) reduced the total number of admissions and temporarily changed the percentage admitted from 3 percent to 2 percent of the foreign-born population of each nation recorded in the 1890 census, when Southern and Eastern European immigrants had yet to arrive in large numbers. The permanent quota formula established in 1929—enacted under the Act of March 2, 1929 (45 Stat.1512)—was based on the percentage of the entire population in the United States of each national origin (both immigrant and native-born alike) in 1920. Such calculations continued to favor populations that could trace their presence in the United States far back into the nation's history, such as those from Northern and Western Europe. Hing, *Defining America*, 68–70; Higham, *Strangers in the Land*, 308–24; Ueda, *Postwar Immigrant America*, 22; Ngai, *Impossible Subjects*, 21–55; LeMay, *Guarding the Gates*, 127–34. On the development of passport controls during and after World War I, see Torpey, *The Invention of the Passport*, 117–18.

12. On the downturn in immigration during the 1930s, see Ueda, *Postwar Immigrant America*, 32. On Mexican repatriation, see Balderrama and Rodriguez, *Decade of Betrayal*, 122. On Filipino repatriation, see Chapter 8 of this volume.

13. On Ellis Island, see Moreno, *Encyclopedia of Ellis Island*, xv–xvi. On the contrast between Ellis Island and Angel Island, see Daniels, "No Lamps Were Lit for Them."

14. Sakovich, "Angel Island Immigration Station Reconsidered," 3, 209.

15. "Picture brides" were young women in Japan and Korea who were married to immigrants in America through the custom of arranged marriage. For more on Japanese and Korean picture bride migration, see Chapters 3 and 5 in this volume. "Paper sons" were Chinese men who falsely claimed to be the sons of exempt-class Chinese immigrants or Chinese American citizens in order to secure admission into the United States during the Chinese exclusion era. See Chapter 2 in this volume.

16. For the migratory routes of Chinese, Russians, South Asians, and Filipinos, see respective chapters. Information on Salvadoran migrants came from Ivan Jimenez, "Immigration through Angel Island 1910–1940: The Salvadoran People." Information on Spanish migrants came from Esther Gray, "Representing Spanish Immigration through Angel Island."

17. On Harry Bridges's hearing, see Soennichsen, *Miwoks to Missiles*, 132–34. On the deportation of resident aliens, see Sakovich, "Angel Island Immigration Station Reconsidered."

18. Olmstead Center for Landscape Preservation, "Cultural Landscape Report," 13–14.

19. Architectural Resources Group, "Hospital Building,"11–12; Olmstead Center for Landscape Preservation, "Cultural Landscape Report," 14–15, 17, 88; Fanning and Wong, *Angel Island*, 15.

20. Barde, *Immigration at the Golden Gate*, 56–59.

21. Ibid., 59–62; Hart Hyatt North to CGI, November 11, 1904, File 52371/004, INS COSCCF; *San Francisco Call*, October 8, 1909.

22. On the location of the shed on the wharf, see Barde, *Immigration at the Golden Gate*, 67–68, 74. On the varied complaints of the shed, see F. H. Larned, Acting CGI, "Supplemental Memorandum to the Assistant Secretary of the Dept. of Commerce and Labor," November 23, 1908, File 52270/21, Richard Taylor to CGI, March 25, 1909, File 52270/21, H. H. North to CGI, September 20, 1909, File 52999/14, and F. H. Larned to Secretary of Commerce and Labor, January 28, 1909, File 5220/71, INS COSCCF; Huey Dow to Collector of Customs, November 1902, File 9903/66, IACF, SF; Wong Ngum Yin, "Composition," enclosed in Inspector in Charge to CGI, October 29, 1906, File 13928, and John Endicott Gardner to J. H. Barbour, April 19, 1902, File 4862, Chinese General Correspondence, NARA, DC; *San Francisco Call*, September 9, 1908, and November 29, 1908.

23. Olmstead Center for Landscape Preservation, "Cultural Landscape Report," 173; *Chung Sai Yat Po*, January 17, 1903; File 5986, Chinese General Correspondence, NARA, DC; Daniel Keefe to Secretary of Commerce and Labor, August 7, 1909, File 52270/21, and William R. Wheeler to Secretary of Commerce and Labor, January 28, 1909, File 51456/056, INS COSCCF.

24. Olmstead Center for Landscape Preservation, "Cultural Landscape Report," 29; Architectural Resources Group, "Hospital Building," 19.

25. Architectural Resources Group, "Hospital Building," 11; H. H. North to George C. Perkins, December. 7, 1903, Box 1, Hart Hyatt North Papers, Bancroft Library, UC Berkeley. For a construction history of the immigration station, see also U.S. Department of Commerce and Labor, *AR-CGI* (1910), 132.

26. Architectural Resources Group, "Hospital Building," 30, 17; Olmstead Center for Landscape Preservation, "Cultural Landscape Report," 29–30, 32–35, 38–40; Toogood, "A Civil History," 409, 406; William R. Wheeler, "Memorandum for the Secretary," January 28, 1909, File 51456/056, INS COSCCF; Barde, *Immigration at the Golden Gate*, 72–73.

27. *San Francisco Chronicle*, August 18, 1908; Toogood, "A Civil History," 376–77.

28. The immigration service kept an office in downtown San Francisco to handle correspondence; to receive applications, affidavits, and some witness testimony; and to issue return certificates and visitors' passes to the island. In addition, notices of all Chinese landings and denials were posted in the office on a daily basis. On the work left to be completed on the immigration station, see Toogood, "A Civil History," 409; William R. Wheeler, "Memorandum for the Secretary," January 28, 1909, File 51456/056, INS COSCCF; and Olmstead Center for Landscape Preservation, "Cultural Landscape Report," 38–40. On the role of the immigration service office in downtown San Francisco, see Hart Hyatt North, "In the Matter of the Chinese Exclusion Law," February 1, 1910, File 52961/26-D, INS COSCCF.

29. *San Francisco Examiner*, January 28, 1898. After his retirement from the service, North authored articles on Chinese and Japanese immigration, such as "Chinese and Japanese Immigration" and "Chinese Highbinder Societies."

30. Hart Hyatt North to CGI, June 9, 1910, File 52961/16A and 16B, INS COSCCF.

31. Lai, "Island of Immortals," 91.

32. Barde, *Immigration at the Golden Gate*, 73; Lai, "Island of Immortals," 91; Hart Hyatt North to CGI, February 3, 1910, File 52961/26-D and Hart Hyatt North to CGI, February 2, 1910, File 52961/24, INS COSCCF. For North's official report on the opening of the station, see Commissioner of Immigration, "Annual Report, San Francisco, 1910," July 19, 1910, File 52967/27; and "Brief on the Situation at the Angel Island Immigrant Station, by H. H. North, Commissioner," c. May 1910, File 52961/16-B, INS COSCCF.

33. Lai, "Island of Immortals," 100. On the vast literature on the Chinese immigrant experience on Angel Island, see, for example, Lai, Lim, and Yung, *Island*; Lee, *At America's Gates*; Hsu, *Dreaming of Gold*; Lau, *Paper Families*; and Barde, *Immigration at the Golden Gate*. The first comprehensive study of other Asian immigrants on Angel Island was Gee, "Sifting the Arrivals." The first to analyze non-Asians on Angel Island was Sakovich, "Angel Island Immigration Station Reconsidered."

34. The reference to Mexico may refer to the fact that Angel Island was used as a detention facility for immigrants in transit to and from Cuba, Mexico, and other Latin American countries. In 1921, Mexico banned the immigration of Chinese laborers into Mexico. "Zu's whip" refers to Zu Di (A.D. 266–321), a Chinese general who was known to be a fierce warrior and competitor. Lai, Lim, and Yung, *Island*, 134.

35. Previous attempts to quantify the number of immigrants processed through the Angel Island Immigration Station can be found in Askin, "Historical Report;" Daniels, "No Lamps Were Lit for Them;" Sakovich, "Angel Island Immigration Station Reconsidered;" and Barde and Bobonis, "Detention at Angel Island."

36. The numbers for Ellis Island are from 1892 to 1954. Moreno, *Encyclopedia of Ellis Island*, xi, ix; Jacobson, *Roots Too*, 4–10, 59–71.

37. For more on the celebratory mythos of Ellis Island, see Wallace, "Boat People: Immigrant History at the Statue of Liberty and Ellis Island," and Daniels, "No Lamps Were Lit for Them."

38. Gee, "Sifting the Arrivals," 39–40, 52–53, 100; Sakovich, "Angel Island Immigration Station Reconsidered," 221; Gardner, *The Qualities of a Citizen*, 3.

CHAPTER ONE

1. "Angel Island Is Denounced by Clergyman," *San Francisco Chronicle*, June 9, 1916.
2. File 15287/8–17 (Jung Look Moy), IACF, SF.
3. "Angel Island Is Denounced by Clergyman," *San Francisco Chronicle*, June 9, 1916.
4. Gontard, "Second Class on Angel Island," 7.
5. Architectural Resources Group, "Hospital Building," 19.
6. "Transcript of Stenographic Notes," June 6, 1911, File 52961/24-D, INS COSCCF. On public health examinations, see Shah, *Contagious Divides*, 184. On policies regarding which immigrants were sent to the immigration station, see Daniel Keefe, Memorandum for the Secretary of Commerce and Labor, June 17, 1910, File 52961/24A, INS COSCCF; and Sakovich, "Angel Island Immigration Station Reconsidered," 44–45.
7. The *Angel Island* ferry replaced the *Inspector*, which had a limited capacity of fifty passengers, in 1911. Then in 1936, a new diesel launch named the *Jeff D. Milton* replaced it.
8. Architectural Resources Group and Daniel Quan Design, "Final Interpretive Plan," C-3; Olmstead Center for Landscape Preservation, "Cultural Landscape Report," 43; Askin, "Historical Report," 29; Toogood, "A Civil History," 401–2.
9. Lai, Lim, and Yung, *Island*. 73.
10. Gontard, "Second Class on Angel Island," 8–9.
11. The numbers of hospital patients eventually declined in the later years of the immigration station's history. In 1940, fewer than 5,000 immigrants were examined by the Public Health Service. Askin, "Historical Report," 27; Toogood, "A Civil History," 381–83; Architectural Resources Group, "Hospital Building," 19.
12. Moreno, *Encyclopedia of Ellis Island*, 64–70; Shah, *Contagious Divides*, 179–80, 186.
13. There was a very large disinfecting shed at the quarantine station at Ayala Cove, where passenger belongings or clothing received a first disinfection. If further fumigation was needed once individuals arrived at the hospital, it would have been conducted in the small hospital disinfector room, which was added within a year of the station's opening at the request of Dr. W. M. Glover. Architectural Resources Group, "Hospital Building," 36, 44.
14. Architectural Resources Group, "Hospital Building," 24, 33–62; Appendix D: Historic Drawings, in Olmstead Center for Landscape Preservation, "Cultural Landscape Report," 173–74; Toogood, "A Civil History," 368–69; "Transcript of Stenographic Notes," June 6, 1911, File 52961/24-D, INS COSCCF.
15. Shah, *Contagious Divides*, 180; Sakovich, "Angel Island Immigration Station Reconsidered," 45–46.
16. Gontard, "Second Class on Angel Island," 9, 49.
17. Alexandra Hrenoff interview.

18. Architectural Resources Group, "Hospital Building," 25; A. Warner Parker to the Commissioner-General of Immigration, August 21, 1915, File 53438/54, INS COSCCF (italics added).

19. See Files 13241/1-1 (John Stevens), 13241/1-9 (Miguel Gonzalez), and 13241/1-10 (Jose Gutierrez), IACF, SF.

20. The opinion that Angel Island required special medical vigilance can be found in the *San Francisco Chronicle*, August 18, 1907; Walter J. Matthews to CGI, December 6, 1904, File 51456/1-15, INS COSCCF; Olmstead Center for Landscape Preservation, "Cultural Landscape Report," 173–75; and Remarks of Samuel R. Backus, "Minutes of Immigration Consultation at San Francisco," August 9–11, 1916, File 53990/52, INS COSCCF. On comparing the medical inspection at Ellis Island with Angel Island, see Shah, *Contagious Divides*, 185; Fairchild, *Science at the Borders*, 88; and Conway, *Forgotten Ellis Island*, 32–34.

21. On the bacteriological tests as a means for Asian exclusion, see Shah, *Contagious Divides*, 188–89, 196–97; and Architectural Resources Group, "Hospital Building," 19. One exception to the trend of parasitic diseases being found mostly in Asians was the case of Spanish immigrants who had been working in Panama. Almost one-third of Spanish laborers applying for entry between 1913 and 1915 were afflicted with hookworm. See Gray, "Representing Spanish Immigration."

22. Hookworm was reclassified in 1917; liver fluke in 1927. Lai, Lim, and Yung, *Island*, 108; Shah, *Contagious Divides*, 199.

23. Statistics for 1909, 1920, and 1933 from Hart Hyatt North to CGI, May 5, 1909, File 52371/004, Edward White to CGI, June 20, 1920, File 54862/27, and D. W. MacCormack to Edward L. Haff, October 22, 1933, File 55853/219, INS COSCCF. See also Architectural Resources Group, "Hospital Building," 66.

24. Angel Island Immigration Station Foundation, "The Other Side of the Fence," 4–5.

25. The Bureau of Immigration merged with the Bureau of Naturalization in 1933 to create the Immigration and Naturalization Service (INS). In 2003, the INS was abolished and its functions placed under three agencies: U.S. Citizenship and Immigration Services, Immigration and Customs Enforcement, and Customs and Border Patrol—within the newly created Department of Homeland Security. For quote on the "keepers" of the gate, see Edward W. Cahill to Mr. George Fitch, November 9, 1934 and Edward L. Haff to Ted Reindollar, May 14, 1936, File 12030/1, "Historical File Relating to Angel Island," NARA, PR; and Sakovich, "Angel Island Immigration Station Reconsidered," 35.

26. Van Vleck, *The Administrative Control of Aliens*, 25–26; Howe, *The Confessions of a Reformer*, 255; Rak, *Border Patrol*, 10–11. On the new types of officers in the service in San Francisco, see Hart Hyatt North to J. S. Rodgers, June 9, 1909, Folder 3, Box 1, Hart Hyatt North Papers, Bancroft Library, UC Berkeley; and Luther Steward, "Visit Paid the Angel Island Immigration Station," June 6, 1911, 80–81, File 52961/24-D, INS COSCCF.

27. John Birge Sawyer Diaries, January 1907, vol. 1, 41, 46, 55, Bancroft Library, UC Berkeley.

28. Ibid., vol. 2, 89–90, 117–21.
29. "Minutes of Immigration Consultation at San Francisco," August 9–11, 1915, File 53990/52, INS COSCCF.
30. Emery Sims interview; Edwar Lee, interview with Lai, Lim, and Yung.
31. Sakovich, "Angel Island Immigration Station Reconsidered," 109.
32. Lee, *At America's Gates*, 58–61; "Profile of B. C. Haworth as Recalled by His Daughter, Chloe Haworth Smith," March 31, 1981, courtesy of Deak Wooten.
33. On Gardner's work as an interpreter in the immigration service, see Lee, *At America's Gates*, 61–63; and Barde, *Immigration at the Golden Gate*, 203–5. On his family history, see Susan S. Briggs, correspondence to authors, August 11, 2009, and August 17, 2009.
34. Edwar Lee, interview with Lowe.
35. Edwar Lee, interview with Lai, Lim, and Yung.
36. Edwar Lee, interview with Lowe.
37. Both Tye Leung and Fuku Terasawa served as interpreters and assistant matrons. See Chapter 2 for more on Tye Leung and Chapter 3 for more on Fuku Terasawa.
38. Samuel Backus to CGI, November 1, 1911, File 52961/24-E, INS COSCCF; Samuel Backus on the vault as quoted in Architectural Resources Group and Daniel Quan Design, "Final Interpretive Plan," C-4.
39. Emery Sims interview.
40. Gontard, "Second Class on Angel Island," 8.
41. Lee Puey You's case is discussed more fully in Chapter 2 of this volume. Yung, "'A Bowlful of Tears,'" 7, 10.
42. Exceptions to the literacy requirement included married women joining their husbands, women joining a son or grandson, single or widowed daughters coming to join a father, men over age fifty-five coming to join a son or grandson, and individuals coming to the United States to avoid religious persecution. See Smith and Herring, *Bureau of Immigration*, 182; and Sakovich, "Angel Island Immigration Station Reconsidered," 128. A description of the test cards can be found in Architectural Resources Group and Daniel Quan Design, "Final Interpretive Plan," C-10. On the changes after 1918, see *AR-CGI* (1918), 10–11; and Sakovich, "Angel Island Immigration Station Reconsidered," 127.
43. Sakovich, "Angel Island Immigration Station Reconsidered," 113, 151–52.
44. Ibid., 155–60.
45. Ibid., 36; James L. Houghteling to Charles I. Stengel, Esq., December 14, 1937, File 55853/219, INS COSCCF.
46. Sakovich, "Angel Island Immigration Station Reconsidered," 217–18.
47. See File 16598/10–1 (George Griffith) and File 14300/1–14 (Paul Kofend), IACF, SF.
48. Sakovich, "Angel Island Immigration Station Reconsidered," 164, 172.
49. File 13168/5–3 (Juan Rechy Gonzales), IACF, SF.
50. On Mexican immigrants, see Chapter 7 of this volume. The description of wealthy Guatemalan immigrants on Angel Island is drawn from Laura Gutiérrez, "The Guatemalan Experience at Angel Island."

51. Wimbush, "Erbon Delventhal," 3.
52. Gardner, *The Qualities of a Citizen*, 87–99.
53. Files 16949/5–1, 5–2, 5–3 (Emile, Rose, and Alfred Louis), IACF, SF. On domesticity as a fixture of immigration law and the ways in which the LPC clause was uniquely gendered, see Gardner, *The Qualities of a Citizen*, 14, 88.
54. Gee, "Sifting the Arrivals," 204.
55. Salyer, *Laws Harsh as Tigers*, 197–98; Gardner, *The Qualities of a Citizen*, 73–88; Sakovich, "Angel Island Immigration Station Reconsidered," 100–101. On the ways in which the moral turpitude clause was enforced on Ellis Island, see Cannato, *American Passages*, 260–86.
56. File 14033/4–11 (Maria Holmgren, pseud.), IACF, SF.
57. Gardner, *The Qualities of a Citizen*, 1–3.
58. Lai, Lim, and Yung, *Island*, 68.
59. Glover's comments are in Architectural Resources Group, "Hospital Building," 25; "Australians Detained on Angel Island," *San Francisco Chronicle*, August 10, 1922. There is no indication that the immigration station was expanded or remodeled in the 1920s. See Architectural Resources Group and Daniel Quan Design, "Final Interpretive Plan," C-11.
60. Descriptions of the detention facilities can be found in M. W. Glover to Acting Commissioner of Immigration, November 21, 1910, File 52961/26F, INS COSCCF; Architectural Resources Group, "Angel Island Immigration Station Detention Barracks," 12, 18, 24; Askin, "Historical Report," 58; AR-CGI (1917), 199; Wang, "The History and Problem of Angel Island;" Bamford, *Angel Island*, 15; Sakovich, "Angel Island Immigration Station Reconsidered," 64–65; and Architectural Resources Group and Daniel Quan Design, "Final Interpretive Plan," 18–25, C-5, C-7. The Scanlan description is in "Anzacs Resent U.S. Immigration System," *San Francisco Chronicle*, August 17, 1938.
61. Askin, "Historical Report, 7–11; Olmstead Center for Landscape Preservation, "Cultural Landscape Report," 30–31. Information on the guard tower is from Daniel Quan, correspondence to authors, July 22, 2008.
62. Askin, "Historical Report," 9–11, 16–17, 44; Architectural Resources Group, "Angel Island Immigration Station Detention Barracks," 30–31.
63. Angel Island detention figures are based on an analysis of 29,000 passengers listed in the ledgers for 1913–1919 of the Pacific Mail Steamship Company, one of the dominant carriers of passengers between San Francisco and Asia. Barde and Bobonis, "Detention at Angel Island," 113. Information on Ellis Island is from www.ellisisland.org/genealogy/ellis_island_history.asp (accessed September 24, 2008).
64. Barde and Bobonis, "Detention at Angel Island," 113–16; On Quok Shee, see Barde, *Immigration at the Golden Gate*, 26–52.
65. Takahashi quote from Sarasohn, *The Issei*, 52; Maurer quote from *Annual Report of the Woman's Home Missionary Society*, 1921/22, 139, Pacific School of Religion.
66. Isaak, *Our Life Story and Escape*, 129.
67. Kawai, *My Lantern*, 138. On the crowded conditions, see Architectural Resources Group and Daniel Quan Design, "Final Interpretive Plan," C-9.

68. On the protest by German officers, see Architectural Resources Group and Daniel Quan Design, "Final Interpretive Plan," C-9. On the problems relating to the mixing of women of different classes, see Commissioner of Immigration to CGI, May 17, 1911, File 52961/26H, INS COSCCF. On Ivy Gidlow's comments, see Ivy Gidlow to Elsa Gidlow, January 20, 1929, Elsa Gidlow Papers, Gay and Lesbian Historical Society.
69. M. W. Glover to Acting Commissioner of Immigration, November 21, 1910, File 52961/26F, INS COSCCF; Ivy Gidlow to Elsa Gidlow, January 20, 1929, Elsa Gidlow Papers, Gay and Lesbian Historical Society; "7 Aliens Enjoy Workless Winter," *San Francisco Chronicle*, March 5, 1930.
70. Mock Ging Sing interview.
71. "Charge Made of Abuse at Angel Island," *San Francisco Examiner*, May 22, 1917, 1; Wladimir Pruszyaski to Commissioner White, January 7, 1919, File 54462/191, INS COSCCF; Alexander Hrenoff interview; Sakovich, "Angel Island Immigration Station Reconsidered," 68–70; "Australians Detained at Angel Island," *San Francisco Chronicle*, August 10, 1922; M. W. Glover to Acting Commissioner of Immigration, November 21, 1910, File 52961/26F, INS COSCCF; Olmstead Center for Landscape Preservation, "Cultural Landscape Report," 44; Nishi, "Actions and Attitudes of the United States Public Health Service on Angel Island," 29; Architectural Resources Group, "Hospital Building," 25–26.
72. Architectural Resources Group and Daniel Quan Design, "Final Interpretive Plan," C-7.
73. Lai, Lim, and Yung, *Island*, 77–78. On the architectural layout of the administration building dining rooms, see Architectural Resources Group and Daniel Quan Design, "Final Interpretive Plan," C-4.
74. Complaints by Japanese women in Kawai, *My Lantern*, 138. Samuel Backus to CGI, November 1, 1911, File 52961/24-E, INS COSCCF.
75. Architectural Resources Group and Daniel Quan Design, "Final Interpretive Plan," C5-C7.
76. As quoted in Architectural Resources Group and Daniel Quan Design, "Final Interpretive Plan," C-6.
77. "Important for Visitors: Read Carefully before Seeing Prisoners," April 7, 1923, courtesy of Maria Sakovich.
78. "Russian Students in Jail," *Russkii Golos*, October 19, 1923.
79. Katharine R. Maurer, "Immigration Notes from Angel Island," *Woman's Home Missions*, September 1916, 21, and "Busy Days at Angel Island," *Woman's Home Missions*, June 1921, 1, Pacific School of Religion.
80. Katharine R. Maurer, "Angel Island: 'Keeper of the Western Gate,'" *Woman's Home Missions*, May 1937, 4–5, Pacific School of Religion.
81. Lai, Lim, and Yung, *Island*, 166.

CHAPTER TWO

1. Meaning to feed oneself, to make a living.
2. Lai, Lim, and Yung, *Island*, 162.
3. The figure of 178,000 Chinese who were admitted into the United States comes from *AR-CGI*, 1910–1940; and Chen, "Chinese Immigration into the United States," 181. The statistics on Chinese

detainees at Angel Island are based on a study of 29,000 passengers listed in the ledgers of the Pacific Mail Steamship Company for 1913–18, in Barde and Bobonis, "Detention at Angel Island," 113–16. See also Lai, "Island of Immortals," 98; and Chen, "Chinese under Both Exclusion and Immigration Laws," 403.

4. Chan, *This Bitter-sweet Soil*, 51–78; Siu, *The Chinese Laundryman*, 85.

5. Chan, *This Bitter-sweet Soil*, 16–26; Chen, *Chinese San Francisco*, 11–23; Hsu, *Dreaming of Gold*, 18–29; Chen, "Chinese under Both Exclusion and Immigration Laws," 206; Lai, Lim, and Yung, *Island*, 44.

6. Jann, "The Story of a Sojourner in Gold Mountain," 15.

7. Lai, Lim, and Yung, *Island*, 44.

8. Women made up less than 10 percent of the Chinese immigrants to the United States between 1910 and 1940. Chan, "The Exclusion of Chinese Women," 95, 97; Yung, *Unbound Feet*, 55–63.

9. Yung, *Unbound Voices*, 213–14.

10. Eighty-eight percent of all Chinese immigrants coming to the United States on the Pacific Mail Steamship line from 1913 to 1919 came in steerage class, according to Barde, *Immigration at the Golden Gate*, 134; Interview #39, Angel Island Oral History Project, Ethnic Studies Library, UC Berkeley.

11. Lai, Lim, and Yung, *Island*, 47.

12. Kathy Ang, correspondence to authors, June 20, 2009.

13. California State Senate, Special Committee on Chinese Immigration, *Chinese Immigration*, 275.

14. Yung, *Unbound Feet*, 20–21; Lee, *At America's Gates*, 25–30. See also Gyory, *Closing the Gate; and* Saxton, *Indispensable Enemy*.

15. Lee, *Orientals*, 88–89; Chan, "The Exclusion of Chinese Women," 97–99; Yung, *Unbound Feet*, 26–37. See also Pfaelzer, *Driven Out*.

16. Lee, *At America's Gates*, 43–46; Chan, "*The Exclusion of Chinese Women*," 109–32.

17. Pre-exclusion era statistics taken from Yung, *Unbound Feet*, 22. The figure for the exclusion era includes immigrants only from 1882–91 and immigrants and returning citizens from 1894–1940. Statistics for 1892 not available. *AR-CGI*, 1898–1943; Chen, "Chinese Immigration into the United States," 181; Liu, "A Comparative Demographic Study," 223; U.S. Bureau of the Census, *Historical Statistics of the U.S. 1789–1945*, 35.

18. From 1910 to 1924, U.S. citizens made up 41 percent of the total number of Chinese men admitted into the country; returning laborers and returning merchants were 15 percent each; merchant sons were 11 percent; new merchants were less than 1 percent. From 1910 to 1924, wives of U.S. citizens made up 30 percent of the total number of Chinese women admitted into the country; merchant wives were 28 percent; U.S. citizens were 18 percent; merchant daughters were 6 percent; students were 5 percent; and returning laborers were 2 percent. Lee, *At America's Gates*, 115, 98.

19. Jann, "Story of a Sojourner," 15–16.

20. Yung, "'A Bowlful of Tears' Revisited," 10; Jann, "Story of a Sojourner," 15–16.

21. Yu, "Rediscovered Voices," 129; Lai, "Island of Immortals," n28, 102.

22. Shah, *Contagious Divides*, 186, 193–94.

23. See, for example, Files 14894/2–2 (Lee Kan) and 11215, IACF, SF; Lee, *At America's Gates*, 91–92.

24. Gee, "Housewives, Men's Villages, and Sexual Respectability," 94–97.

25. By 1900 the percentage of Chinese women in San Francisco who were listed as prostitutes in the U.S. census had dropped from 71 percent in 1870 to 16 percent, and by 1910, 7 percent. See Yung, *Unbound Feet*, 71–72. For examples of news coverage, see "Chinese Slave Girls Testify at Angel Island, Tell Story of Strange Voyage across Pacific," *San Francisco Chronicle*, December 8, 1910; "Chinese Slave Girls Rescued by Police," *San Francisco Chronicle*, September 21, 1912; and "Six Slaves Caught in Raid, Hidden in Merchant's Home," *San Francisco Chronicle*, May 24, 1913.

26. Barde, *Immigration at the Golden Gate*, 26–52; Barde and Bobonis, "Detention at Angel Island," 106.

27. Hart Hyatt North to CGI, January 27, 1910, and Daniel Keefe to Secretary of Commerce and Labor, February 7, 1910, File 52961/26-C, INS COSCCF; *AR-CGI* (1915), 41–42.

28. Yung, *Unbound Voices*, 282–88.

29. File 12017/1686 (Wong Kim Ark), Return Certificate Application Case Files, NARA, PR (italics added); Lee, *"Wong Kim Ark v. United States*: Immigration, Race, and Citizenship," 89–109.

30. Interview #23, Angel Island Oral History Project, Ethnic Studies Library, UC Berkeley.

31. Interviews #45 and #12, Southern California Chinese American Oral History Project, Asian American Studies Center, UCLA; Hsu, *Dreaming of Gold*, 71–72; Lai, Lim, and Yung, *Island*, 111.

32. Lee, *At America's Gates*, 83.

33. Lai, Lim, and Yung, *Island*, 45; Interview with Mr. Yuen, Angel Island Interviews, Bancroft Library, UC Berkeley.

34. Rule 7, U.S. Department of Commerce and Labor, Bureau of Immigration, "Treaties, Laws, Regulations Relating to the Exclusion of Chinese," May 1905, 47; Smith and Herring, *Bureau of Immigration*, 35–36; Untitled Correspondence, Box 1, Historical File Relating to Angel Island, NARA, PR.

35. "Transcript of Stenographic Notes," June 6, 1911, File 52961/24-D, 28–29, INS COSCCF; John D. Nagle, "Comment on Proposed Chinese General Order No. 11," August 1927, File 55597/912, INS COSCCF.

36. File A18485/7–97 (Fong Hoy Kun, pseud.), IACF, SF.

37. Lai, Lim, and Yung, *Island*, 116.

38. Yung, *Unbound Voices*, 217.

39. Lai, Lim, and Yung, *Island*, 45.

40. Interview #23, Angel Island Oral History Project, Ethnic Studies Library, UC Berkeley.

41. File 55452/385, INS COSCCF.

42. Lai, Lim, and Yung, *Island*, 77–78.

43. Yu, "Rediscovered Voices," 131–32; Interview #23, Angel Island Oral History Project, Ethnic Studies Library, UC Berkeley.

44. Ng, *The Treatment of the Exempt Classes*, 1–2; Charles Jung interview.

45. Lee, *At America's Gates*, 139.

46. On lawyers at the Angel Island Immigration Station, see Lee, *At America's Gates*, 139–40. On Stidger's family background, see Biographical File of

Oliver Perry Stidger, Society of California Pioneers; Barde, *Immigration at the Golden Gate*, 67; Salyer, *Laws Harsh as Tigers*, 174, n165, 292; and "Rites Held for Lawyer O. P. Stidger," *San Francisco Chronicle*, September 5, 1959. For Stidger's critiques of immigration law, see O. P. Stidger, "Our Immigration Law," and "Highlights on Chinese Exclusion and Expulsion." The estimate that Stidger and Kennah handled 85 percent of the immigration cases on Angel Island is from "Attorneys Disbarred in Chinese Port Scandal," *San Francisco Examiner*, August 22, 1917.

47. On the Densmore investigation, see Lee, *At America's Gates*, 200; and Barde, *Immigration at the Golden Gate*, 209–33. "Attorneys Disbarred in Chinese Port Scandal," *San Francisco Examiner*, August 22, 1917; "Attorney Stidger Indicted by U.S.," *San Francisco Examiner*, November 3, 1917; Stidger, "Highlights on Chinese Exclusion and Expulsion," 5, 20, 25–28.

48. Chen, "Chinese under Both Exclusion and Immigration Laws," 105–7. See also Lai, Lim, and Yung, *Island*, 110–11.

49. File 18703/13–5 (Chin Sing), IACF, SF.

50. Statistics on appeals by Chinese immigrants and overall admission rates at the Angel Island Immigration Station taken from *AR-CGI*, 1910–1924. Statistics on Chinese women excluded for prostitution can be found in *AR-CGI*, 1910–1930. Charles Jung quotes taken from Yu, "Rediscovered Voices," 129, 127.

51. No. 23099R, *Ngim Ah Oy v. Edward Haff*, U.S. District Court for the Southern District of California, August 24, 1939; No. 9418, *Ngim Ah Oy v. Haff*, U.S. Court of Appeals for the Ninth Circuit, June 11, 1940; No. 380, *Ngim Ah Oy v. Haff*, Supreme Court of the United States, October 21, 1940.

52. Lee Puey You story and quotes taken from Yung, "'A Bowlful of Tears' Revisited."

53. File 39071/12–9 (Ngim Ah Oy), IACF, SF.

54. Yung, "'A Bowlful of Tears' Revisited," 5.

55. Lai, Lim, and Yung, *Island*, 79.

56. Ibid., 78.

57. Ibid.

58. Interview #39, Angel Island Oral History Project, Ethnic Studies Library, UC Berkeley.

59. Yu, "Rediscovered Voices," 128–29.

60. Lai, Lim, and Yung, *Island*, 73–74.

61. Ibid., 109

62. Interview #35, Angel Island Oral History Project, Ethnic Studies Library, UC Berkeley.

63. Interview #44, Angel Island Oral History Project, Ethnic Studies Library, UC Berkeley.

64. Lai, Lim, and Yung, *Island*, 81.

65. Interview #33, Angel Island Oral History Project, Ethnic Studies Library, UC Berkeley.

66. Lai, Lim, and Yung, *Island*, 75.

67. Yung, "'A Bowlful of Tears' Revisited," 5–6; Yung, *Unbound Feet*, 66–67.

68. "Chinese Hangs Self at Angel Island," *San Francisco Chronicle*, October 7, 1919.

69. Lester Tom quote from Alex Hannaford, "Scarred by an Angel," *South China Morning Post*, May 1, 2004.

70. Interview #39, Angel Island Oral History Project, Ethnic Studies Library, UC Berkeley.
71. Lai, Lim, and Yung, *Island*, 114. Edwar Lee may be referring to the case of Wong Shee, who committed suicide by sticking chopsticks through her ears and cutting her own throat in the bathroom of the immigration station at 801 Silver Avenue on November 19, 1941. See File 41369/11–29 (Wong Shee), IACF, SF.
72. Chan, "The Exclusion of Chinese Women," 95, 97.
73. File A2 283 668, Alien Investigative Case File, Bureau of Citizenship and Immigration Services, FOIA Division, in possession of Kathy and David Ang; Kathy Ang, correspondence to authors, June 20, 2009; File 23550/8–5 (Lim Soon Din), IACF, SF.
74. A team of scholars, including Charles Egan, Wan Liu, Newton Liu, and Xing Chu Wang, was commissioned by the Angel Island Immigration Station Foundation to translate and analyze all the poems and inscriptions on the walls of the detention barracks in 2003. Architectural Resources Group and Daniel Quan Design, "Poetry and Inscriptions;" Charles Egan, "Voices in the Wooden House."
75. Interview #32 (Jann Mon Fong a.k.a. Smiley Jann), Angel Island Oral History Project, Ethnic Studies Library, UC Berkeley.
76. Interview #33 (Tet Yee), Angel Island Oral History Project, Ethnic Studies Library, UC Berkeley.
77. Egan, "Voices in the Wooden House."
78. Yu, "Rediscovered Voices," 134.
79. Yung, "'A Bowlful of Tears' Revisited," 10–11. Lee Puey You's poem translated by Marlon K. Hom.
80. Lai, Lim, and Yung, *Island*, 27–28.
81. Xiangshan (Zhongshan today) is a district in the Pearl River Delta. Lai, Lim, and Yung, *Island*, 66.
82. Lee, *At America's Gates*, 223–32; Chen, "Chinese Immigration," 236.
83. Ngai, "Legacies of Exclusion"; U.S. Department of Justice, *Chinese Investigations*.
84. Chen, "Chinese Immigration," 177. Arthur Lem, correspondence to Erika Lee, January 13, 1996.
85. File A6 824 153, Alien Investigative Case File. Bureau of Citizenship and Immigration Services, FOIA Division, in possession of Daisy Gin.
86. Yung, "'A Bowlful of Tears' Revisited," 12.
87. Interview #32, Angel Island Oral History Project, Ethnic Studies Library, UC Berkeley; Arliss Jann, correspondence to authors, July 18, 2009.
88. Interview #33, Angel Island Oral History Project, Ethnic Studies Library, UC Berkeley; Felicia Lowe, *Carved in Silence*.

CHAPTER THREE

1. Yoneda, *Ganbatte*, 5.
2. Ibid., 10.
3. Daisuke Namba, a twenty-four-year-old communist agitator, was executed in 1924 for attempting to assassinate the Prince Regent Hirohito.

4. This translation, found in the Anne Loftis Papers at Stanford University, is reprinted with permission from the Department of Special Collections, Stanford University Libraries. Our thanks to Charles Egan for pointing out that the poems were evidently revised by Yoneda in later years, as the Japanese text differs substantially from that published in the *Nichibei* on February 21, March 14 and 21, 1927.

5. File 25537/21–18 (Goso Yoneda), IACF, SF.

6. The statistics on Japanese arrivals in San Francisco, detention time on Angel Island, and rejection rate are based on *AR-CGI*, 1910–32; and Passenger Lists of Vessels; Registers of Persons Held for Boards of Special Inquiry; and Registers of Japanese, Filipinos, and Hawaiians Held for Boards of Special Inquiry, NARA, PR.

7. U.S. census reports.

8. Ichioka, *The Issei*, Chapter 2; James Stanlaw, "Japanese Emigration," 35–51.

9. Ito, *Issei*, 33.

10. As quoted in U.S. Congress, *Reports of the Immigration Commission*, "Immigrants in Industries,"14.

11. Ito, *Issei*, 18.

12. Ichioka, *The Issei*, 51–52.

13. U.S. Congress, *Reports of the Immigration Commission*, "Immigrants in Industries,"167.

14. Azuma, *Between Two Empires*, 29–30.

15. *San Francisco Chronicle*, February 23, 1905, 1.

16. As quoted in U.S. Congress, *Reports of the Immigration Commission*, "Abstracts of Reports of the Immigration Commission," 170.

17. Gee, "Sifting the Arrivals," 74.

18. U.S. Congress, *Reports of the Immigration Commission*, "Abstracts of Reports of the Immigration Commission,"661.

19. Daniels, *Asian America*, 121.

20. Margarita Lake of the Woman's Home Missionary Society of the Methodist Episcopal Church to Victor Metcalf, Secretary of Commerce and Labor, March 9, 1905; and letter from Commissioner H. H. North to CGI, June 24, 1908, File 52424/13, INS COSCCF.

21. Azuma, *Between Two Empires*, 37–38.

22. Story and quotes taken from Shiz Hayakawa, interview with Heihachiro Takarabe, San Francisco, CA, November 26, 1972, Issei Oral History Project, California State University, Sacramento; and Sarasohn, *Issei Women*.

23. Story and quotes taken from Iyo Tsutsui, interview with Heihachiro Takarabe, Stockton, CA, February 26, 1975, Issei Oral History Project, California State University, Sacramento; and Sarasohn, *Issei Women*.

24. Sarasohn, *Issei Women*, 71; Takanashi, "Stories of Picture Brides," 217–21; and Yoneda, *Ganbatte*, 1.

25. Sarasohn, *Issei Women*, 73.

26. As quoted in Tanaka, "Japanese Picture Marriage," 216.

27. "A New Project at Yokohama YWCA," *Joshi Seinen-kai* (Young women's world), 12, no. 6 (June 1915): 39–40, translated by Yoshiko Yokochi Samuel.

28. Sarasohn, *Issei Women*, 74, 87.
29. In a letter to the Commissioner-General of Immigration in Washington, D.C., on January 6, 1914, San Francisco Commissioner Samuel Backus reported that only eighteen out of a total of 3,174 "photo brides" had been denied admission during the calendar years 1910 to 1913 inclusive. File 52424/13A, INS COSCCF.
30. "Visit to the Angel Island Detention Center," *Shin-sekai* (New world daily), April 29, 1920, translated by Yoshiko Yokochi Samuel.
31. Sarasohn, *The Issei*, 52
32. Sarasohn, *Issei Women*, 72.
33. Ibid., 74.
34. Our thanks to Don Nakahata for information regarding his grandparents, the Reverend Barnabas and Fuku Terasawa. Nakahata has deposited the original pocketsize, leather-bound register of over 600 picture bride marriages performed by the Reverend Terasawa from 1909 to 1913 in the Japanese American Research Project Collection at the University of California, Los Angeles.
35. "Interview with Mrs. Terasawa, Matron and Interpreter at Angel Island, California," SRR.
36. Constance Willis Camp, "Kuan Yin: Goddess of Mercy of Angel Island," booklet, Woman's Home Missionary Society, Methodist Episcopal Church, n. d., 3.
37. Information about the work of the YWCA on Angel Island was taken from the YWCA publication, *Joshi Seinen-kai* (Young women's world), September 1915, November 1915, February 1917, and September 1919; and "Kaiko nijunen (Looking back at the past twenty years)," San Francisco Japanese YWCA, 1932, translated by Yoshiko Yokochi Samuel.
38. For a class and gender analysis of Japan's emigration policies, see Azuma, *Between Two Empires*, Chapter 2; Tanaka, "Japanese Picture Marriage," Chapter 4; and Sawada, *Tokyo Life, New York Dreams*, Chapter 3.
39. Quotes taken from Kawai, *My Lantern*, 137–38, reprinted with permission from Keisen Jogakuen; and Kawai, "A Day at Angel Island."
40. Besides Fuku Terasawa, other Japanese interpreters who were employed at the Angel Island Immigration Station included Emily Austin, James L. Gardiner, B. C. Haworth, Sadikichi Nomura, F. Scheuten, and A. J. Wiebe.
41. Sarasohn, *Issei Women*, 87.
42. File 10447/11–1 (Yoshi Nakayama), IACF, SF.
43. For a class and gender analysis of the immigration process for Asian women at Angel Island, see Gee, "Housewives, Men's Villages, and Sexual Respectability;"and Gee, "Sifting the Arrivals," Chapter 3.
44. "Picture Brides of the Flowery Kingdom," *San Francisco Chronicle*, May 7, 1911, 3; Tanaka, "Photographs of Japanese Picture Brides."
45. *AR-CGI* (1919), 348.
46. For a discussion of how both exclusion and general immigration laws were applied to Asian immigrants at Angel Island, see Gee, "Sifting the Arrivals," Chapter 1.
47. Files 14255/32–26 (Shichitaro Ikeda, pseud.) and 14255/32–27 (Sumiyo Ikeda, pseud.), IACF, SF.

48. On Japanese prostitution cases found at the National Archives, see Gee, "Sifting the Arrivals," 245–67; and Gee, "Housewives, Men's Villages, and Sexual Respectability," 98–101. On Japanese prostitution on the West Coast, see Ichioka, *The Issei*, 28–39; and Yasutaki, *Transnational Women's Activism*, Chapter 4. On the prostitution raid in Fresno, see *Fresno Morning Republican*, August 8, 1913. On Commissioner White's investigation of Japanese picture brides, see Tanaka, "Photographs of Japanese Picture Brides," 47–48.

49. File 12768/17–20 (Wasaku Honji), IACF, SF.

50. Files 14438/28–7 (Sadaye Hisakuni) and 14586/15–8 (Masaya Onisuke), IACF, SF.

51. File 13443/5–7 (Yoshitsugu Fujita), IACF, SF. For cases of Japanese sons who were permitted to post bonds, see files 14270/29–1 (Tomematsu Ozawa) and 14725/29–18 (Yuji Yamanaka). Adopted sons were admissible according to the Gentlemen's Agreement, although the immigration service suspected that laborers were being brought in under the guise of adopted sons. See U.S. Department of State, *Report of the Honorable Roland S. Morris on Japanese Immigration*, 34.

52. Information about JAA's work on Angel Island was taken from their publication, *Zaibei Nihonjinkai Hokokusho* (Japanese Association of America annual reports), 1911–1918, translated by Yoshiko Yokochi Samuel; Robert Sinclair Murray, "The Japanese Association of America," 1924, SRR; and Azuma, *Between Two Empires*, 43–48.

53. "Japanese Ban Self Preservation, Says Phelan," *San Francisco Examiner*, November 9, 1919, N5; "Photo Brides Used to Evade Law, Is Charged," *San Francisco Examiner*, March 7, 1919, 1, 4.

54. "Japanese Picture Brides Are Swarming Here," *Seattle Times*, July 30, 1919, 1. See also "Japanese from as Far East as Omaha Come to Greet Arriving Picture Brides," *Sacramento Bee*, July 26, 1919; and "Picture Brides Stir Phelan to Plan Exclusion," *San Francisco Chronicle*, July 26, 1919.

55. "Picture Brides' Other Successors: Japanese Ingenuity in Forcing Peaceful Penetration under the Gentlemen's Agreement," *Sacramento Bee*, November 28, 1921, 1. See also "We Are 'Peacefully Penetrated' by Japan," *Sacramento Bee*, June 11, 1919, 1.

56. As quoted in Ichioka, *The Issei*, 173.

57. "Japs Oppose Picture Bride Marriages," *San Francisco Examiner*, November 1, 1919, 8; "Japanese Body Disapproves of Picture Brides," *San Francisco Chronicle*, November 1, 1919, 21.

58. Ichioka, *The Issei*, 173–75; Tanaka, "Japanese Picture Marriage," Chapter 5.

59. Ichioka, *The Issei*, 245–46; "Japs Crowd S.F. Steamers to Beat Ban," *San Francisco Chronicle*, June 12, 1924, 9.

60. Annual Report of Edward Haff, Acting Commissioner, San Francisco District, 1930, File 55727/930, INS COSCCF; Maurer, "Angel Island," 1929, Katharine Maurer Papers, California State Library.

61. Annual Report of John Nagle, Commissioner of Immigration, San Francisco District, 1931, File 55753/930, INS COSCCF.

62. Azuma, *Between Two Empires*, 120–21.

63. Dick Kobashigawa interview; Kobashigawa, *Hitome-Bore*.
64. Jim Ariki interview; File 37622/7–2 (Masayuki Ariki), IACF, SF.
65. File 30309/27–5 (Kaoru Shiibashi), IACF, SF.
66. File 32196/18–2 (Miyono Nojima), IACF, SF.
67. On the immigration service's awareness of the fraudulent practice, see Annual Report of John Nagle, Commissioner of Immigration, San Francisco District, 1931, File 55753/930, and 1932, File 55778/930, INS COSCCF. For other similar fraudulent cases, see Files 30454/11–1 (Haruichi Higashiguchi) and 30500/10–2 (Yuri Abo), IACF, SF.
68. Hideko Nojima Tsukamoto, letter to great-grandson Kenji on December 3, 1997. Our thanks to Alice Murata for this letter.
69. Architectural Resources Group and Daniel Quan Design, "Poetry and Inscriptions: Translation and Analysis," II-6–7, III-331, and III-369.
70. Yoneda, *Ganbatte*, 220. These slogans were also found on the barrack walls by the research team of scholars in 2003. See Architectural Resources Group and Daniel Quan Design, "Poetry and Inscriptions," III-363–64, III-101, and III-293.
71. Yoneda, *Ganbatte*, 12.
72. Our thanks to Jennifer Gee and Eiichiro Azuma for pointing out these parallels between Angel Island detention and Japanese American internment. For examples of Japanese poems written by *issei* internees, see Kazue de Cristoforo, *May Sky*.
73. Shiz Hayakawa interview, Issei Oral History Project, California State University, Sacramento; and Sarasohn, *Issei Women*.
74. Iyo Tsutsui interview, Issei Oral History Project, California State University, Sacramento; and Sarasohn, *Issei Women*.
75. Dick Kobashigawa interview; Kobashigawa, *Hitome-Bore*.
76. Jim Ariki interview.
77. Betty Kawamoto Dunn interview.

CHAPTER FOUR

1. *United States v. Bhagat Singh Thind*, 261 U.S. 204 (1923); López, *White by Law*, 61–77.
2. *San Francisco Examiner*, March 17, 1928.
3. The annual reports for the immigration service recorded 8,055 alien applicants from India through all ports of entry into the United States from 1910 to 1932. The estimate for San Francisco alone is based on the fact that San Francisco was the most important port of entry for South Asians into the United States at the time, though they also entered the country in Seattle, New York, and across the U.S.-Mexico border. Annual reports for the immigration service in San Francisco alone are not available for all of the years that the immigration station was opened, but records from 1910–14 and 1926–27 indicate that 3,498 South Asian applicants came through the port of San Francisco during these years.
4. Until Canada passed discriminatory legislation restricting South Asian immigration in 1908, Vancouver was also a significant port of entry for South Asians coming to North America. Millis, "East Indian Immigration to British Columbia and the Pacific Coast States," 73; Das,

Hindustani Workers, 17. On immigration to Canada, see Jensen, *Passage from India*, 57–82.

5. Chan, *Asian Americans*, 20.

6. Jensen, *Passage from India*, 9, 22–24, 26; Chan, *Asian Americans*, 20; Chan, "European and Asian Immigration," 53–54; Das, *Hindustani Workers*, 7, 17; Millis, "East Indian Immigration to British Columbia and the Pacific Coast States," 72.

7. Chan, *Asian Americans*, 20; Jensen, *Passage from India*, 24–25. Details relating to specific immigrants found in "Brief for Aliens," by Henry F. Marshall, Attorney, c. October 1913, in File 12924/4–6 (Inder Singh), IACF, SF. This document includes details on several immigrants, including 12924/4–6 (Inder Singh), 12924/4–22 (Siroop Singh), and 12924/4–15 (Argen Singh); File 12545/7–1 (Muston Singh), IACF, SF.

8. Millis, "East Indian Immigration to British Columbia and the Pacific Coast States," 74; Jensen, *Passage from India*, 30; U.S. Senate, *Reports of the Immigration Commission*, "Immigrants in Industries," 336.

9. "Today," *San Francisco Chronicle*, February 5, 1928.

10. Hallberg, "Bellingham, Washington's Anti-Hindu Riot," 172; Millis, "East Indian Immigration to British Columbia and the Pacific Coast States," 72, 74–75; Jensen, *Passage from India*, 51–52.

11. "Hindu Cheap Labor a Menace to Prosperity of the Coast," *Chico Enterprise*, December 20, 1909; "Turn Back the Hindu Invasion," *San Francisco Call*, February 1, 1910; "The New Invasion," *San Francisco Call*, February 2, 1910; "Influx of the Fortune Hunting Hindu Hordes Continues Unabated," *San Francisco Call*, February 4, 1910; "Hindoos Not Suited to Western Civilization," *San Francisco Chronicle*, February 6, 1910; Jensen, *Passage from India*, 101, 107.

12. These figures were grossly exaggerated. The 1910 U.S. census recorded fewer than 5,000 South Asians in California, Washington, New York, and Oregon. U.S. Department of Labor Memorandum Regarding Hindu Migration to the United States, c. January 1914, in "Hindu Immigration," File 52903/110C, INS COSCCF; Jensen, *Passage from India*, 107–9, 111; "Hindu Horde Joins 10,000 Countrymen in California," *San Francisco Call*, April 24, 1910; "Uncle Sam's Domain Now Sikh's Mecca," *San Francisco Call*, May 21, 1910.

13. Jacoby, "U.S. Strategies of Asian Indian Immigration Restriction," 37.

14. Frank Ainsworth to CGI, April 18, 1910, File 52961/16-B, 39–41, INS COSCCF; Jensen, *Passage from India*, 108.

15. Jensen, *Passage from India*, 103, 110.

16. For attacks in the news media, see "Horde of Hindus Here to Enjoy Welcome Extended by Hart North," *San Francisco Call*, August 6, 1910; "San Francisco Now Sole Dumping Ground for the Undesirable, Unspeakable Hindu, Barred by His Master from Sister Colonies," *San Francisco Daily News*, June 3, 1910; "Asiatic Exclusion League Acts on Hookworm Discovery Here," *San Francisco Chronicle*, October 17, 1910. For the AEL's campaign against North, see Jensen, *Passage from India*, 105–7, 111; Asiatic Exclusion League, *Proceedings of the Asiatic Exclusion League*, 24; Resolution, included in A. E. Yoell to Daniel Keefe, April 20, 1910, and A. E. Yoell to Secretary of Commerce and Labor, May 17, 1910, File 52961/10, INS COSCCF; "Brief on the Situation at the

Angel Island Immigrant Station, by H. H. North, Commissioner," c. October 1910, File 52961/16-B, and "Protest Hindu Immigration, 1910," File 52903/110, INS COSCCF; Jensen, *Passage from India*, 114–15, 117.

17. Jensen, *Passage from India*, 118–19. Edsell to Immigration Bureau, DC, December 10, 1910, in "Hindu Immigration, 1910," File 52903/110-A, INS COSCCF.

18. Jensen, *Passage from India*, 105. For an example of the cost of hookworm treatment, see the file of Sukumar Chatterji, a student applying for admission in 1913. File 12650/16–3, IACF, SF.

19. On the use of physical defects as a cause for exclusion, see Benjamin S. Cable, Memorandum to CGI, April 25, 1910, and Memorandum for the Acting Secretary of Commerce and Labor, April 26, 1910, in "Hindu Immigration, 1910," File 52903/110, COSCCF.

20. Jensen, *Passage from India*, 105; "Hookworm Is More Potent Than Laws," *San Francisco Chronicle*, October 4, 1910; "Uncle Sam to Stop Hindu Immigration, Hookworm Discovery at Angel Island Takes on Alarming Aspect," *San Francisco Bulletin*, September 30, 1910; "Asiatic Exclusion League Acts on Hookworm Discovery Here," *San Francisco Chronicle*, October 17, 1910; "Hindoo Immigrants Have Hookworm Disease; Hookworm to Stop Hindoo Invasion," *San Francisco Chronicle*, September 29, 1910; and "Glover's Discovery of Hookworm among Hindoos Confirmed," *San Francisco Chronicle*, September 30, 1910; Misrow, *East Indian Immigration on the Pacific Coast*, 32. Statistics drawn from Table VIII, in Das, *Hindustani Workers*, 13.

21. Harjit K. Gosal and Hardeep K. Gosal, "Passage to the Pacific Coast in the Early 1900s," courtesy of Hardeep K. Gosal and the Angel Island Immigration Station Foundation; File 12884/9–02 (Hazara Singh), IACF, SF.

22. File 10445/6–01 (Bhupendra Nath Ray), IACF, SF.

23. Kala Bagai Chandra interview, courtesy of Rani Bagai; "Nose Diamond Latest Fad; Arrives Here from India," unknown San Francisco newspaper, September 17, 1915, courtesy of Rani Bagai.

24. File 12924/4–9 (Karam Singh), IACF, SF.

25. U.S. Department of Labor Memorandum Regarding Hindu Migration to the United States, c. January 1914, in "Hindu Immigration," File 52903/110C, INS COSCCF; Millis, "East Indian Immigration to British Columbia and the Pacific Coast States," 74; Gee, "Sifting the Arrivals," 112.

26. File 13608/18–2 (Robindra Nag), IACF, SF.

27. For the government's rationale in basing exclusion on local labor conditions, see 13233/3–6 (Kehar Singh), IACF, SF; Gee, "Sifting the Arrivals," 126–29.

28. Samuel Backus to CGI, October 22, 1913, Files 12973/8–2 (Sunder Singh) and 12924/4–2 (Kahn Singh), IACF, SF; *Gegiow v. Uhl* (239 U.S. 3, 36 S.Ct. 2, 60 L.Ed. 114); Salyer, *Laws Harsh as Tigers*, 206.

29. File 10739/12–3 (Bela Singh), IACF, SF; Gee, "Sifting the Arrivals," 105.

30. File 10739/12–4 (Lakha Singh), IACF, SF; Gee, "Sifting the Arrivals,"109.

31. Daniel Keefe, Memorandum for the Secretary, April 7, 1913, in "Hindu Immigration, 1910," File 52903/110-A, INS COSCCF.

32. Misrow, *East Indian Immigration on the Pacific Coast*, 32; Statistics drawn from Table VIII, in Das, *Hindustani Workers*, 13.
33. Appendix, Table 3.
34. Das, *Hindustani Workers*, 14–15.
35. The newspaper article is dated August 28, 1910, and was included in American Consulate General, Calcutta, India, to Assistant Secretary of State, September 1, 1910, in "Hindu Immigration, 1910," File 52903/110, INS COSCCF; Jensen, *Passage from India*, 113.
36. U.S. Department of Labor Memorandum Regarding Hindu Migration to the United States, c. January 1914, in "Hindu Immigration," File 52903/110C, INS COSCCF; Inspector, Jacksonville, to CGI, December 5, 1913, in "Hindu Immigration, 1910," File 52903/110-B, INS COSCCF.
37. W. C. Hopkinson to John L. Zurbrick, Inspector in Charge, Vancouver, February 12, 1912, in "Hindu Immigration, 1910," File 52903/110-A, INS COSCCF; Jacoby, "U.S. Strategies of Asian Indian Immigration Restriction," 38. Joan Jensen explains that Chinese and Japanese also used the side door from Hawaii. See Jensen, *Passage from India*, 116.
38. On the policies of the immigration service regarding South Asians applying for admission from the Philippines, see Files 12924/4–2, 12924/4–4 to 12924/4–18, 12924/4–20 to 12924/4–23, all of whom arrived on the *Nippon Maru* on September 22, 1913, IACF, SF; *AR-CGI* (1914), 320–2; "Hindoos Told to Be on Their Way," *San Francisco Chronicle*, March 11, 1914; U.S. Department of Labor Memorandum Regarding Hindu Migration to the United States, c. January 1914, in "Hindu Immigration," File 52903/110C, INS COSCCF.
39. The new rules were instituted on June 16, 1913. Daniel Keefe, Memorandum for the Secretary, April 7, 1913, in "Hindu Immigration, 1910," File 52903/110-A, INS COSCCF. Jensen, *Passage from India*, 147–48; Das, *Hindustani Workers*, 114.
40. Millis, "East Indian Immigration to the Pacific Coast," 181. U.S. Congress, *Reports of the Immigration Commission*, "Immigrants in Industries," 349. On the committee's definitions of "races," see U.S. Congress, *Reports of the Immigration Commission*, "Dictionary of Races or People," 8. The recommendations on South Asian exclusion appear in U.S. Congress, *Reports of the Immigration Commission*, "Abstracts of Reports," 47.
41. Singh, "The Gadar Party," 45; Jensen, *Passage from India*, 32–41; Misrow, *East Indian Immigration on the Pacific Coast*. 14–15, 26–27; Gee, "Sifting the Arrivals," n67, 323; File 12924/4–6 (Inder Singh), IACF, SF.
42. Jensen, *Passage from India*, 154, 157–58; Gee, "Sifting the Arrivals," 92.
43. Files 10414/7–10 (Neva Singh) and 12924/4–20 (Mangal Singh), IACF, SF.
44. File 12973/8–6 (Battan Singh), IACF, SF.
45. The letter from the four male immigrants is from "A Few Extracts from Letters Received by Our Deaconess at Angel Island," typewritten documents, March 24, 1928, Katharine R. Maurer Papers, California State Library; the description of the Sikh men is in "Angel Island," *Annual Report, Women's Home Missionary Society*, 1922/23, 190, Pacific School of Religion; the description of Natio is in "Immigration Notes from Angel

Island," *Women's Home Missions*, September 1916, 21, Pacific School of Religion.

46. Statistics for 1910 from Registers of Persons Held for Boards of Special Inquiry, NARA, PR. Statistics for 1928–1940 from Registers of Japanese, Filipino, and Hawaiians Held for Board of Special Inquiry, NARA, PR. File 35216/2–1 (Banta Singh), IACF, SF.

47. Both carvings translated by Jane Singh in Egan, "Voices in the Wooden House."

48. Liana Belloni, correspondence to authors, June 13, 2009, and August 10, 2009.

49. Bose, *Indian Revolutionaries Abroad*, 55; Jensen, *Passage from India*, 22–23, 30; Singh, "The Gadar Party," 36–37, 45; Brown, *Har Dayal*, 141.

50. File 11120/4–1 (Kartar Singh Sarabha), IACF, SF; Brown, *Har Dayal*, 4, 150; Jensen, *Passage from India*, 177; Singh, "The Gadar Party," 38, 42; Hoover, "The Hindu Conspiracy in California," 249; "Chapter 7: Gadar," in "Echoes of Freedom: South Asian Pioneers in California, 1899–1965," University of California, Berkeley Library, www.lib.berkeley.edu/SSEAL/echoes/chapter7/chapter7.html (accessed May 26, 2009). The entire poem by Kartar Singh Sarabha is from F. C. Isemonger and J. Slattery, *An Account of the Ghadar Conspiracy (1913–1915)* (Berkeley: Reprinted by Folklore Institute, 1998); available at "Pioneer Asian Indian Immigration to the Pacific Coast," www.sikhpioneers.org//gadarpoems.html (accessed May 21, 2009).

51. File 12637/4–3 (Sohon Lal Pathak), IACF, SF; Josh, *Hindustan Gadar Party*, 184; "To the Gallows: A Hero Unsung," *Indian Express*, February 11, 2003, www.indianexpress.com/oldStory/18184/ (accessed May 21, 2009).

52. Hoover, "The Hindu Conspiracy in California," 246; Jensen, *Passage from India*, 158.

53. Brown, *Har Dayal*, 165, 181; File 13443/12–8 (Muhammad Manlavie Baraktullah), IACF, SF.

54. Singh, "The Gadar Party," 38; "Chapter 7: Gadar," in "Echoes of Freedom: South Asian Pioneers in California, 1899–1965," University of California, Berkeley Library, www.lib.berkeley.edu/SSEAL/echoes/chapter7/chapter7.html (accessed May 26, 2009); Jensen, *Passage from India*, 177–78, 184–85; Brown, *Har Dayal*, 153–55; *San Francisco Chronicle*, March 27, 1914.

55. Brown, *Har Dayal*, 156–65; Jensen, *Passage from India*, 187; *San Francisco Examiner*, March 27 and 28, 1914.

56. Jensen, *Passage from India*, 188–89, 220–24; Hoover, "The Hindu Conspiracy in California," 246; Brown, *Har Dayal*, 5; "Chapter 7: Gadar," in "Echoes of Freedom: South Asian Pioneers in California, 1899–1965," University of California, Berkeley Library, www.lib.berkeley.edu/SSEAL/echoes/chapter7/chapter7.html (accessed May 26, 2009).

57. Jensen, *Passage from India*, 159–62; Das, *Hindustani Workers*, 16.

58. Immigration Act of 1917 (39 Stat. 874).

59. Hing, *Making and Remaking Asian America*, 70.

60. Gee, "Sifting the Arrivals," 145–47.

61. File 25338/13–1 (Rasheed Nazar Mehomed Futehally), IACF, SF.

62. From 1921 to 1930, 67 percent were "geographically excluded," 4 percent were excluded for LPC, and 3 percent for medical reasons.

AR-CGI, 1921–1930; File 22731/3–2 (Kartar Singh), IACF, SF; Gee, "Sifting the Arrivals," 131–37, 262–63.

63. Gee, "Sifting the Arrivals," 93–96, 193–94.
64. File 17119/14–1 (Ardjan Singh), IACF, SF; Gee, "Sifting the Arrivals," 96–98.
65. File 22452/8–1 (Raj Singh), IACF, SF; Gee, "Sifting the Arrivals," 93, 56–57, 313.
66. Bhagat Singh, "Kartar Singh Sarabha," GADAR: A Newsletter of the Gadar Memorial Center (San Francisco), November/December 1992, available at "Pioneer Asian Indian Immigration to the Pacific Coast," www.sikhpioneers.org//famous.html#kartar (accessed May 21, 2009).
67. Mahesh Chandra is pictured with his family on page 163; Kala Bagai Chandra interview.
68. Harjit K. Gosal and Hardeep K. Gosal, "Passage to the Pacific Coast in the Early 1900s," courtesy of Hardeep K. Gosal and the Angel Island Immigration Station Foundation. On Punjabi-Mexican families, see Leonard, *Making Ethnic Choices* and the Web site for the documentary by Jayasri Majumdar Hart, *Roots in the Sand*, www.pbs.org/rootsinthesand/ (accessed July 31, 2009).
69. Liana Belloni, correspondence to authors, June 13, 2009, and August 10, 2009; Rani Bagai, correspondence to authors, August 11, 2009. "Kanta Chandra Gupta," in *The Asian American Encyclopedia*, vol. 2, 523.
70. Act of July 2, 1946 (60 Stat. 416).

CHAPTER FIVE

1. Files 12777/18–1 (An Chang Da), 12777/18–2 (Yin Chi Ham), 12777/18–3 (Chung In Kooa), 12777/18–4 (Cho Hin), 12777/18–5 (Lee Chang Soo), and 12777/18–6 (Kim Lyul), IACF, SF.
2. Gee, "Sifting the Arrivals," 330.
3. Sunoo, *Korean Picture Brides*, 66.
4. Houchins, "The Korean Experience in America," 558; William Wilson, Secretary of Labor, to the Secretary of State, April 29, 1913, File 53620/91, INS COSCCF.
5. Background history on Korean immigration taken from Choy, *Koreans in America*; Kim, *Koreans in America*; Moon, "The Korean Immigrants in America"; Houchins, "The Korean Experience in America"; and Chan, "Introduction," in Lee, *Quiet Odyssey*, xxi–lx.
6. Sunoo, *Korean Picture Brides*, 208.
7. Used to make fiber products like rope and hammocks, the henequen plant stood three to four feet tall and bore spiny leaves. See Desmond, "Koreans in Mexico."
8. Report of Young-Soon Pak sent to the Korean National Association in San Francisco, November 17, 1905, as quoted in Kim, *Koreans in America*, 17.
9. As quoted in Moon, "The Korean Immigrants in America," 69.
10. Houchins, "The Korean Experience in America," 554–56.
11. *Sinhan Minbo,* October 19, 1916, translated by Jean Lew.
12. For the full text of Rule 11 and Rule 21 (Executive Order 589), see California State Board of Control, *California and the Oriental,* 180–83.

13. Kim, *Koreans in America*, 23; Moon, "The Korean Immigrants in America," 394–95. Detention time and deportation rates are based on immigration case files at the National Archives and the BSI registers.
14. Whang Sa Sun's story and quotes taken from Desmond, "Memories of My Grandfather;" and Choy, *Koreans in America*, 300–03.
15. Choy, *Koreans in America*, 302.
16. Although the 1910 U.S. census lists only 462 Koreans on the U.S. mainland, based on community sources, Hyung June Moon estimates that there were more likely 1,200 Koreans, with 800 concentrated in California. See Moon, "The Korean Immigrants in America," 92–93.
17. Ibid., 149–61.
18. Ibid., 132, 239.
19. Kim, *Koreans in America*, 18–20; Henry Ahn, correspondence to authors, February 20, 2009.
20. Files 10501.5/6–1 (Yong Li Yuen), 10501.5/6–2 (Lee Kun Yung), 10501.5/6–3 (Kim Eng Su), and 10501.5/6–4 (Yi Beng Um), IACF, SF. Our thanks to Marisa Louie for finding these files for us.
21. Choy, *Koreans in America*, 87–88; Series of fifteen articles about David Lee in *Sinhan Minbo*, from October 5, 1944, to February 1, 1945, translated by Jean Lew; The Reverend Suk-Chong Yu, correspondence to authors, March 5, 2008; Gee, "Sifting the Arrivals," 328–32. Our thanks to Don Lee for sharing what information he had about his grandfather David Lee.
22. Moon, "The Korean Immigrant in America," 306.
23. Quotes and coverage of the Hemet incident taken from Moon, "The Korean Immigrants in America," 377–94.
24. William Jennings Bryan, who was secretary of state from 1913 to 1915, was known to be a pacifist and an anti-imperialist. During his visit to Korea in 1905, he had expressed distress over seeing the large numbers of Japanese soldiers and the royal family's resignation to the incipient fall of Korea. He doubted that any good could come from Japanese colonial rule. Although he was an Asian exclusionist, Bryan welcomed temporary immigrants such as merchants, visitors, and students to the United States. See Moon, "The Koreans in America," 392–93; and Smith, *The Social and Religious Thought of William Jennings Bryan*, 45–49.
25. *Sinhan Minbo*, November 16, 1944, translated by Jean Lew.
26. File 12777/18–2 (Yin Chi Ham), IACF, SF.
27. Amos Weder, Consul-General, to the Secretary of State, February 22, 1913, File 53620/91, INS COSCCF.
28. William Wilson, Secretary of Labor, to the Secretary of State, April 29, 1913, File 53620/91, INS COSCCF.
29. *AR-CGI* (1914), 437.
30. Thomas Sammons, American Consul-General, July 24, 1914, April 15, 1915, and September 27, 1915, File 53620/91, INS COSCCF.
31. Louis F. Post, Assistant Secretary of Labor, to the Secretary of State, May 25, 1915, File 53620/91, INS COSCCF.
32. Salyer, *Laws Harsh as Tigers*, 218–19.

33. F. H. Larned, Acting CGI to Seattle, San Francisco, and Honolulu, October 21, 1914, File 53620/91, INS COSCCF.
34. Files 13734/15–4 (Ho Chyo), 13734/15–5 (Park Syeng Koo), 13734/15–6 (Jong Ki Eun), 13734/15–7 (Park Chung Rai), 13734/15–8 (Cho Eung Sun), 13734/15–9 (Song Nie Keon), 13734/15–10 (Chai Chung Lah), and 13734/15–11 (Song Chuk Yong), IACF, SF.
35. *Sinhan Minbo*, November 12, 1914, translated by Jean Lew.
36. *Sinhan Minbo*, January 7, 1915 and January 28, 1917, translated by Jean Lew.
37. Thomas Sammons, American Consul-General to the Secretary of State, September 27, 1915, File 53620/91, INS COSCCF.
38. File 15701/9–3 (Oh Wan Hyung), IACF, SF.
39. Files 15701/9–3 (Oh Wan Hyung), 15701/9–4 (Lee You Jung), 15701/9–14 (Cho Pyung Mook), 15701/9–18 (In Dyuk Chang), 15701/9–19 (Kiel In Young), 15701/9–21 (Pyun Pong Chick), 15701/9–22 (Chai Il Myung), 15701/9–23 (Kim Kay Chang), 15701/9–24 (Kim Chin Young), 15701/9–25 (Bo Wang So), and 15701/9–26 (Lee Hong Nai), IACF, SF.
40. In the end, Congress exempted aliens escaping religious persecution (but not political persecution) from the literacy requirement of the Immigration Act of 1917. References to European immigrants were made throughout the debate on the immigration bill. See U.S. Congress, House of Representatives, Committee on Immigration and Naturalization, "Immigration of Aliens into the United States," February 8, 1916.
41. File 15701/9–24 (Kim Chin Young), IACF, SF.
42. Commissioner Edward White to CGI, Washington, D.C., November 16, 1915, File 53620/91, INS COSCCF.
43. Files 16658/7–1 (Pak Ni Keun), 16658/7–2 (Oh Dong Woo), 16658/7–3 (Hun Hi Myung), 16658/7–4 (Lyang Sung Ha), 16658/7–5 (Ahn Taik Choo), 16658/7–6 (Suh Kwang Chin), 16658/7–7 (Chung In Cho), 16658/7–8 (Pang Nuih Tung), 16658/7–9 (Pak Ki Suk), 16658/7–10 (Choi Bong Men), 16658/7–11 (Kim Tai Ha), 16658/7–12 (Shinn Tai Young), 16658/7–13 (San Li Do), and 16658/7–14 (Lee Sang Kee), IACF, SF. The joint order was replaced by an act passed by Congress on May 22, 1918, which established the passport/visa system. See *AR-CGI* (1918), 10–11.
44. Also known as the March First Movement, the Mansei (ten thousand years or "long live") Movement was a mass demonstration of Koreans from all walks of life, proclaiming Korea's independence on March 1, 1919. The Japanese retaliated with brute force, killing, arresting, and torturing thousands of Korean protestors. Following the uprising, the Korean Provisional Government was established in the French Settlement of Shanghai and the Korean Commission was established in Washington, D.C., for carrying out diplomatic propaganda on behalf of national independence.
45. Kim Ok Yun story and quotes taken from File 24868–7-1 (Kim Ok Yun), IACF, SF; and Sunoo, *Korean Picture Brides*, 47–48.

46. Telephone conversation with Harold Sunoo, April 14, 2009, Los Angeles, CA.
47. File 24108/20–25 (Choi Kyung-Sik), IACF, SF.
48. Our thanks to Charles Egan, author of "Voices in the Wooden House: Angel Island Inscriptions, 1910–1945," for finding this poem and granting us permission to use it.
49. Gee, "Sifting the Arrivals," 321–43.
50. Kim, *Koreans in America*, 23–27.
51. Our thanks to Charles Egan for finding this poem and granting us permission to use it.
52. Moon, "The Korean Immigrants in America," 110–31; Houchins, "The Korean Experience in America," 559–60.
53. Background information on Korean picture brides taken from Sunoo, *Korean Picture Brides*. For stories of picture brides who made their own arrangements, see Sunoo, *Korean Picture Brides*, 267–84; and Yoon, *The Passage of a Picture Bride*.
54. Shinn Kang-ae's story and quotes taken from Sunoo, *Korean Picture Brides*, 21–55; and Shinn Kang-ae, interview with Sonia Sunoo, July 23, 1975, Korean American Oral History Collection, University of Southern California, translated by Jean Lew.
55. Anh Chang-ho (1878–1938) was a political leader in the national independence movement and in the Korean immigrant community. He immigrated to the United States in 1902 as a student and helped to found the Friendship Society, Young Korean Academy, and Mutual Assistance Association, forerunner of the Korean National Association. After the March First (1919) uprising, he helped to set up the Korean provisional government in Shanghai and served as its secretary of interior, secretary of labor, and prime minister. He was arrested by the Japanese police in 1935 and sentenced to four years in jail. He died in 1938 of poor health suffered while in jail.
56. Kim Suk-eun story and quotes taken from Sunoo, *Korean Picture Brides*, 75–82.
57. Files 12851/21–2 (Kim Suk En), 12581/21–3 (Chang Kang Ei), and 12581/21–4 (Lee Che Hyun), IACF, SF.
58. *Sinhan Minbo*, September 10, 1914, October 24, 1917, and December 5, 1917, translated by Jean Lew.
59. *Sinhan Minbo*, March 25, 1915, translated by Jean Lew.
60. David Lee, president of the Korean National Association of North America, to the Commissioner, U.S. Immigration, Angel Island, December 26, 1917, File 53620/91, INS COSCCF.
61. Louis F. Post, Assistant Secretary of Labor, to the Secretary of State, January 29, 1918, File 53620/91, INS COSCCF.
62. Files 13301/20–20 (Im So See), 13301/20–21 (Pok Kyong Whan), 13301/20–22 (Pok Tong Khan), and 13301/20–23 (Pok Yun Sun), IACF, SF.
63. Rose Paik's story and quotes taken from Sunoo, *Korean Picture Brides*, 219–26; and Lee, *Quiet Odyssey*, 83.
64. Files 21539/14–1 (Pok Sum Oi) and 21539/14–2 (Lyang Ai Shun), IACF, SF.
65. Donald Lyang interview.

66. Paul Whang, interview with Officer N. D. Collaer, August 12, 1940, Angel Island Station, File 12030/24–2, Angel Island General Correspondence, NARA, PR.
67. Lee and Kim, "A Pioneer Pastor's Son."
68. Shinn Kang-ae and Sonia Sunoo's stories and quotes taken from Sunoo, *Korean Picture Brides*, 43–55.

CHAPTER SIX

1. "25 Students Held Here from Russia," *San Francisco Daily News*, August 30, 1932, 1.
2. Our thanks to Maria Sakovich and Eddie Fung for helping us estimate the number of Russians and Jews who were detained on Angel Island. The 8,000 figure was derived from the following sources: Refugee Survey 1937–38, Archives of Chatham House; Passenger Lists of Vessels, NARA, PR; and Registers of Persons Held for Boards of Special Inquiry, NARA, PR.
3. The 2 percent deportation rate was derived from Registers of Persons Held for Boards of Special Inquiry, NARA, PR. The deportation rate for Russian applicants at all ports of entry was 3.6 percent (see Appendix, Table 3).
4. Brownstone, *Island of Hope*, 149. The phrase "a vale of tears" comes from a letter written by a European detainee to Deaconess Katharine Maurer: "Only the recording Angel is qualified to set down the work of your ministry here in this vale of tears; for despite the beauty of this Island and its still more beautiful setting, that's what it is to most of us—just a vale of tears." See Katharine Maurer, "Angel Island," *Woman's Home Missions* (July–August 1936), 9, Pacific School of Religion.
5. U.S. Library of Congress, "Immigration: Polish/Russian."
6. Rischin, *The Promised City*, 20–30; Magocsi, "Russian Americans."
7. Sakovich, "Angel Island Immigration Station Reconsidered," 26–27; "Russians Not Deported," *San Francisco Call*, August 13, 1905.
8. Sakovich, "Angel Island Immigration Station Reconsidered," 27–29.
9. Rossi, "Evdokia Gregorievna Zaharoff."
10. Gatrell, *A Whole Empire Walking*, 15–26.
11. "Russ Jew Tells of Persecution," *San Francisco Chronicle*, May 22, 1916, 3.
12. Magocsi, "Russian Americans." For stories of White Russian refugees who made it to America, see Day, *Russians in Hollywood*.
13. Shapiro, "Autobiographical Material," Box 1, Folder 1, and Shapiro, "The Course of Revolutionary Events at Blagoveschensk," Box 4, Folder 7, Nadia Shapiro Collection, Hoover Institution Archives, Stanford University.
14. Shapiro, "How I Came to Work in English," Box 4, Folder 14, Nadia Shapiro Collection, Hoover Institution Archives, Stanford University.
15. Background information about the Mennonites is taken from Nachtigall, "Mennonite Migration and Settlements of California." Sources for Nick Friesen's story include Nick Friesen interview; Martens, *River of Glass*; and Friesen, "What Has Forced Us with Our Brethren to Leave Soviet Russia."
16. Tolstoy, *Out of the Past*, 311–14.

17. Shapiro, "Chapter 1," Box 5, Folder 38, Nadia Shapiro Collection, Hoover Institution Archives, Stanford University.
18. Isaak, *Our Life Story and Escape*, 128–29.
19. Tolstoy, *Out of the Past*, 312.
20. File 16846/3–20 (Victoria Bogush), IACF, SF.
21. File 29883/13–13 (Nikolai Simonovich), IACF, SF.
22. Files 16782/2–6 (Elia Elterman), 29091/22–1 (David Janzen), and 16363/32–2 (Haim Naber), IACF, SF.
23. Cannato, *American Passage*, 195; Marinbach, *Galveston*, 62.
24. As quoted in Cannato, *American Passage*, 214.
25. Similar results occurred at the port of Galveston. Two days after Keefe issued his directive, immigrant inspectors there excluded eighty-three of the 280 Jewish passengers on the *Hanover*, mainly on the grounds that they were LPC because of their "poor physiques." Marinbach, *Galveston*, 62.
26. Wilson, "Message from the President of the United States," August 23, 1918.
27. Files 12680/12–1 to 12–10 (Nikolai Dudieff, Dimian Druna, Favil Grushin, Peter Tamaieff, Batako Kaitookof, Favil Tzagarieff, Josef Kutzian, Issac Vaitzman, Bibo Kulaeff, and Feodor Oreshin) and 14–1 (Alexander Pietouchkne), IACF, SF.
28. File 13627/20–4 (Aleksei Chakashoff), IACF, SF.
29. Files 12592/3–1 (Andry Hudoshenekoff), 3–3 (Daria Kalandrina), 3–5 (Alexandra Okulova), 3–7 (Bladimir Okulova), and 3–8 (Anesia Chegerova), IACF, SF
30. For a discussion of Noshkin and the Del Mar colony, see Clark, "The Del Mar Ranch," 141–53.
31. File 15153/40–1 (Simon Yankell Sinelnikoff), IACF, SF.
32. Files 14255/22–6 (Solomon Pustilnik), 22–7 (San Mishnyak), 22–9 (Itzck Diablowitzki), 28–3 (Isaac Sabsai), 28–4 (Josef Yesozo-Limchik), 28–5 (Gregory Polekoff), 28–6 (Abram Davidovitch), 28–7 (Manos Livian), 28–8 (Michael Papkoff), and 28–10 (David Stoffman), IACF, SF.
33. These comparisons are based on our review of 100 Hebrew (so labeled by the Bureau of Immigration) and 100 non-Hebrew Russian case files for the 1910–1924 period found at the National Archives, Pacific Regional Branch.
34. The comment was made in reference to Shulim Shwetz, a tailor who was deemed LPC because he came with only $24, had no friends or relatives in the United States, and planned to live in a city with high unemployment. His attorney, Frank Ainsworth, requested a second hearing after he found someone willing to offer Shwetz a job, but his request was denied by Commissioner Backus. See File 14298/18–1 (Shulim Shwetz), IACF, SF.
35. Katharine Maurer, *Annual Report of the Women's Home Missionary Society* (July 1–15, 1916) 27:19–20, Pacific School of Religion.
36. Hebrew Sheltering and Immigrant Aid Society of America, *Annual Report* (1915), 10, and *Annual Report* (1916), 31, YIVO Institute of Jewish Research.
37. Salyer, *Laws Harsh as Tigers*, 158.
38. File 14708/17–3 (Lebe Schneeveis), IACF, SF.

39. Salyer, *Laws Harsh as Tigers*, 206.
40. Hebrew Sheltering and Immigrant Aid Society of America, *Annual Report* (1917), 6–8, YIVO Institute of Jewish Research.
41. File 16723/39–18 (Brucha Punchik), IACF, SF.
42. File 16636/31–16 (Zlota Schneider), IACF, SF.
43. Salyer, *Laws Harsh as Tigers*, 122–35; Higham, *Strangers in the Land*, Chapter 8; Preston, *Alien and Dissenters*, Chapter 8.
44. Sakovich, "Angel island Immigration Station Reconsidered," 144–46; File 54407/17 (Fredrick Harold Berger), INS COSCCF.
45. Sakovich, "Angel Island Immigration Station Reconsidered," 151.
46. Sergei Prokofiev's story and quotes taken from Stephen Press, "Prokofiev's Vexing Entry into the USA."
47. Tolstoy, *Out of the Past*, 313; File 30644/23–1 (Alexandra Tolstoy), IACF, SF.
48. American Consul G. C. Hanson, "Activities of the 'Harbin Committee Rendering Aid to Russian Students' and the Y.M.C.A. in Connection with the Immigration to the United States of Russian Students," March 8, 1923, and "List of Students Who Left Harbin for the United States for the Purpose of Continuing Education," File 55605/130, INS COSCCF.
49. N. M. Hess, "In Re: Harbin Committee Rendering Aid to Russian Students," September 10, 1922, File 55605/130, INS COSCCF.
50. George Day, Pacific Coast Secretary for Foreign Students, to E. T. Colton, Overseas Division, YMCA, September 12, 1922, George Martin Day Papers, Hoover Institution Archives, Stanford University.
51. N. M. Hess, "In Re: Harbin Committee Rendering Aid to Russian Students," September 10, 1922, File 55605/130, INS COSCCF.
52. Commissioner-General W.W. Husband to Commissioner of Immigration, San Francisco, California, October 10, 1922, and Letter from Acting Secretary of State E. J. Henning to the Secretary of State, November 23, 1922, File 55240/18, INS COSCCF; G. C. Hanson, "Activities of the Harbin Committee Rendering Aid to Russian Students and the Y.M.C.A. in Connection with the Immigration to the United States of Russian Students," March 8, 1923, and "List of Students Who Left Harbin for the United States for the Purpose of Continuing Education," File 55605/130, INS COSCCF.
53. Sakovich, "Angel Island Immigration Station Reconsidered," 165–68; Shimkin, "From Golden Horn to Golden Gate."
54. Letter from "all the students" to the Commissioner of Immigration Station at Angel Island, July 27, 1923, File 52700/40, INS COCCF.
55. "Entry Is Refused 57 Russian Aliens," *San Francisco Examiner*, September 12, 1923, 1.
56. Eight of the fifteen refugees made it back and were admitted on October 2, 1923. See "Slavs Enter after Second Trip to U.S.," *San Francisco Chronicle*, October 3, 1923.
57. According to the cover letter from American Consul G. C. Hanson to the Secretary of State, the article appeared in the October 19 and 27, 1923 issues of the local Russian newspaper *Russkii Golos* (Russkii Color) and was being sent to illustrate the great interest in immigration to the United States in Harbin. See File 52700/40, INS COCCF.

58. The students may have been angry with the League of Nations for not doing enough to overthrow the Bolsheviks and to help Russian refugees.

59. "64 Russians Are Allowed to Land Here," *San Francisco Chronicle*, October 12, 1923, 8.

60. "Russians Fearful of Deportation," *San Francisco Examiner*, August 14, 1923, 6.

61. *AR-CGI* (1924), 27.

62. Kranzler, *Japanese, Nazis and Jews*, 58.

63. File 38687/2–1 (Girsh Leibovich Agranovich), IACF, SF.

64. File 39271/4–1 (Paula Georgievna Alexandrova), IACF, SF.

65. Neufeld family's story and quotes taken from Neufeld, *Jacob's Journey*; Files 29662/14–1 to 14–11 (Neufeld, Jacob, Helena, Jakob, Johann, Henrich, Helena, Franz, Wilhelm, David, Abram, and Hermann); and *The Mennonite*, November 13, 1930, 6.

66. Altogether some 250,000 refugees fleeing Nazism reached the U.S. shores between 1933 and 1945, making America the largest recipient of Jewish refugees in the world. Sakovich, "Angel Island Immigration Station Reconsidered," 202–07; Wyman, *Paper Walls*, 36–38.

67. For a discussion of the difficulties Jewish refugees faced in seeking refuge in the United States at this time, see Wyman, *Paper Walls*, 155–68.

68. Wyman, *Paper Walls*, 27–30; Alice Steiner's story and quotes taken from Alice Steiner interviews.

69. File 4041511–7 (Szymon Zuckerman), IACF, SF.

70. Files 40253/2–1 (Alfred Marill), 40253/2–2 (Klara Marill), and 40293/5–1 (Arthur Muller), IACF, SF.

71. Files 39976/12–1 (Isaak Adler) and 12–2 (Mathilde Adler), IACF, SF. From 1938 to 1941, the Nazis were willing to release Jews from the concentration camps as long as they agreed to leave the country promptly and permanently. See Wyman, *Paper Walls*, 35.

72. File 40198/24–1 (Hans Singer), IACF, SF.

73. Wyman, *Paper Walls*, 194, 36.

74. Alice Steiner interviews.

75. Nick Friesen interview.

76. Shapiro, "Autobiographical Material," Box 1, Folder 1, and Shapiro, "Chapter 1," Box 5, Folder 38, Nadia Shapiro Collection, Hoover Institution Archives, Stanford University.

77. Herbert Neufeld interview.

CHAPTER SEVEN

1. Files 15035/1–3, 1–4 (Juan, Frederico, Fortunato, and Antonio Cesana), IACF, SF.

2. Sánchez, *Becoming Mexican American*, 21–22, 65–66; Hoffman, *Unwanted Mexican Americans*, 11.

3. McWilliams, *Southern California Country*, 319; Barkan, *From All Points*, 320; Sánchez, *Becoming Mexican American*, 18–19, 281; Cardoso, *Mexican Emigration to the United States*, 94; Gamio, *Mexican Immigration to the United States*, 1–12; Martinez, *Mexican Emigration to the U.S.*, 78, 88. For an overview of Mexican immigration to the United States through the twentieth century, see Camarillo, "Mexico."

4. On the role of the U.S. economy in facilitating Mexican migration northward, see Cardoso, *Mexican Emigration to the United States*, 71; Sánchez, *Becoming Mexican American*, 39, 67, 19; Reisler, *By the Sweat of Their Brow*, 11; Martinez, *Mexican Emigration to the U.S.*, 3; Barkan, *From All Points*, 196; and García, *Desert Immigrants*, 51. On Mexican labor in California, see Sánchez, *Becoming Mexican American*, 19, 67; Gutiérrez, *Walls and Mirrors*, 44–45; and Martinez, *Mexican Emigration to the U.S.*, 4.

5. Sánchez, *Becoming Mexican American*, 20–23; Balderrama and Rodríguez, *Decade of Betrayal*, 14; Cardoso, *Mexican Emigration to the United States*, 12.

6. Hamilton, *The Limits of State Autonomy*, 57; Lear, *Workers, Neighbors and Citizens*, 3–4; Martinez, *Mexican Emigration to the U.S.*, 8.

7. Balderrama and Rodríguez, *Decade of Betrayal*, 12, 14; Lear, *Workers, Neighbors and Citizens*, 3–4; Sánchez, *Becoming Mexican American*, 20. For portraits of Mexican immigrants during the revolutionary era, see Gamio, *The Life Story of the Mexican Immigrant*.

8. Raat, *Mexico and the United States*, 87; Martinez, *Mexican Emigration to the U.S.*, 42, 44–45, 60; Cardoso, *Mexican Emigration to the United States*, 109–10.

9. Balderrama and Rodríguez, *Decade of Betrayal*, 8–9; Immigration Act of 1917 (39 Stat. 874); Sánchez, *Becoming Mexican American*, 19–20, 61, 52, 133.

10. Sánchez, *Becoming Mexican American*, 42, 34, 28–30, 35–36, 41, 51.

11. Ibid., 35, 41, 59; Cardoso, *Mexican Emigration to the United States*, xiii–xiv, 30; García, *Desert Immigrants*, 40–41.

12. Files 13275/8–10 (Rosa Flores), 13612/10–15 (Elena Rendon), and 12830/8–7 (Moses Galcono), IACF, SF.

13. Michael Lopez interview.

14. Files 12993/2–11 (Angela Vasquez, pseud.) and 13275/8–6 (Maria Gonzalez Clemens), IACF, SF.

15. Galarza, *Barrio Boy*, 214.

16. On the Artesiros family's transport, see Hart Hyatt North to CGI, June 9, 1910, File 52961/16A and 16B, INS COSCCF. For other examples, see Files 14804/1–1 (Humberto Pequeros), 14341/1–2 (Herman Lupio) 12830/8–7 (Moses Galcono), and 14300/1–16 (Jesus Morales) IACF, SF.

17. The PMSS passenger ledgers listed 165 passengers who were identified as being "from Mexico." There were most certainly many more Mexicans among the 29,000 in the data base of PMSS passengers for 1913–19, but few were identified as being "Mexican." Data drawn from the PMSS Angel Island database compiled by Robert Barde. See also Barde and Bobonis, "Detention at Angel Island," 108–9.

18. There is some evidence that fares might have dropped dramatically in the next few years. In 1918, Cecilia Tapia testified that her first-class ticket from Salina Cruz, located much farther south along the West Coast of Mexico, was $75. Files 13294/7–1 (Tito Araica) and 17027/4–8 (Cecilia Tapia), IACF, SF.

19. Files 13787/2–20 (Parcenta Herrera), 13294/7–1 (Tito Araica), 13898/6–2 (Bernardo Fregoso), 14804/1–1 (Humberto Pequeros), and 16502/10–5 (Arturo De Cima), IACF, SF.

20. File 13199/4–3 (Maria Mayin), IACF, SF.

21. Files 13612/10–16 (Maria Salvador) and 15592/5–14 (Margarita Gonzalez), IACF, SF.

22. Files 13898/6–2 (Bernardo Fregoso), 13787/2–20 (Parcenta Herrera), and 13275/8–10 (Rosa Flores), IACF, SF.

23. See the example of Juan Milsen, who arrived in 1914 and was ordered excluded for being afflicted with hookworm. He was treated and finally landed. File 13787/2–19, IACF, SF. For the statistics from 1910 to 1920, see *AR-CGI*, 1910–1920.

24. File 13787/2–21 (Felix Herrera), IACF, SF.

25. See, for example, the case of Luis Algarin, in which the Los Angeles Chinese inspector was assigned the task of interviewing Algarin's Los Angeles-based brother. File 14881/6–1, IACF, SF.

26. Detention data drawn from a review of passenger lists of 104 ships and BSI registers that listed Mexican detainees on Angel Island from 1913 to 1939, and from the PMSS Angel Island database compiled by Robert Barde. See Passenger Lists of Vessels, NARA, PR; Registers of Persons Held for Boards of Special Inquiry, NARA, PR; and Barde and Bobonis, "Detention at Angel Island," 108–9.

27. Files 13898/6–2 (Bernardo Fregoso) and 13199/7–5 (Bonifacio Magana), IACF, SF.

28. The case of the Artesiros family is included in Hart Hyatt North to CGI, June 9, 1910, File 52961/16A and 16B, INS COSCCF.

29. File 17411/14–5 (Christina Alonso), IACF, SF.

30. Files 14300/1–16 (Jesus Morales) and 16033/1–4 (Adolpho Cisneros), IACF, SF. Statistics on the rate of Mexican exclusions under the LPC clause can be found in *AR-CGI*, 1910–1930.

31. File 13275/8–6 (Maria Gonzales Clemens), IACF, SF.

32. Sánchez, *Becoming Mexican American*, 58; Gardner, *Qualities of a Citizen*, 91–92, 190, 95–96.

33. File 17027/4–8 (Cecilia Tapia), IACF, SF.

34. File 14348/12–1 (Maria Cabezud), IACF, SF.

35. File 12993/2–11 (Angela Vasquez, pseud.), IACF, SF.

36. File 19754/8–1–2 (Maria Sanchez, pseud.), IACF, SF.

37. File 13612/10–19 (Simona Gonzales, pseud.), IACF, SF.

38. File 15692/8–3 (Dolores Flores, pseud.), IACF, SF.

39. File 16033/1–4 (Sofia Jiminez, pseud.), IACF, SF.

40. File 13787/2–9 (Dolores Veco), IACF, SF.

41. The three highest groups of women excluded for being suspected prostitutes were: Mexicans (1336), English (621), and French (420). *AR-CGI*, 1910–1930.

42. File 13275/8–1 (George Paulson, pseud.), IACF, SF.

43. Reisler, *By the Sweat of their Brow*, 128, 67; Cardoso, *Mexican Emigration*, 120–22; Hoffman, *Unwanted Mexican Americans*, 10; Ruiz, *From Out of the Shadows*, 29; Barkan, *From All Points*, 327.

44. Sánchez, *Becoming Mexican American*, 19; Hoffman, *Unwanted Mexican Americans*, 10; Foley, *The White Scourge*, 54; Burnham, "The Howl for Cheap Mexican Labor," 48; McClatchy, "Oriental Immigration," 197; "Ban Demanded on Philippine Influx to U.S., *San Francisco Examiner*, September 9, 1930.

45. Files 15035/1–1, 1–2, 1–3, 1–4 (Juan, Frederico, Fortunato, and Antonio Cesana), 14881/6–1 (Luis Algarin), and 14370/7–1 (Eutacia Losano), IACF, SF.

46. Files 12904/4–6 to 4–10 (Lopez family), Case Files of Investigations Resulting in Warrant Proceedings , NARA, PR.
47. Ernesto Galarza, *Barrio Boy*, 214–16. Excerpt reprinted courtesy of University of Notre Dame Press.
48. Reisler, *By the Sweat of their Brow*, 52; Files 15035/1–1 to 1–4, (Juan, Frederico, Fortunato, and Antonio Cesana), IACF, SF.
49. Sánchez, *Becoming Mexican-American*, 55–7; Stern, "Buildings, Boundaries, and Blood," 42, 45–6; Perkins, *Border Patrol*, 61.
50. Balderrama and Rodríguez, *Decade of Betrayal*, 9; Stern, "Buildings, Boundaries, and Blood," 48.
51. Sánchez, *Becoming Mexican American*, 50, 55–56; Stern, "Nationalism on the Line," 302.
52. Hoffman, *Unwanted Mexican Americans*, 30–32.
53. Mirande, *Gringo Justice*, 102, 105–6. Stern, "Nationalism on the Line," 303–5, 306, 312; Hoffman, *Unwanted Mexican Americans*, 30–32; Sánchez, *Becoming Mexican American*, 106; Barkan, *From All Points*, 328, 330.

CHAPTER EIGHT

1. Sobredo, "From American 'Nationals,'" xvi, 53; Cordova and Canillo, eds., *Voices*, n.p.; File 34028/14–20 (Rafael Magno, pseud.), IACF, SF.
2. Sobredo, "From American 'Nationals,'" xvi, 53.
3. File 34028/14–20 (Rafael Magno, pseud.), IACF, SF.
4. Some 583 Filipinos were held for Boards of Special Inquiry between 1928 and 1942 at the immigration station. Another 300–400 repatriates were detained on Angel Island in the late 1930s waiting for ships to take them to the Philippines under the Repatriation Act program. Other documents note that at least seventy-three Filipinos were under care at the hospital in 1939. Many thousands more arrived in San Francisco before 1934 without having to be processed for entry on Angel Island. See Registers of Japanese, Filipinos, and Hawaiians Held for Board of Special Inquiry, NARA, PR; Maurer, "Angel Island," *Woman's Home Missions* (May 1937), 4, Pacific School of Religion; Helen Johnson, "Christmas at Angel Island," February 1939, Katharine R. Maurer Papers, California State Library; Sakovich, "Angel Island Immigration Station Reconsidered," 236.
5. Chan, *Asian Americans*, 25; McKinley, "Benevolent Assimilation;" Francisco Carino, "My Life History," August 1924, and Unknown Filipino to an Americanization Teacher in Los Angeles, "I am Only a Foreigner—So This Is America," SRR; Sobredo, "From American 'Nationals,'" 56.
6. Sobredo, "From American 'Nationals,'" 68; Takaki, *Strangers from a Different Shore*, 50; Mabalon, "Life in Little Manila," 35–37; Bulosan, *America Is in the Heart*, Part I; Cordova and Canillo, *Voices*.
7. Mabalon, "Life in Little Manila," 35, 37; Sobredo, "From American 'Nationals,'" xvii; Lasker, *Filipino Immigration*, 31, 164–65, 207.
8. Mabalon, Reyes, et al., *Filipinos in Stockton*, 11; Mabalon, "Life in Little Manila," 41, 47; Sobredo, "From American 'Nationals,'" n44, 76; Lasker, *Filipino Immigration*, 1, 21, 31, 347–48; Ngai, *Impossible Subjects*, 102–3; España-Maram, *Creating Masculinity*, 4; Cordova, "Voices from the Past," 45, 42.

9. Carino, "My Life History," SRR.
10. Eliseo Felipe interview.
11. Ngai, *Impossible Subjects*, 103; Sobredo, "From American 'Nationals,'" 77; Mabalon, "Life in Little Manila," 1.
12. Lasker, *Filipino Immigration*, 5, 21; Mabalon, "Life in Little Manila," 48.
13. Eliseo Felipe interview.
14. Ngai, *Impossible Subjects*, 105, 97.
15. McClatchy quote from "Ban Demanded on Philippine Influx to U.S.," *San Francisco Examiner*, September 9, 1930. Welch quote from "Welch Assails Invasions of Filipinos Here," *San Francisco Examiner*, November 28, 1930. See also "Filipinos Declared Unfit by Citizenship Speaker," *San Francisco Chronicle*, February 22, 1930.
16. Steiger quote from "Filipinos Declared Unfit by Citizenship Speaker," *San Francisco Chronicle*, February 22, 1930. See also Lasker, *Filipino Immigration*, 42; and Carino, "My Life History," SRR.
17. Ngai, *Impossible Subjects*, 106, 109–11; Sobredo, "From American 'Nationals,'" xix, 112–13; Mabalon, "Life in Little Manila," 60; Melendy, "California's Discrimination," 39, 41. In 1933, the state passed a miscegenation law barring the marriages of "Malays" (Filipinos) and whites. Pascoe, *What Comes Naturally*, 93.
18. Mabalon, "Life in Little Manila," 60–61; Baldoz, "Valorizing Racial Boundaries," 977–79; Ngai, *Impossible Subjects*, 105, 114; Melendy, "California's Discrimination," 40; Takaki, *Strangers from a Different Shore*," 327–28.
19. Ngai, *Impossible Subjects*, 113, 116; Mabalon, "Life in Little Manila," 61, 63; Bulosan, *America Is in the Heart*, 121; Baldoz, "'Valorizing Racial Boundaries,'" 983.
20. Filipino nationalists did express resentment that Filipinos would thereafter be classified as aliens. "Majority in State Want Filipino Ban," *San Francisco News*, February 14, 1939; Ngai, *Impossible Subjects*, 116; Sobredo, "From American 'Nationals,'" 105, 109–11, 114–15, 118, 124–25, xxi, 134, 136.
21. Although the Tydings-McDuffie Act deemed the Philippines a foreign country for purposes of immigration according to the Immigration Act of 1917, the 1917 act's "barred zone" provision did not apply to the Philippines. The Tydings-McDuffie Act dictated that Filipinos would be classified as "aliens ineligible to citizenship" for the purposes of immigration and thus totally excludable by law once the Philippines became fully independent. This section of the act never went into effect, because in 1946, two days before Philippine independence, President Harry Truman signed the law repealing Filipino status as ineligible for naturalization. Ngai, *Impossible Subjects*, 125. However, Filipinos were still classified as "aliens ineligible to citizenship" for the purposes of other laws, such as the alien land laws and those prohibiting them from receiving federal assistance from the federal government. On the 1925 Supreme Court case, *Toyota v. United States* (268 U.S. 402), that declared Filipinos were not "free white persons" eligible for naturalization, see Hing, *Making and Remaking Asian America*, 35, and Ngai, *Impossible Subjects*, 119–20. On the prohibition from receiving assistance from the federal government, see Takaki, *Strangers from a Different Shore*, 332.

22. Excerpt of telegram from Paul Armstrong to Commissioner, INS, March 8, 1935, in File 33994/19–20 (Herman Fagel), IACF, SF; Radiogram from Edward Haff to INS, Washington, D.C., May 10, 1934, File 55853/219, INS COSCCF.

23. For examples of the exclusion and fingerprinting policy, see, Files 34013/2–3, 34028/14–20, and 33994/20–3, IACF, SF.

24. "Discussion of the International Institute as a Private Agency in San Francisco, Presented to the Section on Family Welfare of the Relief Council of the Community Chest," May 10, 1934, Folder 9, Box 34, and Annual Report, 1934, 2, Box 1, Folder 13, IISF, IHRC; Urban, "Rooted in the Americanization Zeal."

25. "Filipino Parole Responsibility," Box 21, Folder 16, "President's Report, February 19, 1935," 2, Box 1, Folder 14, and Mrs. James Reed to Edward Haff, September 18, 1936, Folder 14, Box 1, IISF, IHRC; Vicente Vigillia, Ricardo Ibarra, and Rufo Boromeo to Mrs. Eugenia de Estoita, May 18, 1934 and Grace Love to Mr. W. E. Walsh, February 25, 1935, in File 34028/16–11 (Ricardo Ibarra), IACF, SF.

26. An "Appeal Dismissed" notation with the date of February 27, 1935, is included on every file examined from the six ships that were en route as the Tydings-McDuffie Act was being accepted by the Philippine Legislature. See, for example, "Appeal Dismissed, B/L 55870/774, 2/27/35, C.S.B." in File 34028/14–2, IACF, SF.

27. For cases of Tydings-McDuffie parolees who successfully petitioned for admission, see files 34028/14–14 (Leoncio Abenis), 33994/19–20 (Hermenehildo Fagel), and 34028/16–26, (Juan Meneses), IACF, SF. Annie Clo Watson to Edward Haff, April 11, 1935, Box 21, Folder 16 and Mrs. James Reed to Edward Haff, September 18, 1936, Box 1, Folder 14, IISF, IHRC.

28. Earl Cushing to District Director, San Francisco, January 19, 1937, and R. B. Jones, "Report of Investigation," September 3, 1946, in File 34028/14–20 (Rafael Magno, pseud.), IACF, SF. See also the April 1938 memo from the San Francisco District Director of the INS warning all Pacific Coast offices to be on the lookout for seventy-one Filipinos who had arrived on the *President Taft* and who remained at large. District Director, San Francisco, "Memo to All Ports of Entry on Pacific Coast," April 20, 1938, in File 33994/20–4, IACF, SF.

29. See various documents, 1934–1946 in File 34028/14–13 (Marcelo Domingo, pseud.) IACF, SF.

30. Detention statistics drawn from Registers of Japanese, Filipinos, and Hawaiians Held for Boards of Special Inquiry, NARA, PR.

31. Filipino American Historical Society of Chicago, "Profile of an Immigrant: Ambrosia G. Ravelo," October 1999, courtesy of Estrella Ravelo Alamar; Files 34860/15–7 (Florentino Ravelo) and 15–8 (Ambrosia Ravelo), IACF, SF.

32. File 40041/4–22 (Eliseo Felipe), IACF, SF; Eliseo Felipe interview.

33. The Cable Act (1922) (42 Stat. 1021); *Toyota v. United States* (268 U.S. 402) (1925); Hing, *Making and Remaking Asian America,* 35.

34. File 40008/10–3 (Marie Natividad Gaitos Ellorin), IACF, SF; Joyce Ellorin, correspondence to authors, March 28, 2009.

35. Angel Island officials were correct in their suspicion that Nattie Ellorin should have been expatriated. The Tydings-McDuffie Act had

reclassified all Filipinos, including Flaviano Ellorin, as aliens. By virtue of her marriage to him, Maria Ellorin had lost her citizenship. There is no indication in her immigration file that she was actually expatriated.

36. File 35308/4–1 (Elisa Calloway Hawkins), IACF, SF; Elisa Brooks interview.
37. Joyce Ellorin, correspondence to authors, March 28, 2009.
38. National deportation rates are from Cannato, *American Passages*, 343.
39. Ngai, *Impossible Subjects*, 120–21; Sobredo, "From American 'Nationals,'" 207–8; Lasker, *Filipino Immigration*, 42.
40. On Edward Cahill's remarks on the repatriation program and the International Institute's offer of Filipino interpreters to the U.S. government, see Edward Cahill to Col. MacCormack, April 28, 1936; "Address Given by United States District Commissioner of Immigration and Naturalization Edward W. Cahill, Radio Station KQW, San Jose, August 19, 1935," in Edward Cahill to Col. D. W. MacCormack, January 7, 1936, and Edward Cahill to Col. D. W. MacCormack, August 25, 1935, in "Filipinos, mistreatment by officers of the service," File 55874/464B, INS COSCCF; Katharine R. Maurer, "Angel Island: Keeper of the Western Gate," *Woman's Home Missions* (May 1937), 4, Pacific School of Religion; Takaki, *Strangers from a Different Shore*, 333. The government projections can be found in Sobredo, "From American 'Nationals,'" 207–8; and Lasker, *Filipino Immigration*, 42.
41. Edward Cahill to Col. D. W. MacCormack, August 25, 1935, and Edward Cahill to Richard J. Welch, December 27, 1935, in "Filipinos, mistreatment by officers of the service," File 55874/464B, INS COSCCF.
42. "Address Given by United States District Commissioner of Immigration and Naturalization Edward W. Cahill, Radio Station KQW, San Jose, August 19, 1935," Edward Cahill, District to Col. MacCormack, April 28, 1936, Edward Cahill to Commissioner James Houghteling, June 3, 1938, in "Filipinos, mistreatment by officers of the service," File 55874/464B, INS COSCCF.
43. Pedro B. Buncan, New York City to the Secretary of Labor, June 6, 1935, and other letters from writers across the country, in "Filipinos, mistreatment by officers of the service," File 55874/464B, INS COSCCF.
44. Edward Cahill, District Commissioner to Edward Shaughnessy, April 28, 1937, in "Filipinos, mistreatment by officers of the service," File 55874/464B, INS COSCCF; Ngai, *Impossible Subjects*, 121–22; Sobredo, "From American 'Nationals,'" 209.
45. On complaints by Filipino organizations and the repatriation of Filipino prisoners, see Filipino Seamen's Association, New Orleans, to Quintin Paredes, Resident Commissioner of the Philippines, May 9, 1936, Commissioner of Immigration to Albert Mundt, August 9, 1935, and Edward Cahill to Richard J. Welch, December 27, 1935, in "Filipinos, mistreatment by officers of the service," File 55874/464B, INS COSCCF; and Ngai, *Impossible Subjects*, 124.
46. "Repatriates Pen Protest against Ship Treatment," *Filipino Pioneer*, March 1937, in Edward Cahill to Edward Shaughnessy, April 28, 1937, in

"Filipinos, mistreatment by officers of the service," File 55874/464B, INS COSCCF.

47. Ibid.
48. Maurer, "Angel Island," *Woman's Home Missions* (May 1937), 4, Pacific School of Religion; Helen Johnson, "Christmas at Angel Island," February 1939, Katherine R. Maurer Papers, California State Library. Unfortunately, the Filipino repatriation files relating to the Angel Island Immigration Station were destroyed.
49. Edward Haff to Commissioner, September 13, 1935, Edward Cahill to Richard J. Welch, December 27, 1935, and Edward Cahill, District Commissioner to Commissioner J. L. Houghteling, April 7, 1938, in "Filipinos, mistreatment by officers of the service," File 55874/464B, INS COSCCF; Sobredo, "From American 'Nationals,'" xxv; and Ngai, *Impossible Subjects*, 122.
50. "Injustice Apparent," *San Francisco Call*, February 29, 1940.
51. Files 39384/1–2 to 1–7 (Carmen, Edward, Mercedes, Elizabeth, Maria, Violet, and Fred Wienke), IACF, SF.
52. Takaki, *Strangers from a Different Shore*, 361–62.
53. Ibid., 359, 432; Eliseo Felipe interview; Immigration and Nationality Act, 1965 (79 Stat. 911).

CHAPTER NINE

1. "Statement of Clarence Zieg," August 12, 1940, File 12030/24–2, Angel Island General Correspondence, NARA, PR. The 151 Germans were merchant seamen who had been rescued by an American ship after they scuttled their luxury liner to prevent capture by the British in the Atlantic. They had been waiting for an opportunity to return home by way of the Pacific since January 1940. See Soennichsen, *Miwoks to Missles*, 141–50.
2. Lee Puey You interview.
3. Myron Wong interview.
4. "Statement of Guard William Fields," and "Statement of Captain Frank L. Smith," File 12030/24–2, Angel Island General Correspondence, NARA, PR.
5. Toogood, "A Civil History," 430–31; Askin, "Historical Report," 85; "A Mystery Fire on Angel Island," *San Francisco Chronicle*, August 13, 1940, 26.
6. Myron Wong interview.
7. "150 Angel Isle Aliens Moved to S.F. Post," *San Francisco Chronicle*, November 6, 1940, 20.
8. Alexander Weiss's story and quotes come from his interview with the authors.
9. Connie Young Yu, "Commemoration," *San Francisco Journal*, April 25, 1979, 11.
10. Chris Chow interview; Ad-Hoc Committee meeting minutes and correspondence in Chris Chow's possession.
11. Ow, "Paul Chow's Ghost Stories."

12. According to Philip Choy, the nine members of the UC Asian Architectural Student Society consisted of Bruce Flynn, Maxine Griffith, Ricky Ho, Fred Jang, Dinah Louie, Dennis Mok, Lily Mok, Takiya Nakamoto, and Sylvia Quan, who all helped to measure and evaluate the existing facilities. Fong Chan investigated the structural conditions and Brian W. Choy and Fred Jang provided photographic work.
13. Chris Chow interview.
14. AIISHAC, "Report and Recommendations," 2, 8.
15. Philip Choy interview.
16. Helmich, "Angel Island Immigration Station," 7–14.
17. "President's Message," *Passages*, fall 1998, 2.
18. "National Recognition Continues," *Passages*, fall 1999, 1.
19. AIISF, "Angel Island Immigration Station Visioning Workshop Report."
20. Felicia Lowe interview.
21. Katherine Toy's testimony in U.S. Congress, House of Representatives, *Recreation Land Bills*.
22. Lynn Woolsey and Mark Souder, U.S. Congress, House of Representatives, "Angel Island Immigration Station Restoration and Preservation Act."
23. AIISF, "Angel Island Immigration Station Master Plan."
24. Architectural Resources Group and David Quan Design, "Poetry and Inscriptions"; Daniel Quan, correspondence to authors, December 2, 2009.
25. AIISF, "Road to Restoration," videorecording; Quan, "Angel Island Immigration Station."
26. "Re-opening Speech by AIISF Board President Kathy Lim Ko," February 15, 2009, Angel Island, courtesy of AIISF.
27. Quoted in Jacobson, *Roots Too*, 66.

EPILOGUE

1. Immigration and Nationality Act of 1952 (66 Stat. 163); Hing, *Defining America*, 74; Lee, "A Nation of Immigrants," 14–17; Ngai, *Impossible Subjects*, 234–39.
2. Kennedy, *A Nation of Immigrants*, 85; Reimers, *Still the Golden Door*, 17–20, 71, 77–79, 81, 84–85; Lee, "A Nation of Immigrants," 18–21; Immigration and Nationality Act of 1965 (79 Stat. 911).
3. "Immigration Growth of '90s at Highest Rate in 150 years," *Washington Times*, June 5, 2002; U.S. Census Bureau, "Native and Foreign-Born Population by State: 2007." On the new immigration from Asia, see Zhou and Gatewood, "Transforming Asian America."
4. Reimers, *Still the Golden Door*, 84–85; Daniels, *Guarding the Golden Door*, 52–58; Hing, *Defining America*, 97–100. U.S. Census Bureau, "Native and Foreign-Born Population by State: 2007" and "Foreign-Born Population by Citizenship Status and Place of Birth: 2007." Census statistics from U.S. Census Bureau, "Estimated Unauthorized Immigrants by Selected States and Countries of Origin."
5. U.S. Department of Homeland Security, "Brief Documentary History."
6. Hing, *Defining America*, 266–67; Daniels, *Guarding the Golden Door*, 267.

7. Hing, *Defining America*, 267; Kanstroom, *Deportation Nation*, 8–15; "Suicides Point to Gaps in Treatment; Errors in Psychiatric Diagnoses and Drugs Plague Strained Immigration System," *Washington Post*, May 13, 2008. On the proportion of Latino deportees, see "Enforcement Gone Bad," *New York Times*, February 21, 2009; and Lopez and Light, "A Rising Share." On racial profiling in contemporary immigration law enforcement, see Nguyen, *We Are All Suspects Now*. The quote on current trends in deportation policy is from Kanstroom, *Deportation Nation*, 226.

8. On 1996 statistics of immigrant detention capacity, see U.S. Congress, "Problems with Immigration Detainee Medical Care," 91. On increase in detentions, see "System of Neglect; As Tighter Immigration Policies Strain Federal Agencies, the Detainees in Their Care Often Pay a Heavy Cost," *Washington Post*, May 11, 2008; "City of Immigrants Fills Jail Cells with Its Own," *New York Times*, December 26, 2008; "In-Custody Deaths," Times Topics, *New York Times*, http://topics.nytimes.com/top/reference/timestopics/subjects/i/immigration_detention_us/incustody_deaths/index.html (accessed May 7, 2009); "Immigrant Detention System Ensnares American Citizens," *USA Today*, March 25, 2009; and "Immigrant Detainee Dies, and a Life Is Buried, Too," *New York Times*, April 2, 2009.

9. Statistics and analysis for detentions on Angel Island are drawn from Barde and Bobonis, "Detention at Angel Island," 107, 113. Statistics for Ellis Island are from Pitkin, *Keepers of the Gate*, 73.

10. Human Rights Watch, "Forced Apart;" "Immigrant's Criminal Past Colors a Battle against Detentions," *New York Times*, June 12, 2009; "Piecing Together an Immigrant's Life the U.S. Refused to See," *New York Times*, July 5, 2009; Kanstroom, *Deportation Nation*, 243.

11. On the character of contemporary immigrant detainees, see United States Government Accountability Office, *Alien Detention Standards*, 3. On the government's efforts to locate detention facilities, see "Border Policy's Success Strains Resources; Tent City in Texas among Immigrant Holding Sites Drawing Criticism," *Washington Post*, February 2, 2007; and U.S. Department of Homeland Security, "Immigration Detention Facilities."

12. "Cities and Counties Rely on U.S. Immigrant Detention Fees," *Los Angeles Times*, March 17, 2009; "Marchers Urge End to Immigrants' Jailing," *Boston Globe*, March 28, 2009; "City of Immigrants," *New York Times*, December 26, 2008.

13. "System of Neglect," *Washington Post*, May 11, 2008. For a map of the locations of immigrant detention centers in the United States, see "City of Immigrants," *New York Times*, December 26, 2008, and "A Growing Detention Network," www.nytimes.com/interactive/2008/12/26/us/1227_DETAIN.html (accessed May 15, 2009); "Immigrant Detention System Ensnares American Citizens," *USA Today*, March 25, 2009; Amnesty International USA, "Jailed without Justice."

14. United States Government Accountability Office, *Alien Detention Standards*, 2–3; "Immigrants Can Linger in Detention for Months," *Washington Post*, May 14, 2008; Testimony by Mary Meg McCarthy, director, National Immigrant Justice Center, in U.S. Congress, "Problems with Immigration Detainee Medical Care," 89; Amnesty International

USA, "Jailed without Justice." On rates and lengths of detention on Ellis Island and Angel Island, see Moreno, *Encyclopedia of Ellis Island*, xvii, and Barde and Bobonis, "Detention at Angel Island," 113–16.

15. "City of Immigrants" *New York Times*, December 26, 2008; "System of Neglect," *Washington Post*, May 11, 2008.

16. "Border Policy's Success Strains Resources," *Washington Post*, February 2, 2007; U.S. Government Accountability Office, *Alien Detention Standards*, 2; "System of Neglect," *Washington Post*, May 11, 2008; "City of Immigrants," *New York Times*, December 26, 2008; "Cities and Counties Rely on U.S. Immigrant Detention Fees," *Los Angeles Times*, March 17, 2009; "Marchers Urge End to Immigrants' Jailing," *Boston Globe*, March 28, 2009.

17. Amnesty International USA, "Jailed without Justice;" "System of Neglect," *Washington Post*, May 11, 2008.

18. The most comprehensive report on the nation's broken detention system is National Immigration Law Center, et al., "A Broken System." See also "System of Neglect," *Washington Post*, May 11, 2008; "In Custody, in Pain," *Washington Post*, May 12, 2008; and "Studies Point to Gaps in Treatment; Errors in Psychiatric Diagnoses and Drugs Plague Strained Immigration System," *Washington Post*, May 13, 2008. On the government's failure to follow its own National Detention Standard for Medical Care, see U.S. Department of Homeland Security, *Immigration and Customs Enforcement's Tracking and Transfers of Detainees*, 9–10. The most recent statistics on detainee deaths can be found in "Officials Say Detainee Fatalities Were Missed," *New York Times*, August 17, 2009; Detention Watch Network, "Press Conference for National Week of Action;" "Few Details on Immigrants Who Died in Custody," *New York Times*, May 5, 2008; and "New Scrutiny as Immigrants Die in Custody," *New York Times*, June 26, 2007. Jason Hiu Lui Ng's case is covered in "Ill and in Pain, Detainee Dies in U.S. Hands," *New York Times*, August 12, 2008.

19. U.S. Congress, "Problems with Immigration Detainee Medical Care," 83–85.

20. Ibid., 97–111.

21. Ibid., 2.

22. "Immigration Growth of '90s at Highest Rate in 150 years," *Washington Times*, June 5, 2002; U.S. Census Bureau, "Native and Foreign-Born Population by State: 2007."

23. Hing, *Defining America*, 269.

24. Amnesty International USA, "Jailed without Justice."

25. Lai, Lim, and Yung, *Island*, 159.

BIBLIOGRAPHY

ARCHIVAL COLLECTIONS
Archives of Chatham House, London
Refugee Survey, 1937–38

Asian American Studies Center, University of California, Los Angeles
Southern California Chinese American Oral History Project

Bancroft Library, University of California, Berkeley
Angel Island Interviews
Hart Hyatt North Papers
John Birge Sawyer Diaries

California State Library
Katharine R. Maurer Papers

Special Collections, California State University, Sacramento
Issei Oral History Project

Ethnic Studies Library, University of California, Berkeley
Angel Island Oral History Project

Gay and Lesbian Historical Society, San Francisco

Elsa Gidlow Papers

Pacific School of Religion, Berkeley, California

Annual Reports of the Woman's Home Missionary Society of the Methodist
  Episcopal Church
Woman's Home Missions

Society of California Pioneers, San Francisco

Biographical File of Oliver Perry Stidger

Hoover Institution Archives, Stanford University

Survey of Race Relations Collection
Nadia Shapiro Collection
George Martin Day Papers

Department of Special Collections, Stanford University Libraries

Anne Loftis Papers

*United States National Archives and Records Administration, Pacific
Regional Branch*

Records of the Immigration and Naturalization Service. RG 85. Angel Island
  General Correspondence, 1915–41, San Francisco.
Records of the Immigration and Naturalization Service. RG 85. Case Files of
  Investigations Resulting in Warrant Proceedings, 1912–50, San Francisco.
Records of the U.S. Immigration and Naturalization Service. RG 85. Densmore
  Investigation Files, 1917, San Francisco.
Records of the Immigration and Naturalization Service. RG 85. Historical File
  Relating to Angel Island, 1894–1941.
Records of the Immigration and Naturalization Service. RG 85. Investigation
  Arrival Case Files, 1884–1944.
Records of the Immigration and Naturalization Service. RG 85. Passenger Lists
  of Vessels Arriving in San Francisco, California, 1893–1953 (Microfilm
  M1410). Washington, DC, National Archives.
Records of the Immigration and Naturalization Service. RG 85. Registers
  of Japanese, Filipinos, and Hawaiians Held for Boards of Special Inquiry
  at San Francisco, September 1928–February 1942 (Microfilm A3408).
  Washington, DC, National Archives, 2004.
Records of the Immigration and Naturalization Service. RG 85. Registers of
  Persons Held for Boards of Special Inquiry at the San Francisco, California,
  Immigration Office, February 1910–May1941 (Microfilm M1388),
  Washington, DC, National Archives, 2004.
Records of the Immigration and Naturalization Service. RG 85. Return Certificate
  Application Case Files of Chinese Departing, 1913–44, San Francisco.

Records of the U.S. District Court, Northern California. RG 21. Admiralty Case
Files, 1851–1934.

*United States National Archives and Records Administration,
Washington, DC*

Records of the Immigration and Naturalization Service. RG 85. Chinese
General Correspondence, 1898–1908.
Records of the Immigration and Naturalization Service. RG 85. Entry 9. INS
Central Office Subject Correspondence and Case Files, ca. 1906–57.
Records of the Immigration and Naturalization Service. Series A: Subject
Correspondence Files, Part 1: Asian Immigration and Exclusion, 1905–13.
Bethesda, MD: University Publications of America, 1996.

University of Minnesota, Immigration History Research Center

International Institute of San Francisco Records, 1922–92

University of Southern California, USC Korean Heritage Library

Korean American Oral History Collection

YIVO Institute of Jewish Research, New York City

Hebrew Sheltering and Immigrant Aid Society of America Annual Reports

Oral History Interviews

Jim Ariki, interview with Judy Yung, October 3, 2006, Gilroy, CA.
Elisa Brooks, interview with Judy Yung, December 10, 2008, South Bend, IN.
Kala Bagai Chandra, interview with Inder Bagai, Ram Bagai, and Rani Bagai,
November 26, 1982, Los Angeles, CA, courtesy of Rani Bagai.
Chris Chow, interview with Judy Yung, November 29, 2009, San Francisco, CA.
Philip P. Choy, interview with Judy Yung, August 2, 2009, San Francisco, CA.
Betty Kawamoto Dunn, interview with Alice Murata, December 2, 2007,
Chicago, IL.
Eliseo Felipe, interview with Judy Yung, April 13, 2009, Salinas, CA.
Nick Friesen, interview with Judy Yung, October 8, 2008, Reedley, CA.
Alexandra Hrenoff, interview with Maria Sakovich, January 7 and 8, 2001,
Santa Rosa, CA.
Dick Kobashigawa, interview with Judy Yung, October 7, 2006, San
Francisco, CA.
Charles Jung, interview with Connie Young Yu, November 11, 1976, San
Francisco, CA.
Edwar Lee, interview with Felicia Lowe, April 9, 1984, San Francisco, CA.
Edwar Lee, interview with Him Mark Lai, Genny Lim, and Judy Yung, May
8,1976, Oakland, CA.
Lee Puey You, interview with Judy Yung and Him Mark Lai, December 14,
1975, San Francisco, CA.
Law Shee Low, interview with Judy Yung, October 20, 1988, San
Francisco, CA.

Michael Lopez, interview with Katherine Toy, December 16, 2009, Palo Alto, CA.

Felicia Lowe, interview with Judy Yung, August 18, 2009, San Francisco, CA.

Donald Lyang, interview with Judy Yung, November 23, 2008, Hillsborough, CA.

Mock Ging Sing, interview with Felicia Lowe, April 9, 1984, San Francisco, CA.

Herbert Neufeld, interview with Judy Yung, December 4, 2008, Bakersfield, CA.

Emery Sims, interview with Him Mark Lai, Genny Lim, and Judy Yung, June 29, 1977, San Francisco, CA.

Alice Steiner, interview with Nora Steiner Mealy, January 19, 2002, Davis, CA.

Alice Steiner, interview with Poonam Sachdev, December 7, 2004, Davis, CA.

Alexander Weiss, interview with Judy Yung, July 30, 2009, Oakland, CA.

Myron Wong, interview with Kevin Kalhoefer, December 11, 2004, Los Angeles, CA.

Videorecordings

Angel Island Immigration Station Foundation. "Road to Restoration." San Francisco: AIISF, 2009.

Felicia Lowe Productions. "Carved in Silence." San Francisco: CrossCurrents, NAATA, 1987.

Unpublished Materials

Angel Island Immigration Station Foundation. "Angel Island Immigration Station Master Plan," California State Parks, 2000.

Angel Island Immigration Station Foundation. "Angel Island Immigration Station Visioning Workshop Report," 1999.

Angel Island Immigration Station Historical Advisory Committee. "Report and Recommendations on the Angel Island Immigration Station," 1976.

Architectural Resources Group. "Angel Island Immigration Station Detention Barracks Historic Structure Report." Prepared for National Park Service, California State Parks, Angel Island Immigration Station Foundation, 2002.

Architectural Resources Group. "Historic Structures Report: Hospital Building, Angel Island Immigration Station." Prepared for the National Park Service, California State Parks, Angel Island Immigration Station Foundation, 2002.

Architectural Resources Group and Daniel Quan Design. "Poetry and Inscriptions: Translation and Analysis." Prepared for the California Department of Parks and Recreation and Angel Island Immigration Station Foundation, 2004.

Architectural Resources Group and Daniel Quan Design. "Final Interpretive Plan, Phase 1 Project Area, Angel Island Immigration Station." Commissioned by the California Department of Parks and Recreation, 2006.

Askin, Dorene. "Historical Report, Angel Island Immigration Station." California Department of Parks and Recreation, Interpretive Planning Unit, 1977.

Chen, Helen. "Chinese Immigration into the United States: An Analysis of Changes in Immigration Policies." PhD diss., Brandeis University, 1980.

Chen, Wen-hsien. "Chinese under Both Exclusion and Immigration Laws." PhD diss., University of Chicago, 1940.

Susan Clark. "The Del Mar Ranch: From the German Rancho to the Sea Ranch, California, 1845 to 1964." M.A. thesis, California State University, Sonoma, 1990.

Egan, Charles. "Voices in the Wooden House: Angel Island Inscriptions, 1910–1945" (unpublished manuscript).

Friesen, Johann. "What Has Forced Us with Our Brethren to Leave Soviet Russia" (unpublished manuscript). Record Group M312, Center for Mennonite Brethren Studies, Fresno Pacific University.

Gee, Jennifer. "Sifting the Arrivals: Asian Immigrants and the Angel Island Immigration Station, San Francisco, 1910–1940." PhD diss., Stanford University, 1999.

Gosal, Harjit K., and Hardeep K. Gosal. "Passage to the Pacific Coast in the Early 1900s." Angel Island Immigration Station Foundation.

Gray, Esther. "Representing Spanish Immigration through Angel Island." History 201, Stanford University, 2009.

Gutiérrez, Laura. "The Guatemalan Experience at Angel Island." History 201, Stanford University, 2009.

Helmich, Mary, "Angel Island Immigration Station, Interpretive Plan, Phase II." Interpretive Planning Section, Office of Interpretive Services, 1987.

Jimenez, Ivan. "Immigration through Angel Island 1910–1940: The Salvadoran People." History 201, Stanford University, 2009.

Liu, Fu-ju. "A Comparative Demographic Study of Native-born and Foreign-born Chinese Populations in the United States." PhD diss., University of Michigan, 1953.

Mabalon, Dawn Bohulano. "Life in Little Manila: Filipinas/os in Stockton, California, 1917–1972." PhD diss., Stanford University, 2003.

Moon, Hyung June. "The Korean Immigrants in America: The Quest for Identity in the Formative Years, 1903–1918." PhD diss., University of Nevada, 1976.

Nachtigall, Gary B. "Mennonite Migration and Settlements of California." M.A. thesis, California State University, Fresno, 1972.

Nishi, Thomas. "Actions and Attitudes of the United States Public Health Service on Angel Island, San Francisco Bay, California, 1891–1920." M.A. thesis, University of Hawaii, Manoa, 1982.

Ow, Jeffrey. "Paul Chow's Ghost Stories." Asian American Studies 200A, University of California, Los Angeles, 1994.

Sakovich, Maria. "Angel Island Immigration Station Reconsidered: Non-Asian Encounters with the Immigration Laws, 1910–1940." M.A. thesis, California State University, Sonoma, 2002.

Sobredo, James D. "From American 'Nationals' to the 'Third Asiatic Invasion': Racial Transformation and Filipino Exclusion (1898–1934)." PhD diss., University of California, Berkeley, 1998.

Tanaka, Kei. "Japanese Picture Marriage in 1900–1924: California Construction of Japanese Race and Gender." PhD diss., Rutgers University, 2002.

Toogood, Anna Coxe. "A Civil History of Golden Gate National Recreation Area and Point Reyes National Seashore, California." 2 vols. Historic Resource Study, U.S. National Park Service, 1980.

Urban, Andrew. " 'Rooted in the Americanization Zeal': The San Francisco International Institute, Race, and Settlement Work, 1918–1939." University of Minnesota, 2005.

Published Materials

Amnesty International USA. "Jailed without Justice: Immigration Detention in the USA." March 25, 2009, www.amnestyusa.org/immigrant-detention/page.do?id=1641031 (accessed May 16, 2009).

Angel Island Immigration Station Foundation. "The Other Side of the Fence." *Passages: The Quarterly Newsletter of the Angel Island Immigration Station Foundation* 4, no. 4 (2001): 4–5.

Asiatic Exclusion League. *Proceedings of the Asiatic Exclusion League, San Francisco, June, 1910.* San Francisco: Allied Printing, 1910.

Azuma, Eiichiro. *Between Two Empires: Race, History, and Transnationalism in Japanese America.* New York: Oxford University Press, 2005.

Balderrama, Francisco E., and Raymond Rodriguez. *Decade of Betrayal: Mexican Repatriation in the 1930s.* Albuquerque: University of New Mexico Press, 1995.

Baldoz, Rick. "Valorizing Racial Boundaries: Hegemony and Conflict in the Racialization of Filipino Migrant Labour in the United States." *Ethnic and Racial Studies* 27, no. 6 (November 2004): 969–86.

Bamford, Mary. *Angel Island: The Ellis Island of the West.* Chicago: Woman's American Baptist Home Mission Society, 1917.

Barde, Robert Eric. *Immigration at the Golden Gate: Passenger Ships, Exclusion, and Angel Island.* Westport, CT: Praeger, 2008.

Barde, Robert, and Gustavo J. Bobonis. "Detention at Angel Island: First Empirical Evidence." *Social Science History* 30, no. 1 (Spring 2006): 103–36.

Barkan, Elliot. *From All Points: America's Immigrant West, 1870s–1952.* Bloomington: University of Indiana Press, 2007.

Bose, Arun Coomer. *Indian Revolutionaries Abroad, 1905–1922: In the Background of International Developments.* Patna (India): Bharati Bhawan, 1971.

Brown, Emily C. *Har Dayal: Hindu Revolutionary and Rationalist.* Tucson: University of Arizona Press, 1975.

Brownstone, David, Irene Franck, and Douglass Brownstone. *Island of Hope, Island of Tears.* New York: Barnes and Noble, 2000.

Bulosan, Carlos. *America Is in the Heart.* New York: Harcourt, Brace, 1943.

Burnham, Frederick Russell. "The Howl for Cheap Mexican Labor." In *The Alien in Our Midst or Selling Our Birthright for a Mess of Pottage*, edited by Madison Grant and Charles Stewart Davison. New York: Galton, 1930.

California State Board of Control. *California and the Oriental: Japanese, Chinese and Hindus.* Sacramento: California State Board of Control, 1922.

California State Senate. Special Committee on Chinese Immigration. *Chinese Immigration: Its Social, Moral, and Political Effect.* Sacramento: State Office of Printing, 1878.

Camarillo, Albert M. "Mexico." In *The New Americans: A Guide to Immigration since 1965*, edited by Mary C. Waters and Reed Ueda with Helen B. Barrow. Cambridge: Harvard University Press, 2007.

Cannato, Vincent J. *American Passage: The History of Ellis Island.* New York: Harper, 2009.

Cardoso, Lawrence A. *Mexican Emigration to the United States, 1897–1931: Socio-Economic Patterns*. Tucson: University of Arizona Press, 1980.

Chan, Sucheng. *Asian Americans: An Interpretive History*. Woodbridge, CT: Twayne, 1991.

———. *This Bitter-sweet Soil: The Chinese in California Agriculture, 1860–1910*. Berkeley: University of California Press, 1986.

———. "The Exclusion of Chinese Women, 1870–1943." In *Entry Denied: Exclusion and the Chinese Community in America, 1882–1943*, edited by Sucheng Chan. Philadelphia: Temple University Press, 1991.

———. "European and Asian Immigration into the United States." In *Immigration Reconsidered: History, Sociology, and Politics*, edited by Virginia Yans-McLaughlin. New York: Oxford University Press, 1990.

Chen, Yong. *Chinese San Francisco, 1850–1943: A Trans-Pacific Community*. Palo Alto, CA: Stanford University Press, 2000.

Chew, Ng Poon. *The Treatment of the Exempt Classes of Chinese in the United States: A Statement from the Chinese in America*. San Francisco: Chung Sai Yat Po, 1908.

Choy, Bong-Youn. *Koreans in America*. Chicago: Nelson-Hall, 1979.

Conway, Lorie. *Forgotten Ellis Island: The Extraordinary Story of America's Immigrant Hospital*. New York: HarperCollins, 2007.

Cordova, Dorothy. "Voices from the Past: Why They Came." In *Making Waves: An Anthology of Writings by and about Asian American Women*, edited by Asian Women United of California. Boston: Beacon Press, 1989.

Cordova, Joan May T., and Alexis S. Canillo, eds. *Voices: A Filipino-American Oral History*. Santa Rosa, CA: Northwestern Graphics, 1984.

Daniels, Roger. *Asian America: Chinese and Japanese in the United States since 1850*. Seattle: University of Washington Press, 1988.

———. *Guarding the Golden Door: American Immigration Policy and Immigrants since 1882*. New York: Hill and Wang, 2004.

———. "No Lamps Were Lit for Them: Angel Island and the Historiography of Asian American Immigration." *Journal of American Ethnic History* 17, no. 1 (Fall 1997): 3–18.

Das, Rajani Kanta. *Hindustani Workers on the Pacific Coast*. Berlin, Germany: Walter DeGruyter, 1923.

Day, George Martin. *The Russians in Hollywood: A Study in Culture Conflict*. Los Angeles: University of Southern California Press, 1935.

Desmond, Gail Whang. "Koreans in Mexico." In *Korean American Writings*. New York: Insight, 1975.

———. "Memories of My Grandfather: Rev. Whang Sa Sun." In *Korean American Writings*. New York: Insight, 1975.

Detention Watch Network. "Press Conference for National Week of Action to Hold DHS Accountable." April 10, 2009, www.detentionwatchnetwork.org/node/2398? (accessed May 11, 2009).

España-Maram, Linda. *Creating Masculinity in Los Angeles's Little Manila: Working-Class Filipinos and Popular Culture, 1920s–1950s*. New York: Columbia University Press, 2006.

Fairchild, Amy L. *Science at the Borders: Immigrant Medical Inspection and the Shaping of the Modern Industrial Labor Force*. Baltimore, MD: Johns Hopkins University Press, 2003.

Fanning, Branwell, and William Wong. *Angel Island*. Charleston, SC: Arcadia, 2006.

Foley, Neil. *The White Scourge: Mexicans, Blacks, and Poor Whites in Texas Cotton Culture*. Berkeley: University of California Press, 1997.

Gabaccia, Donna. "Great Migration Debates: Keywords in Historical Perspective." Social Science Research Council. "Border Battles: The U.S. Immigration Debates." July 28, 2006, http://borderbattles.ssrc.org/Gabaccia/index.html (accessed October 9, 2009).

Galarza, Ernesto. *Barrio Boy*. Notre Dame: University of Notre Dame Press, 1977.

Gamio, Manuel. *Mexican Immigration to the United States: A Study of Human Migration and Adjustment*. Chicago: University of Chicago Press, 1930.

———. *The Life Story of the Mexican Immigrant*. Berkeley: University of California Press, 1971.

García, Mario. *Desert Immigrants: The Mexicans of El Paso, 1880–1920*. New Haven, CT: Yale University Press, 1981.

Gardner, Martha. *The Qualities of a Citizen: Women, Immigration, and Citizenship, 1870–1965*. Princeton, NJ: Princeton University Press, 2005.

Gatrell, Peter. *A Whole Empire Walking: Refugees in Russia during World War I*. Bloomington: Indiana University Press, 1999.

Gee, Jennifer. "Housewives, Men's Villages, and Sexual Respectability: Gender and the Interrogation of Asian Women at the Angel Island Immigration Station." In *Asian/Pacific Islander American Women: A Historical Anthology*, edited by Shirley Hune and Gail M. Nomura. New York: New York University Press, 2003.

Gontard, Jean. "Second Class on Angel Island: Immigrant Hell." Translated and introduced by Glenn Farris. *The Californians: Magazine of California History* 12, no. 4 (July 1986): 6–9, 49.

Gutiérrez, David. *Walls and Mirrors: Mexican Americans, Mexican Immigrants, and the Politics of Ethnicity*. Berkeley: University of California Press, 1995.

Gyory, Andrew. *Closing the Gate: Race, Politics, and the Chinese Exclusion Act*. Chapel Hill: University of North Carolina Press, 1998.

Hallberg, Gerald L. "Bellingham, Washington's Anti-Hindu Riot." *Journal of the West* 12 (January 1973): 163–171.

Hamilton, Nora. *The Limits of State Autonomy: Post-Revolutionary Mexico*. Princeton: Princeton University Press, 1982.

Higham, John. *Strangers in the Land: Patterns of American Nativism, 1860–1925*. 2nd ed. New York: Antheneum, 1978.

Hing, Bill Ong. *Defining America through Immigration Policy*. Philadelphia, PA: Temple University Press, 2004.

———. *Making and Remaking Asian America through Immigration Policy, 1850–1990*. Stanford, CA: Stanford University Press, 1994.

Hoffman, Abraham. *Unwanted Mexican Americans in the Great Depression: Repatriation Pressures, 1929–1939*. Tucson: University of Arizona Press, 1974.

Hoover, Karl. "The Hindu Conspiracy in California, 1913–1918." *German Studies Review* 8, no. 2 (May 1985): 245–61.

Houchins, Lee, and Chang-su Houchins. "The Korean Experience in America, 1903–1924." *Pacific Historical Review* 43, no. 4 (November 1974): 548–75.

Howe, Frederic C. *Confessions of a Reformer*. New York: C. Scribner's Sons, 1925.

Hsu, Madeline. *Dreaming of Gold, Dreaming of Home: Transnationalism and Migration between the United States and South China, 1882–1943*. Stanford, CA: Stanford University Press, 2000.

Human Rights Watch. "Forced Apart (By the Numbers): Non-Citizens Deported Mostly for Nonviolent Offenses" (Overview). April 15, 2009, www.hrw.org/en/reports/2009/04/15/forced-apart-numbers (accessed May 16, 2009).

Ichioka, Yuji. *The Issei: The World of the First Generation Immigrants, 1885–1924.* New York: Free Press, 1998.

Isaak, H. P. *Our Life Story and Escape.* Dinuba, CA: H. P. Isaak, 1977.

Ito, Kazuo. *Issei: A History of Japanese Immigrants in North America.* Seattle: Japanese Community Service, 1973.

Jacobson, Matthew Frye. *Roots Too: White Ethnic Revival in Post–Civil Rights America.* Cambridge: Harvard University Press, 2006.

Jacoby, Harold S. "U.S. Strategies of Asian Indian Immigration Restriction, 1882–1917." In *From India to America: A Brief History of Immigration; Problems of Discrimination; Admission and Assimilation,* edited by S. Chandrasekhar. La Jolla, CA: A Population Review Book, 1982.

Jann Mon Fong. "The Story of a Sojourner in Gold Mountain." *Ren Jian Shi* (People's world), January 16, 1935, 15–16. Translated by Him Mark Lai and Marlon K. Hom.

Jensen, Joan. *Passage from India: Asian Indian Immigrants in North America.* New Haven, CT: Yale University Press, 1988.

Josh, Sohan Singh. *Hindustan Gadar Party: A Short History.* New Delhi, India: People's Publishing House, 1977.

Kanstroom, Daniel. *Deportation Nation: Outsiders in American History.* Cambridge, MA: Harvard University Press, 2007.

Kazue de Cristoforo, Violet. *May Sky, There is Always Tomorrow: An Anthology of Japanese American Concentration Camp Kaiko Haiku.* Los Angeles: Sun and Moon Press, 1997.

Kawai, Michi. "A Day on Angel Island." *Joshi Seinen-kai* (Young women's world) 12, no. 8–9 (September 1915): 49–53.

———. *My Lantern.* Tokyo: Kyo Bun Kwan, 1939.

Kim, Warren Y. *Koreans in America.* Seoul: Po Chin Chai Printing Company, 1971.

Kobashigawa, Dick Jiro. *Hitome-Bore; A Kibei-Nisei Story.* San Francisco: Dick Kobashigawa, 2001.

Kennedy, John F. *A Nation of Immigrants.* New York: Harper & Row, 1964.

Kranzler, David. *Japanese, Nazis and Jews: The Jewish Refugee Committee of Shanghai, 1938–1945.* Hoboken, NJ: KTAV Publishing, 1988.

Lai, Him Mark. "Island of Immortals: Chinese Immigrants and the Angel Island Immigration Station." *California History* 57, no. 1 (Spring 1978): 88–103.

Lai, Him Mark, Genny Lim, and Judy Yung. *Island: Poetry and History of Chinese Immigrants on Angel Island, 1910–1940.* San Francisco: HOC-DOI, 1980; Seattle: University of Washington Press, 1991.

Lasker, Bruno. *Filipino Immigration to Continental U.S. and to Hawaii.* Chicago: University of Chicago Press, 1931.

Lau, Estelle. *Paper Families: Identity, Immigration Administration, and Chinese Exclusion.* Durham, NC: Duke University Press, 2007.

Lear, John. *Workers, Neighbors and Citizens: The Revolution in Mexico City.* Lincoln: University of Nebraska Press, 2001.

Lee, Erika. "A Nation of Immigrants / A Gatekeeping Nation: American Immigration Law and Policy, 1875–Present." In *A Companion to American*

Immigration History, edited by Reed Ueda. Malden, MA: Blackwell Publishers, 2006.

———. "American Gatekeeping: Race and Immigration Law in the Twentieth Century." In *Not Just Black and White: Immigration, Race, and Ethnicity, Then to Now*, edited by George Fredrickson, Nancy Foner, and Josh DeWind. New York: Russell Sage Foundation, 2004.

———. *At America's Gates: Chinese Immigration during the Exclusion Era, 1882–1943*. Chapel Hill: University of North Carolina Press, 2003.

———. "*Wong Kim Ark v. United States*: Immigration, Race, and Citizenship." In *Race Law Stories*, edited by Devin Carbado and Rachel Moran. New York: Foundation Press, 2008.

Lee, K. W., with Dr. Luke and Grace Kim. "A Pioneer Pastor's Son." *KoreAm Journal*. March 2007, www.koreamjournal.com (accessed June 1, 2007).

Lee, Mary Paik. *Quiet Odyssey: A Pioneer Korean Woman in America*, edited with an introduction by Sucheng Chan. Seattle: University of Washington Press, 1990.

Lee, Robert. *Orientals: Asian Americans in Popular Culture*. Philadelphia: Temple University Press, 1999.

LeMay, Michael C. *Guarding the Gates: Immigration and National Security*. Santa Barbara, CA: Praeger, 2006.

LeMay, Michael, and Elliott Barkan. *U.S. Immigration and Naturalization Laws and Issues*. Westport, CT: Greenwood Press, 1999.

Leonard, Karen. *Making Ethnic Choices: California's Punjabi Mexican American*. Philadelphia: Temple University Press, 1992.

López, Ian Haney. *White by Law: The Legal Construction of Race*. New York: New York University Press, 2006.

Lopez, Mark Hugo, and Michael T. Light. "A Rising Share: Hispanics and Federal Crime." February 18, 2009, Pew Hispanic Center, http://pewhispanic.org/reports/report.php?ReportID=104 (accessed May 16, 2009).

Mabalon, Dawn B., Rico Reyes, the Stockton Chapter, Filipino American National Historical Society, and the Little Manila Foundation. *Filipinos in Stockton*. Charleston, SC: Arcadia Publishing, 2008.

Magocsi, Paul Robert. "Russian Americans." www.everyculture.com/multi/Pa-Sp/Russian-Americans.html (accessed January 25, 2010).

Marinbach, Bernard. *Galveston: Ellis Island of the West*. Albany: State University of New York Press, 1983.

Markowitz, Peter L. "Straddling the Civil-Criminal Divide: A Bifurcated Approach to Understanding the Nature of Immigration Removal Proceedings." *Harvard Civil Rights—Civil Liberties Law Review* 43 (Summer 2008): 289–351.

Martens, Wilfred. *River of Glass*. Scottsdale, PA: Herald Press, 1980.

Martinez, John Ramon. *Mexican Emigration to the U.S., 1910–1930*. San Francisco: R and E Research Associates, 1971.

McClatchy, V. S. "Oriental Immigration." In *The Alien in Our Midst or Selling Our Birthright for a Mess of Pottage*, edited by Madison Grant and Charles Stewart Davison. New York: Galton, 1930.

McKinley, William. " 'Benevolent Assimilation' Proclamation of President William McKinley, December 21, 1898." *The Statutes at Large of the United States of America from March 1897 to March 1899 and Recent Treaties, Conventions, Executive Proclamations, and the Concurrent Resolutions of the*

Two Houses of Congress. Vol. XXX. Washington, DC: Government Printing Office, 1899.

McWilliams, Carey. *Southern California Country: An Island on the Land*. New York: Duell, Sloan, and Pearce, 1946.

Melendy, H. Brett. "California's Discrimination against Filipinos, 1927–1935." In *Letters in Exile: An Introductory Reader on the History of Pilipinos in America*, edited by the UCLA Asian American Studies Center. Los Angeles: UCLA Asian American Studies Center, 1976.

Millis, H. A. "East Indian Immigration to British Columbia and the Pacific Coast States." *American Economic Review* 1, no. 1 (1911): 72–76.

———. "East Indian Immigration to the Pacific Coast." *Survey* 28 (June 1912): 379–86.

Mirande, Alfredo. *Gringo Justice*. Notre Dame, IN: University of Notre Dame Press, 1987.

Misrow, Jogesh C. *East Indian Immigration on the Pacific Coast*. San Francisco: R and E Research Associates, 1971. First published 1915.

Moreno, Barry. *Encyclopedia of Ellis Island*. Wesport, CT: Greenwood Press, 2004.

National Association of Hispanic Journalists. "NAHJ Urges News Media to Stop Using Dehumanizing Terms When Covering Immigration." www.nahj. org/nahjnews/articles/2006/March/immigrationcoverage.shtml (accessed September 25, 2009).

National Immigration Law Center, American Civil Liberties Union of Southern California, and Holland & Knight Law Firm. "A Broken System: Confidential Reports Reveal Failures in U.S. Immigrant Detention Centers." www.nilc.org (accessed August 23, 2009).

Neufeld, Herb. *Jacob's Journey: Escape from Communist Russia*. New York: Vantage Press, 2000.

Ng, Franklin, ed. *The Asian American Encyclopedia*. New York: Marshall Cavendish, 1995.

Ngai, Mae M. *Impossible Subjects, Illegal Aliens and the Making of Modern America*. Princeton: Princeton University Press, 2004.

———. "Legacies of Exclusion: Illegal Chinese Immigration during the Cold War Years," *Journal of American Ethnic History* 18:1 (1998): 3–35.

Nguyen, Tram. *We Are All Suspects Now: Untold Stories from Immigrant America after 9/11*. Boston, MA: Beacon Press, 2005.

North, Hart Hyatt. "Chinese and Japanese Immigration to the Pacific Coast." *California Historical Society Quarterly* 28, no. 4 (1949): 343–50.

———. "Chinese Highbinder Societies in California." *California Historical Society Quarterly* 27, no. 1 (1948): 19–31.

Odo, Franklin S. *In Movement: A Pictorial History of Asian America*. Los Angeles: Visual Communications/Asian American Studies Central, 1977.

Olmsted Center for Landscape Preservation. "Cultural Landscape Report for Angel Island Immigration Station, vol. 1: Site History." Brookline, MA: Olmsted Center for Landscape Preservation, 2002.

Pascoe, Peggy. *What Comes Naturally: Miscegenation Law and the Making of Race in America*. New York: Oxford University Press, 2009.

Peffer, George Anthony. "Forbidden Families: Emigration Experiences of Chinese Women under the Page Law, 1875–1882." *Journal of American Ethnic History* 6 (1986): 28–46.

Perkins, Clifford. *Border Patrol: With the U.S. Immigration Service on the Mexican Boundary, 1910–54.* El Paso: Texas Western Press, 1978.

Pfaelzer, Jean. *Driven Out: The Forgotten War against Chinese Americans.* Berkeley: University of California Press, 2008.

Pitkin, Thomas M. *Keepers of the Gate: A History of Ellis Island.* New York: New York University Press, 1975.

Press, Stephen. "Prokofiev's Vexing Entry into the USA." www.sprkfv.net/journal/three06/vexing1.html (accessed November 7, 2009).

Preston, William. *Aliens and Dissenters: Federal Suppression of Radicals, 1903–1933.* Urbana: University of Illinois Press, 1963.

Quan, Daniel. "Angel Island Immigration Station: Immigration History in the Middle of San Francisco Bay." *CRM,* no. 8 (1999): 16–19.

Raat, W. Dirk. *Mexico and the United States: Ambivalent Vistas.* 3rd ed. Athens: University of Georgia Press, 2004.

Rak, Mary Kidder. *Border Patrol.* Boston: Houghton Mifflin, 1938.

Raymond, Boris and David R. Jones. *The Russian Diaspora, 1917–41.* Lanham, MD: Scarecrow, 2000.

Reimers, David. *Still the Golden Door: The Third World Comes to America.* New York: Columbia University Press, 1992.

Reisler, Mark. *By the Sweat of Their Brow: Mexican Immigrant Labor in the United States, 1900–1940.* Westport, CT.: Greenwood Press, 1976.

Rischin, Moses. *The Promised City: New York's Jews, 1870–1914.* Cambridge: Harvard University Press, 1962.

Rossi, Jean. "Evdokia Gregorievna Zaharoff: Her Life and Flight from Russia." *Pacific Historian* 14, no. 1 (1970): 41–47.

Ruiz, Vicki. *From Out of the Shadows: Mexican Women in Twentieth-Century America.* New York: Oxford University Press, 1998.

Salyer, Lucy. *Laws Harsh as Tigers: Chinese Immigrants and the Shaping of Modern Immigration Law.* Chapel Hill: University of North Carolina Press, 1995.

Sánchez, George. *Becoming Mexican American: Ethnicity, Culture, and Identity in Chicano Los Angeles, 1900–1945.* New York: Oxford University Press, 1995.

Sarasohn, Eileen Sunada, ed. *Issei Women: Echoes from Another Frontier.* Palo Alto, CA: Pacific Books, 1998.

———. *The Issei: Portrait of a Pioneer, an Oral History.* Palo Alto, CA: Pacific Books, 1983.

Sawada, Mitziko. *Tokyo Life, New York Dreams: Urban Japanese Visions of America, 1890–1924.* Berkeley: University of California Press, 1996.

Saxton, Alexander. *The Indispensable Enemy: Labor and the Anti-Chinese Movement in California.* Berkeley: University of California Press, 1971.

Shah, Nayan. *Contagious Divides: Epidemics and Race in San Francisco's Chinatown.* Berkeley: University of California Press, 2001.

Shimkin, Michael and Mary. "From Golden Horn to Golden Gate: The Flight of the Russian Siberian Flotilla." *California History* 64, no. 4 (Fall 1985): 290–94.

Singh, Jane. "The Gadar Party: Political Expression in an Immigrant Community." In *Asian American Studies: A Reader,* edited by Jean Yu-wen Shen Wu and Min Song. New Brunswick, NJ: Rutgers University Press, 2000.

Siu, Paul C. *The Chinese Laundryman: A Study in Social Isolation,* edited by John Kuo Wei Tchen. New York: New York University Press, 1987.

Smith, Darrell Hevenor, and H. Guy Herring. *Bureau of Immigration: Its History, Activities, and Organization.* Institute for Government Research Service Monographs of the United States Government, No. 30. Baltimore, 1924.

Smith, Willard H. *The Social and Religious Thought of William Jennings Bryan.* Lawrence, KS: Coronado Press, 1975.

Soennichsen, John. *Miwoks to Missiles: A History of Angel Island.* Tiburon, CA: Angel Island Association, 2005.

Stanlaw, James. "Japanese Emigration and Immigration: From the Meiji to the Modern." In *Japanese Diasporas: Unsung Pasts, Conflicting Presents, and Uncertain Futures,* edited by Nobuko Adachi. New York: Routledge, 2006.

Stern, Alexandra Minna. "Buildings, Boundaries, and Blood: Medicalization and Nation-Building on the U.S.-Mexico Border, 1910–1930." *Hispanic American Historical Review* 79, no. 1 (February 1999): 41–81.

———. "Nationalism on the Line: Masculinity, Race and the Creation of the U.S. Border Patrol, 1910–1940." In *Continental Crossroads: Remapping U.S-Mexico Borderlands History,* edited by Samuel Truett and Elliot Young. Durham, NC: Duke University Press, 2004.

Stidger, O. P. "Highlights on Chinese Exclusion and Expulsion: The Immigration Law of 1924 as It Affects Persons of Chinese Descent in the United States, Their Business Interests, Their Rights and Their Privileges." San Francisco: Chinese Chamber of Commerce, 1979, 1924.

———. "Our Immigration Law, Its Menace to American Citizenship, Commentary on Proposed Immigration and Exclusion Law." San Francisco, CA: Allen, 1913.

Stolarik, M. Mark, ed. *Forgotten Doors: The Other Ports of Entry to the United States.* Philadelphia: Balch Institute Press, 1988.

Sunoo, Sonia Shinn. *Korean Picture Brides: A Collection of Oral Histories.* Bloomington, IN: Xlibris Corporation, 2002.

Takaki, Ronald. *Strangers from a Different Shore: A History of Asian Americans.* Boston: Little, Brown, 1989.

Takanashi, Takako. "Stories of Picture Brides." *Joshi Seinen-kai* (Young women's world) 16, no. 4 (April 1919): 217–21. Translated by Yoshiko Yokochi Samuel.

Tanaka, Kei. "Photographs of Japanese Picture Brides: Visualizing Immigrants and Practicing Immigration Policy in Early Twentieth-Century United States." *American Studies* (Seoul National University) 3, no. 1 (2008): 27–55.

Tolstoy, Alexandra. *Out of the Past.* New York: Columbia University Press, 1981.

Torpey, John. *The Invention of the Passport: Surveillance, Citizenship, and the State.* New York: Cambridge University Press, 2000.

Ueda, Reed. *Postwar Immigrant America: A Social History.* Boston, MA: Bedford/St. Martin's Press, 1994.

U.S. Census Bureau. *Historical Statistics of the United States, 1789–1945: A Supplement to the Statistical Abstract of the United States.* Washington, D.C.: Government Printing Office, 1949.

———. "Estimated Unauthorized Immigrants by Selected States and Countries of Origin." *The 2010 Statistical Abstract.* www.census.gov/compendia/statab/cats/population/native_and_foreign-born_populations.html (accessed January 5, 2010).

———. "Foreign-Born Population by Citizenship Status and Place of Birth: 2007" U.S. Census Bureau, *The 2010 Statistical Abstract.* www.census.gov/compendia/

statab/cats/population/native_and_foreign-born_populations.html (accessed January 5, 2010).

———. "Native and Foreign-Born Population by State: 2007." U.S.Census Bureau, *The 2010 Statistical Abstract*. www.census.gov/compendia/statab/ cats/population/native_and_foreign-born_populations.html (accessed January 5, 2010).

U.S. Congress, House of Representatives. "Angel Island Immigration Station Restoration and Preservation Act—H.R. 4469." *Congressional Record* 150 (2004): 7663–7664. Text from Congressional Record Permanent Digital Collection (accessed January 13, 2010).

U.S. Congress, House of Representatives. "Immigration Station on Angel Island, Cal.," 59th Cong., 1st sess., House Report 4640. Washington, D.C.: Government Printing Office, 1906.

U.S. Congress, House of Representatives. "Problems with Immigration Detainee Medical Care"; Hearing before the Subcommittee on Immigration, Citizenship, Refugees, Border Security, and International Law of the Committee on the Judiciary, June 4, 2008. http://judiciary.house.gov/ hearings/hear_060408.html (accessed May 11, 2009).

U.S. Congress, House of Representatives. *Recreation Land Bills*. Hearing before the Subcommittee on National Parks, Recreation and Public Lands, July 15, 2004. Text in LexisNexus Congressional Hearings Digital Collection (accessed January 13, 2010).

U.S. Congress. House of Representatives. Committee on Immigration and Naturalization. "Immigration of Aliens into the United States—H.R. 10384." Text from U.S. Congressional Serial Set (accessed April 3, 2010).

U.S. Congress. Senate. Committee on Immigration. *Reports of the Immigration Commission*, Part 25, "Immigrants in Industries: Japanese and Other Immigrant Races in the Pacific Coast and Rocky Mountain States," vol. 1: "Japanese and East Indians." Washington, DC: Government Printing Office, 1911.

———. *Reports of the Immigration Commission*, Part 5: "Dictionary of Races or People." Washington, DC: Government Printing Office, 1911.

———. *Reports of the Immigration Commission*, Part 1–2: "Abstracts of Reports of the Immigration Commission, with Conclusions and Recommendations." Washington, DC: Government Printing Office, 1911.

U.S. Department of Commerce and Labor. Bureau of Immigration. "Treaties, Laws, Regulations Relating to the Exclusion of Chinese, May, 1905." Washington, DC: Government Printing Office, 1905.

U.S. Department of Labor. Bureau of Immigration and Naturalization. *Annual Report of the Commissioner-General of Immigration to the Secretary of Labor*. Washington, DC: Government Printing Office, 1910–1912.

U.S. Department of Labor. Bureau of Immigration. *Annual Report of the Commissioner-General of Immigration to the Secretary of Labor*. Washington, DC: Government Printing Office, 1913–1932.

U.S. Department of Homeland Security, History Office. "Brief Documentary History of the Department of Homeland Security, 2001–2008." www.dhs. gov/xabout/history/ (accessed May 13, 2009).

———. U.S. Immigration and Customs Enforcement. "Immigration Detention Facilities." www.ice.gov/pi/dro/facilities.htm (accessed May 15, 2009).

———. U.S. Immigration and Customs Enforcement. "Operations Manual ICE Performance Based National Detention Standards (PBNDS), 2008." www.ice.gov/partners/dro/PBNDS/index.htm (accessed May 16, 2009).

———. Office of Inspector General. *Immigration and Customs Enforcement's Tracking and Transfers of Detainees*. Washington, DC: Government Printing Office, 2009.

U.S. Department of Justice, Immigration and Naturalization Service. *Chinese Investigations: Investigator's Reference Bulletin No. 3*. Washington, DC: Government Printing Office, 1957.

U.S. Department of Labor. *Annual Report of the Secretary of Labor*. Washington, DC: Government Printing Office, 1933–1940.

U.S. Department of State. *Report of the Honorable Roland S. Morris on Japanese Immigration and Alleged Discriminatory Legislation against Japanese Residents in the United States*. New York: Arno Press, 1978.

U.S. Government Accountability Office. *Alien Detention Standards: Observations on the Adherence to ICE's Medical Standards in Detention Facilities*. Washington, DC: Government Printing Office, 2008.

U.S. Library of Congress. "Immigration: Polish/Russian." www.memory.loc.gov/learn/features/immig/alt/polish.html (accessed November 7, 2009).

Van Vleck, William C. *The Administrative Control of Aliens*. New York: Commonwealth Fund, 1932.

Wallace, Mike. "Boat People: Immigrant History at the Statue of Liberty and Ellis Island." In *Mickey Mouse History and Other Essays on American Memory*. Philadelphia: Temple University Press, 1996.

Wilson, Woodrow. "Message from the President of the United States," August 23, 1918. Text from U.S. Congressional Serial Set (accessed April 1, 2010).

Wimbush, Adam. "Erbon Delventhal: Bond Collector." *Passages: The Quarterly Newsletter of the Angel Island Immigration Station Foundation* 5, no. 3 (Summer 2002): 3.

Wyman, David. *Paper Walls: America and the Refugee Crisis, 1938–1941*. New York: Pantheon Books, 1985.

Yans-McLaughlin, Virginia, and Marjorie Lightman, with the Statue of Liberty-Ellis Island Foundation. *Ellis Island, the Peopling of America: The Official Guide*. New York: New Press, 1997.

Yasutaki, Rumi. *Transnational Women's Activism: The U.S., Japan, and Japanese Immigrant Communities in California, 1859–1920*. New York: New York University Press, 2004.

Yoneda, Karl. *Ganbatte: Sixty-Year Struggle of a Kibei Worker*. Los Angeles: UCLA Asian American Studies Center, 1983.

Yoon, Won Kil. *The Passage of a Picture Bride*. Loma Linda, CA: Pacific Rim Press, 1994.

Yu, Connie Young. "Rediscovered Voices: Chinese Immigrants and Angel Island." *Amerasia Journal* 4, no. 2 (1977): 123–39.

Yung, Judy. "'A Bowlful of Tears' Revisited: The Full Story of Lee Puey You's Immigration Experience at Angel Island." *Frontiers: A Journal of Women's Studies* 25, no. 1 (2004): 1–22.

———. *Unbound Feet: A Social History of Chinese Women in San Francisco*. Berkeley: University of California Press, 1995.

———. *Unbound Voices: A Documentary History of Chinese Women in San Francisco*. Berkeley: University of California Press, 1999.

Zhou, Min and James Gatewood. "Transforming Asian America: Globalization and Contemporary Immigration to the United States." In *Contemporary Asian America: A Multidisciplinary Reader*, edited by Min Zhou and James Gatewood. New York: New York University Press, 2007.

Zolberg, Aristide R. *A Nation by Design: Immigration Policy in the Fashioning of America*. Cambridge, MA: Harvard University Press, 2006.

INDEX

African detainees, 18, 38, 50, 52–53
Ahn Chang-ho, 201, 358 n. 55
Ainsworth, Frank, 22, 129, 151,
 166–68, 193, 195–96, 206–07
Akaka, Daniel, 309
Alien Contract Labor Law (1885), 7
Alien Land Law, 130, 132, 145–46,
 156
alien radicals, 48, 165–69, 211,
 228–33
aliens ineligible to citizenship. *See*
 U.S. citizenship
American Red Cross, 234, 252, 258
Angel Island ferry, 33–34
Angel Island Immigration Station
 administration building, 15, 28,
  34, 298, 311
 dedication of monument (April
  28, 1979), 306
 detention life, 55–64, 95–102,
  111–12, 120, 122–24, 235
 employee cottages, 40, 303
 employees, 39–46
 fire, 298–300
 food, 60–62, 96–97, 123–24,
  154–55, 225
 grand reopening (February 15,
  2009), 312–13
 hospital, 36–38
 location, 11–12
 National Angel Island Day
  (January 21, 2020), 314
 National Historic Landmark
  celebration (May 16, 1998), 308
 opening day (January 21, 1910), 14
 poetry and wall inscriptions, 16, 17,
  69, 103–05, 107, 108, 112–13,
  139, 140, 162–63, 197–99,
  235–36, 302–03, 311, 324

 recreation yards, 56, 63, 98
 segregation policy, 34, 36–37, 56,
  58, 60–61, 290, 299
 suicides, 5, 101–02, 346. n. 71
 visitors, 56, 59, 63, 64, 97, 98,
  235, 266–68
Angel Island Immigration Station
 Foundation (AIISF), 308
Angel Island Immigration Station
 Historical Advisory Committee
 (AIISHAC), 305, 307
Angel Island Liberty Association, 89,
 98–99
Araki, George, 301
Ariki, Masayuki (Jim), 134–36,
 141–42
Asiatic Barred Zone, 7, 169
Asiatic Exclusion League (AEL), 50,
 116, 147, 149–52, 155, 193
Assyrian detainees, 22, 50
Austin, Emily, 45–46, 135
Australian detainees, 22, 29, 50,
 56, 60
Ayala, Juan Manuel de, 9

Backus, Samuel W., 42, 46, 156,
 166, 184, 225, 226, 265
Bagai, Vaishno Das and Kala,
 145–46, 153–55, 173
Bamford, Mary, 56
Baraktullah, Muhammad Manlavie,
 165–66
Bergeron, Victor "Trader Vic," 306
bonds and bonding, xxiii, 51, 130,
 133–34, 220, 226, 237, 239–40
Border Patrol, 7, 250–51, 271, 317
Bracero Program, 316
Brachmann, Josef, 224
Bridges, Harry, 9

Bryan, William Jennings, 186–87, 356 n. 24
Burton, John, 309

Cable Act of 1922, 288
Cahill, Edward, 291–93
California State Parks, 301, 311
Caminetti, Anthony, 127–28, 159–60, 165, 189, 229
Canadian detainees, 5, 19, 59
Chandra, Kanta. *See* Gupta, Kanta Chandra
Chinese Exclusion Act of 1882, xvi, 6–7, 10, 75, 206
Chinn, Ngoot P., 306
Choi Kyung Sik, 197–98
Chow, Chris, 304, 305
Chow, Paul, 303, 305, 306, 308, 313
Choy, Philip, 305, 307, 309, 313
citizenship. *See* U. S. citizenship
coaching books and notes, 88–90, 99
Confession Program, 106, 107, 108
contagious diseases, 36, 152, 219, 255–56
    hookworm, 37, 39, 118, 122–23, 129, 152, 196, 339, n. 21
    liver fluke, 37, 39, 78
    trachoma, 37, 39, 122–23, 128–29, 152, 213, 218, 219
contract laborer, 157, 268

Daughters of the American Revolution (DAR), 66
Day, George Martin, 232
Dayal, Har, 164, 166–69
Delventhal, Erbon, 51
Densmore investigation, 91–92
deportation of alien residents, xxiii, 9, 105, 158, 167–68, 228–29, 284–85, 290–93, 318, 319–20, 334 n. 4
detention life. *See* Angel Island Immigration Station
detention shed, 10–11, 13
Dill, Anna and Alexandra, 37, 60

Edelstein, Alice, 240–42, 243–44
Ellen Stark Ford House for Japanese and Korean Women and Children, 127

Ellis Island, 8, 12, 22–23, 57, 212, 221, 302, 307, 309, 310, 313–14, 319
Ellis, Sarah, 122
Ellorin, Flaviano and Maria Natividad (Nettie) Gaitos, 287–88, 290
Estoita, Eugenia de, 283
Executive Order 589. *See* immigration laws

Fallon, Joseph P., 51
Feinstein, Dianne, 310
Felipe, Eliseo, 276–77, 278–79, 286–87, 296
Foran, John, 304–05, 306, 307
Fort McDowell, 10, 96, 234, 300
Friesen, Nick, 216–17, 218, 244

Gadar Party, 145, 154, 163–69
Galarza, Ernesto, 266–68
Gardner, John Endicott, 43–44
Gegiow v. Uhl (1915), 157, 226
Gentlemen's Agreement (1907–08), 6, 113, 116, 127, 132, 190
German detainees, 10, 18, 58, 299, 300, 369, n. 1
Gidlow, Ivy, 5, 59
Glover, M. W., 38, 39, 60, 152
Gontard, Jean and Bertha, 31–35, 37, 47
Guhuthakurta, Leelabati and Seeta, 171
Gupta, Kanta Chandra, 163, 174

Haff, Edward, 95
Hanson, G. C., 233
Harbin Committee Rendering Aid to Russian Students, 231
Hawaii, 114–15, 179, 180, 214, 276
Hawkins, Basilio and Elisa Calloway, 288–90
Haworth, B. C., 43
Hayakawa, Shizu, 117–18, 119, 120, 140
Hebrew Immigrant Aid Society (HIAS), 220, 221, 224–28, 242
Hemet incident, 185–87, 188
Hess, N. M., 231–33
Hindu-German Conspiracy, 168

Hindus, xxiii, 149
hookworm. *See* contagious diseases
Hopkinson, W. C., 159, 166
Hrenoff, Michael, 234

Im So See, 176, 204–05
immigrant inspection
  and inspectors, 41–43
  and interpreters, 43–46, 81–82,
    120–21, 184–85, 221–22, 282
  and interrogation, 30, 46–48,
    85–90, 124–27, 153–58, 187–88,
    191–92, 202–03, 205–07, 222,
    230–31, 260–263, 287
  and medical examination, 35–38,
    77–78, 152–53, 218–20, 255–56
  and primary inspection, 31–35
Immigration and Customs
    Enforcement (ICE), 317
immigration laws, 6–8, 48–49
  Act of August 3, 1882, 7
  Act of March 2, 1929, 7–8, 335,
    n. 11
  Act of May 22, 1918, 48, 357,
    n. 43
  Act of May 24, 1934, 294–95
  Alien Contract Labor Law
    (1885), 7
  Cable Act of 1922, 288
  Chinese Exclusion Act of 1882,
    xvi, 6–7, 10, 75, 206
  Executive Order 589 (March 14,
    1907), 116, 180, 184
  Filipino Repatriation Act (July 10,
    1935), 290–91
  Gentlemen's Agreement (1907–08),
    6, 113, 116, 127, 132, 190
  Immigration Act of 1891, 7
  Immigration Act of 1903, 7, 228
  Immigration Act of 1907, 159,
    190, 193
  Immigration Act of 1917, 7, 48,
    117, 147, 169, 226–27, 228, 251
  Immigration Act of 1924, 7, 76, 105,
    132–33, 138, 169–70, 196, 237,
    241, 285, 335, n. 11
  Immigration Act of 1965, 174,
    296, 316–17
  Immigration Reform and Control
    Act of 1986, 317
  Joint Order (July 26, 1917), 195,
    204, 357, n. 43
  Ladies Agreement (1920), 118,
    132, 199
  Luce-Celler Act (1946), 174, 296
  McCarran-Walter Act of 1952,
    141, 316
  Page Law (1875), 6, 75
  Patriot Act (2001), 318
  Quota Act of 1921, 7, 48–49,
    233–37, 270–71, 335, n. 11
  Rule 11 (February 14, 1913), 181,
    192–93, 195
  Tydings-McDuffie Act (1934), 8,
    273–74, 281–85, 287–88, 366,
    n. 21
  War Brides Act of 1945, 148
immigration lawyers, 91–95, 225
immigration raids, 105, 318
International Institute, 282–84, 291
internment, Japanese American,
    139–43
interpreters. *See* immigration
    inspection
interrogation. *See* immigrant
    inspection
Isaak, H. P., 58, 218

Jann Mon Fong (Smiley Jann), xvi,
    71–72, 76–77, 103, 107
Japanese Association of America
    (JAA), 119, 125, 130, 131–32,
    134
Jung Look Moy, 30–31
Jung, Charles, 90–91, 93, 97

Kawai, Michi, 58, 122–24
Keefe, Daniel, 50, 157, 220–21
Kim Chin Young, 193–95
Kim Ok Yun, 196–97
Kim Suk-eun, 200–03
Ko, Kathy Lim, 308, 313
Kobashigawa, Jiro (Dick), 134–35,
    141
Korean National Association (KNA),
    177, 183–87, 191–95, 196, 198,
    204

Ladies Agreement, 118, 132, 199
Lai, Him Mark, xvi, 305

Lal, Gobind Behari, 164
Law Shee Low, 72–73, 88
Lee, Chi Yet, xvii
Lee, David, 182, 184–86, 188–89,
    191–92, 195, 200, 202, 204
Lee, Edwar, 43, 44–45
Lee, Ira, 96
Lee, Mabel, 45, 46
Lee Puey You, 48, 77, 93–95, 96,
    100–01, 104, 106–07, 299
Leung, Tye, 46, 81–82
Levin, Solomon, 215
likely to become a public charge
    (LPC), 50, 52, 151, 155–57,
    220–25, 237–40, 242–43, 251,
    258, 265–69
Lim, Genny, xvi, 305
Linton, Hugh and Lillian, 29–30
literacy test, 48, 117, 170–71, 226–28,
    251, 259–60, 340, n. 42
liver fluke. See contagious diseases
Lopez, Catarino and Esther Galzarza,
    4–5, 265–68
Lopez, Maria, 252–53
Louis, Rose and Emile, 52–53
Lowe, Felicia, 108, 308, 310
Luce-Cellar Act (1946), 174, 296
Lyang, Hong, 206–07

Manzanar, 140, 141, 304, 309
Masloff, Nicolas, 235–36
Matthews, Walter J., 12–13
Maurer, Katharine, 4–5, 43, 44,
    64–66, 80, 100, 122, 161–62,
    210, 291
Mayerson, H., 43
McCarran-Walter Act of 1952, 141,
    316
McClatchy, V. S., 131, 132, 264, 279,
    280
medical examination. See immigrant
    inspection
Mennonites, 216–17, 220, 238–40,
    244
merchants, 1, 79, 84–85, 206–07
Mexico border. See U.S.-Mexico
    border
Mexico, Koreans in, 180, 183–84
Miwok American Indians, 9–10
Mock Ging Sing, 59

Molokans, 213
Mooney, Hugh, 40
moral turpitude, 53–55, 128, 138,
    262–63
Morris, C. D., 192, 194

Nagle, John, 86, 236
Nakayama, Yoshi and Sakaki,
    125–27
National Historic Landmark status,
    307, 308–09
Neufeld, Jacob and Helena, 238–40,
    244–45
New Zealand detainees, 22, 50
Ng Poon Chew, 90
Nojima, Miyono, 137–39, 142–43
North Garrison, 301, 302,
North, Hart Hyatt, 12, 13, 14–15, 22,
    41, 81–82, 101, 150–51
Noshkin, Emelian, 223

Okada, Kichiko, 110
O'Neill, Brian, 308
Oriental Exclusion League, 131

Pacific Mail Steamship Company
    (PMSS), 10–11, 253
Page Law (1875), 6, 75
Paik, Rose, 176, 205–06
Pak Sum Oi, 206–07
Palmer, A. Mitchell, 229
paper sons, xvi, 84–90, 335, n. 15
parasitic diseases. See contagious
    diseases
Pathak, Sohon Lal, 165, 166
Patriot Act (2001), 318
Perry, Alonzo, 40
Phelan, James D., 115, 130–32
picture brides, 110, 117–27, 130–32,
    140–41, 199–204, 335, n. 15
Pierson, Carrie, 82
poetry. See Angel Island Immigration
    Station
Pok Kyang Whan, 176, 205
Polish detainees, 59–60, 219, 224
political radicals, 48, 165–69, 211,
    228–33
Post, Louis F., 190, 204, 229
primary inspection. See immigrant
    inspection

Prokofiev, Sergei, 229–30
prostitution. *See* women

Quan, Daniel, 308–09, 311
quarantine station, 10, 213
Quok Shee, 57, 81
Quota Act of 1921. *See* immigration
    laws

radical aliens. *See* alien radicals
Ravelo, Florentino and Ambrosia
    Galutera, 285–86
refugees, 22, 193, 196, 221, 234,
    240–43, 248, 251–53, 317
repatriations, xviii, 8, 271, 274,
    290–96
returning alien residents, 128,
    137–39, 171–72, 285–87
returning U.S. citizens, 82–84,
    92–93, 134–37, 256, 287–90
Roosevelt, Theodore, 116, 179, 180
Rule 11 (February 14, 1913). *See*
    immigration laws

Sakovich, Vladimir, 235
Samborisky, Evdokia and Anton,
    214
Sarabha, Kartar Singh. *See* Singh,
    Kartar Sarabha
Sawyer, John Birge, 41–42
Schulze, Charles Frederick, 82
servants, domestic, 254–55
Shapiro, Nadia, 211, 215–16, 218,
    231–32, 244
Shiibashi, Kaoru, 136–37
Shinn, Kang-ae, 196, 200–01, 202,
    208
Sikhs, xxiii, 149, 160
Sims, Emery, 42–43, 45, 46–47
Singh, Hazara, 152–53, 173
Singh, Karam, 155
Singh, Kartar Sarabha, 164–65, 166,
    172–73
Singh, Tara, 162–63
Soto Shee, 5, 73, 101–02
Souder, Mark, 310
Spanish detainees, 9, 37, 38, 339,
    n. 21
Stidger, Oliver P., 91–92
Strand, Joseph, 231, 232–33, 239

students, 164, 170–71, 181, 187–199,
    231–36
suicides, 5, 11, 101–02, 145–46, 346,
    n. 71
Sun Yat-sen, 71, 91
Sunoo, Sonia Shinn, 200, 201,
    208–09

Takahashi, Mak, 301
Tapia, Cecilia, 259–60
Terasawa, Fuku, 46, 120–21
Thau, Albert, 40
Thind, Bhagat Singh, 145–46
Tolstoy, Alexandra, 218–19,
    230–31
Tom Yip Jing, xvi, 306
Tom, Henry, 98
Toy, Katherine, 308, 310
trachoma. *See* contagious diseases
Traube, William, 225
Troitsky, Vasily, 235
Tsutsui, Iyo, 118, 119, 124–25,
    140–41
Tydings-McDuffie Act (1934), 8,
    273–74, 281–85, 287–88, 366,
    n. 21

undocumented immigrants, xxii,
    271, 317, 318
U.S. citizenship, 7, 82–84, 132,
    145–46, 174, 288, 294–95, 316
U.S.-Mexico border, 247, 250, 256,
    259, 269–70, 317

War Brides Act of 1945, 148
Weiss, Alexander, xv, 16, 302–04,
    313
Welch, Richard J., 279, 281
Whang Sa Sun, 181–82, 202, 207
Whang Sa Yong, 182, 183, 202
Whang, Paul, 182, 207–08
White, Edward, 193, 195, 196, 229
Wienke, Ludwig and Carmen,
    293–95
Willacy Detention Center, 320, 321
Williams, William, 221
Wilson, William, 189
Wilson, Woodrow, 22, 221, 252
Wolff, Harry, 227, 228
Wolff, Simon, 225

women
  and domesticity, 52, 127
  and literacy test, 117, 170–71,
    226–28, 259–60
  and prostitution, 58–59, 75, 80–81,
    128, 204, 260–63, 364, n. 41
  as dependents, 52–53, 79–80, 128,
    219, 223, 260
Won, Gerald, 97, 101
Wong Chung Hong, 1, 4
Wong Kim Ark, 82–83
Wong Shee, 78, 97
Wong, Douglas, 98
Wong, Myron, 299, 300
Woolsey, Lynn, 310

Yee, Tet, xvi, 99, 103, 107–08
Yoneda, Goso (Karl), 111–14,
    139–40
Young, Mary Lee, 97
Young Men's Christian Association
    (YMCA), 66, 98, 156, 223,
    231–33
Young Women's Christian
    Association (YWCA), 66, 119,
    122–24, 266
Yu, Connie Young, 304, 305, 306
Yung, Judy, 305, 306

Zizhihui (Angel Island Liberty
    Association), 89, 98–99